The Monarchs of Europe
and some claimants

A EUROPEAN FAMILY

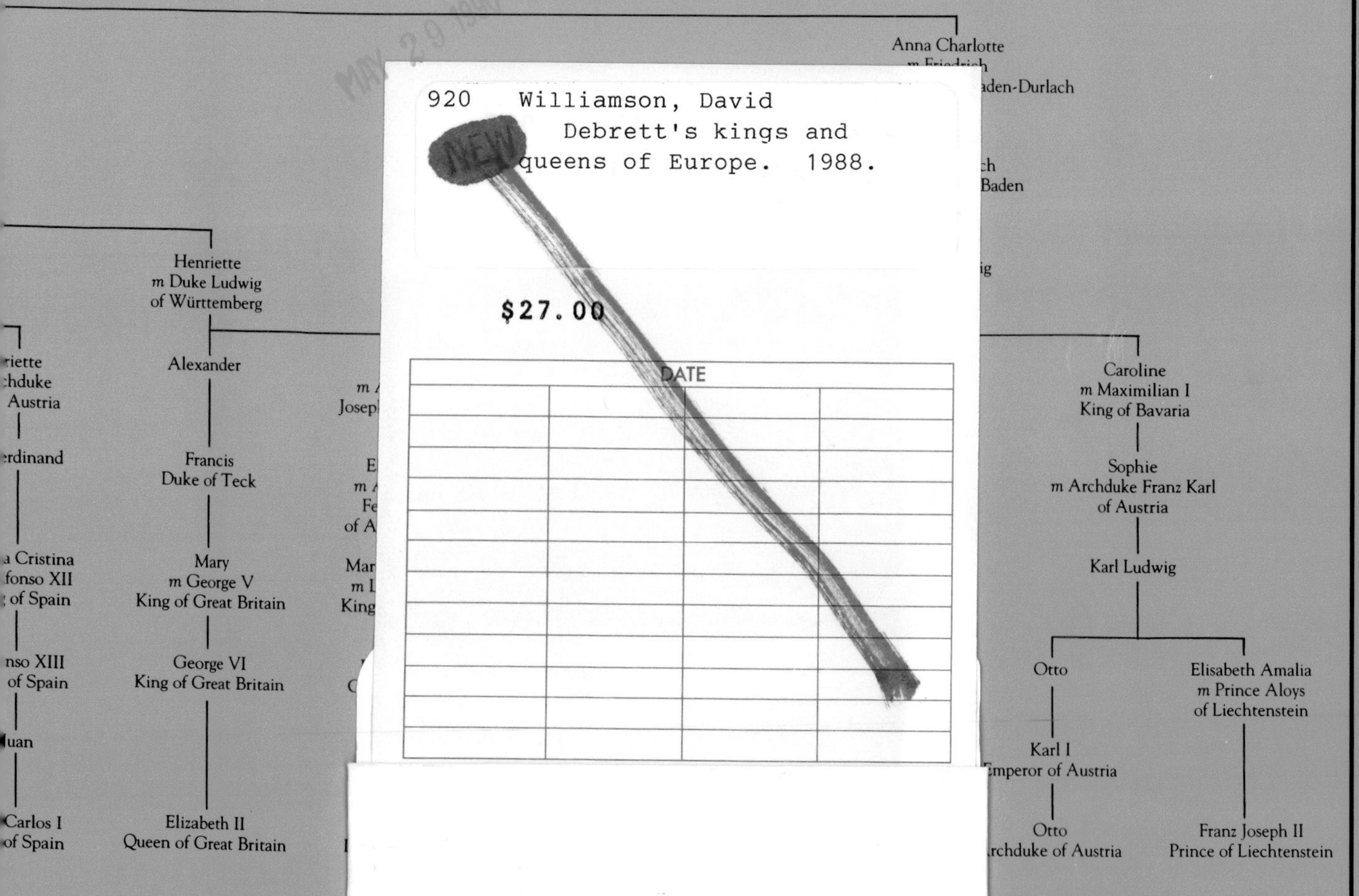

Anna Charlotte
m Friedrich
Baden-Durlach

Baden

Henriette
m Duke Ludwig
of Württemberg

Alexander

riette
chduke
Austria

Francis
Duke of Teck

rdinand

Joseph

a Cristina
fonso XII
of Spain

Mary
m George V
King of Great Britain

nso XIII
of Spain

George VI
King of Great Britain

uan

Carlos I
of Spain

Elizabeth II
Queen of Great Britain

Caroline
m Maximilian I
King of Bavaria

Sophie
m Archduke Franz Karl
of Austria

Karl Ludwig

Otto

Elisabeth Amalia
m Prince Aloys
of Liechtenstein

Karl I
Emperor of Austria

Otto
Archduke of Austria

Franz Joseph II
Prince of Liechtenstein

Debrett's
Kings and Queens
of Europe

Europe in 1914.

Debrett's Kings and Queens of Europe

DAVID WILLIAMSON

Salem House Publishers
Topsfield, Massachusetts

FOR MY MOTHER

First published in the United States
Salem House Publishers, 1988, 462 Boston Street,
Topsfield, Massachusetts 01983

Created by Richard Webb and Delian Bower

Designed by Vic Giolitto

Production by Nick Facer/Rob Kendrew

Picture research by Anne-Marie Ehrlich

Text copyright © 1988 David Williamson

Debrett Trade Mark Copyright
© 1988 Debrett's Peerage Limited

Library of Congress Cataloging-in-Publication Data

Williamson, David.
    Debrett's kings & queens of Europe.

    Includes index.
        1. Europe—Kings and rulers—Genealogy.
I. title. II. Title: Debrett's kings and queens of
Europe. III. Title: Kings & queens of Europe.
CS404.W5   1988   940′.09′92 [B]   87-37618
ISBN 0-88162-364-4

Typeset in Great Britain by P&M Typesetting Ltd, Exeter, Devon

Colour and mono reproduction by Peninsular Repro Services,
Exeter, Devon

Printed and bound in Great Britain
by Purnell Book Production Ltd, Paulton, Bristol

CONTENTS

INTRODUCTION

This book is a companion volume to *Debrett's Kings and Queens of Britain*, published in 1986. In planning it I have had to face several problems. In the first place I toyed with the idea of presenting each country dealt with in alphabetical order, but soon rejected this in favour of a geographical arrangement. I have taken a trip across Europe from west to east, starting on the Atlantic seaboard with Portugal and ending on the shores of the Black Sea with the Balkan countries. In covering such a wide field and so many countries it has, of course, been impossible to treat each individual monarch in as much detail as I did in *Kings and Queens of Britain*, but I hope I have been able to convey something of the characters and personalities of the many very different men and women who have reigned over parts of Europe for over a thousand years. I have tried to show them as human beings, possessing human feelings and human failings, and only too often the unwitting victims of unscrupulous politicians and other forces beyond their control. It has also struck me in the course of writing the book how great a part climate and environment play in shaping people's lives. The rulers of warm, sunny Portugal, Spain and Italy being for the most part warm-blooded, happy-natured extroverts, taking their pleasures with gusto, whereas the further one travels eastwards and northwards to colder climes austerity and restraint appear and the rulers of the Scandinavian countries, for example, take themselves and their pleasures far more seriously. It is hardly surprising that the Protestant Reformation made such headway in the north of Europe while the south and west remained virtually untouched by it.

The book is entitled *Kings and Queens of Europe*, and I have interpreted that to the letter by omitting the Holy Roman Emperors, Emperors of Austria, German Emperors (as such) and Emperors of Russia. To include them would have made the book of inordinate length. Similarly, I have had to exclude all the minor sovereigns, Grand Dukes, Electors, Dukes and Princes, except in so far as in several cases they later became Kings. Also,

for reasons of length I have given only a glance at the middle European kingdoms of Hungary, Bohemia and Poland, and at the medieval kingdoms of Naples, Sicily, Serbia and Bulgaria.

Some readers may be disappointed to find no mention of the Kings of Cyprus, the Kings of Armenia and the Kings of Georgia in these pages. Properly speaking, these now vanished Christian kingdoms belong to Asia rather than to Europe. Others, who might have figured in the book but for reasons of space, include the Kings of Majorca, for a short while independent of Aragon, and that intriguing figure King Theodore of Corsica, the German adventurer Baron von Neuhoff, who almost succeeded in establishing his island kingdom in the mid-eighteenth century, but died in poverty in London, where his monument can be seen to this day on the surviving west wall of St Anne's Church, Soho.

The problem of dealing with proper names, which can vary so much from country to country, has been solved by using either the English forms or the forms most familiar to English readers. This is far from satisfactory and many inconsistencies will be found, but it is, I think, preferable to a slavish and pedantic attempt to give the names in their correct form for each country which would render many of them quite unpronounceable to most English readers.

The inclusion of some thirty genealogical tables in the Appendix will, it is hoped, both elucidate and supplement the text.

In a book of this type it is inevitable that there will be some errors of fact and I shall be grateful to any readers who come across one to point it out so that it may be corrected in any future editions.

Again I must thank the very many people who helped me in the preparation of this book but will single out only one name, that of Pamela Milne who typed my manuscript impeccably while at the same time coping with the ravenous demands of a new baby.

DAVID WILLIAMSON

The Iberian Peninsula

PORTUGAL

The House of Burgundy

ALFONSO I 1139–1185

b Guimaraens July 1110; *s* his father as Count of Portugal 1 May 1112; proclaimed King 25 July 1139 (confirmed by papal bull 23 May 1179); *m* 1146 Mafalda (*d* 4 Nov 1158), dau of Amadeus III, Count of Savoy, Maurienne and Piedmont, and Mafalda of Albon; 4 sons, 3 daus; *d* Coimbra 6 Dec 1185; *bur* Priory of Santa Cruz, Coimbra

SANCHO I THE CITY-BUILDER 1185–1211

b 2 Nov 1154, 3rd but only surv son of Alfonso I; *s* his father 6 Dec 1185, having been associated in the government for several years previously; *m* 1174 Dulce (*d* 1 Sept 1198), dau of Raymond Berengar IV, Count of Barcelona, and Petronilla, Queen of Aragon; 5 sons, 6 daus; *d* Alcobaça 26 March 1211; *bur* Priory of Santa Cruz, Coimbra

ALFONSO II THE FAT 1211–1223

b 23 April 1185, 2nd but eldest surv son of Sancho I; *s* his father 26 March 1211; *m* 1206 Urraca (*b* 1190; *d* 3 Nov 1220), dau of Alfonso VIII, King of Castile, and Eleanor of England; 4 sons, 1 dau; *d* Santarém 25 March 1223; *bur* Alcobaça

SANCHO II 1223–1248

b 8 Sept 1207, eldest son of Alfonso II; *s* his father 25 March 1223; replaced by his brother Alfonso as Regent and went into exile Jan or Feb 1246; *m ca* 1245 Mencia (*d* after 1270), widow of Alvares Peres de Castro, and dau of Diego Lópes de Haro and Urraca, natural dau of Alfonso IX, King of Leon; *d* Toledo 8 Jan 1248

ALFONSO III 1248–1279

b 5 May 1210, 2nd son of Alfonso II; declared himself Defender of the Kingdom Jan 1246; *s* his brother Sancho II 8 Jan 1248; *m* (1) in France 1235 (repudiated 1245), Matilda, in her own right Countess of Boulogne (*d* 1262), dau of Renaud, Count of Dammartin, and Ida of Boulogne; 2 sons (both *d* young); *m* (2) *ca* 3 June 1254 (regularized 1263) Beatrice (*b* 1242; *d* 27 Oct 1303), natural dau of Alfonso X, King of Castile, and Maria de Guzman; 4 sons, 4 daus; *d* 16 Feb 1279; *bur* Alcobaça

DENIS THE LABOURER 1279–1325

b 9 Oct 1261, eldest son of Alfonso III by his 2nd marriage; *s* his father 16 Feb 1279; *m* 2 Feb 1282 Isabel (*b* 1271; *d* Coimbra 4 July 1336; canonized as St Isabel of Portugal), dau of Pedro III, King of Aragon, and Constance of Sicily; 1 son, 1 dau; *d* Lisbon 7 Jan 1325; *bur* Convent of Odivelas, nr Lisbon

ALFONSO IV THE BRAVE 1325–1357

b 8 Feb 1291, only legitimate son of Denis; *s* his father 7 Jan 1325; *m* 12 Sept 1309 Beatrice (*b* 1293; *d* 25 Oct 1359), dau of Sancho IV, King of Castile, and Maria de Molina; 4 sons, 3 daus; *d* Lisbon 28 May 1357; *bur* Lisbon Cathedral

PEDRO I THE SEVERE 1357–1367

b Coimbra 18 April 1320, 3rd but only surv son of Alfonso IV; *s* his father 28 May 1357; *m* (1) 1328 (*m* annulled 1333) Blanche (*d* 1345), dau of Infante Pedro of Castile and Maria of Aragon; *m* (2) Lisbon 24 Aug 1340 Constance (*d* 13 Nov 1345; *bur* Santarém), dau of Juan Manuel, Count of Penafiel, and Constance of Aragon; 3 sons, 1 dau; *m* (3) secretly 1 Jan 1354 Ines (*d* (murdered) Coimbra 7 Jan 1355), dau of Pedro Fernando de Castro and Beatrice of Portugal (granddau of Alfonso III); 2 sons, 2 daus; *d* Estremoz 18 Jan 1367; *bur* Alcobaça

FERDINAND I THE HANDSOME 1367–1383

b 31 Oct 1345, 2nd but eldest surv son of Pedro I; *s* his father 18 Jan 1367; *m* Oporto 1371 Leonor (*d* Convent of Tordesillas 27 April 1386), formerly wife of João Lourenço da Cunha, Lord of Pombeiro, and dau of Martin Alfonso Telles de Meneses; 2 sons (both *d* young), 1 dau; *d* 22 Oct 1383; *bur* Santarém

[BEATRICE 1383–1385]

b Coimbra 1372; only dau of Ferdinand I; proclaimed Queen under her mother's regency 22 Oct 1383, but never effectively reigned; *m* Badajoz 13 May 1383, as his 2nd wife, Juan I, King of Castile (*d* 9 Oct 1390); *d* after 1409

Portugal, the westernmost country of Europe, may be likened to a rectangle standing on end, bordered on the north and east by Spain and on the west and south by the Atlantic, a fact which was to make it one of the foremost nations of seagoing explorers in the world.

Until 1095, Portugal had no separate history from the rest of the Iberian peninsula. In that year Alfonso VI, King of Castile, gave the county of Portugal to Henry of Burgundy with the hand of his natural daughter Theresa, whose mother was one Ximena Nunes. Henry was a grandson of Robert, Duke of Burgundy, and thus a scion of the Capetian Royal House of France. He was a typical warrior of the time and left his capable wife in charge of their country while he journeyed to Palestine to take part in the Second Crusade from 1103 to 1105. Theresa, we are told, was not only an extremely able administrator but also beautiful, passionate and a patroness of poetry and music. On the death of Alfonso VI in 1109 all his dominions were claimed by his legitimate daughter Urraca and several years of civil war and war with the ever-troublesome Moors ensued. Henry died at Astorga on 30 April or 1 May 1112 leaving an only surviving son Alfonso, then less than two years old. The Countess Theresa, styling herself Infanta, at once resumed the regency and set about consolidating the country from her capital of Guimaraens. She was also constantly at war with her half-sister Urraca and was ably supported by her lover Fernando Peres de Trava. Her love, however, was also to prove her downfall, for her son Alfonso as he grew to manhood came to resent his mother's paramour. At the age of seventeen he raised an army, defeated his mother at São Mamede in July 1128 and drove her and her lover into exile, where she died in poverty on 1 November 1130. Her body was brought back to Portugal and buried beside that of Count Henry in Braga Cathedral.

The young Alfonso set about gaining the complete independence of his country. Traditionally a man of large stature with a flowing black beard and endowed with a strength to match, he conducted a series of raids into Galicia, harrying his cousin and overlord Alfonso VII of Leon. After several years of border skirmishing, however, the cousins concluded a treaty and banded together to fight the Moors. On 25 July 1139 Alfonso won a great victory over the Muslim forces at the battle of Ourique (the exact locality of which is still disputed) and thereafter assumed the title of King. It should be noted, however, that the titles of King and Queen were at that period used quite indiscriminately among the Christian dynasties in Spain and were often synonymous with those of Prince and Princess and not indicative of an independent sovereign ruler.

Alfonso's long reign was occupied throughout in fighting the Moors. An abortive attempt to capture Lisbon with English and Norman aid in 1140 or 1142 was followed in March 1147 by the capture of the important town of Santarém, leading to the final capture of Lisbon with the help of an English fleet *en route* to the Crusades after a siege of several months in October of the same year. Further conquests followed until Alfonso had gained all Portugal north of the Tagus.

A year before the conquest of Lisbon, Alfonso had made an advantageous marriage with Mafalda of Savoy, who bore him a large family whose eventual marriages were to cement further notable alliances for Portugal. He also had several natural children (as did almost all the early Portuguese Kings), who also played a role in affairs of state. Relations between Portugal and Leon remained uneasy for many years and in the course of a skirmish in 1169 Alfonso was captured after breaking his leg, and held prisoner for two months by his own son-in-law Ferdinand II of Leon. His freedom was only purchased by the surrender of the towns he had captured in Galicia and a considerable ransom. He returned to Coimbra, but as a result of his injury was never able to ride a horse again and future campaigning was conducted by his son Sancho. The culminating triumph of Alfonso's reign was the issue by Pope Alexander III of the bull *Manifestis probatum* (23 May 1179), which recognized his title as King and confirmed his possession of all his Moorish conquests. Alfonso died after a reign of fifty-seven years on 6 December 1185 and was succeeded by his eldest surviving son Sancho I.

Sancho I was already an experienced warrior and continued fighting the Moors until the conclusion of a truce in 1192 gave him the opportunity to repair the old city walls and found new towns, earning himself the sobriquet of *O Povoador* (the City-builder) by which he has gone down in history. The latter part of his reign was taken up with ecclesiastical disputes, between the King on one side and the Portuguese Bishops backed by Pope Innocent III on the other, chiefly over the matter of church revenues, although there were some surprising undercurrents, such as the Bishop of Coimbra accusing Sancho of harbouring a witch in his palace.

The King's imprisonment of the Bishop of Oporto for five months until he escaped and fled to Rome led to the country being placed under a papal interdict, which was only lifted in 1210 when Sancho submitted, received the Bishop back and paid the Pope 100 marks in gold. He died at Alcobaça in March of the following year. Sancho's Queen, Dulce of Barcelona, had predeceased him by over twelve years. The King concluded some brilliant matches for their many children, the most remarkable being that of the youngest daughter Berengaria, who, marrying far afield, became Queen of Denmark. The transition from warm, sunny Portugal to the gloomy north must have been a rude shock to the poor girl.

Sancho's successor was his eldest son Alfonso II, nicknamed the Fat. Unlike his father and grandfather, he was no soldier, and his comparatively short reign of twelve years saw a renewal of the ecclesiastical disputes, brought about by the avaricious King's appropriation of church revenues. This led to another papal interdict, which was still in force when the King died in March 1223.

Sancho II was a boy of fifteen when he succeeded his father. His mother, Urraca of Castile, was already dead and the government was taken over by the Archbishop of Lisbon and the King's pious aunts (one of whom, Sancha, was to be canonized in 1705), who succeeded in getting the interdict lifted and Sancho's succession recognized by Pope Honorius III. When he grew to manhood Sancho set about reconquering territory which had been lost to the Moors, but while he

The marriage of King John I of Portugal and Philippa of
Lancaster at Oporto in February 1387. This magnificent
illuminated manuscript is in the British Museum.

D. JOÃO II

John II, King of Portugal, a portrait in the Naval Museum at Lisbon.

Alfonso X the Wise, King of Castile, dictating his book on chess, depicted in a manuscript in El Escorial. Note the King's robe displaying the canting arms of Castile (a castle) and Leon (a lion).

Philip the Handsome, who became titular King of Castile in right of his wife Juana: a panel of the Netherlands School in the National Gallery, London. The right-hand panel depicts his sister Margaret who became Regent of the Netherlands.

*King Carlos I of Spain, better known as the Emperor
Charles V. This fine equestrian portrait by Titian is in
the Prado Museum at Madrid.*

did so the country lapsed into anarchy, the great barons and ecclesiastics becoming all-powerful and exacting crippling tithes from the people. A state of discontent grew throughout the land and the King became a scapegoat. His marriage to Dona Mencia Lópes de Haro did not help, for they were held to be within the prohibited degrees of kinship with each other and not lawfully dispensed (although only second cousins once removed). This gave the Bishops a lever to act against Sancho and a papal bull was obtained authorizing the King's brother to take over the kingdom as 'Defender and Visitor ... for the Supreme Pontiff' early in 1246. The unfortunate King went into exile and Alfonso, Count of Boulogne in right of his wife, became the effective ruler. Sancho died at Toledo in January 1248, deserted by the wife for whom he had lost his throne.

The 'Defender and Visitor' now became King Alfonso III. He continued and completed the reconquest of lands lost to the Moors and was the first Portuguese monarch to be styled 'King of Portugal and the Algarves'. He had no surviving issue from his marriage to the heiress of Boulogne, and with singular bravado (especially in view of his brother's unfortunate matrimonial escapade) contracted a bigamous marriage with Alfonso X of Castile's natural daughter Beatrice. There was, of course, a great political motivation for the marriage, which gained Alfonso X's recognition of his new son-in-law's extended kingdom. The Countess of Boulogne died in 1262 and in the following year Pope Urban IV regularized the King's marriage to Beatrice and legitimated their son Denis. Alfonso III was the first Portuguese sovereign to call a Cortes, so initiating a form of parliamentary government, and he prepared the way for the consolidation of the kingdom which was to be completed by his son and successor.

Denis had rebelled against his father in 1277 and a state of civil war continued until the latter's death (hastened by sorrow at this unfilial behaviour) brought about the former's accession in 1279. His legitimacy was at once disputed by his brother Alfonso, who had been born after the regularization of their parents' marriage, but a compromise was reached. Denis had been well educated by French and Portuguese scholars and one of his most memorable acts was to be the founding of the University of Lisbon (later moved to Coimbra). After a succession of warlike and troubled reigns, Denis's was one of comparative peace. The King saw the necessity to encourage agriculture, earning himself the sobriquet *O Lavrador*, the labourer or farmer. His long reign of nearly fifty years was a real golden age for Portugal. He strengthened the leading cities and built towns, and still found time to write lyric poetry. Denis married Isabel of Aragon, later to be canonized as St Isabel of Portugal for her outstanding piety and charitable works. She bore him one son and one daughter, but extramarital affairs produced several other sons greatly favoured by their father. The moral tone of the court was very lax and Denis's sister Branca, Abbess of Las Huelgas, was notorious for her love affair with a carpenter, by whom she had a son later to become Master of the Order of Calatrava and to be beheaded by Pedro the Cruel of Castile. Denis's favouring of his natural sons led to a bitter dispute with his legitimate son and heir Alfonso, who took up arms against his father and

marched on Lisbon. A battle was only prevented by the action of the saintly Queen Isabel in riding between the armies and forcing her husband and her son to make an uneasy peace which lasted until Denis's death in January 1325.

Alfonso IV began his reign by pursuing his vendetta against his illegitimate half-brothers, beheading one and confiscating all the property of another, who had prudently taken refuge in Castile. In other respects he continued his father's policy of peaceful development. His daughter Maria was married to Alfonso XI of Castile, who neglected her for his favourite Leonor de Guzman and treated her so cruelly that her father felt impelled to invade Castile. Queen Isabel again intervened to act as peacemaker, coming from her convent at Coimbra and returning to die there later the same year. Her death removed a great influence for good. In 1340 a Moorish army crossed the straits of Gibraltar to aid their fellows in Granada. The differences between the Christian kingdoms were put aside and Castile and Portugal banded together to vanquish the Moors at the battle of Salado on 29 October 1340, where Alfonso IV earned his sobriquet of 'the Brave'.

Alfonso's eldest surviving son and heir Pedro had a somewhat chequered matrimonial career. His first wife Blanche of Castile, to whom he was married at the age of eight, proved to be mentally retarded and the marriage was annulled. At the age of sixteen, he was married by proxy to his second wife, Constance Manuel, the marriage being concluded four years later. Constance brought with her as one of her maids of honour a beautiful Castilian girl, Ines Pires de Castro, known as *Colo de Garça* (Heron's neck). Pedro fell madly in love with her and after Constance's death in childbirth in 1345, lived openly with Ines, who bore him four children. Frequently urged by his father to remarry, Pedro refused on the grounds of his attachment to the memory of his late wife. Suspicions that he had married Ines secretly were said to have been denied by her declaring that 'she never was, nor could be, his wife'. She was probably referring to the fact that she had been deliberately chosen by Constance to act as godmother to her son Luis, thus bringing about an 'affinity' which the church would have considered a bar to any subsequent marriage with Pedro. Be that as it may, Pedro fell under the political influence of Ines's two brothers, a pair of intriguers who induced him to claim the throne of Castile. This alarmed Alfonso IV, who also feared an attempt might be made to set aside Constance's children in favour of those of Ines. He allowed himself to be persuaded to put her to death and is said to have ridden to Coimbra to do the deed himself but to have been dissuaded by his little grandchildren pleading for their mother's life. Three courtiers were made of sterner stuff and returned to complete the mission. Pedro, who was absent in the north, on hearing the news immediately raised an army and prepared to march against his father. A short and bloody civil war was terminated by Queen Beatrice emulating her mother-in-law St Isabel and effecting a reconciliation. Alfonso IV died soon after in May 1357.

Pedro I's first act on his accession was to avenge Ines. Two of her murderers were handed over to him by Castile and duly executed before his eyes, their hearts being drawn out of their bodies, one through the chest and one through the back. The third murderer managed to escape to England and evade this fate. Pedro now declared that he had been secretly married to Ines on 1 January 1354, a year before her murder, and ghastly scenes were to follow. The murdered woman's body was disinterred from its grave at Coimbra and taken to the convent of Alcobaça, where, on 24 April 1361, arrayed in royal robes and propped up on a throne, it was solemnly crowned in the presence of the whole court and then reinterred. A magnificent tomb was erected by Pedro and his own tomb was constructed at its feet in such a way that the first thing he and Ines might see on the day of resurrection would be each other.

Pedro's reign was short and comparatively unremarkable. He loved to dispense justice in person and to frequent the courts incognito to flush out corrupt and unjust judges. He thus earned his sobriquet of 'the Severe'. When not engaged in these pursuits he gave himself up to hunting, feasting and dancing. Like most of his predecessors he was also a great womanizer and one of his natural sons was to become the first King of the House of Avis.

On Pedro's death in 1367 he was succeeded by his only surviving son by Constance, Ferdinand I the Handsome, 'a bold, merry and lusty youth, fond of women and an accoster of them', says the historian Fernão Lopes. His attempt to claim the thrones of Castile and Leon in 1369 led to a war with Henry of Trastamara, who emerged as the successful candidate in 1371, and continued intermittently until 1382. Like his father and Sancho II before him, Ferdinand completely lost his head over a woman. She was Leonor Telles de Meneses, the wife of João Lourenço da Cunha, and he met her at the wedding of his half-sister Beatrice, the daughter of Ines de Castro, to Sancho, Count of Albuquerque. Leonor has been represented as a cross between Messalina and Lucrezia Borgia. So infatuated was Ferdinand that he married her in Oporto in 1371, conveniently ignoring the fact that she had a husband still living and her marriage had not been annulled. The acquiescent nobility acknowledged her as Queen, the only one to dissent being Ines de Castro's son Denis, who boldly said that he would not kiss her hand but that she might kiss his and then prudently sought refuge in Castile. Denis's brother John had fallen in love with Queen Leonor's sister Maria and married her secretly. As he was extremely popular the Queen feared that he might be preferred to her only surviving child Beatrice as heir to the throne. The thought of her sister thus becoming Queen in her place was too much for her. She played cleverly on John's ambitions, pointing out that had he married her daughter rather than her sister he would have had an indisputable right to the throne and hinting at his wife's infidelity. She did this to such an extent that the wretched man was finally induced to kill his wife in cold blood at her house in Coimbra. Almost needless to say, he was not rewarded with Beatrice's hand although pardoned for his crime. He joined his younger brother in Castile.

Queen Leonor continued to manipulate her weak husband, aided and abetted by her lover the Count of Ourém, and brought about the conclusion of a treaty of peace with Castile on 2 April 1383 whereby the Princess Beatrice, who had been recognized as heiress to the throne in 1376, was to marry King Juan I of Castile and in the event of King Ferdinand's death without male issue the regency was to be exercised by Queen Leonor until Beatrice's eldest son came of age. The marriage of the eleven-year-old girl took place at Badajoz in May and her father, who was too ill to attend, died six months later on 22 October 1383, bitterly lamenting on his deathbed 'that God gave me these realms to maintain with peace and justice, and I for my sins have acted in such wise that I shall give him very ill account of them'.

Queen Leonor at once set about securing the regency, neglecting to attend her husband's burial, which took place with scant ceremony. Her daughter and son-in-law were publicly proclaimed Queen and King of Portugal and the Algarves, giving occasion to unrest and rioting in several towns. Leonor's Galician lover Ourém was hated by the nobles as much as she was and, determined to rid themselves of the man, they found a leader in Dom John, Master of Avis, an illegitimate son of King Pedro I by one Theresa Lourenço and consequently a half-brother of the late King. His life had been threatened by Leonor and he willingly placed himself at the head of an insurrection in Lisbon, which on 6 December stormed the palace and killed Ourém, who was stabbed to death by Dom John's own hand. The Bishop of Lisbon was also killed, and several other murders were perpetrated in the provinces. Queen Leonor fled to Santarém and Dom John assumed the title of Defender and Governor of the Kingdom.

In 1384 King Juan of Castile entered Portugal with a large army and joined his mother-in-law at Santarém, but they soon fell out over plans for the future government of Portugal and Leonor, treacherous to the last, was discovered in an attempt to poison her son-in-law, who thereupon despatched her to the Convent of Tordesillas in Castile, where she remained until her death in April 1386. Juan of Castile went on to besiege Lisbon but an attack of pestilence in his camp forced him to retire for the time being. Meanwhile, a Cortes assembled at Coimbra in March 1385 to discuss the succession to the throne. The claims of Beatrice and of the children of Ines de Castro were set aside on the grounds of their illegitimacy, but the claim of the equally illegitimate Master of Avis was preferred and on 6 April 1385 he was acclaimed King.

The House of Avis

JOHN I THE GREAT	1385–1433

b 11 April 1358; Grand Master of the Order of Avis; Defender and Governor of the Kingdom December 1383; acclaimed King 6 April 1385; *m* Oporto 2 February 1387 Philippa (*b* Leicester 31 March 1360; *d* Odivelas, nr Lisbon 19 July 1415; *bur* Batalha), eldest daughter of John of Gaunt, Duke of Lancaster, and his 1st wife, Blanche of Lancaster; 6 sons, 2 daus; *d* Lisbon 14 August 1433; *bur* Batalha

DUARTE I 1433–1438

b Viseu 31 October 1391, 2nd but eldest surviving son of King John I; *s* his father 14 August 1433; *m* 22 September 1428 Leonor (*d* Toledo 19 February 1445), dau of Ferdinand I, King of Aragon, and Leonor of Albuquerque (granddau of Pedro I and Ines de Castro); 3 sons, 3 daus; *d* Tomar 18 September 1438; *bur* Alcobaça

ALFONSO V THE AFRICAN 1438–1481

b Cintra 15 January 1432, 2nd but eldest surviving son of King Duarte I; *s* his father 18 September 1438; *m* 6 May 1447 his 1st cousin, Isabel (*b* 1432; *d* Evora 2 December 1455; *bur* Batalha), eldest dau of Dom Pedro, Duke of Coimbra (3rd son of King John I), and Isabel of Urgel; 2 sons, 1 dau; *d* Cintra 24 August 1481; *bur* Batalha

JOHN II THE PERFECT 1481–1495

b Lisbon 3 May 1455, yr and only surviving son of King Alfonso V; *s* his father 24 August 1481; *m* Setubal 18 January 1471 his 1st cousin, Leonor (*b* 2 May 1458; *d* 17 November 1525; *bur* Convent of St Clara, Lisbon, which she had founded), eldest dau of Dom Ferdinand, Duke of Viseu, Constable of Portugal (3rd son of King Duarte I), and Beatrice of Portugal; 2 sons (who *dvp*); *d* Alvor 25 October 1495; *bur* Batalha

MANUEL I THE FORTUNATE 1495–1521

b Alconchette 1 June 1469, 6th and yst son of Dom Ferdinand, Duke of Viseu, Constable of Portugal (3rd son of King Duarte I), and Beatrice of Portugal; *s* his brother as Duke of Viseu 22 August 1484; *s* his 1st cousin (and brother-in-law) King John II 25 October 1495; *m* (1) Valencia October 1497 Isabel (*b* 2 October 1470; *d* Saragossa 24/25 August 1498; *bur* Saragossa or Toledo), widow of Alfonso, Prince of Portugal (son of King John II), and eldest dau of Ferdinand II, King of Aragon, and Isabel I, Queen of Castile; 1 son (*d* young); *m* (2) Alcazar de Sol 30 October 1500 Maria (*b* 29 June 1482; *d* 7 March 1517), sister of his 1st wife, being 3rd dau of Ferdinand II, King of Aragon, etc; 7 sons, 3 daus; *m* (3) Lisbon 7 March 1519 Leonor (*b* Brussels 24 November 1498; *m* (2) 8 July 1530, Francis I, King of France; *d* Talavera 18 February 1558), niece of his 1st and 2nd wives, being eldest dau of Philip I and Juana, King and Queen of Castile; 1 son, 1 dau; *d* Belem 13 December 1521

JOHN III 1521–1557

b Lisbon 6 June 1502, 2nd but eldest surviving son of King Manuel I; *s* his father 13 December 1521; *m* Estremoz 7 February 1525 Catherine, Regent of Portugal 1557–62 (*b* Torquemada 14 January 1507; *d* Lisbon 12 February 1578), 4th and yst dau of Philip I and Juana I, King and Queen of Castile; 6 sons, 3 daus; *d* Lisbon 11 June 1557; *bur* Belem

SEBASTIAN 1557–1578

b (posthumously) Lisbon 19 January 1554, only child of John, Prince of Portugal (5th son of King John III), and Joana, 2nd dau of Emperor Charles V (Carlos I, King of Spain); *s* his grandfather King John III 11 June 1557; *d* Alcazar-Kebir, Morocco 4 August 1578; eventually *bur* Belem

HENRY 1578–1580

b Lisbon 31 January 1512, 6th son of King Manuel I; *cr* Cardinal by Pope Paul III 16 December 1545; Archbishop of Lisbon 1564; *s* his grandnephew King Sebastian 4 August 1578; *d* Almeirim 31 January 1580; *bur* Evora, transferred to Belem 1582

[ANTONIO I JUNE–AUGUST 1580]

b 31 Jan 1531, natural son of Dom Luis, Duke of Beja (3rd son of King Manuel I), and Violante Gomes; Prior of Crato 1555; Governor of Tangier 1574; proclaimed King at Santarém 19 June 1580; defeated at Alcantara 26 August 1580 and fled to France; *d* Paris 26 August 1595

King John I and Philippa of Lancaster from their monumental effigies at Batalha.

Dom John, Grand Master of Avis, who ascended the Portuguese throne at the age of twenty-seven in 1385 was to prove one of the outstanding rulers of his age and well worthy of the epithet of 'Great' with which he has gone down in history. The reign commenced with the decisive defeat of the Castilians at the battle of Aljubarrota on 14 August 1385, a battle to be commemorated by the foundation of Batalha Abbey, which was to become the burial place of John and his Queen and many of their descendants. The victory ensured Portuguese independence.

Throughout his reign John was ably assisted by Dom Nuno Alvares Pereira, Constable of Portugal, who became known as 'the Holy Constable' and was a model of knightly chivalry and perfection until he finally retired into a monastry as Brother

Nuno de Santa Maria, dying two years before the King in 1431.

The battle of Aljubarrota had been won with the help of English archers and on 9 May the following year, 1386, John concluded the treaty of Windsor with King Richard II of England. This stipulated that there should be 'an inviolable, eternal, solid, perpetual and true league of friendship, alliance and union' between the kingdoms. It has never been violated and to this day Portugal is often described as 'England's oldest ally'. The alliance was further cemented by John's marriage to Philippa of Lancaster, daughter of John of Gaunt, which was celebrated at Oporto in February 1387. 'Dona Filipa', as she was known in Portugal, was to become the country's best loved Queen. Austere and pious by nature, she brought about a much needed reform in court life and she and the King brought up their large family with care. John had two natural children by one Ines Pires born before his marriage, and the son Alfonso, who married the daughter of 'the Holy Constable', was to be the ancestor of the future Bragança monarchs. After his marriage John appears to have remained faithful to Philippa although on one occasion court gossip informed the Queen that he had strayed. He was able to convince her that this was not so and wryly commemorated the event by having one of the royal apartments decorated with a design of chattering magpies.

The best known of John and Philippa's children was their fourth son Henry 'the Navigator', Duke of Viseu, Grand Master of the Order of Christ and Governor of the Algarves, who, from his residence at Sagre, near Cape St Vincent, directed voyages of discovery in attempts to prove his theory that a passage to India could be found by sailing round Africa. Despite his name, he never sailed on any expedition in person and the route he sought was not to be discovered in his lifetime, but the encouragement he gave to voyagers and the improvements in shipbuilding which he sponsored and financed paved the way for later explorers such as Vasco da Gama.

John I's reign accomplished a complete reorganization of the kingdom in spite of continuing warlike forays with Castile which did not end until 1411. Four years later the King's three eldest surviving sons were clamouring for a chance to prove their mettle, having been too young to serve earlier. They would not be put off by their father's offer to hold a tourney for them and eventually prevailed upon him to launch an attack on the port of Ceuta in North Africa. An expedition was fitted out and was about to sail when Queen Philippa was struck by plague. From her deathbed she armed and exhorted her sons and the fleet put out from the Tagus six days after her death on 25 July 1415. Ceuta fell after one day to become the first Portuguese possession in Africa. The King rewarded his sons by knighting them in the captured mosque and conferring the Dukedoms of Coimbra and Viseu (the first to be created in Portugal) on Dom Pedro and Dom Henry.

The rest of the King's reign was peaceful and uneventful. He died after a long illness on the forty-eighth anniversary of the battle of Aljubarrota, 14 August 1433.

Prince Duarte, who succeeded his father, was a man of forty-two, highly cultured and sensitive. He was so overwhelmed with grief at his father's death that he had to be persuaded by his brother Pedro to assume the government, in which he had already been associated for several years. Pedro was to become the power behind the throne. At a Cortes summoned at Evora in 1434, King Duarte propounded the *Lei Mental*, so called because it was said to have been in the mind of his father at the time of his death. It decreed that grants of land made to the nobility could only descend in the direct male line of the original grantee and should revert to the crown on the failure of such heirs. The law remained in force until its abolition in 1832. In 1437 the King's youngest and favourite brother Ferdinand, seized with the same ardour which had filled his elder brothers in 1415, begged to be allowed to lead another expedition to Africa, against the infidels. A fleet was duly collected and the King and his brother set sail with the object of taking Tangier. The town was three miles from the coast and the King with 8,000 soldiers was cut off by the Moors from retreating to Ceuta and reduced to extremities in three days. The situation was only saved by Ferdinand offering himself as a hostage, when the King and his troops were allowed to return to their ships and sail back to Lisbon. Ferdinand, who became known as 'the Constant Prince', never regained his freedom and died at Fez in June 1443. Duarte, who was devoted to his family, never recovered from the ignominious episode, which probably hastened his death. He fell victim to plague and died at Tomar in September 1438 after a reign of five years. His wife, Leonor of Aragon, had borne him nine children and it was the eldest surviving son Alfonso, a child of six, who succeeded to the throne.

Alfonso V's reign began with a dispute over the regency. King Duarte had stipulated in his will that Queen Leonor was to be Regent, but she was inexperienced and, as an Aragonese, unpopular with the people, who preferred the late King's brother Pedro, Duke of Coimbra. Negotiations for a compromise arrangement were drawn out over several months, complicated by the interference of the Count of Barcelos (John I's natural son) and the Archbishop of Lisbon, by the Queen giving birth to a posthumous daughter in March 1439, and by the death in the same month of her eldest daughter Philippa. Eventually the Cortes appointed Pedro the sole Regent. Queen Leonor continued conspiring, but was forced to go into exile in Castile in December 1440. She died at Toledo in February 1445.

Alfonso V attained his legal majority at the age of fourteen in January 1446 and the following year married his cousin Isabel, the eldest daughter of the former Regent. Soon after his marriage the young King fell under the influence of his half-uncle the Duke of Bragança (Count of Barcelos), who persuaded him that the Duke of Coimbra had poisoned both his parents. The former Regent was ordered to leave the court and withdraw to his estates. Bragança, still not satisfied, led an army after him but was defeated at Penella. He now persuaded the weak King to declare Dom Pedro an outlaw and, rallying his forces, defeated him at the hard fought battle of Alfarrobeira, in which on 21 May 1449 Pedro lost his life. The

Bragança line was to remain in virtual control of the kingdom until the reign of John II.

Alfonso V's long reign saw a great increase by conquest of Portugal's possessions in Africa, earning the King the epithet of 'the African', while his uncle Prince Henry continued to work tirelessly in his promotion of voyages of discovery until his death in 1460.

It was Alfonso's great ambition to secure the throne of Castile and on the death of his brother-in-law King Henry IV in 1474 he mounted an expedition to further his claim. The rather pathetic Queen Isabel, who had pleaded in vain for her father's life, had died in childbirth in 1455, and Alfonso now planned to marry his own niece, the thirteen-year-old Joanna, who was undoubtedly the daughter of his sister the Queen of Castile, although it was more than doubtful that King Henry had been her father. (We shall hear more of this when dealing with that kingdom later.) The Castilians rallied round Henry IV's half-sister Isabel, who had married King Ferdinand of Aragon, and inflicted an ignominious defeat on the Portuguese forces at Toro in 1476. Alfonso sought help from Louis XI of France, but it was not forthcoming and in 1478 he was forced to sign the treaty of Alcantara renouncing all claim to Castile and Leon. Joanna, the unfortunate pawn in the game, was despatched to a Portuguese nunnery where she survived for many years.

Alfonso V, King of Portugal: one of a series of stylized engraved portraits of European monarchs.

Alfonso was now a broken man. He lost his hair, grew fat and coarsened, and gave himself up to melancholia. Death overtook him before his resolve to abdicate could be ratified by the Cortes in 1481. Although his aspirations had brought him disaster, Alfonso must not be dismissed as a worthless King. He was a patron of literature and an able writer himself on a variety of subjects, assembling a great library at Evora. When the chronicler Acenheiro asked him how he should write the history of his reign, Alfonso's reply was 'Tell the truth'. Alfonso V founded the Order of the Tower and Sword and introduced the titles of Baron and Marquis into the Portuguese nobility.

John II who succeeded his father and was known, paradoxically it would seem to us today, as 'the perfect Prince', has been likened both in appearance and character to Henry VIII of England. His first act as King was to summon a Cortes to meet at Evora to hold an inquiry into all titles to landed property and to ensure that only the royal judges should dispense criminal justice throughout the land. This, of course, gave great offence to the nobility who combined together to oppose the King, finding a ready leader in Ferdinand, 3rd Duke of Bragança, now the powerful and immensely rich head of the bastard line descended from John I. The Duke and his equally powerful brothers began the almost inevitable intriguing with Castile.

King John's only son Alfonso was being educated at the border town of Moura under the tutelage of his maternal grandmother the Duchess of Viseu, in accordance with the terms of a treaty concluded by Alfonso V. John now determined to withdraw the boy into the safety of his own custody. The Bragança faction was able to delay the execution of this plan until 1483. When it finally came about the Duke of Bragança undertook to escort the young Prince to Evora. Here, after two days of celebrations, when the Duke went to take leave of the King he was told that his duplicity was known and that he was to be arrested and stand trial for treason. He was tried by twenty-nine judges, headed by the King, and after a trial lasting twenty-two days was found guilty on twenty-two counts and beheaded in the main square of Evora on 29 June 1484. His two brothers had managed to escape to Castile, but the elder, the Marquis of Montemór, was quaintly decapitated in effigy complete with imitation blood. The King's vengeance then turned on his brother-in-law the Duke of Viseu, whom he stabbed to death with his own hand at Setúbal in August 1484. The Duke's brother and successor Manuel prudently swore allegiance to John and was declared next heir to the throne after Prince Alfonso. (There had been so many intermarriages between the descendants of John I both legitimate and illegitimate that the reader is referred to the genealogical table in the appendix for an elucidation of the very complex relationships which existed. King John II and the Duke of Bragança, for example, were both married to sisters of the Duke of Viseu.) Many other nobles were executed and the power of the feudal nobility gave way to royal absolutism.

A conflict with Rome, when Pope Sixtus IV accused John of 'usurping religious liberty and the rights of the church', was settled by the sending of an embassy to the papal court protesting the King's complete submission and thereby gaining a bull promoting expansion into Africa as a 'crusade'.

In November 1490 the fifteen-year-old Prince Alfonso was married to the twenty-year-old daughter of Ferdinand of Aragon and Isabel of Castile, but he died childless less than a year later. John's cousin and brother-in-law Manuel now became heir presumptive, but John sought to promote his illegitimate son Jorge, a boy of ten, and gave him the Grand Masterships of Avis and Santiago. A complacent Queen Leonor had brought the boy up, but when the King removed him from her care into his own household she became incensed that her brother's rights should be infringed and a rift between the King and Queen developed and was only healed when John fell ill with dropsy. Feeling himself to be at death's door and urged by his confessor, John drew up a will naming Manuel as the rightful heir.

The King sought relief from his ailments at the spa of Monchique, but the waters proved ineffective and he moved to Alvor, where he died on 25 October 1495, aged only forty. Leonor survived as Queen Dowager until 1525. The comparatively short reign of John II saw a great expansion of Portugal's overseas possessions and the conclusion of the treaty of Tordesillas with Spain in 1494 agreed the division of future possessions in the new world between Spain and Portugal. Because of his suppression of feudalism John was loved by the people, who ignored the brutal side of his character.

Manuel 'the Fortunate', who succeeded his cousin and brother-in-law at the age of twenty-six, owed his name to the fact that he had been born on the feast of Corpus Christi at the exact moment when the Sacred Host was being borne in procession before his father's palace at Alconchette on the Tagus. Manuel's reign of twenty-five years was a golden age for Portugal, seeing progress in exploration and a flowering of literature, although the King himself did little beyond amassing the riches which his fleets brought home to him. One of his first acts was to pardon the exiled nobles and restore their lands. The new Duke of Bragança was among them and the King's aim was to surround himself with a magnificent court.

Like his immediate predecessors, Manuel cherished the idea of succeeding to the throne of Spain and to this end he married the widow of his nephew Prince Alfonso, the Infanta Isabel, although he only gained the consent of her parents 'the Catholic Kings' by expelling the Jews and unbaptized Moors from his dominions. The wedding took place in Valencia in October 1497 and the King and Queen took part in prolonged celebrations before commencing a slow progress through the towns of Castile to show themselves as the future heirs of that kingdom. Queen Isabel had become pregnant within a month of her marriage and the junketing probably cost her her life for she was taken ill in Toledo and died in August 1498 after giving birth to a son Miguel, who in his turn died a month short of his second birthday in 1500. Manuel then obtained the hand of his first wife's sister Maria, who bore him ten children before she died in 1517. On the second anniversary of her death Manuel married his third and last wife Leonor,

the niece of her two predecessors. She bore him a son who died in infancy and a daughter who died unmarried. After Manuel's death she was to become the second wife of Francis I of France, so we shall meet her again hereafter. King Manuel is said to have been 'fair, smiling, thinnish and long-armed'. He was of abstemious habits when it came to eating, drinking and the pleasures of the flesh, but enjoyed splendour and was extremely fond of music and dancing. Manuel's reign, which saw the acquisition of Brazil, Goa and yet more territory in Africa, ended with his death from plague at Belem on 13 December 1521.

The new King, John III, was aged nineteen and in 1525 married his stepmother's sister Catherine. The brother of these two Queens, the Emperor Charles V (Carlos I of Spain) was to marry John's eldest sister Isabel the following year and the marriage was to have far-reaching consequences for Portugal. John is generally represented as possessing a limited intellect. A religious fanatic of the worst sort, he introduced the Inquisition and the Jesuits into Portugal, and occupied himself with the founding of new Bishoprics. Although it was not apparent on the surface, the reign was an era of decline.

Of John's nine children, the only one to survive was a sickly youth, John, who in 1552 was married at the age of fifteen to his double first cousin Joana, daughter of the Emperor Charles V. The bridegroom was subject to recurrent attacks of fever, which were treated by blood-letting, weakening him still further. Eventually his physicians decided to separate him from his wife (who had, however, become pregnant) and forbade him to drink more than one cup of water a day. On the night of 1 January 1554 the young Prince woke crazed by thirst and, disobeying his medical advisers, soaked a towel in a pool of rainwater outside his window, wrang it out, and drank the resulting liquid. The foolhardy act proved fatal and, falling to the ground unconscious, he died the following day. His widow, herself still in her sixteenth year, was nearing the end of her pregnancy and it was decided to keep the news of her husband's death from her. Court mourning was deferred for three weeks and on 19 January the Princess was safely delivered of a son, who was named Sebastian after the Saint on the eve of whose feast day he was born. Joana returned to Spain soon after, leaving the baby in the care of his grandparents.

John III never fully recovered from the blow of his last surviving child's death and died of apoplexy on 11 June 1557, a few days after his fifty-fifth birthday.

The succession now passed to the three-year-old Sebastian. John had left no directions about the regency, but a hastily convened council of nobles declared that it had been his wish that Queen Catherine should undertake the office and she was duly appointed. She was almost as bigoted as her husband had been and was so aggressively Spanish that her rule became unpopular with all classes.

It was widely believed that she was intriguing to secure the eventual succession of her nephew Philip II of Spain. The Regent had a rival in the person of her brother-in-law Cardinal Henry, who felt the regency should have been his. Catherine was not a bad ruler, but apparently grew weary of the business. She first voiced her intention to resign in favour of Henry in December 1560, but the plan was not put into effect and approved by the Cortes until two years later, when Henry took over on the proviso that Sebastian, who was to remain in his grandmother's care, should come of age at fourteen.

The Cardinal's regency was comparatively uneventful, enlivened only by his quarrels with his bastard nephew Antonio who, although in Deacon's orders and destined for the priesthood, led a dissolute life which scandalized the chastely austere Cardinal, who eventually banished him from court.

Sebastian duly came of age in January 1568. He had already exhibited signs of religious mania and was completely under the influence of his Jesuit tutor Luis Gonçalves da Câmara and his brother Martim. It must be remembered that Sebastian was the child of double first cousins so that instead of eight different great-grandparents he only had four and the two great-grandmothers were sisters, one of them being the unbalanced Queen Juana of Castile. It was not a heritage which boded well for either his mental stability or his physical well-being. Hunting, military exercises and an excess of religious observances were the daily occupations of the King. All this seriously undermined his health and led to a breech in the relationship between the King and his grandmother when she urged him to desist from his violent exercises, and quarrels between them were to exist on and off until the old Queen's death in February 1578. Many proposals were put forward for Sebastian's marriage to various ladies, chief among them being his cousin the Infanta Isabel Clara Eugenia of Spain, daughter of Philip II. However, they all came to nothing and there were serious rumours of his probable impotence.

Sebastian's one overwhelming ambition was to be able to lead a 'crusade' against the Moors. In 1574 he made a preliminary expedition of reconnaissance, followed in 1578 by a full-scale invasion which ended in disaster. At Alcazar-Kebir on 4 August 1578, Sebastian was killed and his army annihilated. His body was recovered and eventually returned to Portugal and interred in the Convent of the Jeronimos at Belem in 1582. However, rumours that he had survived were to persist for many years, giving rise to four false Sebastians, the last appearing in Venice in 1603. The idea of the 'hidden King' then became a cult comparable to that of Arthur in Britain and Sir Richard Burton the explorer was to encounter remnants of it in remote areas of Brazil in the second half of the nineteenth century.

News of the disaster reached Lisbon in about a week, Sebastian's death was confirmed on 24 August, and the crown of Portugal devolved on the Regent, the sixty-six-year-old Cardinal Henry. The new King was a man of exemplary character, but his health was failing and it was apparent that he could not reign for long. He valiantly offered to resign his orders and marry to provide an heir, but the Holy See was reluctant to grant a dispensation and Philip of Spain, who coveted the succession for himself, sent Spanish theologians to dissuade him from taking such a step. The Cardinal King's health deteriorated rapidly; he took to his bed, began to cough

blood and could only take liquid nourishment. The end came on his sixty-eighth birthday (31 January 1580), after a reign of only seventeen months.

Henry had failed to nominate a successor from the several claimants to the throne. These were Antonio, Prior of Crato, the illegitimate son of his brother Luis, Duke of Beja; the Duke of Parma, who claimed through his late mother Maria, elder daughter of Duarte, Duke of Guimaraens, Henry's younger brother; Catherine, Duchess of Bragança, the younger daughter of the Duke of Guimaraens; Philip II, King of Spain, son of Henry's eldest sister Isabel; and Emmanuel Philibert, Duke of Savoy, son of Henry's second sister Beatrice. The best claim and that most favoured by the people was that of the Duchess of Bragança, she being not only Portuguese herself but also the wife of a direct descendant in the male line (albeit illegitimate) of King John the Great. The Cortes, however, allowed itself to be bought by the money and lavish promises of the Spanish King, who also managed to buy off the Duke of Bragança by promises of the sovereignty of Brazil, much to the Duchess's chagrin. At this juncture the Prior of Crato proclaimed himself King at Santarém on 19 June 1580 and at once proceeded to Lisbon, where he was welcomed with enthusiasm and set about striking money and raising any army.

The self-proclaimed King was the natural son of Dom Luis, Duke of Beja, the third son of King Manuel I, and a famous beauty Violante Gomes, known as 'the Pelican', to whom he now alleged his father had been secretly married in much the same manner as Pedro I and Ines de Castro. Antonio's rule was to prove a short one, for Philip's army under the Duke of Alba invaded Portugal and routed his forces at the battle of Alcantara on 26 August 1580. Antonio managed to make his getaway and after evading the Spanish forces for several months made his way to France in May 1581. Philip, meanwhile, had been proclaimed King Philip I of Portugal and made his solemn entry into Lisbon in December 1580 to receive the homage of the nobility and the submission of the Duchess of Bragança. The sixty years of Portugal's 'Babylonian captivity' had begun.

The rest of Dom Antonio's story is an adventurous one. The Azores had remained staunchly loyal to him and an invading force of 600 men was repelled at Terceira by the expedient of the islanders driving their semi-wild bulls into them. Meanwhile, Antonio was seeking aid from England, but the time was not yet ripe for Elizabeth I to wage war on Philip, so he returned to France where the Queen Regent Catherine de'Medici renounced her own very tenuous rights to Portugal in exchange for a future cession of Brazil and fitted him out with a fleet and army to fight the Spaniards. Antonio was certainly a brave man and returned in person to defend the Azores, which eventually fell to the superior forces of Spain in June 1583. Antonio had left the previous November to enlist more help and was to spend the rest of his life evading capture and assassination and endeavouring to interest others in his cause, even seeking the aid of Morocco. All his attempts proved fruitless and he died in Paris in 1595. He is in some ways a romantic and attractive figure, the 'Bonnie Prince

Charlie' of Portugal. As an ecclesiastic in minor orders, he was not free to marry, but he left a large illegitimate progeny. His four daughters became nuns and two sons died young, but the eldest surviving son, Manuel, married Emilia, daughter of William the Silent, Prince of Orange, and founded a family which continued in the male line until 1687 and the female until 1731. All proudly styled themselves 'of Portugal'.

Portugal remained under Spanish rule for sixty years, the Kings Philip II, Philip III and Philip IV of Spain being numbered Philip I, Philip II and Philip III of Portugal. They ruled through governors and viceroys and visited the country but rarely. When they did so they were received in a lavish style calculated by the Portuguese to gain concessions from the crippling taxes levied against them, but it was of no avail. Discontent grew and by the late 1630s, during the viceroyalty of the Duchess of Mantua, a strong movement for independence from Spain developed and received the backing of France. The obvious candidate for the throne was the Duke of Bragança, grandson of that Duchess who had claimed it in 1580. Failing him, there were still descendants of the Prior of Crato to fall back on. In 1639 the Duke was appointed Governor of the Arms of Portugal in a crafty move to attach him to the Spanish faction. In 1640 the attention of the Spaniards was deflected by a rebellion in Catalonia and the Portuguese conspirators seized the opportunity to stage a coup, the Duke having agreed in secret that he would accept the crown if offered to him. On 1 December the palace in Lisbon was stormed, almost without bloodshed, the Duchess of Mantua was held prisoner and her secretary of state, Miguel de Vasconcelos, who was generally detested, was found cowering in a cupboard, dragged out, shot and thrown from a window. In a few hours all was calm and the city settled down to await the arrival of Portugal's new King.

The House of Bragança

JOHN IV THE FORTUNATE   1640–1656

b Vila Viçosa 18 March 1604, eldest son of Teodosio, 7th Duke of Bragança, and Ana de Velasco; s his father as 8th Duke of Bragança 29 November 1630; proclaimed King of Portugal and the Algarves 1 December 1640; crowned at Lisbon 15 December 1640; accession confirmed and ratified by the Cortes 19 January 1641; m 12 January 1633 Luisa Maria, Queen Regent of Portugal 6 November 1656 to 21 June 1662 (b Sanlucar de Barrameda 13 October 1613; d Grillo, nr Lisbon 27 February 1666), dau of Juan Manuel Domingo Perez de Guzman, 8th Duke of Medina Sidonia, and Juana de Sandoval; 4 sons, 3 daus; d Lisbon 6 November 1656

ALFONSO VI   1656–1683

b Lisbon 21 August 1643, 3rd, but 1st surv, son of King John IV; s his father 6 November 1656, under his mother's regency until 21 June 1662, when he declared himself of age; forcibly placed under restraint 23 November 1667; m Lisbon 2 August 1666 (m annulled 24 March 1668) Maria Francisca Luisa Isabel (b Paris 21 June 1646; d Palhavaa 27 December 1683), yr dau of Charles Amadeus of Savoy, Duke of Nemours, and Elisabeth de Bourbon-Vendôme; no issue; d Sintra 12 September 1683

PEDRO II   1683–1706

b Lisbon 26 April 1648, 4th and yst son of King John IV; assumed the regency for his brother King Alfonso VI 23 November 1667, recognized by the Cortes 1 January 1668; s his brother 12 September 1683; resigned the regency to his sister the Queen Dowager of England 1704, but resumed power on her death 31 December 1705; m (1) Alcantara 2 April 1668 Maria Francisca Luisa Isabel (b Paris 21 June 1646; d Palhavaa 27 December 1683), formerly wife of his brother King Alfonso VI; 1 dau; m (2) Lisbon 11 August 1687 Maria Sophia Elisabeth (b Schloss Benrath, nr Düsseldorf, 6 August 1666; d Lisbon 4 August 1699), dau of Philipp Wilhelm, Elector Palatine of the Rhine, and his second wife Elisabeth Amalie of Hesse-Darmstadt; 5 sons, 2 daus; d Alcantara 9 December 1706

JOHN V   1706–1750

b Lisbon 22 October 1689, 2nd but eldest surv son of King Pedro II; s his father 9 December 1706; acclaimed Lisbon 1 January 1708; granted the style of Most Faithful Majesty by Pope Benedict XIV 21 April 1749; m Lisbon 27 October 1708 his first cousin, Maria Anna Josepha (b Linz 7 September 1683; d Lisbon 14 August 1754), dau of Leopold I, Holy Roman Emperor, King of Hungary and Bohemia, etc, and his 3rd wife Eleonore Magdalene Theresia, dau of Philipp Wilhelm, Elector Palatine of the Rhine; 5 sons, 1 dau; d Lisbon 31 July 1750

JOSEPH I   1750–1777

b Lisbon 6 June 1714, 2nd but eldest surv son of King John V; s his father 31 July 1750; acclaimed Lisbon 7 September 1750; m (proxy) Madrid 27 December 1727 and (in person) Elvas 19 January 1728 Mariana Victoria, Regent of Portugal 29 November 1776 to 24 February 1777 (b Madrid 31 January 1718; d Ajuda Palace, Lisbon 15 January 1781; bur São Francisco de Paula, Lisbon), dau of Philip V, King of Spain, and his 2nd wife Elisabeth Farnese; 1 son (stillborn), 6 daus; d Ajuda Palace, Lisbon 24 February 1777; bur São Vicente de Fora

MARIA I   1777–1816
AND
PEDRO III   1777–1786

Maria Francisca, b Lisbon 17 December 1734; s her father 24 February 1777; m Ajuda, nr Lisbon 6 June 1760 her uncle, Pedro, titular King jointly with her as Pedro III (b Lisbon 5 July 1717; d Ajuda 5 March 1786; bur São Vicente de Fora), 4th son of King John V; 4 sons, 3 daus; became mentally incapacitated and resigned under her son's regency from 1792; left Portugal 29 November 1807 and landed in Brazil 7 March 1808; d Rio de Janeiro 20 March 1816; bur Convent of Ajuda, Rio de Janeiro, returned to Portugal and re-bur Basilica of Estrela, Lisbon 1821

JOHN VI 1816–1826

b Lisbon 13 May 1767, 4th and yst but only surv son of Queen Maria I and King Pedro III; assumed the regency for his mother 16 February 1792; proclaimed Prince Regent of Portugal 15 July 1799; *s* his mother 20 March 1816; acclaimed as King of Portugal and Brazil Rio de Janeiro 6 February 1818; returned to Portugal 1821; recognized the independence of Brazil under his son Pedro 29 August 1825, while assuming the title of Emperor of Brazil himself for life; *m* (proxy) Madrid 27 March, (in person) Lisbon 9 June 1785 Carlota Joaquina (*b* Aranjuez 25 April 1775; *d* Queluz 7 January 1830; *bur* São Vicente de Fora), eldest dau of Carlos IV, King of Spain, and Maria Luisa of Bourbon-Parma; 3 sons, 6 daus; *d* Lisbon 10 March 1826; *bur* São Vicente de Fora

PEDRO IV MARCH–APRIL 1826

b Queluz 12 October 1798, 2nd but elder surv son of King John VI; proclaimed Perpetual Defender and Protector of Brazil 13 May 1822, and Emperor of Brazil (as Pedro I) 12 October 1822; crowned Rio de Janeiro 1 December 1822; *s* his father as King of Portugal 10 March 1826; abdicated the throne of Portugal in favour of his eldest daughter Maria da Gloria 29 April 1826; abdicated the throne of Brazil in favour of his only surv son Pedro (II) 7 April 1831, and returned to Europe to assist his daughter in establishing her throne; Regent of Portugal for his daughter 1834; *m* (1) (proxy) Vienna 13 May, (in person) Rio de Janeiro 5 November 1817 Maria Leopoldina (*b* Vienna 22 January 1797; *d* Rio de Janeiro 11 December 1826; *bur* São Paulo), 5th dau of Francis I, Emperor of Austria, and (4th dau of) his 2nd wife Maria Theresa of Bourbon-Two Sicilies; 3 sons, 4 daus; *m* (2) (proxy) Munich 2 August, (in person) Rio de Janeiro 17 October 1829 Amelia (*b* Milan 31 July 1812; *d* Lisbon 26 January 1873), 3rd dau of Eugène de Beauharnais, 1st Duke of Leuchtenberg and Prince of Eichstadt, and Augusta of Bavaria; 1 dau; *d* Queluz 24 September 1834; *bur* São Vicente de Fora, Lisbon, reinterred São Paulo, Brazil 1972

MARIA II (FIRST REIGN) 1826–1828

MIGUEL I 1828–1834

b Queluz 26 October 1802, 3rd but yr surv son of King John VI; nominated Regent of Portugal for his niece Queen Maria II 3 July 1827 and assumed office 26 February 1828; declared himself King 30 June 1828 and was proclaimed by the Cortes 11 August 1828; deposed by the Convention of Evora-Monte 26 May 1834; lived in exile in Germany from 1851; *m* Kleinheubach 24 September 1851 Adelheid (*b* Kleinheubach 3 April 1831; *d* St Cecilia's Convent, Ryde, Isle of Wight 16 December 1909), dau of Constantin, Hereditary Prince of Löwenstein-Wertheim-Rosenberg, and Agnes of Hohenlohe-Langenburg; 1 son, 6 daus; *d* Bronnbach 14 November 1866

MARIA II (SECOND REIGN) 1834–1853

b Rio de Janeiro 4 April 1819, eldest dau of King Pedro IV; *s* her father on his abdication 29 April 1826, under the regency of her aunt the Infanta Isabel Maria until 3 July 1827, then under that of her uncle Dom Miguel until his usurpation of the throne 11 August 1828;

reinstated on his deposition 26 May 1834; *m* (1) (proxy) Munich 5 November 1834, (in person) Lisbon 26 January 1835 August, 2nd Duke of Leuchtenberg and Prince of Eichstadt, *cr* Prince of Portugal, peer, and General-in-Chief of the Portuguese Armies 1 December 1834 (*b* Milan 9 December 1810; *d* Lisbon 28 March 1835), brother of her stepmother the Empress Amelia of Brazil; *m* (2) (proxy) Coburg 1 January, (in person) Lisbon 9 April 1836 Prince Ferdinand of Saxe-Coburg and Gotha, *cr* King Consort of Portugal 16 September 1837, Regent of Portugal for his son King Pedro V 19 December 1853 to 16 September 1855 (*b* Vienna 29 October 1816; *d* Lisbon 15 December 1885); 7 sons, 4 daus (and a stillborn child of unspecified sex); *d* Lisbon 15 November 1853; *bur* São Vicente de Fora

PEDRO V 1853–1861

b Lisbon 16 September 1837, eldest son of Queen Maria II; *s* his mother 15 November 1853, under the regency of his father until 16 September 1855; *m* (proxy) Berlin 29 April, (in person) Lisbon 18 May 1858 Stephanie (*b* Dresden 15 July 1837; *d* Lisbon 17 July 1859), elder dau of Karl Anton, Prince of Hohenzollern-Sigmaringen, and Josephine of Baden; no issue; *d* Lisbon 11 November 1861; *bur* São Vicente de Fora

LUIS I 1861–1889

b Lisbon 31 October 1838, 2nd son of Queen Maria II; *s* his brother King Pedro V 11 November 1861; *m* (proxy) Turin 27 September, (in person) Lisbon 6 October 1862 Maria Pia (*b* Turin 16 October 1847; *d* Stupinigi, nr Turin 5 July 1911), dau of Victor Emmanuel II, King of Italy, and Adelaide of Austria; 2 sons (and 1 stillborn); *d* Cascais 19 October 1889; *bur* São Vicente de Fora

CARLOS I 1889–1908

b Lisbon 28 September 1863, elder son of King Luis I; *s* his father 19 October 1889; *m* Lisbon 22 May 1886 Amelia (*b* Twickenham, Middlesex, England 28 September 1864; *d* Château de Bellevue, Le Chesnay, nr Versailles 25 October 1951), eldest dau of Louis Philippe, Count of Paris, and Marie Isabelle of Montpensier; 2 sons, 1 dau; assassinated Lisbon 1 February 1908; *bur* São Vicente de Fora

MANUEL II 1908–1910

b Lisbon 15 November 1889, yr son of King Carlos I; *s* his father 1 February 1908; deposed by revolution 5 October 1910; *m* Sigmaringen 4 September 1913 Augusta Victoria (*b* Potsdam 19 August 1890; *m* (2) Langenstein 23 April 1939 Count Carl Robert Douglas; *d* Munchhof, Baden 29 August 1966), only dau of Wilhelm, Prince of Hohenzollern and his 1st wife Maria Theresa of Bourbon-Two Sicilies; no issue; *d* Fulwell Park, Twickenham, Middlesex 2 July 1932

The first Bragança King of Portugal, who ascended the throne at the age of thirty-six, would have been far happier leading the simple and orderly life of a country gentleman, pursuing his favourite pastimes, hunting and composing music. He was,

King John IV, the first Bragança King, from a contemporary print.

however, the obvious candidate for the throne, being thoroughly Portuguese, and he had the determined backing of his Andalusian wife, Luisa de Guzman. His accession was hailed with rejoicing and, after entering Lisbon, he was publicly crowned on a platform erected before the Cathedral. It was the last actual coronation to take place in Portugal, as John was later to dedicate his crown to the Blessed Virgin and place it on her statue in the church at Vila Viçosa. One of the new King's first – and most popular – acts was to declare that the revenues from his patrimonial estates were sufficient to supply his needs and those of his household and that the revenues of the crown lands should in future be devoted to national needs.

The revolution had occurred so suddenly and successfully that the last person to be informed of it was King Philip IV of Spain, the erstwhile Philip III of Portugal. The news was broken to him by the Count-Duke of Olivares in an all-time masterpiece of tact. 'I have to congratulate your majesty on a most fortunate event,' he said, 'whereby you have just obtained a powerful dukedom and some magnificent estates.' 'By what means?' asked the King. 'The Duke of Bragança has madly allowed himself to be seduced by the populace, who have proclaimed him King of Portugal. His vast estates are therefore forfeited and become the property of your majesty, who, by the annihilation of this family, will in future reign securely and peaceably over that kingdom', was the reply. The might of Spain could, of course, have easily crushed the Portuguese rebellion but was deflected by a Catalan one instead. The new regime obtained the recognition of Sweden and England and concluded a treaty with France in June 1641.

Bearing in mind that the Queen of France, Anne of Austria, was Philip IV's sister, the Portuguese delegates had been doubtful of the success of their mission and allowed their surprise to be shown, provoking the Queen's remark: 'True it is, that I am the sister of his Catholic Majesty, but am I not also the mother of the Dauphin?' A treaty was also concluded with the Dutch States-General, who agreed to help in the war against Spain in return for being allowed to retain the Portuguese colonies already seized by them. The Brazilians, however, preferred to return to Portuguese rule and sent a fleet to help recapture the West African colonies of Angola and São Tome, thus alienating the Dutch. The state of affairs thus brought about had the effect of depressing John, who, in 1647, made a strange proposal to abdicate and retire to the Azores, leaving the choice of a successor to the Queen Regent of France. Nothing came of this scheme and border clashes with Spain continued in desultory fashion until the King, long debilitated by attacks of gout and kidney-stones, died on 6 November 1656. His eldest son Teodosio, whom he had created Prince of Brazil, had predeceased him at the age of nineteen in 1653, providentially it would seem as he already exhibited signs of religious mania similar to those manifested by King Sebastian. The heir to the throne, therefore, was the thirteen-year-old Alfonso, and the regency was assumed by Queen Luisa.

Alfonso VI suffered both physical and mental disabilities. An illness at the age of three (perhaps a form of poliomyelitis) had left him partially paralysed in the right side and the state of his mind was such that many doubted if he would ever be fit to rule. His mother the Queen Regent, however, was a born ruler and a Moorish astrologer is said to have prophesied her great destiny at her birth. She pursued the war against Spain with vigour and successfully married off her only surviving daughter Catherine to King Charles II of England, having failed to capture Louis XIV. English troops and arms were forthcoming as a result of the marriage and the struggle with Spain was finally to be resolved in 1668 with Spain's recognition of Portugal's independence. Meanwhile, Alfonso had come of age. Opinions and contemporary descriptions of him are much at variance, some representing him as 'of agreeable presence, fair, blue-eyed, with a perfect nose' and others as a moronic, wine-bibbing somnambulist, savagely killing animals for pleasure. He eschewed all attempts to educate him and gave himself to the company of low companions, the chief of these being one Antonio Conti, whom he had spotted from his window selling ribbons outside the Palace when, as was his wont, he was watching the street boys throwing stones. Installed in the Palace, Antonio became the King's inseparable companion, defying the Queen and leading him out into the city on night escapades damaging the property of respectable citizens in a gang of riff-raff similar to himself. This state of affairs could not be allowed to continue and eventually the Duke of Cadaval and a small band of nobles arrested Conti and some other of the King's companions and shipped them off to Brazil. When the King finally realized what had happened he flew into a rage and rode off to Alcantara, where he gathered together a band of some four hundred armed men, declaring that the time had come for him to assume the reins of government. Queen Luisa, who had been planning to resign the regency in two months' time, gave in with a good grace and retired to a Carmelite convent where she died in February 1666. She had asked Alfonso to come to her bedside, but he was hunting at Salvaterra and tarried so long on his return journey that he arrived too late to see his mother alive. The affairs of government were in the capable hands of the Count of Castelo Melhor, who continued and concluded the final outcome of the Spanish war.

Negotiations for the King's marriage to Marie Françoise Louise Elisabeth of Savoy, styled Mademoiselle d'Aumale, a spirited nineteen year old, were begun in 1665 and concluded the following year. The bride arrived in Lisbon on 2 August 1666 and the marriage took place immediately. The King, however, found the festivities boring, and left to dine in his own apartments. The new Queen was politically ambitious and requested and obtained admission to state council meetings. She soon realized that she must get rid of Castelo Melhor to gain an ascendancy and found a ready ally in her brother-in-law Dom Pedro, who had bcome infatuated with her. Their intrigue against the minister proved so successful that he was forced to flee from Lisbon and eventually find refuge in England, where he entered the service of Queen Catherine. The sister- and brother-in-law now set about a plan to dissolve her marriage to the King and bring about their own union. The Queen's first move was to remove with her entire household to the Esperança Convent in November 1667, leaving a letter for the King in which she regretted she had been unable to fulfil her marital duties and begged for permission to return to France, taking her dowry with her. The King, who seems to have been genuinely fond of her, rushed to the convent and demanded admission, only to be told by the Abbess that the Queen held the keys. Dom Pedro then appeared on the scene and persuaded his brother to return to Lisbon and leave him to negotiate with the Queen. The following day Maria Francisca (as she was known in Portugal) petitioned the ecclesiastical authorities for the annulment of her marriage on the grounds that it had never been consummated. Evidence of Alfonso's alleged incapacity was given in minute and intimate detail and he himself, ill advisedly, swore an oath that he had made every possible attempt to consummate the marriage. The Queen made a similar oath the same day and the next day the marriage was declared null and void without further examination of the two spouses as demanded by canon law. Within a week Pedro and Maria Francisca were married and he was confirmed in the regency, Alfonso being declared completely incapable of governing. The unfortunate Alfonso was at first confined in Lisbon. In June 1669 he was taken to the Azores, where he remained until 1674, when the fear of plots to restore him to power caused the Regent to have him returned to the mainland. He spent the last nine years of his life in close confinement at Sintra and died there in September 1683.

The Regent now ascended the throne as King Pedro II. Maria Francisca, Queen once again, was only to enjoy that

King Pedro II, from a print.

dignity for three months, dying in December 1683. She left one daughter, Isabel Luisa Josefa, born in January 1669, who was declared heiress to the throne. Pedro showed no great inclination to marry again, but his minister and great friend, the Duke of Cadaval, finally persuaded him to do so, and in 1687 he married the Elector Palatine's daughter, Maria Sophia of Neuburg, who bore him seven children. When the War of the Spanish Succession broke out in 1700, Pedro was inclined at first to side with France and recognize Philip V as King of Spain, but soon saw the expediency of taking the side of Portugal's oldest ally, England, treating with the Right Honourable John Methuen, who was sent to Lisbon to negotiate a political and commercial treaty with Portugal. The famous Methuen treaty, whereby Portuguese wines were to be imported into England at a lower rate of duty than those of France and Germany in return for similar concessions on English merchandise, was signed 27 December 1703. From that day, port became the Englishman's drink, and a large colony of English wine merchants and shippers settled in Oporto, while an English 'factory' was established in Lisbon.

The Austrian candidate for the Spanish throne, the Archduke Charles (later Emperor Charles VI) arrived in Lisbon with a large English fleet and 10,000 English troops on 7 March 1704, and on 30 April Philip V declared war on Portugal. The English troops conducted a successful campaign, taking Gibraltar, and the Archduke advanced to Barcelona. Meanwhile, Pedro had fallen ill and, believing himself to be dying, resigned the regency into the hands of his sister the Queen Dowager of England, who had returned to Portugal in 1693. She governed wisely for a year until her death on 31 December 1705, when Pedro was obliged to resume power until his own death a year later on 9 December 1706. He is regarded as one of Portugal's best Kings and the alliance with England, cemented by the Methuen treaty, was to be the leading influence on Portuguese history for the next century.

The seventeen-year-old boy who succeeded his father as John V and was to reign for nearly half a century, was to prove a flamboyant figure. A patron of literature and the arts and a lover of music and the theatre, he used Portugal's great new wealth (derived from Brazilian silver and gold) to import the best artists, architects and theatrical performers from all over Europe. The Patriarchal Church in Lisbon, the Convent Palace of Mafra, the Library of Coimbra University and the Royal Academy of History at Lisbon all owe their foundation or construction to John V.

The war of the Spanish succession dragged on until peace was signed between Spain and Portugal on 6 February 1715 and thereafter John's foreign policy was to maintain friendly relations with England in pursuance of the terms of the Methuen treaty and to establish a close relationship by the marriages of his daughter and eldest surviving son to the eldest son and daughter of Philip V of Spain. John himself had married the Archduchess Maria Anna of Austria, sister of the Archduke Charles, Philip's rival for the Spanish throne.

John was both as highly sexed and religious as any of his ancestors. So religious, in fact, that he chose nuns to be his mistresses, one of them being Mother Paula of the Convent of Odivelas, whose visits from the King produced a son José who was to become Inquisitor-General of the kingdom. Several other children were the result of similar liaisons and another of John's natural sons, Gaspar, was to become Archbishop of Braga. In 1716 John obtained the creation of the Patriarchate of Lisbon from Pope Clement XI, ostensibly as a reward for Portugal's services against the Turks. Vast sums of money found their way in the papal coffers and finally, a little over a year before his death, John was rewarded with the title of 'Most Faithful Majesty' for himself and his successors by Pope Benedict XIV, thus putting him on a par with the 'Most Christian Majesty' of France and the 'Most Catholic Majesty' of Spain. By this time, however, a decline both in public affairs and in the King's health had set in. His 'dropsy of the chest' (perhaps emphysema) finally failed to respond to the healing waters of Caldas and he died 'a pious death' on 31 July 1750.

The period in which Queen Maria Anna administered affairs during King John's long illness saw the rise of Portugal's greatest statesman, Sebastião José de Carvalho e Melo, better known to history by the title of Marquis of Pombal which he was to receive in 1770. John V had disliked him, but as the Queen's protégé he was appointed Minister of Foreign Affairs and War three days after the King's death.

John's son and successor, Joseph I, was aged thirty-six and was completely untrained for his role, his sole interests being hunting, riding and gambling. He followed these pursuits all day and only saw his ministers for a short time in the late evening, when he would sign whatever papers were put before him without enquiring into their content. His wife, Mariana Victoria of Spain shared his interests and was an ardent horsewoman and huntress, on one occasion accidentally peppering her husband with stray shot.

On 1 November 1755 Lisbon was devastated by a severe earthquake and tidal wave which occurred without any warning. Within seven minutes ten thousand buildings were destroyed and from 5,000 to 8,000 lives had been lost. The court was at Belem, where the shock was only mildly felt, and the King's immediate reaction was to seek the solace of religion with all the extravagant observances to which so many of Portugal's monarchs were unfortunately prone.

The King's indolence left the country's affairs almost completely in the hands of Pombal, who checked the Inquisition and sought to crush the power of the Jesuits. In September 1758 there was an attempt on the King's life when he was returning by carriage from Belem and was shot at by three mounted men, receiving injuries in his shoulder, arm and chest, which however were not serious. The crime was attributed to the Tavora family, five of whose members were arrested together with some other noblemen and brought to trial. No motive was established but there seems to be a strong assumption that it was a crime of passion brought about by the fact that the young Marchioness of Tavora was the King's mistress and her husband had only just discovered the fact. Some of those arrested confessed under torture and all those charged were found guilty, the old Marquis and Marchioness of Tavora, their two sons and six others being executed in January 1759. The Jesuits were implicated in the plot by the confession of one of those executed, conveniently giving Pombal the excuse he was looking for to banish them from the kingdom. Now Prime Minister, Pombal embarked on a remarkable programme of enlightened reform, abolishing slavery in Brazil, establishing a good educational system, reorganizing the army, encouraging agriculture and improving the country's finances. He was also energetic in the rebuilding of Lisbon. He received the title of Marquis of Pombal from his grateful sovereign in 1770.

Queen Mariana Victoria had borne no living son and of her six daughters, only four survived. The eldest of these, Maria Francisca, Princess of Brazil, was declared heiress-presumptive and in order to save Portugal from the possibility of again falling under the sway of a foreign monarch, was married by dispensation to her uncle, King Joseph's brother Pedro. He was seventeen years her senior, but temperamentally they were well suited and lived together quite happily, producing a large family. King Joseph lived just long enough to see the incestuous marriage pattern repeated when his eldest grandson-nephew, the fifteen-year-old Prince of Beira, married his thirty-year-old aunt Dona Maria Benedita, King Joseph's youngest daughter. Mercifully, there were to be no children of this marriage.

Queen Maria I of Portugal: a portrait at Queluz painted before madness had overtaken her.

Joseph apparently suffered a stroke which deprived him of speech in November 1776 and Queen Mariana Victoria assumed the regency. She, her daughter and son/brother-in-law were antagonistic to Pombal and when the aged though still active statesman arrived at the palace on the morning following the King's death in February 1777, he was met in the antechamber by Cardinal da Cunha with the words: 'Your Excellency no longer has anything to do here.'

The new Queen and King, Maria I and Pedro III, were in their forty-third and sixtieth years when they ascended the throne. Although coins were struck in their joint names and all acts and deeds mentioned them both, the Queen was the real sovereign and her uncle/husband but her consort. Both were pious, hearing several masses every day, devoted to each other and with little aptitude for or interest in governing. They passed their days at their favourite palace of Queluz with racing, bullfights, musical evenings and the everlasting religious observances, leaving affairs in the capable hands of the Queen Mother Mariana Victoria, who like them was fanatically religious and had always hated Pombal and his progressive policies. Her first act was to see to his dismissal and free all the imprisoned nobles who had opposed him. The old man was banished to his estates at Pombal and died there in May 1782, aged eighty-three, having at least had the satisfaction of surviving his persecutor Queen Mariana Victoria by more than a year.

While Pedro III employed his energies in efforts to re-establish the Jesuits, his wife, under the influence of her confessor, raised large sums of money to send to the Latin convent in Jerusalem. The sovereigns' one important act was to meet with the Spanish court at Badajoz in 1785, when the dispute over the frontier in South America was settled and their younger surviving son, Dom John, was betrothed to the Spanish Infanta Carlota Joaquina, the marriage taking place the same year.

Pedro III died in March 1786 and two years later, in September 1788, his elder son, Joseph, Prince of Brazil, died of smallpox. He was said to have been a young man of great promise. He was survived by his aunt-wife by over forty years. The deaths of her husband and son, coupled with the disquieting news of the outbreak of the French Revolution in 1789, had a disturbing effect on Queen Maria I. She sank into a state of melancholia, suffering terrible nightmares and Dr Willis, who had treated King George III of England with some success, was summoned to Portugal to attend her. His skill was of no avail and the poor Queen, convinced that she was damned, ran about the palace corridors pitifully wailing 'Ai Jesus!' in a state of delirium. Her only surviving son, Dom John, assumed the government in 1792 and was formally proclaimed Prince Regent of Portugal in July 1799, when it finally became obvious that his mother would never recover her faculties. It was the same year in which Napoleon Bonaparte became the effective ruler of France as First Consul. He regarded Portugal as a province of England and fully realizing its possible importance as a base for English troops, sent his brother Lucien to Madrid in 1800 with instructions to negotiate with Portugal for the abandonment of the alliance with England and the opening of its ports to France among other things, while offering Spain the assistance of French troops if the terms were rejected. Dom John did reject them and declared war on Spain in February 1801. A short campaign followed and after several Portuguese losses, the Prince Regent sued for peace which was concluded by the treaty of Badajoz on 6 June 1801, whereby some territory was ceded to Spain. It was followed soon after by another by which French Guiana was extended to the Amazon. Napoleon, however, was completely dissatisfied by these treaties, having determined to bring about the end of Portuguese independence, and only ratified them after many months.

At the age of eighteen, Dom John, still then the younger son, had been married to the ten-year-old Spanish Infanta Carlota Joaquina, a political marriage first arranged some seven years earlier. At the same time John's sister Mariana Victoria married the Infante Dom Gabriel, Carlota Joaquina's uncle. The Spanish Princess was so ugly and contrasted so unfavourably with the Portuguese one that the people of Lisbon, on first seeing her, said that they had exchanged a whiting for a sardine. Carlota Joaquina was indeed very ugly and even her portraits fail to flatter her. She was dwarfish, beady-eyed, hook-nosed, hirsute and pockmarked, and grew worse as she grew older. She was precocious and vivacious but possessed of an extremely malevolent nature. Portugal seems to have had more than its fair share of malicious, ill-disposed Queens and Carlota Joaquina was probably the worst of them.

The court to which she came, from the much happier atmosphere of Aranjuez, was sombre in the extreme as has already been noted. Her mother-in-law Queen Maria was already exhibiting signs of madness and having visions of her father burning in hell for having permitted Pombal to suppress the Jesuits.

Dom John was good-natured, indolent, corpulent, and almost as ugly as his wife. Like his mother, he was much given to religious observances which bored Carlota Joaquina. In fact, the couple were completely incompatible. The marriage was consummated when Carlota Joaquina was fourteen and she duly produced nine children. Unlike their parents, the children were all handsome and although rumour had it that the younger ones were not Dom John's, there was no denying that Carlota Joaquina was their mother. After the birth of the last child the couple virtually lived apart, he at Mafra and she at Queluz, or at the quinta she had purchased as a retreat and where she was alleged to indulge in sexual orgies rivalling those of Messalina.

The Palace of Queluz in 1856.

Such was the state of affairs in the Portuguese royal family when France and Spain (now both under the domination of Napoleon) demanded that Portugal should close all her ports to the English and that all English residents should be arrested and have their property confiscated. The Prince Regent and the Portuguese government realized that an invasion was imminent and on the advice of the British determined to remove themselves across the Atlantic to the rich colony of Brazil. Carlota Joaquina was violently opposed to the idea and wished to join her mother in Madrid, but her pleas to be allowed to do so were ignored and in November 1807 the mad Queen, Dom John, Carlota Joaquina, their children, and the rest of the royal family with practically the whole court and their servants to the number of 16,000 to 18,000 people embarked on the Tagus in a fleet ill equipped to receive them and set sail for the new world. Dom John and his wife sailed in separate ships, he taking his sons and she the daughters. The voyage was a long and arduous one and everyone, including the royal family, soon became verminous and had to shave

their heads. Rio de Janeiro was finally reached in March 1808 and the royal family received a tumultuous welcome from the Brazilians.

Dom John settled down very happily in Brazil, where he took up residence in the former Viceroy's palace. Carlota Joaquina, on the other hand, detested the country and the people (as, indeed, she did most things which were not Spanish), and found an alternative residence for herself in the Palace Square, where she was able to give full range to 'that asperity, violence and vindictiveness of character from which so much is to be apprehended', as Sir William à Court wrote. She also acquired a country residence at Santa Cruz in a former Jesuit convent and her progresses between her residences became the occasion of much display, all other travellers on the road being obliged to alight from their carriages and kneel in respect as the Princess passed by.

Dom Pedro, the elder surviving son of the royal pair, lived with his father, but Dom Miguel, the younger, lived with his mother and became her spoilt darling, being indulged in every possible youthful excess and escapade. Both boys were exceptionally handsome – young Adonises in fact – and they soon embarked on a series of amorous adventures, Dom Pedro's in particular being reminiscent of those of Henry IV and Louis XIV of France and Charles II of England, and he became the father of many bastards, most of whom he recognized and later ennobled. Carlota Joaquina spent a considerable amount of her time plotting to become Regent of the Spanish colonies in South America and even to be recognized as heir to the Spanish throne, but fortunately she was thwarted in all of them.

Queen Maria I died in March 1816, one month after Brazil had been declared a kingdom, and the Prince Regent became King John VI of the United Kingdom of Portugal, Brazil and the Algarves. In the following year the heir-apparent Dom Pedro, Prince of Brazil, was married to the Archduchess Leopoldina of Austria, a younger sister of Napoleon's Empress Marie Louise. She arrived at Rio in November and the marriage ceremony took place immediately with great pomp and rejoicing including fireworks, bullfights, illuminations, and land and river processions. There were further celebrations in the following February when Dom John was acclaimed King (the ceremony which had superseded the rite of coronation) in the Palace Square.

Dom John VI would have been content to live out the rest of his life in Brazil, but peace had been restored in Europe and the Portuguese began to agitate for the royal family to return to Lisbon. The King was unable for some time to make up his mind whether to return himself or send Dom Pedro. In February 1821 a threatened revolution forced the proclamation in Rio of a Constitution, the initiative being taken by Dom Pedro, and the King decided to return to his Portuguese realm, sadly setting sail in April. Carlota Joaquina was delighted and as she stepped on board ship, removed her shoes and symbolically shook the Brazilian dust from them. The King and Queen were accompanied by Dom Miguel and their daughters and took with them the corpse of old Queen Maria I.

The royal party arrived in Lisbon in July and, on disembarking, the King, after attending a Te Deum in the Cathedral, drove to the Cortes, where he was hailed as 'Constitutional King', and thence to Queluz. The gruesome business of the final burial of the old Queen took place shortly after. Her triple coffin was opened, the noisome effluvia causing one of the Princesses to faint, and the six-year dead, unembalmed corpse, the face quite blackened but the limbs still flexible, was lifted out and completely reclothed, then laid in state while the nobility filed past to kiss its gloved hand.

Since the King and Queen found living in close proximity at Queluz intolerable, he moved to the Palace of Bemposta with two of his daughters, and resumed the old court ceremonials of 'hand-kissing', or public audience. Carlota Joaquina lived quietly at Queluz becoming more and more deeply eccentric in her dress and behaviour.

The Constitution was soon found to be unworkable and Carlota Joaquina caused a scandal by refusing, on the grounds of ill-health, to appear in the Cortes to take the oath to uphold it as required of all members of the royal family. Instead she retired to her Quinta de Ramalhão to plot the return of absolutism and the replacement of Dom John by Dom Miguel. Her attempts were all frustrated in one way or another as the King was popular in spite of his unprepossessing appearance and slothfulness.

Meanwhile, things had been on the move in Brazil. The country sought its independence and Dom Pedro, left behind as Regent, was first proclaimed 'Perpetual Defender and Protector' in May 1822 and Constitutional Emperor in October of the same year, being crowned at Rio in a magnificent display on 1 December. When the news reached Portugal Dom John refused to accept it, and it was not until August 1825 that he was persuaded by the British to recognize Brazilian independence and his son's sovereignty, at the same time reserving the title of Emperor for himself for life. The following March, Dom John, who although only fifty-nine was prematurely aged and a martyr to gout, was taken ill shortly after supping at Belem, where he had gone to witness another interminable religious procession. He was driven back to Bemposta and died six days later after suffering a series of convulsions. The Queen pleaded that her own ill-health prevented her from attending the King's deathbed and started a rumour that he had been poisoned by the Freemasons. Dom John's character has been well summed up by Sir Marcus Cheke in his biography of Carlota Joaquina: 'He was charitable, intensely loyal to his friends, loyal to his country's allies, sentimental, easy-going, much attached to familiar faces and familiar scenes... The defects of his character were mostly the excess of his good qualities. A less kindly man might have freed himself of his difficulties by a divorce, or by severity might have established discipline among his sons.'

The death of John VI meant that his elder son, now the Emperor Pedro I of Brazil, became King Pedro IV of Portugal. A few days before his death the old King had appointed his daughter the Infanta Isabel Maria Regent, knowing that the question of succession would have to be settled in some way as it was unthinkable that Portugal and Brazil could again be united. Pedro kept everyone guessing his intentions until the end of April, then abdicated the Portuguese throne in favour of his eldest daughter, the seven-year-old Maria da Glória, conditional on her betrothal to her uncle Dom Miguel and the acceptance by Portugal of the new liberal Constitution he had promulgated. The little girl did not set sail from Rio until the 5 July 1828, and on arrival at Gibraltar on 2 September received the news that Dom Miguel had returned from abroad, taken over the regency from his sister and been proclaimed King by the Cortes on 11 August. There was nothing for it but to press on to England, where she was recognized by the British government and received a royal salute on arriving at Falmouth. The little Queen was an engaging child and was at once taken up by London society, winning all hearts, including that of George IV when she flung her arms about his portly figure and reached up to kiss him. She also attended a children's party with her exact contemporary, the British heiress-presumptive Princess Victoria, whom Greville considered 'a short, vulgar-looking child, and not near so good-looking as the Portuguese'.

Meanwhile, in Lisbon the absolutist usurper King Miguel I was enjoying a *succès fou*. His dashing good looks and swashbuckling ways made him popular with the people, but he was a man of little education, limited intellect and narrow outlook. His mother, of course, was in the seventh heaven of delight to see her darling on the throne, but her triumph was shortlived. Although only in her fifty-fifth year she became suddenly old and ill and lay for many weeks stretched on a mattress, ill-kempt, racked with pain and often delirious, until death came on 7 January 1830. Her funeral sermon by the fanatical Benedictine monk João Bonaventura was a masterpiece of hyperbole, extolling her 'heroic virtues'.

Miguel's reign in Portugal was favourably regarded by the rest of Europe until 1831, when two liberal risings were rigorously put down with the loss of many lives. At the same time opposition to Pedro's rule in Brazil forced him to abdicate the imperial throne in favour of his son Pedro II and he determined to return to Europe to fight for the restoration of his daughter Maria da Glória in Portugal.

Pedro's character was a strange one. Not as handsome or dashing as his younger brother Miguel, he nevertheless surpassed him in the number of love affairs he conducted, many of them simultaneously. The most famous of his mistresses, the Marqueza dos Santos, dominated him for many years and bore a large family. Pedro treated his first wife, the rather plain Empress Leopoldina, with great cruelty, finding her dumb admiration too cloying, and her death in childbirth was rumoured to have been the result of physical violence on his part. However, he put up a great show at her funeral, frequently interrupting his partaking of the cold collation which had thoughtfully been provided in his tribunal to bend tearfully over his missal. By one of those strange twists of fate which make history and genealogy so fascinating, Pedro's second wife, Amelia of Leuchtenberg, was a granddaughter of Napoleon's first Empress Josephine, whereas his first wife, it will be recalled, was the sister of Napoleon's second wife Marie

Louise. The Empress Amelia was a complete contrast to Leopoldina and won all hearts, including her husband's, from the moment of her landing in Brazil. Pedro founded the Order of the Rose in her honour and she proved a loving mother to her legitimate stepchildren, although steadfastly refusing to have anything to do with the bastard ones. Pedro adored all his children and in a macabre fashion, worthy of some of his ancestors, kept the coffin of one of his infant natural daughters in his study. It was only buried after he returned to Europe.

Travelling as Duke of Bragança, Pedro sailed to England where he set about borrowing money and raising mercenaries to assist his cause. By March 1832 he was able to set up a government in the Azores and plan the invasion of mainland Portugal, which took place in June. With French and British aid the liberal forces were soon able to overcome the numerical superiority of the absolutists and by September Pedro and Maria were back in Lisbon. Military action continued in the north for some months, but Miguel's cause was now hopeless and peace was concluded at the Convention of Evora-Monte, 26 May 1834, whereby Miguel agreed to go into exile for life in exchange for a generous annual pension. He left Portugal on 1 June and, as was only to be expected, immediately renounced the Convention which he claimed to have signed under compulsion.

Pedro's exertions on his daughter's behalf brought about his death. He contracted a galloping consumption in the course of the campaign and died at Queluz in the same room in which he had been born on 24 September 1834, aged only thirty-six.

Queen Maria II now commenced her effective reign at the age of fifteen. Negotiations for her marriage were begun immediately and in November 1834 she was married by proxy to her stepmother's brother, August, Duke of Leuchtenberg, who was naturalized and created Prince of Portugal and General-in-Chief of the Portuguese Armies. The marriage in Lisbon was solemnized in January, but the young husband only survived two months, dying at the end of March. Plans for the Queen's remarriage were begun with almost indecent haste and this time King Leopold of the Belgians took a hand in the matter, putting forward his own nephew Prince Ferdinand of Saxe-Coburg and Gotha. The proxy marriage was concluded at Coburg on 1 January 1836 and the nineteen-year-old bridegroom set out for Portugal accompanied by his father and younger brother. They visited England en route to see their cousin Victoria, soon to be Queen, who gave a vivid description in her diary: 'Ferdinand ... has a very slight figure, rather fair hair, beautiful dark brown eyes, a fine nose and a very sweet mouth; he has a dear good and clever expression in his face ... speaks through his nose in a slow funny way, which is at first against him, but it very soon wears off.... It is impossible to see or know him without loving him.' Ferdinand went on to Lisbon to marry Maria da Glória in April and the following year was proclaimed King Consort of Portugal. As such, he is sometimes styled Ferdinand II. The marriage was a happy one, although the Queen soon lost her youthful good looks and was worn out by childbearing. Maria's reign was fraught with troubles and constant uprisings and she died at the birth of her twelfth child in November 1853.

Maria da Glória's eldest son, who became King Pedro V, was only sixteen when his mother died, so his father King Ferdinand reigned as Regent until he came of age at eighteen in September 1855. Ferdinand had been well grounded in statesmanship by his astute uncle King Leopold of the Belgians and saw to it that his sons received a good education and went on a round of European tours. Their good manners greatly impressed their cousins Victoria and Albert in England. When Pedro took over the reins he showed himself to be a conscientious young man and won universal approval by staying in Lisbon throughout the terrible cholera and yellow fever epidemics which raged for fourteen months, killing over 8,000 people. In May 1858, Pedro, who had inherited the fair hair and good looks of the Coburgs, married the charming young Princess Stephanie of Hohenzollern, but their happiness was to be shortlived as she died of diphtheria fourteen months later. The King remained a widower. In September 1861 he went on a hunting expedition to Vila Viçosa with his two youngest brothers Ferdinand and Augustus. On their return to Lisbon they all fell ill with typhoid fever. Ferdinand died on 6 November and the King on 11 November. Pedro's immediate younger brothers, Luis and John, were recalled from a foreign tour which they had undertaken and the latter also succumbed to typhus on 27 December. Of the five brothers, only Luis, the new King, and Augustus, Duke of Coimbra remained. The shocking news of the deaths of the King and Dom Ferdinand is said to have hastened that of the Prince Consort in England.

King Luis I was slightly less handsome and slightly less brilliant than his brother, but he proved a good King and his long reign saw many reforms and improvements. Luis himself

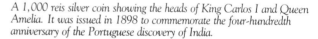

A 1,000 reis silver coin showing the heads of King Carlos I and Queen Amelia. It was issued in 1898 to commemorate the four-hundredth anniversary of the Portuguese discovery of India.

Philip II, King of Spain. This portrait by Titian in the Prado Museum gives a strong impression of the King's character as well as emphasizing his Habsburg lip.

Philip IV, King of Spain, by Velazquez.

King Carlos III of Spain, a superb portrait by Mengs in the Prado Museum.

Opposite
*Maria Anna of Austria, second wife of King Philip IV of Spain and mother of
Carlos II. This portrait by Carreño Miranda in the Prado shows her in
widow's weeds.*

*King Carlos IV of Spain ready to go shooting with his
faithful dog. This telling portrait by Goya is in the
Capodimonte Palace at Naples.*

was something of a scholar and translated several of Shakespeare's plays into Portuguese. His father King Ferdinand remained as his adviser until his death in 1885, having been put forward as a candidate for the Spanish crown after the revolution of 1868. In 1869 he had found great happiness in a second marriage with a Viennese lady, Elise Hensler, whom his cousin the Duke of Saxe-Coburg and Gotha obligingly created Countess von Edla. She was destined to survive the downfall of the Portuguese monarchy, dying at Lisbon in May 1929 on the eve of her ninety-third birthday. King Luis was married in 1862 to Maria Pia of Savoy, daughter of King Victor Emmanuel II of Italy. Small, dark and vital, she bore two surviving sons (a third was stillborn), Carlos, who succeeded his father, and Alfonso, Duke of Oporto.

When King Luis died in October 1889, he was succeeded by his elder son King Carlos I, a large, ebullient man with a magnificent moustache, who has been described as the Portuguese counterpart of King Edward VII, with whom he was on very good terms. Although a worldly *bon viveur*, the King was also a shrewd diplomat and a talented, if somewhat flamboyant, amateur artist. He was married to the statuesque and rather masculine Queen Amelia, a Princess of Orleans, and both enjoyed great popularity. Unfortunately, however, Portugal's political stability was not to last. Economic crises added to the deterioration and the royal family voluntarily donated a fifth of their yearly income to help the country's finances. In spite of this a republican movement began to grow and an abortive revolution took place on 28 January 1908. On 1 February the King and Queen and their two sons returned to Lisbon from Vila Viçosa and entered an open carriage at the Terreiro do Paco to complete the journey to the Necessidades Palace. As they drove off some shots were heard and in the general confusion a man stepped forward and shot the King twice in the head. The Crown Prince pulled out a revolver, but as the carriage proceeded a bearded man shot him dead and turned to despatch the younger Prince. His aim was deflected by the Queen, who with great presence of mind thrust her bouquet into his face so that Dom Manuel only received an injury in the arm.

At the age of eighteen, Dom Manuel thus found himself King of a tottering throne. An attractive though somewhat weak young man of scholarly pursuits was not the right person to save the situation. The monarchy lasted another twenty months until swept away by the revolution of October 1910, when the King and his mother embarked on the royal yacht for Gibraltar and thence to England. The Republic of Portugal was proclaimed on 5 October 1910.

King Manuel settled down quite happily in England. In 1913 he married Princess Augusta Victoria of Hohenzollern, but there were to be no children of the marriage, a result, it was rumoured, of Dom Manuel having contracted a venereal disease during the course of a youthful infatuation with the notorious actress Gaby Deslys. He settled at Fulwell Park, Twickenham, where he devoted himself to producing a monumental work on early Portuguese printed books, and endeared himself to the people of Twickenham by his generous support of local charities. He was also passionately fond of tennis and always to be seen at Wimbledon, his last visit taking place only a few days before his death, which was a tragic one. A sudden throat infection necessitating a tracheotomy caused Dom Manuel to choke before his physician could arrive to carry out the operation. His body was returned to Portugal for burial with his ancestors.

Until his death in 1920, King Manuel II's heir was his uncle Alfonso, Duke of Oporto, but he had seen fit to marry (as her fourth husband) an American lady, Nevada Hayes, who gave herself great airs and graces as 'Crown Princess of Portugal and Duchess of Oporto'. When it became obvious that there were to be no children from King Manuel's marriage an agreement was reached with the descendants of the absolutist King Miguel and in consequence when Manuel died in 1932 all Portuguese monarchists acknowledged as his successor Miguel's grandson Duarte (in theory King Duarte II), who bore the title of Duke of Bragança. In 1950 the Portuguese National Assembly repealed the laws of exile and Dom Duarte and other members of the royal family were allowed to return and take up residence in Portugal, where they enjoyed and still enjoy much popularity. The present pretender to the Portuguese throne is Duarte's son, also Duarte, who was born in 1945 and is unmarried.

King Manuel II.

SPAIN

The Kings of the Suevi

The Iberian peninsula was occupied by many tribes of Celtic origin from about 500BC and was settled by Rome from the second century BC, becoming the Roman Province of Hispania. After the break-up of the Roman Empire a Germanic tribe from the region of Swabia (to which they gave their name) invaded Gaul and Spain and established a kingdom in the northern and central parts of the peninsula. Hermeric, the first King, was succeeded by his son Rechila, who made further conquests southwards from Seville to Cartagena. His son and successor Rechiar married a daughter of Theodoric I, King of the Visigoths, but later fell out with his brother-in-law Theodoric II and was killed in battle with him in 456. The throne was then usurped by Ataulf, one of his governors, but he in turn was murdered by one Maldras, who proclaimed himself King. His rule was challenged by Frumar in the south and Richimund in the north, but both were eventually overcome by Maldras's son Remismund, who married a Visigothic Princess to gain support. Thereafter the history of the Suevi is obscure for nearly a hundred years until we hear of a King Carriaric, who was followed by his son Theodimir and he in turn by his son Miro, who allied himself with the Visigothic Prince Hermenegild in his revolt against his father Leovigild I, but was defeated by the latter, he and his son and successor Eboric being forced to become Visigothic vassals. The last Suevian King was Andeca, the husband of a daughter of Miro, and the kingdom was completely absorbed into the Visigothic kingdom in 585.

The Kings of the Visigoths

The Visigoths, the western division of the Goths, invaded Greece and Italy under their King Alaric and captured Rome in 410. Alaric's brother and successor Ataulf pressed on into Gaul, established his capital at Toulouse and succeeded in conquering most of Spain. Ataulf married Galla Placidia, daughter of the Emperor Theodosius I. After his murder at Barcelona in 415 she was returned to Rome in exchange for 600,000 measures of corn and later married Constantius, who was associated in the Empire with her half-brother Honorius. She acted as a very able Regent of the Western Empire for her son Valentinian III and died at Rome in 450.

After an attempted usurpation by one Sigeric, Ataulf was succeeded by Wallia, who was elected by the people. He planned an invasion of Africa but was thwarted by the destruction of his fleet in a storm. His elected successor, Theodoric I, was married to a daughter of the great Alaric and had a long reign of over thirty years. Three of his six sons

followed him in succession, while one of his daughters was married to the Vandalic King Himeric (who treated her badly and sent her back to her father with her nose cut off) and another to Rechiar, King of the Suevi.

Euric, the last of Theodoric's sons to rule, was succeeded in 484 by his son Alaric (II) who married Theudicoda, daughter of Theodoric, King of the Ostrogoths in Italy. Alaric was killed in battle with the Franks, losing almost all his possessions in France, including Toulouse, and thereafter Toledo became the Visigothic capital.

Amalaric, Alaric's younger son who succeeded his brother Gesalaric in 511, concluded an alliance with the Franks by marrying Clotilda, daughter of the Frankish King Clovis and thereby receiving Toulouse back as part of her dowry. She was a Catholic Christian, whereas the Visigoths adhered to the Arian heresy, and this occasioned her receiving such abuse from the people that she wrote to her brothers to complain of her ill-treatment. They at once formed an expedition to march into Spain. The cowardly Amalaric fled before them but, returning to Barcelona to attempt to rescue some of his treasure, was recognized and killed by a soldier as he sought shelter in a church. Clotilda returned to France but died soon after.

After Amalaric's death his Ostrogothic tutor, Theudis, was elected King. Two further elected Kings followed. The latter of these, Agila, had to contend with a usurping rival Athanagild, who finally murdered him and reigned turbulently until his death at Toledo in 568. He married a lady named Goiswinth and had two daughters, Galswinth and Brunhild, who both married Merovingians and of whom we shall hear more later. Athanagild's death was followed by a short interregnum and then Liuva was elected to the throne. He nominated his brother Leovigild as co-ruler a year later. Leovigild had been married to Theodosia, daughter of Severianus, Governor of Cartagena, and the sister of three Saints, Leander, Isidore and Fulgens. By her he had two sons, Hermenegild and Reccared. After Theodosia's death, Leovigild married Goiswinth, the widow of King Athanagild. The Queen was a fanatical Arian and having arranged the marriage of her granddaughter Ingund to her elder stepson Hermenegild, turned against the girl because of her refusal to abjure Catholicism and persecuted her with physical violence, on one occasion pushing her into a fish pond where she nearly drowned. She also fomented hatred between Leovigild and his son to such an extent that finally Hermenegild was beheaded on 14 April 586 on refusing to receive the sacrament according to the Arian rite. He was later canonized. The unfortunate Ingund fled to Africa with her baby son Theodoric, but their subsequent fate is unknown. Probably both perished there.

Leovigild survived his son barely a year, dying in 587, and was succeeded by his son Reccared, who was converted to

Catholicism by his uncles St Leander and St Fulgens, all his subjects following his example. Queen Goiswinth also feigned conversion but was seen to spit out the consecrated wafer. Although implicated in a plot against her stepson's life, she escaped punishment and died a natural death. Reccared married twice; first to Bada, said to be daughter of Fontus, Count of the Patrimonii, by whom he had Liuva, his successor; and secondly, in 594, to a lady named Clodosind, by whom he had two sons, Geila and Swinthila. Reccared died in 601 and was succeeded by his son Liuva II, who only reigned two years and was followed by a succession of elected Kings.

Chindaswinth, who was elected King in 642, married a lady named Riceberga, who bore him three sons, Recceswinth, Theodofrid and Favila, and one daughter. Recceswinth was associated on the throne with his father in 649 and succeeded as sole ruler in 653, reigning until his death in 672. He was followed by three elected Kings of different families, the last being Egica (687–702), who by his wife Cixilona was the father of Witiza, his associate from 700, Bishop Oppas, and a daughter who married Count Julian. Witiza reigned until 710 and was something of a tyrant. On his death Roderic, son of Duke Theodofrid of Cordova and grandson of King Chindas-

winth, was elected King to the exclusion of Witiza's sons. He immediately had to cope with the Islamic invasion from Africa which began in July 710 with a plundering raid. The following year Roderic was engaged in a campaign against the Basques in the north when the news of a further Moorish incursion made him hurry south to meet the new enemy. A battle was waged on the road to Cordoba between Medina Sidonia and Vejer de la Frontera on 19 July 711. Bishop Oppas and Count Julian, the brother and brother-in-law of King Witiza, both deserted from the Visigothic army to vent their personal spite against the King, who fell in the battle, his forces utterly routed, leaving the whole of southern Spain to fall into the hands of the infidel.

Roderic was married to a lady named Egilona but had become captivated by Florinda, the daughter of Count Julian, and made her his mistress. She was not unwilling, it would seem, but perhaps in an attempt to justify herself had complained to her father that the King had raped her, thus giving further cause for his disaffection. Later the Moors were to dub her *Cava* (Wicked woman). Queen Egilona subsequently became the wife of Abdul-Aziz, the Moorish governor of Seville. Two further Visigothic Kings, Achila and Ardo, held sway in Narbonne before it also fell to the Arabs in 720.

The Kings of the Asturias and Leon

PELAYO	718–737

Son of Favila and grandson of King Chindaswinth; rallied the Christian remnants and was elected King in the Asturias 718; *m* Gaudiosa; 1 son, 1 dau; *d* 737; *bur* Church of St Eulalia, Cangas de Onis

FAVILA	737–739

Son of Pelayo; *s* his father 737; *m* Froiluba; 1 dau; *k* in a boar hunt June 739

ALFONSO I	739–757

Son of Pedro, Lord of Biscay, an alleged descendant of King Reccared; elected King in succession to his brother-in-law Favila 739; *m* Ormesinda, dau of Pelayo; 2 sons, 1 dau; *d* 757

FRUELA I	757–768

b 732, eldest son of King Alfonso I; *s* his father 757; *m* Munia, said to have been a dau of Aznar, Duke of Aquitaine; 1 son, 1 dau; murdered at Cangas de Onis 14 January 768

AURELIUS	768–774

Son of Fruela, brother of King Alfonso I; *s* his cousin King Fruela I 768; *d unm ca* June 774; *bur* Church of St Martin, Iagueza

SILO	774–783

Of unknown parentage; *s* King Aurelius 774; *m* Adosinda (retired to a nunnery in widowhood), dau of King Alfonso I; *dsp* 783

MAUREGATO	783–788

Illegitimate son of King Alfonso I; *s* King Silo 783; *d* 788

BERMUDO I THE DEACON	788–791

Brother of King Aurelius; elected to *s* King Mauregato 788; *m* Ursinda; 2 sons, 2 daus; abdicated 791; *d* 797

ALFONSO II THE CHASTE	791–842

Only son of King Fruela I; *s* on the abdication of King Bermudo I 791; *m* Berta, said to be a daughter of Pepin, King of the Franks; *dsp* 20 March 842; *bur* Oviedo Cathedral

RAMIRO I   842–850

Elder son of King Bermudo I; *s* King Alfonso II 20 March 842 *m* (1) Paterna; 2 sons; *m* (2) Urraca (*d* 861); 1 son, 1 dau; *d* 1 February 850; *bur* Church of St Mary, Oviedo

ORDOÑO I   850–866

Son of King Ramiro I and Paterna; *s* his father 1 February 850; King of Leon 855; *m* Nuña; 5 sons; *d* 27 May 866

ALFONSO III THE GREAT   866–910

b 848, eldest son of King Ordoño I; *s* his father 27 May 866; *m* 870 Ximena (*d* after 910), dau of Garcia Iñiguez, Prince of Navarre; 6 sons, 3 daus; *d* 20 December 910

GARCIA I   (IN LEON) 910–914

Eldest son of King Alfonso III; *s* his father in Leon 20 December 910; *m* Nuña, dau of Nuño Fernandez, Count of Castile; *dsp* Zamora 19 January 914

ORDOÑO II   (IN GALICIA) 910–924

2nd son of King Alfonso III; *s* his father in Galicia 20 December 910; *m* (1) Elvira; 4 sons; *m* (2) 922 (*m* diss 923) Angota (*d* 974); *m* (3) 923 Sancha, dau of Garcia III, King of Navarre; *d* after January 924; *bur* Leon Cathedral

FRUELA II THE CRUEL   (IN ASTURIAS) 910–924
       (IN LEON, GALICIA AND ASTURIAS) 924–925

4th son of King Alfonso III; *s* his father in the Asturias 20 December 910; *m* Nunilo Ximena; 6 sons; *d* March 925

ALFONSO IV THE MONK   925–931

Eldest son of King Ordoño II and Elvira; *s* his uncle King Fruela II March 925; *m* Urraca (*d* 926), dau of Sancho I, King of Navarre, and his 2nd wife Toda Aznarez; 2 sons; abdicated in favour of his brother Ramiro 931 and became a monk; *d* Monastery of St Julian, nr Leon 933

RAMIRO II   931–950

2nd son of King Ordoño II and Elvira; *s* on the abdication of his brother King Alfonso IV 931; *m* (1) Urraca (*d* 931); (2) *ca* 934 Teresa Florentina, dau of Sancho I, King of Navarre, and his 2nd wife Toda Aznarez; 2 sons, 2 daus; *d* 950

ORDOÑO III   950–955

Elder son of King Ramiro II and Teresa Florentina; *s* his father 850; *m* (1) 941 (*m* diss 952) Urraca, dau of Fernan Gonzalez, Count of Castile, and his 1st wife Urraca; *m* (2) 952, Elvira, dau of Count Gonzalo; 2 sons, 1 dau; *d* Zamora August 955

SANCHO I THE FAT   955–966

Younger son of King Ramiro II and Teresa Florentina; *s* his brother King Ordoño III August 955; *m* 961, Teresa, dau of Aznar Fernandez, Count of Monzoa; 1 son, 1 dau; *d* December 966

ORDOÑO IV THE WICKED   958–960

Elder but only surviving son of King Alfonso IV; set up as King in opposition to Sancho I 958; *m* 958 Urraca (*d* 965), divorced wife of King Ordoño III and dau of Fernan Gonzalez, Count of Castile; driven out 960

RAMIRO III   966–982

b 961, only son of King Sancho I; *s* his father December 966 under his mother's regency; *m* Urraca; abdicated in favour of his cousin Bermudo II 982; *d* Leon 984

BERMUDO II   982–999

Elder son of King Ordoño III and his 2nd wife Elvira; *s* on the abdication of his cousin King Ramiro III 982; *m* (1) (*m* diss) Velasquita; 1 dau; *m* (2) Elvira; 2 sons, 2 daus; *d* 999

ALFONSO V   999–1028

b 994, elder son of King Bermudo II and his 2nd wife Elvira; *s* his father 999; *m* 1014, Elvira (*d* 1052), dau of Don Melindo Gonzalez, Count of Galicia, and his wife Doña Mayor; 1 son, 1 dau; *k* in battle with the Moors 5 May 1028

BERMUDO III	1028–1037

b ca 1015, only son of King Alfonso V; *s* his father 5 May 1028; *m* 1028 Urraca Teresa, dau of Don Sancho Garcez, Count of Castile; 1 son (*d* young); *k* in battle with King Ferdinand I of Castile on the banks of the river Carrion 1037

After the crushing defeat of the Visigoths by the Moorish invaders, the Christian remnant who survived made their way northwards into the Asturias and there chose as their leader Pelayo (Pelagius), a grandson of King Chindaswinth and cousin of Roderic. He established his capital at Canga de Onis and in 718 won the battle of Covadonga over the Moors, securing the independence of his embryo state. His son and successor Favila reigned for two years only and was killed by a wild boar while hunting. He had no son and was succeeded by his brother-in-law Alfonso I, who enlarged his realm and annexed Galicia to the west and Leon to the south, while to the east his dominions extended as far as Navarre. Very little has come down to us concerning the characters and personalities of these early Kings and their successors. Alfonso's son Fruela I is represented as a cruel tyrant, who murdered his brother Bimarano, whom he wrongly suspected of aspiring to the throne. He was killed by his own people after a reign of eleven years and succeeded by Aurelius, a nephew of Alfonso I, who managed to live in peace with his Moorish neighbours, though probably at the cost of paying them tribute. Alfonso I's son-in-law Silo was the next King and all that is known of him is that he moved his capital to Pravia. His successor, Mauregato, was an illegitimate son of Alfonso I, allegedly by a slave. He was reputed to have paid a yearly tribute of one hundred beautiful maidens to the Moorish rulers, but the story is almost certainly apocryphal – for one thing the maidens of the Asturias are not and never have been noted for their beauty. Mauregato was followed by Bermudo I, a brother of Aurelius. He had taken Deacon's orders and is said to have accepted the throne and a wife reluctantly. After a short reign of three years he abdicated in favour of Alfonso II, the only son of Fruela I, who had been excluded from the throne earlier because of his youth and latterly because it was feared he might seek to avenge the murder of his father. The legend of the hero Bernardo del Carpio is set in Alfonso's reign but has little or no foundation in fact. Alfonso, although married, took a vow of chastity and after reigning for over fifty years and transferring the capital to Oviedo was succeeded by the son of Bermudo I.

Ramiro I's succession was not undisputed and he found it necessary to dispose of several rivals by blinding them and shutting them in monasteries. He fought several battles with the Moors and also dealt successfully with Norman raiders who landed at Corunna, repelling them and burning seventy of their ships.

On Ramiro's death in 850 the throne passed peacefully to his son Ordoño I, a restorer and fortifier of towns, who extended his kingdom further south as far as Salamanca. He was the first ruler to be styled King of Leon as well as of the Asturias.

Ordoño's son and successor, Alfonso III the Great, is regarded as the second founder of the state, and in the course of a reign of forty-four years consolidated his realm, which now comprised the whole of the Asturias, Biscay, Galicia, and northern Portugal, as well as a great part of Navarre. Fighting with the Moors was continued and several notable victories were won. At the end of his life, however, Alfonso was plagued by domestic troubles, with his wife and sons intriguing and plotting against him. Shortly before his death he partitioned the kingdom between his sons; Garcia received Leon, Ordoño Galicia, and Fruela Oviedo.

The reigns of the brothers were warlike and the state was again reunited under Fruela II in 924. He died of leprosy a year later and was succeeded by his nephew Alfonso IV, the eldest son of Ordoño II. He was, we are told, 'totally unfit to govern' and abdicated in favour of his brother Ramiro, entering the monastery of Sahagun as a monk. He soon regretted this decision and attempted a comeback but was speedily put down by Ramiro and imprisoned with his wife and the sons of his predecessor King Fruela in the Monastery of St Julian, near Leon. Deprived of his sight, he died there soon after.

Ramiro II was followed in turn by his sons Ordoño III and Sancho I. The latter was forced into exile for a time when the powerful Count of Castile, Fernan Gonzalez, set up Ordoño IV, the son of Alfonso IV, marrying him to his daughter Urraca, who had previously been married to and divorced from Ordoño III. Sancho regained the throne two years later. His excessive corpulence caused him great trouble and he sought help from the Moorish physicians at the court of Abdul-Rahman III of Cordoba, all else having failed. They were able to prescribe a diet and a distillation of herbs which reduced his girth considerably. He is said to have died after eating a poisoned apple given to him by a vassal. Sancho's son Ramiro III succeeded him at the age of five under the regency of his mother Teresa, 'a lady of extraordinary beauty and superior intellect'. Ramiro's reign was troubled by further Norman raids which succeeded in destroying and burning many towns and castles and carrying off much plunder. The King's ineffectual dealing with this problem, which was finally resolved by the Count of Castile, caused great discontent and led to a rebellion in Galicia which finally forced Ramiro, still only twenty-one, to resign the crown to his cousin Bermudo, son of Ordoño III. He died two years later in 984.

Bermudo II, though plagued with gout, proved as warlike as any of his predecessors, but was unable to stop the Moors from encroaching as far as the city of Leon. On his death in 999 the crown passed to his five-year-old son Alfonso V and the regency into the hands of Don Melindo Gonzalez, Count of Galicia. The Moorish leader Almanzor died in 1002 and the Omayyad dynasty in Spain fell in 1009, thus mitigating the threat from the Caliphate of Cordova. The struggle from now on was with petty Moorish princes, to one of whom Alfonso even gave his sister in marriage. He was able to devote some time to restoring Leon before he was killed at the siege of Viseu in Portugal in May 1028.

Alfonso's son and successor, Bermudo III, was married to a daughter of the powerful Count of Castile, and his sister Sancha to Ferdinand, son of King Sancho III of Navarre. Bermudo's only child, Alfonso, died young. Bermudo's brother-in-law had become King of Castile in 1035 and Bermudo in an attempt to recover some territory from him was killed in a battle on the banks of the river Carrion in 1037. His kingdom passed to the victor in right of his wife, Bermudo's sister and heiress.

The Kings of Aragon

RAMIRO I	1035–1063

Natural son of Sancho III, King of Navarre, and Urraca, 'a Navarrese lady of rank'; bequeathed Aragon by his father and assumed the title of King 1035; *m* 1036 Gisberga (*d* 1 December 1059; *bur* Church of San Juan de la Peria), dau of Bernard Roger, Count of Bigorre, and his wife Garsenda, heiress of Bigorre; 3 sons, 2 daus; *k* in battle 8 May 1063; *bur* Church of San Juan de la Peria

SANCHO I	1063–1094

b 1045, eldest son of King Ramiro I; *s* his father 8 May 1063; *s* his cousin Sancho IV as (Sancho V) King of Navarre 4 June 1076; *m* 1063 Felicia (*d* 24 April 1068; *bur* Church of San Juan de la Peria), dau of Hilduin IV, Count of Montdidier and Rameru, and Alice de Roucy; 3 sons ; *k* at the siege of Huesca June 1094; *bur* Church of San Juan de la Peria

PEDRO I	1094–1104

b ca 1068, eldest son of King Sancho I; *s* his father in Aragon and Navarre June 1094; *m* 1081 Agnes (*d* after 1110), dau of William VIII, Duke of Aquitaine, and Aldegarde of Burgundy; 1 son, 1 dau (both *dvp*); *d* 28 September 1104

ALFONSO I THE WARRIOR	1104–1134

b ca 1073, 2nd son of King Sancho I; *s* his brother King Pedro I as King of Aragon and Navarre 28 September 1104; *m* 1108 (*m* annulled 1114) Urraca, Queen of Castile, *qv* (*d* 8 March 1126); no issue; *d* Fonga 7 September 1134

RAMIRO II THE MONK	1134–1137

Third and yst son of King Sancho I; *s* his brother King Alfonso I 7 September 1134; *m* 1134 Agnes (probably *d* in childbirth 1136), dau of William IX, Duke of Aquitaine, and Philippa of Toulouse; 1 dau; abdicated and retired into a monastery 1137; *d* 16 August 1147

PETRONILLA	1137–1163

b 1136, only child of King Ramiro II; *s* her father as Queen of Aragon on his abdication 1137; *m* 1151 Raymond Berengar IV, Count of Barcelona (*d* 8 August 1162); 3 sons, 2 daus; abdicated in favour of her son Alfonso 1163; *d* Barcelona 13 October 1173

ALFONSO II	1163–1196

b May 1152, eldest son of Queen Petronilla; *s* his mother on her abdication 1163; *m* 18 January 1174 Sancha (*b* 21 September 1154; *d* Monastery of Xinena November 1208), dau of Alfonso VII, King of Castile and Leon, and his 2nd wife Rixa of Poland; 3 sons, 4 daus; *d* 25 April 1196

PEDRO II	1196–1213

b 1176, eldest son of King Alfonso II; *s* his father 25 April 1196; *m* 5 June 1204 Maria (*d* 1219; *bur* St Peter's, Rome), dau of William VIII, Count of Montpellier, and Eudocia Comnena; 1 son; *k* in battle at Muset 13 September 1213

JAMES I THE CONQUEROR	1213–1276

b 2 February 1208, only son of King Pedro II; *s* his father 13 September 1213; conquered Majorca 1228; *m* (1) Agreda 6 February 1221 (*m* diss 1229) Eleanor (*b* 1195; *d* 1253), dau of Alfonso VIII, King of Castile, and Eleanor of England; 1 son; *m* (2) 8 September 1235 Yolande or Violante (*d* 1255), dau of Andrew II, King of Hungary, and Yolande de Courtenay; 4 sons, 5 daus; *m* (3) Teresa Gil de Vedaura (*d* as a nun after 1276); 2 sons; *d* 25 July 1276

PEDRO III THE GREAT	1276–1285

b ca 1239, 2nd but eldest surviving son of King James I and eldest son by his 2nd wife Yolande of Hungary; *s* his father 25 July 1276; King of Sicily *jure uxoris* and by conquest 1282; *m* 13 June 1262 Constance (*d* Barcelona 1302), dau of Manfred, King of Sicily, and Beatrice of Savoy; 4 sons, 2 daus; *d* 11 November 1285; *bur* Church of the Holy Cross, Villa Franca

ALFONSO III THE DO-GOODER	1285–1291

b ca 1263, eldest son of King Pedro III; *s* his father in Aragon 11 November 1285; *d unm* 18 June 1291

James II the Just 1291–1327

b ca 1264, 2nd son of King Pedro III; *s* his father in Sicily 11 November 1285; *s* his brother King Alfonso III in Aragon 18 June 1291; renounced the crown of Sicily 1295; *m* (1) 1 November 1295 Blanche or Blanca (*d* 14 October 1310), dau of Charles II (of Anjou), King of Naples, and Maria of Hungary; 4 sons, 3 daus; *m* (2) 16 November 1315 Maria (*d* March 1321), dau of Hugh III, King of Cyprus, and Isabella d'Ibelin; *m* (3) 25 December 1321 Elisenda de Moncada; *d* 5 November 1327

Alfonso IV the Debonair or the Good 1327–1336

b 1302, eldest son of King James II; *s* his father 5 November 1327; *m* (1) 10 November 1314 Teresa (*d* 18 October 1327), dau of the Count of Urgel; 4 sons, 2 daus; *m* (2) 5 February 1329 Leonor (*b* 1307; *d* 1359), dau of Ferdinand IV, King of Castile, and Constance of Portugal; 2 sons; *d* 24 January 1336

Pedro IV the Ceremonious 1336–1387

b 5 September 1319, 2nd but eldest surviving son of King Alfonso IV and his 1st wife Teresa of Urgel; *s* his father 24 January 1336; *m* (1) 1342 Maria (*d* 29 April 1347), dau of Philip, Count of Evreux and *jure uxoris* King of Navarre, and Jeanne I, Queen of Navarre; 1 son, 3 daus; *m* (2) Barcelona November 1347 Leonor (*b* 1328; *d* Xerica 29 October 1348), dau of Alfonso IV, King of Portugal; no issue; *m* (3) 13 June 1349 Leonor (*d* 10 June 1374), dau of Peter II, King of Sicily, and Elizabeth of Tyrol; 2 sons, 1 dau; *m* (4) 1379 Sibila de Forcia, crowned at Saragossa 1381 (*d* 4 November 1406), widow of Don Artal de Foges; 1 son, 1 dau; *d* 5 January 1387

Juan I 1387–1395

b 27 December 1350, 2nd but eldest surviving son of King Pedro IV and eldest son of his 3rd wife Leonor of Sicily; *s* his father 5 January 1387; *m* (1) 1372 Mahaud or Marta (*d* 1380), dau of John I, Count of Armagnac; 1 dau; *m* (2) 1384 Violante or Yolande (*b* Val de Cassel 1363; *d* 13 July 1431), dau of Robert I, Duke of Bar, and Marie of France; 2 sons (*d* young), 1 dau; *d* Saragossa 15 May 1395

Martin the Humane 1395–1410

b 1353, 3rd but 2nd surviving son of King Pedro IV; *s* his brother King Juan I 15 May 1395; crowned at Saragossa April 1399; *s* his son Martin as King (Martin II) of Sicily 1409; lost that throne 1410; *m* (1) 1372 Maria (*d* 29 December 1406), dau of Don Lope de Luna and Doña Brianda de Agaout; 3 sons, 1 dau; *m* (2) 16 December 1409 Margarita, dau of the Count de Prades; *d* 31 May 1410

Interregnum 1410–1412
Ferdinand I the Just 1412–1416

b 27 November 1380, son of Juan I, King of Castile, and his 1st wife Leonor, dau of Pedro IV, King of Aragon; elected to succeed his maternal uncle King Martin at Alcañiz 1412; *m* 1393 Urraca, later called Leonor (*b* 1374; *d* Medina del Campo December 1435), dau of Sancho, Count of Albuquerque (illegitimate son of King Alfonso XI of Castile), and Beatrice of Portugal (dau of King Pedro I); 5 sons, 2 daus; *d* Igualada 2 April 1416

Alfonso V the Magnanimous 1416–1458

b 1394, eldest son of King Ferdinand I; *s* his father 2 April 1416; *m* 12 June 1415 Maria (*b* 14 November 1401; *d* Valencia 4 September 1458), dau of Henry III, King of Castile, and Catherine of Lancaster; no issue; *d* 27 June 1458

Juan II 1458–1479

b 28 June 1397, 2nd son of King Ferdinand I; *s* his brother King Alfonso V 27 June 1458; *m* (1) 18 June 1420 Blanche, Queen of Navarre (*b* 1386; *d* Santa Maria de Nieva 1 April 1441), widow of Martin I, King of Sicily, and dau of Charles III, King of Navarre, and Leonor of Castile; 1 son, 2 daus; *m* (2) Calatayud 13 July 1447 Juana (*b* 1425; *d* 13 February 1468; *bur* Poblete), dau of Don Fadrique Henriquez, Count of Melgar, High Admiral of Castile, and Marina de Cordova; 1 son, 3 daus; *d* Barcelona 19 January 1479

Ferdinand II the Catholic 1479–1516

b Sos 10 March 1452; *m* Isabel, Queen of Castile, thus bringing about the union of Castile and Aragon into the kingdom of Spain (*see hereafter*)

The kingdom of Aragon in the eastern part of the Iberian peninsula came into being when Sancho III, King of Navarre, left it as a patrimony to his natural son Ramiro who assumed the title of King. He soon attempted to extend his borders northwards, encroaching upon his half-brother Garcia III's kingdom while the latter was absent in Rome; but Garcia returned in time to drive him back. Ramiro then turned his attention to his Moorish neighbours to the east and was able to extend his realm as far as the Pyrenees and exact tribute from the Emirs of Saragossa, Tudela and Lerida. A dispute concerning the tribute exacted from Saragossa led to a war with Castile in the course of which Ramiro was defeated and killed in May 1063.

Ramiro's son and successor Sancho, 'an excellent and brave Prince', won several towns from the Moors and reached the north bank of the Ebro. In 1076 he became King of Navarre also in succession to his cousin Sancho IV. He was killed besieging Huesca in 1094 and his son and successor, Pedro I, carried on the siege for another two years, winning a great victory over a combined Moorish and Castilian relief army at Alcoraz in 1096 and setting the seal on Aragonese independence. St George is said to have appeared on the field of battle to help Pedro's forces. Pedro's death is said to have been hastened by grief at the deaths of his two children, Pedro and Isabel, who both died on the same day, 18 August 1104. He survived them by one month and was succeeded by his brother Alfonso.

Alfonso the Warrior married in 1108 Urraca, who the following year became Queen of Castile. She was the widow of Count Raymond of Burgundy, and Alfonso laid claim to Castile and Leon in her right. The Castilians and Leonese objected and another violent war between the two Christian kingdoms ensued. Urraca was practically a nymphomaniac and her loose behaviour soon led to a separation from Alfonso who repudiated her in 1111, the Pope obligingly annulling the marriage on grounds of consanguinity (Alfonso and Urraca were second cousins by descent from King Sancho III of Navarre). The end of the marriage ended Alfonso's claims on Castile and he turned his attention to other matters, fighting some twenty-nine battles with Christians and Moors in the course of his thirty-year reign. His greatest achievement was the capture of Saragossa in September 1118. Alfonso died at the siege of Fonga in September 1134 and his death ended the union of Aragon with Navarre. Alfonso, being childless, had attempted to bequeath Navarre to the Knights of St John and Aragon to the Knights Templar, but neither country would consent to this strange arrangement, Navarre electing Garcia Ramirez as King, and Aragon forcing Alfonso's brother Ramiro to leave the monastery where he had lived as a monk for forty years, and ascend the throne as Ramiro II. The reluctant monarch did his duty, renounced his orders (with dispensation from Pope Innocent II), married, begot a daughter and after betrothing her to Raymond Berengar IV, Count of Barcelona, retired again to the monastic life (his wife appearing conveniently to have died at the birth), leaving his intended son-in-law in charge of the kingdom.

Queen Petronilla's marriage to the Count of Barcelona was consummated in 1151 when she was fifteen and the following year she gave birth to her first child, Raymond Alfonso, later King Alfonso II of Aragon. Raymond Berengar reigned well in his wife's name, never assuming the title of King, until his death in August 1162. Petronilla reigned alone for one year, then abdicated in favour of her eldest son, deeming him old enough to rule at the tender age of eleven.

Alfonso II was heir to Aragon through his mother and to Catalonia through his father and thus ruled a considerably extended realm. The King was no mean poet of the Provençal school and was able to enjoy a more peaceful reign than any of his predecessors. His wife Sancha of Castile, whom he married in 1174, bore him a numerous family, but appears to have been a difficult lady as she several times fell out with her son King Pedro II, who succeeded his father in 1196, over matters to do with her jointure and was even prepared to take up arms against him. Naturally, there were plenty of nobles to take

sides and foment the trouble. The Queen finally retired into the convent she had founded at Xinena and died there in November 1208.

Pedro II was one of those royal personages who crop up from time to time 'delighting in low company'. He conceived a great aversion to his wife, Maria of Montpellier, although she appears to have been quite blameless, and sought an annulment of his marriage to her both before and after the birth of their only child James in 1208. His antipathy also extended to the child and he wished to proclaim his brother heir to the crown. The Queen went to Rome to plead her cause with Pope Innocent III and obtained a judgment enjoining Pedro to live in peace with her and treat her with affection. Before she could return, however, Pedro was killed in battle with Simon de Montfort in September 1213.

James I owed his name to his mother's strange whim of placing twelve lighted candles, named for the twelve Apostles, around his cradle and determining that the last to burn out should be his patron. St James was the winner. Only five years old at his accession, James was placed in the guardianship of the Grand Master of the Templars, while Aragon was governed by his great-uncle Sancho, as Regent. The Regent's misrule was such that James staged a coup and took over the kingdom at the age of eleven. It seems astounding that a boy so young could successfully rule a kingdom, but one must remember that life was short in those days and men and women matured early, often becoming parents in their early teens. James was to become Aragon's greatest King, conquering Murcia, Valencia and the Balearic Islands, founding a navy and bringing about a number of governmental reforms, while many stories are told of his acts of personal bravery. His matrimonial career was also quite spectacular. His first marriage, for political reasons, to Eleanor (Leonor) of Castile, contracted when he was thirteen and she twenty-six, was annulled in 1229 on the usual grounds of consanguinity after the birth of one son. The divorced Queen returned to Castile and occupied the rest of her life in founding religious orders and monasteries. James married his second wife, Yolande of Hungary, in 1236 and fathered a large family by her. After her death in 1255, James secretly married his mistress, Doña Teresa Gil de Vedaura, who also bore him two sons. There is a story, which may be discounted, that James had actually married her after his divorce from Eleanor and before his marriage to Yolande. Whatever the truth, Teresa was never acknowledged as Queen and took the veil after James's death in July 1276. James was a tall, muscular man, graceful, dignified, and 'the perfection of manly beauty'. He was blessed with a strong constitution, never knew a day's illness, and was remarkable for his clemency in an age of violence.

Pedro III, who succeeded his father, was fighting the Moors at the time and did not proceed to Saragossa for his coronation for several months. Through his wife he laid claim to the kingdom of Sicily and the Sicilian Vespers incident in 1282 gave him the opportunity to conquer the island, earning the epithet of 'the Great'. He was soon obliged to return home to deal with unrest in Aragon and left his wife Constance and second son James to rule Sicily. Pedro's death in November 1285 is said to have been the result of a wound in the eye received during an engagement with the French, but most Aragonese historians deny this. He was succeeded in Aragon by his eldest son Alfonso and in Sicily by his second son James.

Alfonso III's reign was short, but he earned himself the name of 'the Do-gooder' by granting his subjects the right to carry arms. He also made some important conquests of land from the Moors and engaged in almost continuous disputes with the Pope. He was succeeded by his brother, James II, who was soon compelled to resign the kingdom of Sicily to his next brother Fadrique. His reign saw the suppression of the Knights Templar in 1312. James was married three times, but only had issue by his first wife, Blanche of Anjou, whom he married in an attempt to settle the differences between their families with regard to Naples and Sicily.

Alfonso IV, who succeeded his father at the age of twenty-eight, had just become a widower through the death of his wife Teresa in childbirth. He was married again early in 1329 to Leonor of Castile, who became a wicked stepmother in the classic mould and constantly intrigued against her stepson Pedro. Alfonso spent most of his reign squabbling with the Genoese over Corsica and Sardinia and died of dropsy in January 1336, when he was succeeded by Pedro, now in his seventeenth year.

Pedro IV's first act was to order the arrest of his stepmother, but she managed to escape to Castile, where she continued to stir up trouble. Pedro celebrated his coronation with great pomp and magnificence, earning himself the epithet of 'the Ceremonious', and 10,000 guests are said to have sat down to the coronation banquet. The King was 'of small stature, and spare form', but as spirited and warlike as any of his ancestors, regaining Sicily and warring with rebel barons at home. He married four times and had children by all but his second wife. His death in January 1387 was said to have been the result of having his face slapped by St Thecla, who appeared before him in a vision when he was attempting to deprive the Archbishop of Tarragona of his archiepiscopal dominions, the good saint being the patron of the see.

Juan I, who succeeded his father at the age of thirty-six, was both physically and mentally feeble, and left the management of the government in the hands of his Queen, Yolande of Bar, a woman of great beauty and culture, who surrounded herself with poets, singers and dancers to such an extent that the nobles demanded a curtailment of the almost perpetual festivities and in particular the banishment from court of a female favourite who had gained great ascendancy over both King and Queen. In May 1395 the King was gored by a wild boar while out hunting and died of his injuries a few days later. His two sons by Queen Yolande both died in infancy and he was survived by one daughter from each marriage. Yolande, in order to delay matters and perhaps to secure her daughter's accession to the throne, declared herself to be pregnant. Obviously, the deception could not be maintained and she was obliged to yield to her brother-in-law Martin.

At the time of his accession, King Martin was in Sicily securing the throne of that kingdom for his only surviving son and namesake, who had married the heiress of King Frederick III. His Queen Maria was in Aragon, however, and undertook the regency until he was able to return two years later to be crowned at Saragossa in April 1397. Queen Maria died, 'greatly regretted by the whole nation' in December 1406, and her death was followed three years later by that of her only surviving son King Martin of Sicily. As Martin of Sicily's only child had died in infancy, the curious situation arose of a son, Martin I, being succeeded by his father as King Martin II of Sicily. The older Martin now contracted a second marriage in the hope of getting an heir and three months after his son's death and his accession to the throne of Sicily he married Doña Margarita de Prades. Sadly, no child arrived and the King died in May 1412, having failed to nominate an heir to the throne of Aragon from among his many kinsmen with a claim to it. This resulted in an interregnum which lasted for two years until nine commissioners were appointed to elect a new King and chose Martin's nephew, the Infante Ferdinand of Castile, son of Martin's sister Leonor, who had married King Juan I of Castile.

King Ferdinand I was thirty-two years old when he was elected and had already ruled Castile as Regent for his nephew King Juan II since 1406. He was a staunch supporter of the anti-Pope Benedict XIII until 1415, when the Emperor Sigismund persuaded him otherwise; the withdrawal of his support was instrumental in ending the Great Schism. Ferdinand died in April 1416, still only in his thirty-sixth year. His wife, Leonor of Albuquerque, was one of the greatest heiresses of Castile and inevitably – queens and princesses are almost always eulogized in this manner by medieval chroniclers – 'as beautiful in person as she was graceful and attractive in manner'. She spent her widowhood in Castile, where she played a prominent part at the court of her son-in-law King Juan II, and died in December 1435.

Ferdinand was succeeded by his eldest son Alfonso V, a prototype of the Renaissance Prince, who earned his epithet of 'the Magnanimous' by refusing to be told even the names of those involved in an abortive plot against him at the time of his accession, so that they went unpunished. He was more interested in his Italian realms of Naples and Sicily than in Aragon, where he left his Queen, Maria of Castile, as Regent. She proved herself an able administrator, but became estranged from the King after a fit of jealousy (she being childless) led her to cause his pregnant mistress, one of her own ladies-in-waiting, to be strangled. Alfonso never forgave her or saw her again for the remaining twenty-six years of their marriage, though strangely they died within a few months of each other in 1458.

Alfonso bequeathed his Italian dominions to his natural son Ferdinand, but was succeeded in Aragon by his brother Juan, who had been King of Navarre since 1425, having married Blanche, the heiress of that kingdom. She had died in 1441, however, and in 1447, at the age of fifty, he had married the twenty-two-year-old Juana Henriquez, a masterful lady who was suspected of poisoning her stepson to pave the way for the accession of her own son Ferdinand. Juan's great coup was to arrange the marriage of Ferdinand to the Infanta Isabel of Castile in 1469. Five years later Isabel succeeded to the throne of Castile and Juan knew that on his own death his son and daughter-in-law would rule together over a united Spain.

The Kings of Castile and Leon

FERDINAND I THE GREAT	1035–1065

b ca 1017, 2nd son of Sancho III, King of Navarre, and his second wife Munia Elvira, dau of Sancho Garces, Count of Castile; received Castile on his father's death February 1035; defeated and killed his brother-in-law King Bermudo III, thereby becoming King of Leon 1037; *m* 1033 Sancha (*d* 13 December 1067; *bur* Church of St Isidore, Leon), dau of Alfonso V, King of Leon, and Elvira Melendez; 3 sons, 2 daus; *d* Leon 27 December 1065; *bur* Church of St Isidore, Leon

SANCHO II THE STRONG	1065–1072

b ca 1038, eldest son of King Ferdinand I; *s* his father as King of Castile 27 December 1065; *m* Alberta; murdered near Zamora 7 October 1072; *bur* Monastery of St Salvador of Ona

ALFONSO VI THE BRAVE	1072–1109

b spring 1040, 2nd son of King Ferdinand I; *s* his father in Leon and the Asturias 27 December 1065; *s* his brother King Sancho II 7 October 1072; *m* (1) before 16 June 1074 (*m* diss 1079) Agnes (*b ca* 1054; *d* 1080), dau of William VIII (VI), Duke of Aquitaine, and Matilda of Toulouse; *m* (2) 1081 Constance (*b ca* 1046; *d* 1092), widow of Hugh II, Count of Châlons, and dau of Robert I, Duke of Burgundy, and his 1st wife Hélie de Sémur-en-Brionnais; 1 dau; *m* (3) by 25 November 1093 Berta (*d* 14 January 1095), dau of William I, Count of Burgundy (Franche-Comté), and Stephanie of Barcelona; *m* (4) 1096 Zayda, baptized as Isabel (*d* 1103), dau or dau-in-law of Muhammad II al-Mu'tamid, the Moorish King of Seville; 1 son, 1 or 2 daus; *m* (5) 1105 Beatrice, of unknown origin; *d* 30 June 1109

URRACA	1109–1126

b 1082, dau of King Alfonso VI and Constance of Burgundy; *s* her father 30 June 1109; *m* (1) *ca* 1095 Raymond, Count of Burgundy (*d* Leon 26 March 1107); 1 son; *m* (2) Muñon 30 June 1109 (*m* diss 1114) Alfonso I, King of Aragon; *d* Saldaña 8 March 1126

ALFONSO VII	1126–1157

b ca 1104, only son of Queen Urraca and Raymond of Burgundy; *s* his mother 8 March 1126; *m* (1) Saldaña November 1128 Berengaria (*d* 3 February 1149; *bur* Church of St James the Apostle, Galicia), widow of Bernard III, Count of Besalü, dau of Raymond Berengar III, Count

of Barcelona, and Duke of Provence, and Maria Rodriguez de Bivar, dau of El Cid; 4 sons, 2 daus; *m* (2) July 1152 Rixa, or Richilde (*m* (2) by 1162 Raymond Berengar II, Count of Provence; *m* (3) 1166 Raymond V, Count of Toulouse; *d* 1167/75), dau of Wladyslaw II, King of Poland, and Agnes of Austria; 1 son, 1 dau; *d* Fresneda 21 August 1157; *bur* Toledo

SANCHO III THE DESIRED	(IN CASTILE) 1157–1158

b ca 1134, eldest son of King Alfonso VII; *s* his father in Castile 21 August 1157; *m* 4 February 1151 Blanca (*d* 24 June 1158), dau of Garcia VI, King of Navarre, and his 1st wife Marguerite de l'Aigle; 2 sons; *d* 31 August 1158

FERDINAND II	(IN LEON) 1157–1188

b ca 1145, 2nd son of King Alfonso VII; *s* his father in Leon 21 August 1157; *m* (1) 1165 (*m* diss 1175) Urraca (*b ca* 1151; *d* 16 October 1188), dau of Alfonso I, King of Portugal, and Mafalda of Savoy; 1 son; *m* (2) 1176 Teresa (*d* 7 February 1180), widow of Don Nuño Perez de Lara and dau of Don Ferdinand de Trava, Count of Trastamara; *m* (3) 1184 Urraca, dau of Don Diego Lopez de Haro, Lord of Biscay, and Doña Aldonza Ruiz de Castro; 2 sons; *d* Benavente 21 January 1188

ALFONSO VIII	(IN CASTILE) 1158–1214

b 11 November 1155, only surviving son of King Sancho III; *s* his father 31 August 1158; *m* Taragona September 1179 Eleanor (*b* Damfront, Normandy, 13 October 1162; *d* Burgos 31 October 1214; *bur* Las Huelgas), dau of Henry II, King of England, and Eleanor of Aquitaine; 4 sons, 8 daus; *d* Burgos 6 October 1214; *bur* Las Huelgas

ALFONSO IX	(IN LEON) 1188–1230

b 1166, son of King Ferdinand II and his 1st wife Urraca of Portugal; *s* his father 21 January 1188; *m* (1) 1190 (*m* diss 1198) (St) Teresa (*b* 1181; *d* Coimbra 18 June 1250; canonized by Pope Clement XI 1705), dau of Sancho I, King of Portugal, and Dulce of Barcelona; 1 son, 2 daus; *m* (2) Valladolid 1197 (*m* diss 1209) Berengaria (*b* 1181; *d* 8 November 1245), eldest dau of Alfonso VIII, King of Castile, and Eleanor of England; 2 sons, 3 daus; *d* Villanueva de Saria 23 September 1230

HENRY I	(IN CASTILE) 1214–1217

b 14 April 1204, yst but only surviving son of King Alfonso VIII and Eleanor of England; *s* his father 6 October 1214; *d* as the result of an accident Burgos 6 June 1217

St Ferdinand III (in Castile) 1217–1252 (and Leon from 1230)

b nr Salamanca 1200, eldest surv son of King Alfonso IX of Leon and his 2nd wife Berengaria of Castile; *s* his maternal uncle Henry I as King of Castile 6 June 1217, and his father as King of Leon 24 September 1230, thus re-uniting the two kingdoms; *m* (1) Burgos 27 November 1219 Beatrice (*b ca* 1202; *d* Toro 30 November 1235), dau of Philip of Swabia, King of the Romans, and Irene Angela; 7 sons, 2 daus; *m* (2) Burgos 1237 Jeanne, Countess of Ponthieu (*m* (2) 1260 Jean de Nesle; *d* 16 March 1278), dau of Simon, Count of Dammartin and Boulogne, and Marie, Countess of Ponthieu; 2 sons, 1 dau; *d* Seville 30 May 1252; *bur* Seville Cathedral; canonized by Pope Clement X 1671

Alfonso X the Wise and the Astrologer 1252–1284

b Toledo 23 November 1220, eldest son of King Ferdinand III; *s* his father 30 May 1252; elected King of the Romans 1257; *m* 26 November 1246 Violante or Yolande (*d* Roncesvalles 1300), dau of James I, King of Aragon, and his 2nd wife, Violante of Hungary; 5 sons, 5 daus; *d* Seville 4 April 1284

Sancho IV the Brave 1284–1295

b 13 May 1258, 2nd son of King Alfonso X; *s* his father 4 April 1284; *m* Toledo 1282 Maria, Queen Regent of Castile for her son King Ferdinand IV and her grandson King Alfonso XI (*d* Valladolid 1 June 1322), dau of Infante Don Alfonso, Lord of Molina (yst son of King Alfonso IX), and his 1st wife Doña Mayor Alfonso de Meneses; 5 sons, 2 daus; *d* Toledo 26 April 1295

Ferdinand IV the Summoned 1295–1312

b Seville 6 December 1285, eldest son of King Sancho IV; *s* his father 26 April 1295; *m* Valladolid January 1302 Constance (*b* 3 January 1290; *d* Sahagun 17 November 1313), only dau of Denis, King of Portugal, and Isabel of Aragon; 1 son, 1 dau; *d* Jaén 7 September 1312

Alfonso XI the Just 1312–1350

b 11 August 1311, only son of King Ferdinand IV; *s* his father 7 September 1312; *m* September 1328 his double first cousin Maria (*b* 1313; *d* Evora 18 January 1357), eldest dau of Alfonso IV, King of Portugal, and Beatrice of Castile; 2 sons; *d* nr Gibraltar 26 March 1350

Pedro I the Cruel 1350–1366 1367–1369

b Burgos 30 August 1334, yr but only surv son of King Alfonso XI and Maria of Portugal; *s* his father 26 March 1350; *m* Valladolid 3 June 1353 Blanche (*b* 1338; *d* Medina Sidonia 1361; *bur* Tudela, Navarre), dau of Peter I, Duke of Bourbon, and Isabelle de Valois; deposed by his illegitimate half-brother Henry of Trastamara 1366, restored 1367; *d* (murdered) Montiel 23 March 1369; *bur* Seville Cathedral

Henry II the Bastard 1366–1367 1369–1379

b Seville 13 January 1334, illegitimate son of King Alfonso XI and Leonor Perez de Guzman; created Count of Trastamara by his father; deposed his half-brother King Pedro I 1366 and usurped the throne; deposed in turn by Pedro 1367; regained the throne after murdering Pedro at Montiel 23 March 1369; *m* 1350 Juana (*b* 1339; *d* Salamanca 27 March 1381; *bur* Toledo), dau of Juan Manuel, Count of Penafiel, and Doña Blanca de la Cerda y Lara; 1 son, 1 dau; *d* Burgos 29 May 1379; *bur* Church of St Mary, Toledo

Juan I 1379–1390

b Epila 24 August 1358, only son of King Henry II; *s* his father 29 May 1379; *m* (1) Soria 18 June 1374 Leonor (*b* 1358; *d* Cuellar 13 September 1382), dau of Pedro IV, King of Aragon, and his 3rd wife Leonor of Sicily; 2 sons, 1 dau; *m* (2) Badajoz 17 May 1383 Beatrice (*b* Coimbra 1372; *d* after 1409), dau of Ferdinand I, King of Portugal, and Leonor Telles; *d* Alcala 9 October 1390; *bur* Toledo

Henry III the Infirm 1390–1406

b Burgos 4 October 1379, elder son of King Juan I; *s* his father 9 October 1390; *m* Burgos 1393 Catherine (*b* Hertford by 31 March 1373; *d* 2 June 1418; *bur* Toledo), yst dau of John of Gaunt, Duke of Lancaster, and his 2nd wife Constance of Castile (dau of King Pedro I); 1 son, 2 daus; *d* Toledo 25/26 December 1406

Juan II 1406–1454

b Toro 6 March 1405, only son of King Henry III; *s* his father 25/26 December 1406; *m* (1) 20 October 1418 Maria (*d* Villacastin February 1445), dau of Ferdinand I, King of Aragon, and Leonor of Albuquerque; 1 son, 2 daus; *m* (2) Madrigal August 1447 Isabel (*b* 1430; *d* Arevalo 15 August 1496; *bur* Miraflores, nr Burgos), dau of John, Prince of Portugal, and Isabel of Bragança; 1 son, 1 dau; *d* Valladolid 22 July 1454

HENRY IV   1454–1474

b Valladolid 5 January 1425, son of King Juan II and his 1st wife Maria of Aragon; *s* his father 22 July 1454; *m* (1) Valladolid 15 September 1440 (*m* annulled 1453) Blanca (*b* 1420; *d* 1464), dau of Juan II, King of Aragon, and his 1st wife Blanca of Navarre; *m* (2) Cordoba 21 May 1455 Joana (*b* March 1439; *d* Toro 13 June 1475), dau of Duarte I, King of Portugal, and Leonor of Aragon; 1 dau (?); *d* Madrid 11 December 1474

ISABEL I THE CATHOLIC   1474–1504
AND
FERDINAND V THE CATHOLIC   1474–1516

under whom Castile and Aragon became united to form the kingdom of Spain (*see hereafter*).

Castile, which was to become predominant among the medieval Christian kingdoms of Spain, began as a small dependency of Leon under a line of Counts founded by Fernan Gonzalez around the year 923. His son Garcia founded Burgos and made it his capital in 982. Sancho III, King of Navarre, married the sister and heiress of Count Garcia II and added Castile to his dominions in 1028, later bestowing it on his son Ferdinand, the first to be styled King of Castile.

Ferdinand added Leon and the Asturias to his kingdom, as we have seen, fought with his brothers and the Moors successfully, and on his death in 1065 made the all too common mistake of again dividing up his lands among his children. Sancho got Castile; Alfonso, the favourite, got Leon and the Asturias; Garcia got Galicia and Portugal as far as the Douro; Urraca got Zamora; and Elvira got Toro. Within three years war broke out between the siblings and the legendary exploits of Spain's national hero El Cid belong to this period. Eventually Sancho was murdered by a traitor in his own camp while besieging his sister Urraca in her fortress of Zamora and Alfonso VI became King of Castile.

Alfonso's valiant exploits against the Moors were to make him a national hero, but he was completely overshadowed by the personality of El Cid, with whom his relationship was often strained. The great event of Alfonso's reign was the recovery of Toledo from the Moors in 1085.

Alfonso VI is also noted for his complicated matrimonial entanglements. The number of his wives (five or six), their names, order and provenance are still the subject of controversy. He certainly had one wife of Muslim origin, Zayda, baptized as Isabel, who was the daughter or daughter-in-law (there are conflicting versions) of the conquered King of Seville. She bore Alfonso's only son, Sancho, who fell in battle with the Almoravides during his father's lifetime. Alfonso pursued a careful policy in marrying off his daughters, legitimate and illegitimate. His eldest daughter and destined heiress, Urraca, was married to Raymond of Burgundy; Sancha to the Count of Lara; Elvira to King Roger II of Sicily; another

Effigies of (left to right):

Queen Urraca of Castile and Leon, in the Church of San Vicente, Avila

Berengaria of Castile, second wife of Alfonso IX, King of Leon, in Toledo Cathedral

St Ferdinand III, King of Castile, in the cloisters of Burgos Cathedral.

(illegitimate) Elvira to Raymond IV, Count of Toulouse; and the illegitimate Teresa to Henry of Burgundy, Count of Portugal.

Alfonso died at the then great age of seventy in June 1109 and was succeeded by Urraca, who after the death of Raymond had made a disastrous marriage with King Alfonso I of Aragon, which has already been referred to. Most of the reign was spent in warring with Alfonso and with Urraca's own only son (by Raymond), another Alfonso. Urraca was noted for her 'levity and imprudence', chiefly characterized by her penchant for handsome young Castilian noblemen.

Alfonso VII, who succeeded his mother in 1126 and reigned until 1157, styled himself 'Emperor of all Spain' in 1135. It was a title, almost needless to say, which could hardly be substantiated.

After Alfonso's death Castile and Leon were again divided between his two sons and were not to be re-united until 1217 in the person of St Ferdinand III. This King captured Jaen, Murcia, Cordoba and Seville from the Moors, so that only

Granada remained unconquered. In England he is remembered as the father of one of our best loved Queens, Eleanor, for whom the Eleanor Crosses were built. In between fighting the Moors, Ferdinand founded the University of Salamanca and was a great patron of learning. In his private life he practised a rigid austerity, and this and his constant campaigning wore him out. He died at Seville on 30 May 1252 and lies in a magnificent tomb in the Cathedral there.

His son and successor Alfonso X is known as 'the Wise' or 'the Astrologer' and compiled the 'Alfonsine Tables', a series of astrological charts, as well as a digest of laws and a great chronicle. He also wrote poems in the Calician dialect. Apart from all this, however, he was not a good King and, having managed to get himself elected King of the Romans, wasted much time and far too much money in endeavouring to secure the Imperial Crown. His last years were embittered by squabbles among his heirs. His eldest son Ferdinand de la Cerda (so called from a tuft of hair (*cerda*) growing from a mole on his face) died in 1275, leaving two young sons. Their rights were set aside in favour of their uncle Sancho, which led to a declaration of war by France, the boys' mother being a French Princess. The issue completely divided the royal family, the Queen taking up the cause of her grandsons and fleeing into Aragon with them and their mother. Two years later, however, she had a change of heart and returned to Castile to side with Sancho, who had rebelled against his father, winning the support of the Cortes. A reconciliation was eventually effected and Alfonso died of grief and anxiety when he heard that the erstwhile rebel had suddenly been taken ill.

Sancho's illness was not serious and he soon found himself having to deal with the claims of his dispossessed nephew, which he did successfully. Sancho's greatest asset was his highly talented wife Maria de Molina, who came to be known as Maria la Grande, and when he died in 1295 leaving the throne to his ten-year-old son Ferdinand IV, she became a very able Regent, dealing capably with all rivals and arranging advantageous marriages for her children.

Ferdinand IV was something of a nonentity, a man of little ability and weak character. His sobriquet of 'the Summoned' refers to the circumstances of his death. Two brothers were accused of the murder of one of the King's gentlemen and, although the evidence against them was slight, Ferdinand ordered their execution without trial. As they went to their deaths, protesting their innocence, they summoned the King to appear before God's judgement seat within thirty days. Ferdinand, who was only twenty-six, paid little heed to this, but on the thirtieth day after the incident lay down in the afternoon for a short rest and was found dead by his attendants when they became alarmed by his prolonged absence and went to investigate. The throne of Castile now passed to a year-old child, Alfonso XI. His grandmother Queen Maria again took over the regency and exercised it wisely until her death in 1322. Alfonso assumed the sovereignty in 1324 at the age of thirteen and a few years later mounted a campaign against the Moors of Granada, culminating in the battle of Salado which inflicted enormous losses on them. It is said to have been the first battle in Europe at which cannon were used. Alfonso next laid siege to Algeciras, which surrendered in March 1344. A ten-year truce was made between Granada and Castile, but Alfonso soon found a pretext to break it and he was besieging Gibraltar when the Black Death overtook his camp and he became one of its victims in March 1350.

Alfonso had married Maria of Portugal in 1328, but his heart had already been won by Doña Leonor de Guzman, a young widow of noble birth and acknowledged to be the most beautiful woman in the kingdom, with intellectual abilities to match. She was to be Queen of Castile in all but name throughout Alfonso's reign and bore the King a large family. Queen Maria was shamefully neglected and virtually completely abandoned after giving birth to two sons, of whom only the younger survived. She bided her time and brooded on her revenge. No sooner was Alfonso dead than Leonor was arrested on the Queen's orders, conveyed to the Castle of Talavera, and there strangled. At the same time all the members of her family were subjected to a virulent persecution.

The new King Pedro I was only in his sixteenth year and in the strange way which history has of repeating itself had already formed an attachment similar to that of his father for Leonor. The object of his attention was a girl of noble birth named Maria de Padilla and Pedro was later to claim that he had married her secretly in 1351 or 1352 and that consequently the four children she bore him were legitimate and heirs to the crown. Be that as it may, Pedro yielded to pressure from the Cortes to marry Blanche of Bourbon, a cousin of the King of France. The marriage was celebrated at Valladolid with great splendour in June 1353, but within two days Pedro left his bride and returned to the arms of Maria. His mother, mortified by his conduct, gave her support to a league of nobles who forced the King to dismiss all Maria's relations and supporters from his service and replace them with their own nominees. In 1355, however, Pedro was able to turn the tables and had four of the principal leaguers stabbed and bludgeoned to death at Toro in the very presence of the Queen Mother, whose garments were spattered with their blood and brains. She, horrified by the deed, retired to her native Portugal the following year, where the discovery of her own indulgence in a licentious affair, caused her father King Alfonso IV to order her to be put to death in January 1357. Pedro was unable to remain completely faithful to Maria de Padilla and in 1354 conceived a passing fancy for Juana de Castro, a beautiful young widow. To win her he arranged a mock marriage, persuading two complaisant Bishops to perform the ceremony at Cuellar, declaring that as King he might marry whom and when he chose. Pedro tired of her almost immediately and again returned to Maria. He did, however, have the grace to endow Juana with the town of Dueñas, and she retired there insisting on her title of Queen until her death in 1374.

Most of Pedro's reign was taken up in playing a cat and mouse game with his half-brothers and their supporters, many of whom became his victims. Although there have been attempts to show Pedro in a more favourable light as a lover of justice and a champion of the people's rights, a modern historian has said 'it is impossible to clear Pedro's memory of a load of iniquity, of base perfidy, meanness, and wanton and inhuman brutality, greater than belongs to any other monarch in modern history, except Ivan the Fourth of Russia', and further that: 'He was as devoid of generosity as of pity, as reckless of the truth as of life, as greedy of gain as of blood – a false knight, a perjured husband, a brutal son – not even loyal to the love which was the one bright gleam in his dark history – the love for the hapless Maria de Padilla, of whom there is none to speak a word of ill.' In 1361 the abandoned Queen Blanche died in the castle of Medina Sidonia, where she was held prisoner, poisoned it is said by the governor who was ordered to 'give her herbs so that she should die'. Maria de Padilla died very shortly afterwards and Pedro convoked a Cortes at Seville to declare that she had been his only lawful wife and that her four children were his legitimate heirs. Alfonso, the only son, died a year after his mother, but the three girls, Beatrice, Constance and Isabel survived.

Pedro's eldest surviving half-brother, Henry, Count of Trastamara, now set himself up in opposition to him, placed himself at the head of the disaffected nobles who had fled into Aragon, and with French support drove Pedro out of Seville and seized the throne. Pedro sought refuge in Bayonne, where he found a champion in the person of Edward 'the Black Prince', eldest son and heir of King Edward III of England, who resided there as Governor of Aquitaine for his father. With Edward's aid, Pedro's throne was re-won at the great battle of Najera in April 1367. He reigned uneasily for two more years during which the struggle with Henry continued. In March 1369, on a pretext arranged by Bernard du Guesclin, Henry's French ally, Pedro was persuaded to leave the castle of Montiel and visit du Guesclin's tent to discuss the terms of a treaty. His half-brother was waiting for him there and in a short sharp struggle between the two, Pedro was stabbed to death. He was in his thirty-fifth year.

The fratricide, who has been described as 'almost as cruel and perfidious as his predecessor' secured his throne with the aid of French mercenaries, but soon had to contend with a rival claimant in the person of John of Gaunt, Duke of Lancaster, the Black Prince's brother, who had married Pedro's daughter Constance and claimed Castile in her right. Fortunately for Henry, John's preparations to invade Spain were frustrated by the need to defend the English possessions in Guienne from the French. Henry reigned without further interruption until his death at the age of forty-five in May 1379, following an illness of twelve days supposedly caused by poison. He was 'below the middle height, well made, with a fair complexion and brown hair'. He had been married by his father Alfonso XI to Doña Juana Manuel, a lady descended from St Ferdinand through her father and from the dispossessed de la Cerdas through her mother. She bore Henry one son and one daughter and the marriage was apparently happy in spite of Henry's many flagrant infidelities which provided him with numerous illegitimate offspring as well. Queen Juana assumed the habit of a Poor Clare after Henry's death and survived him until March 1381.

Juan I, Henry's only legitimate son, was in his twenty-first year when he succeeded his father and had already been married for four years to Leonor of Aragon, a match carefully arranged by Henry and bringing a dowry of 80,000 florins. The new King and Queen were crowned at Las Huelgas de Burgos, Juan knighting one hundred young noblemen on the occasion, and in October the Queen gave birth to her first child, Henry. Her second son, Ferdinand, later to become King of Aragon as we have seen, was born in the November of the following year; but the birth of her third child, a daughter Leonor who did not long survive, cost her her life on 13 September 1382. She was much eulogized for her piety and many charitable acts. Juan's second marriage, which took place at Badajoz in May 1383, was to the child Beatrice, heiress of King Ferdinand I of Portugal and Juan's efforts to gain the crown of that country have already been told. In October 1390, while taking part in some military exercises, Juan rode his horse across some recently ploughed land which caused it to stumble, throw its rider and roll on him. The King, who was small and of extremely delicate constitution, was found to be dead when his attendants extricated him. The Archbishop of Toledo, with great presence of mind, caused the news of the King's death to be concealed until the Queen had been informed and the succession of the young heir secured. In contrast to his two immediate predecessors, Juan had been 'kind-hearted, gentle ... and tinctured by no vices'. He was only thirty-two years old when he died. Beatrice of Portugal, by whom he had no children, remained devoted to his memory, and refused all offers of remarriage. She is last mentioned in 1409, but the date of her death is unrecorded.

The new King of Castile, Henry III, was a boy of eleven and was the first heir apparent to receive the title of Prince of the Asturias. The Cortes appointed twelve governors to exercise the royal authority until Henry came of age at fourteen in 1393. Unfortunately, he had inherited his father's delicacy of constitution and has gone down in history with the sobriquet 'the Infirm'. His father had cleverly arranged a marriage for him with Catherine of Lancaster, the daughter of John of Gaunt and Constance, the daughter of Pedro the Cruel, thus restoring the semblance of legitimacy to the line of Trastamara. The first two children of the marriage were daughters, but in March 1405 the Queen gave birth to a son Juan, whose arrival caused excessive rejoicing. The delicate King succumbed to his ailments in December of the following year, having by his will appointed Queen Catherine and his brother Ferdinand as co-Regents for the infant Juan II. Ferdinand, who was elected King of Aragon in 1412, died in 1416, leaving Queen Catherine as sole Regent. Though still a young woman she had become exceedingly stout through over indulgence in eating and drinking and succumbed to a paralytic stroke on 2 June 1418, leaving Juan at the age of thirteen to the mercy of a band of self-seeking courtiers. Almost immediately, the Archbishop of Toledo negotiated for the young King's marriage to his first cousin Maria of Aragon which was solemnized at Medina del Campo in October 1418. A Cortes summoned to meet in Madrid declared Juan of age and he undertook the government in March 1419. Throughout his reign he was to be dominated by favourites, the most notorious being Don Alvaro de Luna. The same age as the King, he inspired such affection in him that they became inseparable companions and there were many dark hints as to the possible sexual nature of the relationship. The favours heaped on Don Alvaro, who was made Constable of Castile, aroused much resentment and a league was formed against him and became powerful enough to have him removed from court in 1427 for a period of eighteen months. However, his influence was strong enough to bring about his recall and the King went in person to meet him on his triumphant return. It must be admitted that the Constable's rule was a vigorous one and brought a long period of peace and prosperity to the realm, but eventually a new faction rose in opposition and Don Alvaro was arrested in his house at Burgos, brought to trial on trumped-up charges and condemned to death. He was taken to Valladolid for his execution, which was made a great public spectacle, and died bravely protesting his loyalty to his King to the end. So fickle was the populace that it is said a great wail arose from the crowd assembled to see the execution, 'men and women weeping as they who had lost a father or some one whom they much loved'. The ungrateful King survived his erstwhile favourite but a year and died lamenting that 'he had not been born the son of a mechanic instead of King of Castile'.

Juan's first wife, Maria of Aragon, had died in 1445. She had borne two daughters, who both died young, and then, in January 1425, a son Henry, who was destined to succeed his father. Within five months of Queen Maria's death, Don Alvaro began negotiations for the King's marriage to Isabel of Portugal and the ceremony took place at Madrigal in August 1447. The new Queen gave Juan two more children, Isabel, who was to bring about the unity of Spain, and Alfonso.

Henry IV, who succeeded his father in July 1454 at the age of twenty-nine, is a strange, pathetic figure. He was tall and gangling with an oversized head, a strangely flattened nose, and enormous, clumsy hands and feet. He was also shy and retiring and only happy in the society of his male favourites and his many pet animals. Completely guileless, kind, forgiving and well-meaning, Henry could have been a great King under happier circumstances and in a different age. He had been married at the age of fifteen to his first cousin Blanca of Aragon, but found it impossible to consummate the marriage, although it was claimed that he was not similarly impotent with other women. The failure to achieve intercourse with his wife was attributed to witchcraft and after a lengthy process an annulment of the marriage was secured in 1453. Two years later Henry contracted another marriage to another first cousin, Joana (in Spain Juana) of Portugal. The pair could not have presented a greater contrast: she dainty and fastidious with a passion for fine clothes and parties; he uncouth and ungainly, unmindful of his dress or personal hygiene and with a strange penchant for repulsive smells. Sad to say, Henry was no more successful in his attempts to consummate this marriage than he had the first and 'the Queen remained intact as she arrived'. In desperation to beget an heir, the royal couple had recourse to the best available

medical advice of the day. A German physician, Münzer, who was called into consultation, has left a vivid description of the poor King's ill-proportioned genitalia and of the crude attempt at artificial insemination for which a solid gold tube was constructed. What became of that artefact, one wonders?

Meanwhile, the King and Queen had both become infatuated with a handsome young courtier, Don Beltran de la Cueva, who was soon rumoured to be the lover of both. In 1461 the Queen at last became pregnant and in March 1462 gave birth to a daughter, Juana, of whom it was universally believed Beltran was the father so that the poor child was dubbed 'La Beltraneja'. In May Henry called a Cortes to recognize Juana as heir to the throne, but several of the cities represented, as well as many of the nobles, refused to do so. Henry spent the rest of his reign vacillating over the recognition and non-recognition of Juana. A year after the birth the Queen again became pregnant, but the shock she received when her hair caught fire from the heat of the sun while she was seated in a window caused her to miscarry a male infant in the sixth month. Shortly after this Henry recognized his half-brother Alfonso as his heir on condition that he would eventually marry La Beltraneja.

The affairs of the kingdom had long been in the hands of the chief minister, Juan Pacheco, Marqués of Villena, who had enforced a humiliating treaty with France and now sided with the rebellious nobles against the King. In 1465 an extraordinary scene was enacted at Avila when a throne was set up on a platform with an effigy of Henry crowned and robed. A herald recited the complaints against the King and declared him deposed, whereupon the Archbishop of Toledo solemnly removed the crown from the effigy, which was then hurled from the throne and torn to pieces by the excited crowd. The eleven-year-old Infante Alfonso was proclaimed King and carried shoulder high from the field. Alfonso is not, however, regarded as a sovereign of Castile and following his death in July 1468, under the usual suspicion of poison, his sister Isabel was put forward as a candidate for the throne. Terms were reached with Henry and on 9 September 1468 he met Isabel at Toros de Guisando, received the homage of the nobles and recognized Isabel as the future Queen. The question of Isabel's marriage was settled in 1469, when, in spite of some opposition from her half-brother, she married Ferdinand, the heir of Aragon. The rest of Henry's life was one of abject misery. Queen Juana had left him, not surprisingly, and had produced two further sons by her new lover Pedro de Castilla, although she still maintained that her daughter was the King's. Henry, who had contracted a painful and distressing disease which defies diagnosis, in the last months of his life conceived an overwhelming passion for Diego Pacheco, the son of his treacherous minister, visiting the boy daily, sitting on his bed and struggling to play the guitar and sing to him. He died after suffering a massive haemorrhage on 11 December 1474, a month short of his fiftieth birthday. Queen Juana survived him six months only, dying at Madrid on 13 June 1475, aged thirty-six. As for Juana, 'La Beltraneja', she never succeeded in finding a husband, although promised for a time to her uncle King

Alfonso V of Portugal, who had hopes of obtaining the succession to Castile and Leon through her. She died in a convent in Lisbon in 1530.

The Kings of Navarre

The tiny kingdom of Navarre in the north-east corner of Spain was destined to be the cradle from whence all the Spanish monarchs sprang. It first gained independence under Count Sancho Iñigo, who conquered Pamplona and made it his capital in about 873. His son, Garcia I, who succeeded him in about 880 was the first to style himself King. King Sancho III the Great acquired Castile and Aragon and successfully battled against the Moors. When he was murdered on 15 October 1035, he left his dominions divided between his sons, Garcia V receiving Navarre, Ferdinand I receiving Castile, and the illegitimate Ramiro I receiving Aragon. Thereafter Navarre had a chequered history often being united with other countries. From 1076 to 1134 it was united with Aragon, then became independent again under Garcia VI. A hundred years later it passed by marriage to the house of Champagne and in 1284 Queen Jeanne I conveyed it to her husband Philip IV of France. It remained united with France until 1328, when another heiress, Queen Jeanne II, conveyed it to her husband Philip, Count of Evreux (Philip III of Navarre). Their great-granddaughter Queen Blanche married King Juan II of Aragon, who was succeeded in Navarre by his daughter Leonor, the wife of Gaston, Count of Foix and Bigorre. She only survived her father by one month and, dying in February 1479, was succeeded by her grandson Francis Phoebus. He was poisoned in January 1483 and was succeeded by his sister Catherine, Duchess of Nemours, who was crowned at Pamplona with her husband Jean d'Albret (Jean III of Navarre) in 1494. During their reign Upper (or Spanish) Navarre was seized by Aragon in 1512, leaving only a French-Basque fragment north of the Pyrenees, to which their son Henry II succeeded in 1517. His little court at Pau in Béarn became one of the most cultured of its day. Henry's daughter and successor, Queen Jeanne III, was a staunch Huguenot and much involved in the religious wars in France. Her son, Henry III of Navarre, became King Henry IV of France in 1589 and he and all his successors until 1830 styled themselves Kings of France and Navarre.

The Kings of Spain

ISABEL I THE CATHOLIC | 1474–1504

---

b Madrigal 22 April 1451, dau of Juan II, King of Castile, and his second wife Isabel of Portugal; s her half-brother King Henry IV 11 December 1474; m Valladolid 19 October 1469 Ferdinand II, King of Aragon (see below); 1 son, 4 daus; d Medina del Campo 26 November 1504

FERDINAND V THE CATHOLIC | 1474–1516

---

b Sos 10 May 1452, son of Juan II, King of Aragon, and his second wife Juana Henriquez; titular King of Castile jure uxoris 11 December 1474; s his father as King of Aragon 19 January 1479; conquered Navarre 1512; Regent of the Kingdom of Castile 25 September 1506 to 23 January 1516; m (1) Valladolid 19 October 1469 Isabel I, Queen of Castile (see above); 1 son, 4 daus; m (2) Denia 22 March 1506 Germaine (m (2) March or April 1519 John, Margrave of Brandenburg-Ansbach, Viceroy of Valencia (d Valencia 5 July 1525); m (3) Valencia 1526, Ferdinand of Aragon, Duke of Calabria (d Valencia 26 October 1550); d Leira 15 October 1536), dau of Jean de Foix, Comte d'Etampes, Governor of the Dauphiné, and Marie of Orleans; 1 son; d Madrigal 23 January 1516

JUANA I THE MAD | 1504–1555
AND
PHILIP I THE HANDSOME | 1504–1506

---

b Toledo 6 November 1479, 2nd dau of Ferdinand and Isabel; s her mother as Queen of Castile 26 November 1504; s her father as Queen of Aragon 23 January 1516; m Lille 21 August 1496 Philip I the Handsome, King of Castile jure uxoris (b Bruges 22 June 1478; d Burgos 25 September 1506), son of Maximilian I, Holy Roman Emperor, and his 1st wife Maria of Burgundy; 2 sons, 4 daus; d Tordesillas 13 April 1555

CARLOS I | 1516–1556

---

b Ghent 24 February 1500, son of Queen Juana and King Philip I; s his maternal grandfather King Ferdinand II (V) 23 January 1516 as joint sovereign with his mother; s his paternal grandfather Emperor Maximilian I in Austria and the Netherlands 12 January 1519; elected King of the Romans (as Charles V) 28 June 1519; ceded the Austrian hereditary possessions to his brother Ferdinand 1521; crowned Holy Roman Emperor 24 February 1530; s his mother in Castile 13 April 1555; abdicated 27 August 1556; m Seville 11 March 1526 Isabel (b Lisbon 4 October 1503; d Toledo 1 May 1539; bur Granada), dau of Manuel I, King of Portugal, and Maria, 3rd dau of Ferdinand and Isabel; 3 sons, 2 daus; d San Geronimo de Yuste 21 September 1558; bur El Escorial

---

PHILIP II | 1556–1598

---

b Valladolid 21 May 1527, eldest son of King Carlos I; s his father on his abdication 27 August 1556; s his maternal uncle King Henry as King of Portugal 13 January 1580; m (1) Salamanca 15 November 1543 Maria (b Coimbra 15 October 1527; d Valladolid 12 July 1545), dau of John III, King of Portugal, and Catherine of Castile (dau of Queen Juana and King Philip I); 1 son; m (2) Winchester 25 July 1554 Mary I, Queen of England (b Greenwich 18 February 1516; d St James's Palace, London, 17 November 1558; bur Westminster Abbey), dau of Henry VIII, King of England, and his first wife Catherine of Aragon (yst dau of Ferdinand and Isabel); no issue; m (3) Toledo 2 February 1560 Elisabeth (b Fontainebleau 2 April 1545; d Madrid 3 October 1568), dau of Henry II, King of France, and Catherine de'Medici; 3 daus; m (4) Segovia 12 November 1570 his

King Ferdinand VII of Spain, a state portait by Goya.

King Alfonso XIII of Spain, a portrait in the Museum of Modern Art at Madrid.

The Spanish royal family. A recent photograph of King Juan Carlos, Queen Sofía and their three children.

St Louis of France
embarking on the Seventh
Crusade in 1248, from
an illuminated manuscript
in the Louvre.

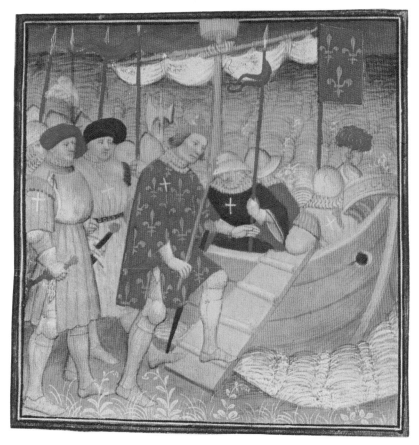

The marriage of King Philip III of
France to his second wife Marie
of Brabant at Vincennes in
1274, from a manuscript in the
British Museum.

*A spirited rendering in a manuscript in the British
Museum of Philip IV of France being gored by a wild boar.
The King's leg was broken but he actually died of a stroke in November 1314.*

niece Anna (*b* Cigales 2 November 1549; *d* Badajoz 26 October 1580), dau of Maximilian II, Holy Roman Emperor, and Maria of Austria (dau of King Carlos I); 4 sons, 1 dau, *d* El Escorial 13 September 1598; *bur* El Escorial

---

PHILIP III   1598–1621

b Madrid 14 April 1578, yst but only surviving son of King Philip II and his fourth wife Anna of Austria; *s* his father 13 September 1598; *m* Valencia 18 April 1599 Margarita (*b* Graz 25 December 1584; *d* El Escorial 3 October 1611), dau of Archduke Charles of Austria and Maria of Bavaria; 4 sons, 4 daus; *d* Madrid 31 March 1621; *bur* El Escorial

---

PHILIP IV   1621–1665

b Valladolid 8 April 1605, eldest son of King Philip III; *s* his father 31 March 1621; lost Portugal 1640; *m* (1) Bordeaux 25 November 1615 Elisabeth (*b* Fontainebleau 22 November 1602; *d* Madrid 6 October 1644), dau of Henry IV, King of France and Navarre, and his second wife Marie de'Medici; 2 sons, 6 daus; *m* (2) Navalcarnero, nr Madrid, 7 October 1649 his niece Maria Anna (*b* Wiener Neustadt 24 December 1635; *d* Madrid 16 May 1696), dau of Ferdinand III, Holy Roman Emperor, and Maria Anna Margarita, dau of King Philip III; 3 sons, 3 daus; *d* Madrid 17 September 1665; *bur* El Escorial

---

CARLOS II   1665–1700

b Madrid 11 November 1661, yst and only surviving son of King Philip IV; *s* his father 17 September 1665; *m* (1) Quintanapalla, nr Burgos 19 November 1679, Marie Louise (*b* Paris 27 March 1662; *d*. Madrid 12 February 1689), dau of Philip, Duke of Orleans, and his first wife Henrietta Anne of England; no issue; *m* (2) Valladolid 14 May 1690, Maria Anna (*b* Benrath, nr Düsseldorf 28 October 1667; *d* Guadalajara 16 July 1740), dau of Philip William, Elector Palatine, and Elizabeth Amelia of Hesse-Darmstadt; no issue; *d* Madrid 1 November 1700; *bur* El Escorial

Ferdinand and Isabel, 'the Catholic Kings', who were to unite Spain, finally expel the Moors, and set the foundation for a vast colonial empire in the new world, do not appear such attractive personalities today as they did two or three generations ago. Isabel, Queen at twenty-three, was tall, red-haired, fresh-complexioned, blue-eyed and placidly serene in appearance. Ferdinand, a year younger than his wife, was shorter, with a lean and athletic appearance. Until 1479 they had to contend with King Alfonso V of Portugal championing the cause of La Beltaneja, but a peace treaty was finally concluded and the eldest daughter of Ferdinand and Isabel, named after her mother, was promised to Alfonso's son and heir. In the same year, Ferdinand succeeded his father in Aragon and Spain became united under its co-rulers.

Under the influence of her confessor Torquemada, Isabel requested the Pope for a bull to introduce the Holy Office, the Inquisition, into Castile (it had already been established in Aragon for some time). She then turned her attention to the conversion of the Jews. Those who refused to be converted were burnt alive or expelled, but some two-thirds accepted at least nominal conversion and made a valuable contribution to the country's economy. The conquest of Granada, the last remaining Moorish kingdom in Spain, was finally accomplished on 2 January 1492 after a long campaign in the course of which Isabel accompanied the army mounted on a mule.

Isabel has been much extolled as a patron of the arts, literature and science and Francis Bacon was to eulogize her as 'an honour to her sex and the corner-stone of the greatness of Spain'. It is probably as the patron of the Genoese explorer, Christopher Columbus, that she is best remembered, and she is said to have sold her jewels to finance his voyages.

Ferdinand and Isabel had five children who grew to maturity and they were all married in their mother's lifetime. The eldest child, Isabel, born in 1470 was married to Alfonso, Prince of Portugal, and then to Manuel I, King of Portugal. After Isabel there was a gap of eight years (during which the Queen suffered at least one miscarriage) until the birth of the only son, Juan, in 1478. He was married in April 1497 to Margaret of Austria, daughter of the Emperor Maximilian I, but died of fever at Salamanca in October of the same year. His widow gave birth to a stillborn child some months later. The birth of Juan was followed in 1479 by that of Juana, destined to succeed her mother in Castile. In June 1482 Isabel was delivered of twins at Cordoba, but only one, Maria, survived and later married her brother-in-law King Manuel I of Portugal, widower of the Infanta Isabel. The family was completed in 1485 with the birth of Catherine, who, as Catherine of Aragon, is well known as the first wife of Henry VIII of England.

In November 1504 Ferdinand and Isabel both fell ill with fever (probably malaria) and although his strong constitution pulled him through, she, being less robust, weakened and died. She was fifty-three years old. Ferdinand, in spite of vowing to his dying wife that he would never marry again, did

A curious old woodblock engraving of Ferdinand and Isabel, the 'Catholic Kings'.

so two years later. His bride was the rather obscure Germaine (or Germana) de Foix, a nonentity who is almost forgotten. She bore Ferdinand one son, who died young, and survived him to marry two more times.

Isabel was succeeded as Queen of Castile by her second daughter Juana, who had married Philip, son of the Emperor Maximilian I, in 1496. He became titular King of Castile with his wife and is reckoned as Philip I of Spain. He was extremely handsome and his wife adored him, although she was mentally unstable and prone to fly into jealous rages without cause. The sudden death of Philip from typhoid in September 1506 brought about her complete collapse and for a long while she refused to have his body buried, carrying his coffin about with her on her journeyings and expecting him to come to life again. She was quite incapable of ruling so her father became Regent or guardian of Castile during the minority of her son Carlos. King Ferdinand completed the unification of Spain with the conquest of Navarre in 1512 and died in January 1516, when his grandson Carlos came to power just a month before his sixteenth birthday.

Carlos, better known to history as the Emperor Charles V, had been brought up in Flanders and arrived in Spain in 1517, Cardinal Jimenez de Cisneros having acted as Regent in the meantime. He was surrounded by a large Flemish entourage who showed their disdain for everything Spanish and his election as Emperor in 1519 added to the dissatisfaction of his Spanish subjects, who objected to his leaving the country while using its resources to further his interests elsewhere. In spite of involving Spain in European affairs, Carlos continued the policy of his grandparents and the country was efficiently governed. Gold was pouring in from South America and it was a golden age, too, for literature and art. Carlos was a great imperial dreamer with visions of a united states of Europe and worked long and hard to that end without achieving final success. Throughout most of his reign his mad mother, kept in close confinement, nominally shared the Spanish throne with him until her death in April 1555.

In the following year, conscious of the failure of his ideal, Carlos resolved on abdicating and on 16 January 1556 he resigned Spain and Sicily to his son Philip, to whom he had already handed over the sovereignty of the Netherlands the preceding October. Carlos settled in a small house at Yuste in Estremadura, where he led a comfortable life until his death in September 1558, reading much, receiving visits from his relations and friends, and enjoying the pleasures of the table.

Carlos did not inherit his father's good looks, possessing the jutting lower jaw and 'Habsburg lip' which marked so many of his family, but he had a good figure and fine eyes. He was brave and fearless in battle (though afraid of mice and spiders) and a just and merciful ruler. He was devoted to his wife, Isabel of Portugal, who died in childbirth in 1539, and he did not remarry. His natural daughter, Margaret, Duchess of Parma, who achieved fame as Governor of the Netherlands, was born some years before his marriage; while his natural son, Don John of Austria, who achieved fame as a soldier, winning the famous naval battle of Lepanto against the Turks on 7 October 1571, was not born until 1547.

Whereas Carlos had always been Flemish in temperament, his son and successor Philip II was a complete Spaniard and spent most of his reign in Spain, leaving his Flemish possessions to be governed by his able half-sister. Philip was dignified, serious, hard-working and autocratic. He was, moreover, a religious fanatic determined to stamp out Protestantism, and the persecution and burning of 'heretics' was pursued with vigour throughout his reign. At the age of sixteen Philip had been married to his cousin Maria of Portugal, who died in childbirth nearly two years later, leaving one son, Carlos. Philip remained a widower for nine years, then in 1554 his father arranged for his marriage to Queen Mary I of England, his first cousin once removed and his senior by eleven years. Philip sailed to England and was married to Mary at Winchester in July. As titular King of England, Philip's bust appeared on the English coinage facing that of his wife and all Acts of Parliament were enacted in their joint names. Mary adored him with a girlish ardour, but he found her physically repellent and complained of the disgusting odour from her nose. In August 1555 he returned to Spain, leaving the thirty-nine-year-old Mary deluding herself with a false pregnancy. He returned to England in 1557 to enlist Mary's aid in his war against France to which she readily agreed and as a result lost Calais, England's last Continental possession. Philip left England for good in July 1557. Mary, sadly disillusioned, died of influenza in November 1558, saying on her deathbed: 'When I am dead you will find the words "Philip" and "Calais" engraved upon my heart'.

Seven months after Mary's death Philip married again. His new bride was Elisabeth of France and their marriage cemented the treaty of peace concluded with that country. She bore Philip three daughters and was suspected, probably unjustly, of having an affair with her stepson Don Carlos, who was the same age as herself. At any rate, Carlos was a difficult young man exhibiting signs of derangement and had to be kept in confinement, where he died in July 1568, put to death at his father's instance it was rumoured. The Queen, whether guilty or not, died in October the same year. The story has provided the theme for a play and an opera.

Philip had definitively established Madrid as his capital in 1560 and three years later commenced the building of El Escorial, the vast palace, monastery and mausoleum constructed in the shape of a gridiron in honour of its patron St Laurence, who had been martyred by being grilled alive.

In November 1570 Philip married his fourth and last wife Anna Maria of Austria, who was his own niece and twenty-two years his junior. She became the mother of four sons and one daughter, all of whom died young with the exception of the youngest son, Philip, who lived to succeed his father. The Queen died in 1580, the year in which Philip added Portugal to his dominions.

Philip had entertained designs on England since the death of his second wife Mary in 1558, feeling that he had as much right to the throne as Mary's half-sister and successor Elizabeth. He was further enraged by the growth of the reformed religion, the aid given by England to his rebellious Dutch subjects, and by piratical raids carried out on Spanish treasure ships. The execution of Mary, Queen of Scots, in 1587 brought matters to a head and Philip assembled and equipped the Great Armada to sail against England. The story of its ignominious defeat by Sir Francis Drake is well known. Philip never fully recovered from the blow to his pride and spent more and more time in withdrawal at El Escorial. He was finally afflicted with a long and painful illness, which he bore with the utmost stoicism, and died, covered in boils and in a verminous condition, on 13 September 1598, aged seventy-one.

Philip III, who ascended the throne at the age of twenty, was melancholy, retiring and deeply religious and his father is said to have bitterly lamented that God had not given him a son better capable of governing his realm. Philip fulfilled his father's forebodings, devoting himself to religious observances and court festivities and leaving the government in the hands of his favourite the Duke of Lerma and the latter's son the Duke of Uceda. The year after his accession he married Margarita of Austria, who presented him with four sons and four daughters before her death in childbirth in 1611. Philip's own death ten years later was brought about by the rigid adherence to court etiquette which prevailed in Spain. He was asphyxiated in his bedroom by the fumes of a charcoal brazier, which would normally have been removed but was left in

Philip III, King of Spain, as a young man, wearing a very finely engraved suit of armour and the Order of the Golden Fleece.

An interesting engraving of Philip III, King of Spain, at the age of thirty-one with his wife Margarita of Austria, surrounded by the coats-of-arms of all the countries over which they ruled or to which they had pretensions.

Elisabeth of Valois, the third wife of King Philip II of Spain, depicted in a portrait by Sanchez Coello in the Prado. She looks self-consciously fashionable.

An older King Philip III on horseback.

A world-weary King Philip IV of Spain as depicted by Velazquez.

place because the person whose office it was to remove it was not at hand and nobody else dared to do so.

The next King, Philip IV, was a boy of sixteen at his accession. He and his family are well known to us from the charming canvases of Velazquez, whose patron he was. Philip was a far more attractive figure than his father, though like him he was content to leave all political matters in the hands of his favourite the Count-Duke of Olivares, a far more able and scrupulous man than the Duke of Lerma in the previous reign. However, Olivares was unable to halt the steady decline into which Spain had fallen and the Catalan revolt and the loss of Portugal in 1640 led to his dismissal in 1643. The King was quite unable to direct the administration and soon allowed it to fall into the hands of other favourites. His patronage of Velazquez as well as of dramatists such as Lope de Vega and Calderón was his redeeming feature. Apart from that he loved horsemanship and hunting and indulged in much crude horseplay with his boon companions. In public, however, he affected a regal bearing of great dignity and it is said that he was only seen to laugh three times in his life.

The French had given support to the Catalan revolt and war dragged on for many years with Spain suffering a number of defeats. It was finally ended by the treaty of the Pyrenees on 7 November 1659, whereby Spain ceded its frontier fortresses in Flanders and Artois as well as Roussillon and Cerdagne to France and Philip's daughter Maria Teresa was betrothed to Louis XIV. It was a marriage which was to have far-reaching consequences for Spain.

Philip married twice and fathered many children, most of whom died in infancy. He also had several natural children, the most noteworthy being the younger Don John of Austria. Philip's eldest legitimate son, Don Baltasar Carlos, an attractive boy of great promise, died prematurely in 1646 at

the age of seventeen, worn out by debaucheries which had been encouraged by his preceptors. Three years after his death the King married again to provide for the succession. Disastrously, he chose his own niece, thirty years his junior; but there had already been too much inbreeding and the degeneracy of the next generation was to be only too apparent. Philip died at the age of sixty in September 1665, leaving the throne to his four-year-old son Carlos.

Carlos II, the last Habsburg King of Spain, began his reign under the regency of his mother Maria Anna of Austria, who was completely under the influence of the Jesuits and had a strong preference for foreigners. Opposition to her rule was led by the late King's natural son Don John and she was forced to relinquish the regency in 1676. Don John took over and was in control until his death in 1679.

Carlos was sadly degenerate with an enormous misshapen head and the heavy Habsburg underjaw exaggerated to almost caricature-like proportions and rendering eating a difficulty, while his intellect was similarly disabled. He had been fed by wet nurses until the age of five or six and was not allowed to walk until almost fully grown. In 1679 he was married to the attractive and vivacious Marie Louise of Orleans, niece of Louis XIV. It would seem that he was afflicted in the same way as King Henry IV of Castile and the marriage was never consummated. The rigid etiquette of the Spanish court nearly broke the spirit of the young Queen, but she fought against it bravely and on one occasion caused great consternation by publicly boxing the ears of her officious *camarera mayor* (mistress of the robes) after she had reprimanded the Queen over some minor infringement. Marie Louise died a victim of Spanish doctors in 1689, having almost completed her twenty-seventh year, and in the following year Carlos married again. His second wife was a German Princess from the Palatinate and doubtless it was felt that an influx of new blood might be a good thing for the dynasty; but like the first marriage this one too remained unconsummated. The near imbecile King became convinced that he had been bewitched and gave himself up to the ministrations of exorcists. Towards the end of his life he had the morbid fancy to order the coffins of his ancestors and relations to be opened so that he might gaze upon them. The sight of the body of his first wife, whom he had loved in his own strange fashion, provoked paroxysms of grief.

Carlos had hoped that he might be succeeded by one of the Austrian Habsburgs, but the Archbishop of Toledo induced him to make a will designating as his successor Philip, Duke of Anjou, the grandson of Louis XIV and Carlos's half-sister Maria Teresa. Having done so, Carlos died on 1 November 1700 at the age of thirty-nine in an advanced state of senile decay. His death was to be followed by the War of the Spanish Succession in which most of Europe was to be involved.

There has been no attempt to cover up the physical degeneracy in this portrait of King Carlos II of Spain by Carreño.

The House of Bourbon

| PHILIP V | 1700–JANUARY 1724 |
| | SEPTEMBER 1724–1746 |

b Versailles 19 December 1683, 2nd son of Louis, Dauphin of France (son of Louis XIV, King of France and Navarre, and Maria Teresa, dau of King Philip IV); *s* his great-uncle King Carlos II 1 November 1700; declared King of Spain at Fontainebleau 16 November and proclaimed at Madrid 24 November 1700 and again February 1701; abdicated in favour of his eldest son 15 January 1724; resumed the throne following the latter's death 6 September 1724; *m* (1) proxy Turin 11 September, in person Figueras 3 November 1701, Maria Luisa Gabriela (*b* Turin 17 September 1688; *d* Madrid 14 February 1714), 3rd dau of Victor Amadeus II, King of Sardinia, and his first wife Anne Marie of Orleans (sister of the first wife of King Carlos II); 4 sons; *m* (2) proxy Parma 16 September, in person Guadalajara 24 December 1714, Elizabeth (*b* Parma 25 October 1692; *d* Aranjuez 11 July 1766; *bur* San Ildefonso), dau of Odoardo Farnese, Hereditary Prince of Parma, and Dorothea Sophia of the Palatinate (sister of the second wife of King Carlos II); 4 sons, 3 daus; *d* Palace of Buen-Retiro, Madrid 9 July 1746; *bur* San Ildefonso

| LUIS I | JANUARY–AUGUST 1724 |

b Madrid 25 August 1707, eldest son of King Philip V; *s* his father on his abdication 15 January 1724; *m* Lerma 20 January 1722 Louise Elisabeth (*b* Versailles 11 December 1709; *d* Paris 16 June 1742), dau of Philip (II), Duke of Orleans, Regent of France, and Françoise Marie de Bourbon, legitimated natural dau of Louis XIV, King of France and Navarre; no issue; *d* Madrid 31 August 1724; *bur* El Escorial

| FERDINAND VI | 1746–1759 |

b Madrid 23 September 1713, 4th son of King Philip V; *s* his father 9 July 1746; *m* Badajoz 20 January 1729 Maria Barbara (*b* Lisbon 4 December 1711; *d* Aranjuez 27 August 1758), dau of John V, King of Portugal, and Maria Anna of Austria; no issue; *d* Villaviciosa 10 August 1759; *bur* Church of Santa Barbara, Madrid

| CARLOS III | 1759–1788 |

b Madrid 20 January 1716, 5th son of King Philip V, and eldest son of his second wife Elisabeth Farnese; *s* his maternal great-uncle as Duke of Parma 29 December 1731; conquered Naples and became King of Naples and Sicily 15 May 1735, resigning Parma to his brother Philip; *s* his half-brother King Ferdinand VI as King of Spain 10 August 1759, and resigned Naples and Sicily to his third son Ferdinand; *m* proxy Dresden 9 May, in person Gaeta 19 June 1738, Maria Amelia (*b* Dresden 24 November 1724; *d* Buen Retiro 27 September 1760), eldest surviving dau of Frederick Augustus II, Elector of Saxony and King of Poland, and Maria Josepha of Austria; 6 sons, 6 daus; *d* Madrid 14 December 1788; *bur* El Escorial

| CARLOS IV | 1788–1808 |

b Portici 11 November 1748, 2nd son of King Carlos III, *s* his father 14 December 1788; abdicated in favour of his eldest surviving son 19 March 1808; retracted the abdication 21 March 1808; ceded the crown of Spain to Napoleon I, Emperor of the French 6 May 1808; *m* San Ildefonso 4 September 1766 Maria Luisa (*b* Parma 9 December 1751; *d* Rome 2 January 1819), yr dau of Philip, Duke of Parma, and Louise Elisabeth of France; 8 sons, 6 daus; *d* Naples 19 January 1819; *bur* El Escorial

| JOSEPH NAPOLEON | 1808–1813 |

b Corte, Corsica 7 January 1768, 2nd but eldest surviving son of Charles Marie Bonaparte and Marie Laetitia Ramolino; French Prince on the proclamation of the Empire by his brother Emperor Napoleon I 18 May 1804; King of Naples 30 March 1806 to 6 June 1808; King of Spain 6 June 1808 to 11 December 1813; *m* Cuges, nr Marseilles, 1 August 1794 Marie Julie (*b* Marseilles 26 December 1771; *d* Florence 7 April 1845; *bur* Santa Croce), dau of François Clary, of Marseilles, and his 2nd wife Françoise Rose Somis; 3 daus; *d* Florence 28 July 1844

| FERDINAND VII | MARCH–MAY 1808 |
| | 1813–1833 |

b San Ildefonso 13 October 1784, 5th but eldest surviving son of King Carlos IV; *s* his father on his abdication 19 March 1808; renounced his rights in favour of his father and with him ceded Spain to Napoleon I, Emperor of the French 6 May 1808; restored as King by the treaty of Valençay 11 December 1813; *m* (1) proxy Naples 16 August, in person Barcelona 6 October 1802, Maria Antonia (*b* Caserta 14 December 1784; *d* Aranjuez 21 May 1806), dau of Ferdinand I, King of the Two Sicilies, and Maria Carolina of Austria; no issue; *m* (2) proxy Cadiz 4 September, in person Madrid 29 September 1816, his niece Maria Isabel (*b* Queluz 19 May 1797; *d* Madrid 26 December 1818), dau of John VI, King of Portugal, and Carlota Joaquina of Spain (eldest dau of King Carlos IV); 2 daus (*d* in infancy); *m* (3) proxy Dresden 7 October, in person Madrid 20 October 1819, Maria Josepha (*b* Dresden 6 December 1803; *d* Aranjuez 17 May 1829), 4th dau of Prince Maximilian of Saxony and his 1st wife Caroline of Parma; no issue; *m* (4) Madrid 11 December 1829, his niece Maria Cristina, Queen Regent of Spain 29 September 1833 to 17 September 1840 (*b* Portici 27 April 1806; *m* (2) Madrid 28 December 1833 Don Fernando Muñoz y Sanchez, 1st Duke of Riansares (*d* Le Havre 13 September 1873); *d* Le Havre 22 August 1878), dau of Francis I, King of the Two Sicilies, and his 2nd wife Maria Isabel of Spain (5th dau of King Carlos IV); 2 daus; *d* Madrid 29 September 1833; *bur* El Escorial

| ISABEL II | 1833–1868 |

b Madrid 10 October 1830, 3rd but eldest surviving dau of King Ferdinand VII, and elder dau by his 4th wife Maria Cristina of the Two Sicilies; proclaimed Princess of the Asturias and Heiress Presumptive 20 June 1833; *s* her father 29 September 1833, under the regency of her mother until 17 September 1840, then under that of

Don Baldomero Espartero, Duke de la Victoria until 8 November 1843, when she was declared of age; deposed and left the country 30 September 1868; abdicated in favour of her son Alfonso 25 June 1870; *m* Madrid 10 October 1846 Francisco de Asis, titular King of Spain from the day of his marriage (*b* Aranjuez 13 May 1822; *d* Epinay-sur-Seine, France, 16 April 1902), son of Infante Don Francisco de Paula (yst son of King Carlos IV), and Luisa Carlota of the Two Sicilies (sister of Queen Maria Cristina); 3 sons, 6 daus; *d* Paris 9 April 1904; *bur* El Escorial

| COUNCIL OF REGENCY | 30 SEPTEMBER 1868–16 NOVEMBER 1870 |
| AMADEO I | 1870–1873 |

b Turin 30 May 1845, 2nd son of Victor Emmanuel II, King of Italy, and Maria Adelaide of Austria; created Duke of Aosta 1845; elected King of Spain 16 November 1870; abdicated 11 February 1873; *m* (1) Turin 30 May 1867 Maria Vittoria (*b* Paris 9 August 1847; *d* San Remo 8 November 1876), dau of Carlo Emanuele dal Pozzo, Principe della Cisterna, and Countess Louise Ghislaine de Mérode; 3 sons; *m* (2) Turin 11 September 1888 his niece Maria Laetitia (*b* Paris 20 November 1866; *d* Moncalieri 25 October 1926), only dau of Prince Napoleon, Head of the Imperial House of France, and Clotilde of Savoy; 1 son; *d* Turin 18 January 1890

| REPUBLIC | 11 FEBRUARY 1873–29 DECEMBER 1874 |
| ALFONSO XII | 1874–1885 |

b Madrid 28 November 1857, 2nd but eldest surviving son of Queen Isabel II; proclaimed King 29 December 1874; *m* (1) Madrid 23 January 1878 Maria de las Mercedes (*b* Madrid 24 June 1860; *d* Madrid 26 June 1878), yst dau of Prince Antoine of Orleans, Duke of Montpensier, and Infanta Luisa Fernanda of Spain (yst dau of King Ferdinand VII); *m* (2) Madrid 29 November 1879, Maria Cristina, Queen Regent of Spain 25 November 1885 to 17 May 1902 (*b* Gross Seelowitz, Moravia 21 July 1858; *d* Madrid 6 February 1929), elder dau of Archduke Charles Ferdinand of Austria, and Elisabeth of Austria; 1 son, 2 daus; *d* El Pardo, Madrid, 25 November 1885; *bur* El Escorial

| INTERREGNUM | 25 NOVEMBER 1885–17 MAY 1886 |
| ALFONSO XIII | 1886–1931 |

b Madrid 17 May 1886, only (and posthumous) son of King Alfonso XII; *s* his father at birth; left the country without abdicating 14 April 1931; *m* Madrid 31 May 1906 Victoria Eugenia Julia Ena (*b* Balmoral Castle, Scotland, 24 October 1887; *d* Lausanne, Switzerland, 15 April 1969), only dau of Prince Henry of Battenberg and Beatrice, yst dau of Victoria, Queen of Great Britain and Empress of India; 4 sons, 2 daus; *d* Rome 28 February 1941; *bur* Church of Our Lady of Montserrat, Rome, transferred to El Escorial 1980

REPUBLIC	1931–1936
CIVIL WAR	1936–1939
GENERALISSIMO FRANCISCO FRANCO Y BAHAMONDE,	
CHIEF OF STATE	1939–1975

JUAN CARLOS I   1975–

b Rome 5 January 1938, elder son of Infante Don Juan, Count of Barcelona (yst son of King Alfonso XIII), and Maria de las Mercedes of Bourbon-Two Sicilies; designated heir to the throne with the title of Prince of Spain 22 July 1969; proclaimed King 22 November 1975; *m* Athens 14 May 1962 Sofia (*b* Psychiko, nr Athens, 2 November 1938), elder dau of Paul I, King of the Hellenes, and Frederika of Hanover; 1 son, 2 daus

Elizabeth Farnese, the domineering second wife of King Philip V of Spain. Determination shows in every feature.

The news of Carlos II's death reached the French court at Fontainebleau on 9 November 1700. Louis XIV at once ordered court mourning, but delayed acceptance of the Spanish crown on behalf of his grandson until after his return to Versailles a week later. On the morning of 16 November he received the Spanish Ambassador in audience and presented the sixteen-year-old Philip to him with the words, 'This, sir, is the Duke of Anjou, whom you may salute as your King'. The Ambassador sank to his knees and made a fulsome speech in Spanish, of which the new King understood not one word. Louis then led his grandson out of his study into the gallery where the court was assembled and with a magniloquent gesture announced, 'Gentlemen, this is the King of Spain'.

Philip left France, which he was never to see again, in January 1701 and entered Madrid in February. Within the year, however, his grandfather had provoked a European war and a Grand Alliance between the Emperor, Great Britain and the United Provinces declared war on France and Spain, the Emperor's younger son, the Archduke Charles, being put forward as a rival candidate for the Spanish throne. The war dragged on for some fourteen years. In 1704 the British took Gibraltar, which they have retained ever since, and in the following year the Archduke Charles captured Barcelona, which he retained until 1714. For a short time he also occupied Madrid. By the treaty of Utrecht, signed on 11 April 1713, Philip was finally recognized as King of Spain by Great Britain and the United Provinces, provided that the crowns of France and Spain should never be united.

Philip, who was a reasonably attractive young man with fair hair and a fresh, open countenance, was extremely highly sexed but also so religious that his scruples would only allow him to find satisfaction in marriage. Accordingly a wife was found for him in the person of Maria Luisa of Savoy, the third daughter of King Victor Amadeus II of Sardinia and the sister of his sister-in-law the Duchess of Burgundy. She arrived in Spain in November 1701 and the uxorious young King kept her at his side day and night to such an extent that their bodily functions were made to synchronize and they received their courtiers at their levée seated on a double commode. Any separation from his wife, when campaigning for example, was a severe trial to Philip both physically and mentally. The Queen was politically astute and a great asset to her husband, but unfortunately she wore herself out in his cause and died in February 1714 at the age of twenty-five. The quest for a new wife for Philip began at once. Alberoni, the Duke of Parma's

representative in Madrid, put forward the Duke's niece Elizabeth Farnese as a candidate and was able to persuade the Princess des Ursins, a woman who exercised almost complete control over the King while acting as the agent of his grandfather, to believe that the Parmesan Princess was eminently suitable. The proxy marriage in Parma took place in September 1714 and the bride set out for Spain. The twenty-one-year-old Elizabeth was considered good looking, though 'much marked with smallpox', an accomplished horsewoman, and 'passionately fond of music'. She was, through her mother, the niece of the Queen Dowager, widow of Carlos II, but that was not much recommendation as the Dowager was not popular in Spain. The new Queen arrived in December and immediately on her arrival had what can only be described as a flaming row with the Princess des Ursins, who began criticizing her appearance and abusing her for being late until Elizabeth called out, 'Count Alberoni, take away this mad woman who dares to insult me!' The Princess was at once arrested and sent into exile. Thus, the new Queen attained an ascendancy over her husband which she was to maintain for the rest of his life. She was a masterful woman in every way and with the help of Alberoni, later created a Cardinal, set about securing Italian thrones for her sons, who were unlikely to succeed to Spain as two sons of Philip's first marriage were still living.

Philip long entertained a hope of succeeding to the French throne, occupied since 1715 by his young nephew Louis XV, and it was probably with this end in view that he was prompted to abdicate the Spanish throne in favour of his eldest son Luis in January 1724. Luis was a young man of great promise, 'endowed with every kind of virtue and good quality. He carried out all his duties to perfection; he spoke French, Spanish, Italian, and Latin excellently; loved justice and virtue, and hated vice .... [He] would have made a model monarch,' wrote the Duke of Liria. The fly in the ointment was Luis's wife, one of the unruly daughters of Philip, Duke of Orleans, the Regent of France. Her own grandmother described her as 'the most disagreeable person that I have ever seen'. She scandalized the Spanish court by hoisting her petticoats up to her knees and walking about in the rain and was seen running about the gardens of La Granja clad only in a thin dressing-gown which blew up in the wind to reveal her in a state of nature. She was peevish and sulky with her husband, refusing to speak to him, and it was commonly believed that she had refused to consummate their marriage. Immensely stout, she indulged her gluttonous appetite at all hours and forced her ladies in waiting to do the same, pinching and slapping them if they refused. Things became so bad that her father-in-law had her confined in the Alcazar of Madrid for six days until she promised to amend her ways. After a reign of seven months and sixteen days King Luis died of smallpox and his father re-ascended the throne. Queen Louise Elisabeth, now known as the Second Queen Dowager of Spain (Carlos II's widow was still living) was sent back to France, where she continued to lead a scandalous life until her death in 1742.

After re-ascending the throne Philip reigned until his death from apoplexy in July 1746. Towards the end of his life he became careless of his appearance, wore old clothes and lapsed into a kind of premature senility, although only in his early sixties. Elizabeth survived him twenty years and had the satisfaction of seeing her eldest son on the throne of Spain and her second surviving son Duke of Parma, her own paternal inheritance.

Philip V was succeeded by his youngest and only surviving son by his first wife, Ferdinand VI, a serious minded man in his thirty-third year. He was of no particular ability, but a great lover of peace and his thirteen-year reign was a period of tranquillity. He was also a music lover and founded the Academia de San Fernando de Bellas Artes in Madrid. Like his father, he was extremely uxorious and his wife, Maria Barbara of Portugal, had a great influence over him. They had no children and after the Queen's death in August 1758, Ferdinand lapsed into a state of melancholia which steadily worsened until his own death mercifully released him in August 1759.

Ferdinand was succeeded by his half-brother Carlos III, who had been King of Naples and Sicily since 1735. He now resigned that crown to his third son Ferdinand and returned to Spain to take over the government. Carlos is always spoken of as 'the perfect type of the benevolent despot', and he was just that. He had done much to improve the welfare of his Italian subjects and, after handing over Naples to his third son Ferdinand, he returned to Spain to carry out similar policies. One of his most noteworthy acts was to separate church and state and expel the Jesuits in 1767. In foreign policy he sided with France, which involved Spain in the Seven Years' War and resulted in the cession of Florida to Britain in 1763.

Carlos was lean and ascetic in appearance, with the prominent Bourbon nose, and was not a slave to uxoriousness as were his father and half-brother. His Queen, Maria Amelia of Saxony, died in her thirty-sixth year, only a year after they returned to Spain and Carlos did not marry again. He was a great patron of the arts and built the Prado gallery as well as completing the vast Oriente Palace and commissioning Tiepolo to decorate it. His passion was for hunting and shooting and he is said to have worn his hunting clothes beneath his court dress to enable him to hurry away to the chase as soon as the court ceremonies, which he found distasteful, were over.

Carlos III's eldest son, Philip, was an imbecile of a particularly distressing kind, being completely unable to stop himself from molesting any woman with whom he came in contact. For this reason he was excluded from the succession to both Naples and Spain and remained in close confinement in Naples until his death at the age of thirty, eleven years before that of his father.

It was Carlos III's second son who succeeded him as Carlos IV in December 1788. He resembled his father very much in appearance, although somewhat shorter and stouter and had the same placid temperament and passion for hunting and shooting. He is well known to us from the portraits of Goya, who portrayed him and his court, as Velazquez had that of Philip IV. Carlos IV had a masterful and strong-minded wife in the person of his cousin Maria Luisa of Parma, who in spite of her ugliness and toothlessness, took as her lover an impecunious young nobleman, Manuel Godoy, who soon gained a total ascendancy over both King and Queen and became the virtual ruler of Spain for nearly twenty years. He lived in a strange ménage-à-trois with the King and Queen, who was wont to refer to the three of them as 'the Trinity on earth'. To give him an official relationship to the royal family he was married in 1797 to the sovereigns' cousin Doña Maria Teresa de Borbon y Vallabriga, Countess of Chinchon, but it was a loveless marriage and the couple separated in 1808 after producing one daughter. The indolent King was later to describe to Napoleon his daily life at this period: 'Every day, winter and summer, I went shooting till twelve, had dinner, and at once returned to shooting until the fall of the evening. Manuel told me how things were going; and I went to bed to begin again the same life the next day unless any important ceremony prevented me.' The French Revolution induced Godoy to declare war on France which was ended by a humiliating treaty whereby Spain became a tool in the hands of the French revolutionary government. Nevertheless, Godoy was rewarded with the grandiose title of Prince of the Peace for his efforts in negotiating the treaty. Spain remained under French influence after the rise of Napoleon and suffered the disaster of having the whole of its fleet destroyed at Trafalgar in 1805.

The heir to the throne, Ferdinand, Prince of the Asturias, was an unprepossessing doltish young man, thick-set and beetle-browed. At the age of eighteen in 1802 he was married to his cousin Maria Antonia of Naples, but the marriage was not a success and Ferdinand, though by no means impotent, neglected his marital duties to such an extent that the bride complained by letter to her mother, the redoubtable Queen Maria Carolina. After a while matters improved and the Princess of the Asturias, an extremely intelligent young woman, gained a measure of influence over her husband and was able to stimulate him into some opposition to Godoy's pro-French policy. This did not please her mother-in-law Queen Maria Luisa, who referred to her as 'a bloodless little animal all venom and vinegar', 'a poisonous viper', and 'her mother's spittle' among other equally disparaging expressions. She refused to allow the Prince and Princess to have a separate household and when the Princess fell ill in the winter of 1805 and lingered on until May 1806, it was widely rumoured that the Queen and Godoy had had her poisoned.

In March 1808 a popular uprising overthrew Godoy and forced the King to abdicate in favour of Ferdinand, but two months later the young King was called to a meeting with Napoleon at Bayonne, where his parents and Godoy had also been summoned. There he was induced to resign the crown back to his father and the two were then made to cede it to France. The 'Trinity on earth' went first to Compiègne, which had been assigned to them by Napoleon. No special restriction was placed on their movements as they were no longer considered a threat and by 1819, after peace had been restored to Europe, they were in Rome. Carlos went on to Naples to visit his brother King Ferdinand. While he was there, Maria Luisa died, tended to the last by Godoy. Carlos was heartbroken when he received the news and wrote a touching letter to Godoy. It was almost his last act, for in the same month he caught a chill and died in Naples, aged sixty. As for Godoy, he survived until 1852, when he died in Paris.

The departure of the Bourbons left Napoleon free to nominate his brother Joseph to the vacant throne, transferring him from that of Naples which he had occupied since 1806. Joseph was a man of little ability and the whole of his reign was occupied by the Peninsular War which gradually liberated the country. Joseph is known as the first of the 'intruder Kings' and was so unpopular that his coins are often found with a scratch mark across the neck, indicating that his unwilling subjects would like to have seen him hanged. The times were so turbulent that his wife Queen Julie never visited Spain although she made much of her queenly dignity and delighted in appearing at the Imperial court in Paris wearing a miniature crown. Joseph was forced to abdicate in December 1813, and by the treaty of Valençay Ferdinand VII, who had been kept in strict confinement at the Château of that name in France, was restored to the throne and returned to Spain in triumph in March 1814. At first he was forced to accept a radical constitution which had been promulgated by a Cortes meeting at Cadiz, then the only unoccupied Spanish town, in 1812, but he was soon able to overthrow this and establish an absolutism which rendered him an unpopular figure throughout Europe.

Ferdinand continued to be unlucky in his matrimonial ventures. His second wife, who was also his niece, Maria Isabel of Portugal, died in childbirth in 1818, having had two daughters who both died in infancy. Ferdinand then married Maria Josepha of Saxony, who produced no children but attempted to write lyric poetry in the language of her adopted country. Her imperfect knowledge of Spanish led her to write in one of her poems how 'with hasty step I seek the public convenience', which caused much amusement. She died in 1829 and in the same year Ferdinand married another niece, Maria Cristina of Naples, who bore two healthy daughters but no son. This led Ferdinand, whose health was failing although he was only in his late forties, to sign a Pragmatic Sanction appointing his daughters heirs to the throne and abrogating the Salic Law which had been introduced by Philip V. In September 1833 Ferdinand died of apoplexy and by the terms of his will was succeeded by his elder surviving daughter Isabel II under the regency of her mother Queen Maria Cristina.

The Queen Regent, still only twenty-seven, was an attractive and elegant woman with a charming manner which ensured much support, but like most Bourbons she was highly sexed and within three months of being left a widow contracted a second and secret marriage with a Spanish officer. According to her granddaughter the Infanta Eulalia, he was escorting her carriage when she suffered a severe nose bleed and having used up all the handkerchiefs available asked her escort to lend her his. When she returned it to him a few minutes later he raised it to his lips with a courtly gesture and the flame of love was at once kindled in the Queen's heart. The couple somehow managed to keep the marriage secret and the Queen carried out her duties as Regent over a period of seven years in the course of which she managed to conceal several pregnancies (she had nine children altogether by her second marriage), on one occasion driving to open the Cortes within a few hours of giving birth.

The accession of Isabel II was disputed by her uncle Don Carlos, the brother of Ferdinand VII, who refused to recognize the legality of the Pragmatic Sanction and proclaimed himself King as Carlos V. He had voiced his objections to his brother in no uncertain terms when asked to swear allegiance to the infant Isabel as Princess of the Asturias, protesting that he could not give up 'rights which God gave me when He willed my birth, and only God can take them from me by granting you a son, which I much desire, possibly even more than you'. To Carlos, therefore, it was a sacred obligation to oppose the succession of his niece, regardless of the fact that it plunged the country into a civil war which lasted until 1839, when the Carlists were defeated with the aid of Britain, France and Portugal who formed a Quadruple Alliance with constitutionalist Spain. The Convention of Vergara ended the war in August of that year and Don Carlos went into exile in France. In October 1840 the Queen Regent was forced to leave the country following a revolt led by General Espartero, who bore the resounding title of Duke of the Victory. He took over the regency and ruled dictatorially until overthrown in his turn by General Narvaez in June 1843. Isabel was declared of age, although only thirteen, and Narvaez became Lieutenant-General of the Kingdom, and the virtual ruler until 1851.

Queen Maria Cristina returned to Spain in March 1844 and took a hand in arranging marriages for her two daughters. The question of 'the Spanish Marriages' occupied the attention of the British and French foreign offices as much as it did the Spanish government. It was finally settled by the Queen marrying her cousin Don Francisco de Asis, Duke of Cadiz, son of Ferdinand VII's youngest brother Don Francisco de Paula, and the Infanta Luisa Fernanda marrying Antoine, Duke of Montpensier, the youngest son of Louis Philippe, King of the French. The double wedding took place at Madrid on 10 October 1846.

The Queen's consort, who was granted the titular dignity of King on the day of the marriage, was a weak, ineffective, effeminate young man, widely believed to be impotent. Isabel herself was to write years later: 'What can I say of a man, who on his wedding night wore more lace than I did?' Isabel herself was plump with a rather plain face marred by patches of eczema. She was hearty and outspoken in manner and like most of her family highly sexed. Despite the forebodings expressed at the time of her marriage, she produced a large family although it seems doubtful if King Francisco fathered any of them, as Isabel had an unending string of lovers to console her for his shortcomings. Isabel's complete incompetence as Queen and the scandals surrounding her private life finally provoked a revolution and in September 1868 she fled to France and was declared deposed. A provisional government was then formed and in May 1869 the Cortes voted for the continuation of monarchical government. A new constitution was promulgated in June and Marshal Serrano was appointed Regent pending the election of a new monarch. The first choice, Prince Leopold of Hohenzollern-Sigmaringen, accepted and then withdrew his candidature and finally in December 1870 the Duke of Aosta, son of King Victor Emmanuel II of Italy, agreed to accept the Spanish throne and was duly proclaimed as Amadeo I. The second of the 'intruder Kings' was able and well-meaning but the Spaniards found him unacceptable because too foreign. When his Queen appeared dressed in a white mantilla, the Madrid prostitutes did the same, while the society ladies arrayed themselves in black ones as a protest. After two years Amadeo could stand no more and he abdicated and returned to Italy. His abdication was followed by the proclamation of a republic on 11 February 1873. At the same time a second Carlist War was waging in the north led by the grandson of the original Don Carlos, styling himself King Carlos VII. The state of near anarchy was only ended when the Liberal Unionists and Moderates rallied round Isabel's son Alfonso and proclaimed him King. His mother had already abdicated her rights in his favour in June 1870 and early in 1875 Alfonso XII returned to Spain. He was to prove a model King in much the same way as his great-grandson was to do exactly one hundred years later. The Carlist War dragged on until 1876, when Don Carlos fled the country and the Pope, who had supported him, recognized Alfonso. Queen Isabel returned to Madrid in October 1876 and at once began interfering in politics, but Alfonso dealt with her quite firmly.

Alfonso's first wife was his cousin Maria de las Mercedes, the daughter of Montpensier and the Infanta Luisa Fernanda, but sadly she died of typhoid in June 1878, only six months after the wedding. In November of the following year Alfonso married the very plain Archduchess Maria Cristina of Austria and in the first years of the marriage two daughters were born. In November 1885 the Queen was again pregnant when Alfonso died of tuberculosis three days short of his twenty-eighth birthday. There were fears that Queen Isabel might claim the regency, but she was content to leave it to her daughter-in-law. In 1888 she was asked to leave Spain and she departed for Paris, where she died of influenza in 1904.

Queen Maria Cristina's elder daughter Maria de las Mercedes, Princess of the Asturias, was the temporary sovereign until the birth of her mother's child and her position would have been confirmed had it been another girl, but on 17 May 1886 the Queen Regent gave birth to a son, one of the very few people to have been born a King (we shall meet another in France in due course). The baby, named after his father, was immediately hailed as Alfonso XIII. The unlucky implications of the numeral were to be borne out later in his life.

Maria Cristina's regency, which lasted until 1902, was a wise one and she gained universal admiration, particularly for her heroic conduct during the Spanish-American War in 1898, whereby Spain lost Cuba and the Philippines. Alfonso took the oath in the Cortes on his sixteenth birthday but was content to allow his mother to manage the country's affairs in an unofficial capacity for another two years. He had received a very careful education and was probably better equipped to rule the country than any of his predecessors. The question of his marriage soon arose and it was while visiting the English court that he met and immediately fell in love with the blonde, blue-eyed and slightly buxom Princess Victoria Eugenia of Battenberg, popularly known as Princess Ena, Queen Victoria's youngest granddaughter. Alfonso's choice met with a certain amount of opposition. Ena might be the granddaughter of Queen Victoria and the niece of King Edward VII, but on her father's side she was only a morganatic scion of the Grand Ducal House of Hesse, hardly worthy in the eyes of most Spaniards of following in the footsteps of the Bourbons and Habsburgs who had had the monopoly in supplying Spain with Queens for centuries past. This was partially overcome by King Edward VII granting his niece the 'style and attribute' of Royal Highness (she had been but a Serene one before). The objection on religious grounds was removed by her willingness to undergo instruction to be received into the Roman Catholic church. Strangely enough, she had been baptized in the severely Protestant church of Scotland, having been born at Balmoral. By another strange quirk of fate she had a Spanish godmother in the person of the Empress Eugénie, widow of Napoleon III and one of Queen Victoria's greatest, if somewhat unlikely, friends.

Duly converted and raised in rank, Princess Victoria Eugenia, accompanied by her widowed mother Princess Beatrice and her cousins the Prince and Princess of Wales (later King George V and Queen Mary), travelled to Madrid for her wedding to the King in May 1906. The wedding day

Alfonso XIII, King of Spain: a fine photograph of the young King.

nearly ended in tragedy when a bomb was thrown from a balcony as the bride and bridegroom were driving through the narrow streets from the church to the palace. A number of people and the horses drawing the state coach were killed, but the King and Queen were unharmed, although her wedding dress was spotted with blood, and they were able to proceed in another carriage. Their calmness won universal admiration.

Unfortunately for Spain and for the future of the royal marriage, the Queen was a haemophilia carrier. This was not known until her first child, Alfonso, Prince of the Asturias, born in May 1907, was circumcised following a tradition the Spanish Royal House had adopted under Moorish influence centuries before. It was extremely difficult to staunch the bleeding and it was soon realized that the little Prince had the dreaded disease which had first shown itself in Queen Victoria's youngest son Prince Leopold and had already been transmitted through several of her female descendants to their male offspring. The second son of the King and Queen was born with impaired hearing which later rendered him almost dumb; the third son was stillborn (a result, it was thought, of the Queen's grief over the death of her uncle King Edward VII); the fourth, Don Juan, was healthy; the fifth, Don

Gonzalo, was another haemophiliac. There were also two daughters. Alfonso's sorrow over his ailing sons brought about a cooling of his feelings towards the Queen as though he blamed her for their plight and he began to neglect her and look for solace elsewhere, developing quite a penchant for actresses. The poor Queen spent many lonely, boring days in the company of her ladies and found the tiresome etiquette of the Spanish court as irksome as had some of her more spirited predecessors. On one occasion she thought to amuse her ladies by telling them a story about her grandmother Queen Victoria who, if she found an undusted table top or other surface in any of her residences, was in the habit of writing 'Victoria RI' in the dust with her fingertip as a gentle rebuke to the servants. The ladies received the story in absolute silence for a few moments, then one of them remarked, 'A Spanish Queen would never notice dust'. Poor Ena must have felt utterly deflated.

Alfonso's reign was not an easy one and he was beset with difficulties from the outbreak of the First World War (in which Spain remained neutral) onwards. A disastrous campaign in Morocco led to general unrest at home which was ended when General Miguel Primo de Rivera staged a military coup and seized power in September 1923. He abolished the Constitution and was virtually dictator until January 1930, when failing health forced him to resign. The King made an attempt to return to Constitutional government but was unable to stem the tide of growing unrest and the Republican movement and on 14 April 1931 went into voluntary exile, hoping thereby to prevent a civil war.

The Second Republic of Spain had an uneasy existence for five years, vainly struggling against the growing Communist influence, until civil war, which Alfonso had hoped to avert, broke out on 18 July 1936. After a long and bloody struggle, order was restored in March 1939 when Madrid was captured by Generalissimo Don Francisco Franco y Bahamonde, the leader of the Nationalist party. Franco, styled Caudillo of Spain, exercised a harsh dictatorship until his death on 20 November 1975.

Although his friendship with the Fascist regimes in Germany and Italy brought him into disrepute with other nations during and after the Second World War, it cannot be denied that he restored law and order and completely transformed the Spanish economy during his long leadership.

King Alfonso had settled in Rome and was entertaining hopes that his return to Spain might be imminent when he was struck down by coronary heart disease in January 1941. On 14 January he formally abdicated the Spanish throne in favour of his second surviving son Don Juan. The eldest son, Alfonso, had renounced his rights to the throne in 1933 when about to make an 'unsuitable' marriage, and was killed in a motoring accident in Miami in September 1938. The second son, Don Jaime, Duke of Segovia, had also renounced his rights because of his disabilities, so it was Don Juan who had been recognized as Prince of the Asturias since 1933, although he preferred to use the title of Count of Barcelona. King Alfonso lingered on until 28 February 1941.

Queen Victoria Eugenia had parted from the King on

amicable terms and settled in Lausanne, Switzerland. She was to return to Spain just once to hold her great-grandson at the baptismal font in 1968 and was received with overwhelming enthusiasm. She died at Lausanne in April of the year following.

Franco had determined on a restoration of the monarchy, though it was not to take place until after his death. Spain was officially declared a kingdom again on 31 March 1947, but Franco kept people guessing who the next King was to be for twenty-two years. His choice lay between Don Juan, his son Don Juan Carlos, and Don Alfonso, the elder son of the Duke of Segovia. At last, on 22 July 1969, he designated Don Juan Carlos as heir to the throne with the title of The Prince of Spain, and assigned him a residence in Madrid where he could live while the Caudillo 'trained' him in government matters. The Prince was tall, good-looking and with an extremely attractive and elegant wife, the former Princess Sofia of Greece, by whom he had two daughters and a son.

In 1972 it seemed for a time as though Franco might be about to change his mind when his granddaughter married Don Alfonso, who was then Spanish Ambassador to Sweden, and received the title of Duke of Cadiz and the qualification of Royal Highness on the day of the birth of his first child, Franco's great-grandchild. However, Don Alfonso received no further marks of favour and when Franco died after a long, lingering illness, the proclamation of King Juan Carlos I went without a hitch and the transference from dictatorship to monarchy ran smoothly.

King Juan Carlos and Queen Sofia have proved to be ideal sovereigns. Many thought the restoration would be but a flash in the pan and the cheaper type of journalist was ready to dub the King 'Juan Carlos the Short'. However, all the gloomier prognostications have been refuted, the King and Queen have steadily steered Spain back to democracy and won the support and respect of all parties and the admiration of the rest of Europe. They continue to live in the small Zarzuela Palace, only using the Oriente Palace for state receptions, and follow a very simple lifestyle. The Queen has refused to appoint any ladies-in-waiting, doubtless remembering how many former Queens were at the mercy of their *camareras mayores*. This has led to one or two amusing situations as, for example, when she has given her handbag to a uniformed guardsman to hold for her when performing some public duty requiring the use of both hands; or when she broke the heel off one of her shoes on the occasion of a state visit to Windsor Castle. Today the Spanish monarchy is more stable than it has been for centuries and King Juan Carlos seems assured of handing on a secure heritage to his son Felipe, Prince of the Asturias.

FRANCE

The Merovingian Kings

After the break-up of the Roman Empire the kingdom of the Franks gradually emerged in the former Roman province of Gaul. The very legendary Pharamond is claimed to have been the first King of the Franks and to have been followed by Clodion the Hairy, who probably had some historical basis and started the custom followed by the later Kings of his dynasty of growing their hair to an inordinate length as a sign of their royal status. His son and successor was Meroveus (or Merovech), who fought against the Visigoths under the Roman General Aëtius at the battle of Châlons in 451. Meroveus, who gave his name to the dynasty, died about 457 and was succeeded by his son Childeric I, the real founder of the kingdom. He is said to have seduced and carried off Basina, the wife of the King of Thuringia, and by her to have become the father of Clovis. Childeric died about 481 and was buried in his capital, Tournai, where his tomb was discovered in 1653.

Clovis I, Childeric's son and successor, greatly extended his kingdom by the force of arms and established his capital at Paris in about 486. Some years later Clovis sought a political alliance by marriage to Clotilda, daughter of Gondebaud, King of Burgundy, who was a Christian. His own conversion to Christianity under her influence took place in 496, after he had attributed his victory over the Alemanni to his invocation of Christ. He was baptized by St Remi, Bishop of Rheims, and three thousand of his soldiers followed suit. After his conversion Clovis continued his conquests and eventually ruled most of France.

When Clovis died in 511 he made the all too common mistake of dividing his kingdom among his sons. The eldest, Thierry, born of an unknown mother before his father's marriage to Clotilda, received Austrasia; Clodomir, Clotilda's eldest son, received Orleans; Childebert received Paris; and Clotaire, the youngest, received Soissons. By 558 Clotaire had become sole King, having murdered several nephews in the process and managed to outlive his childless brother Childebert.

Clotaire died three years later in 561, when the whole business was repeated again by a division between his four surviving sons (the eldest, Chramm, had rebelled against his father and been burned to death for punishment). Sigebert, King of Austrasia, and Chilperic, King of Soissons, the two youngest brothers, married two sisters, Brunhild and Galswinth, daughters of the King of the Visigoths in Spain. Galswinth was strangled in her bed by Chilperic's jealous mistress Fredegund, whom he then married. A long struggle between Brunhild, anxious to avenge her sister, and Fredegund then ensued and lasted for many years. The whole history of the Merovingians is one of warring brothers and evil rival Queens. Gregory of Tours gives a graphic account of the struggles, to many of which he was an eyewitness, but his history ends in 591, when Brunhild and Fredegund were both still alive. Brunhild managed to survive her rival, but after a lifetime of killing and King-making finally met her just deserts when, an aged great-grandmother, she was tied by one arm and one leg to the tail of a wild horse and dragged and trampled to death through the streets. Her executioner was Fredegund's son Clotaire II who became sole King in 613.

On his death in October 629, Clotaire left a more secure kingdom to his son Dagobert I. The ten year reign of 'le bon roi Dagobert' was a last flowering of the Merovingian dynasty. He was an able man and well served by St Eloi as chief minister. His matrimonial entanglements were as involved as those of most of his predecessors and he had at least three Queens and numerous concubines.

With Dagobert's death in January 639 the rot really set in and the long series of puppet Kings who followed are known to history as 'les rois fainéants', the 'do-nothing Kings'. Power passed into the hands of the quaintly styled Mayors of the Palace, an office which eventually became exclusive to one family. They made and unmade Kings until 751, when Childeric III, the last Merovingian, was shorn of his royal locks and sent into a monastery where he died in 754. The Mayor of the Palace, Pepin, was elected King in his place and crowned at Soissons with papal approval in November 751.

The Carolingian Kings

The Carolingian dynasty sprang from a family of saints. Its founder was St Arnulf, Bishop of Metz, who died in 641. Before entering the church he had been married and had a son Ansegisal, Mayor of the Palace in Austrasia from 632 to 638. He married St Begga, daughter of Pepin of Landen, also sometime Mayor in Austrasia, and sister of St Gertrude, Abbess of Nivelles, a convent founded by their mother Itta. Ansegisal and St Begga were the parents of Pepin of Heristal, who became Mayor of Austrasia and Neustria and died in 714. His natural son Charles Martel was the greatest Mayor of the dynasty and successfully repelled the Moors who had crossed the Pyrenees in 732 and pillaged Bordeaux. He died in 741 and it was his son Pepin the Short who was finally elected King of the Franks in 751. Very little is known of Pepin apart from the fact that he was a good ruler and a brave man. His wife, curiously known as Bertha of the Big Foot, bore him two sons, Charles and Carloman, and seems to have had a strain of Merovingian blood in her veins. Pepin died at St Denis on 24 September 768 and his sons reigned together until 771, when Carloman died leaving Charles as sole ruler.

Charles, reckoned as Charles I in the long list of Kings of France, is better known to history as Charlemagne and the first Holy Roman Emperor after his coronation by Pope Leo III in St Peter's, Rome, on Christmas Day 800, the date regarded as the revival of the Roman Empire in the West. His rule extended over most of Western Europe and when he died in 814 he was succeeded both as Emperor and King by his son Louis I the Pious.

Louis divided his dominions on his death in 840 and France fell to the lot of his youngest son Charles II the Bald, who reigned until his death in 877, having also been elected Emperor in 875. His successors in France became almost as ineffectual as had the Merovingians before them and the sobriquets of Louis II the Stammerer (877–879) and Charles III the Simple (893–923) tell their own sad story.

Just as the Carolingians had risen to power through the weakness of the Merovingians, so a new family, the Capetians, now rose ready to replace them in their turn. The last Carolingian King, Louis V, was killed in a hunting accident in May 987, leaving no direct heir, and in the following month Hugh Capet was elected to succeed him and became the founding father of a dynasty whose descendants in the male line one thousand years later still occupy two European thrones today, those of Spain and the Grand Duchy of Luxembourg.

The Capetian Kings

Hugh Capet 987–996

b Paris ca 940, eldest son of Hugh the Great, Count of Paris (son of King Robert I), and his third wife, Hedwig of Saxony; elected King of France June 987; crowned at Noyon 3 July 987; m 963/68 Adelaide (b ca 945; d 15 June 1006), dau of William III, Duke of Aquitaine, and Adela of Normandy; 1 son, 3 daus; d Les Juifs, nr Chartres, 24 October 996; bur St Denis

Robert II the Pious 996–1031

b Orleans 27 March 972, only son of Hugh Capet; s his father 24 October 996, having been associated with the throne and crowned at Orleans ca 987; m (1) 988 (repudiated 992) Rosala, or Susanna (b ca 955; d Ghent 7 February 1003), widow of Arnulf II, Count of Flanders, and dau of Berengar II of Ivrea, King of Italy, and Willa of Tuscany; m (2) 996 (repudiated 998) Bertha (b ca 964; d after 1001), widow of Odo, Count of Blois, and dau of Conrad III, King of Transjurane-Burgundy, and Mahaut of France (dau of King Louis IV); m (3) ca 1003 Constance (b ca 983; d Melun 25 July 1032; bur St Denis), dau of William II, Count of Provence, and Adelais of Anjou; 4 sons, 2 daus; d Melun 20 July 1031; bur St Denis

Henry I 1031–1060

b April/May 1008, eldest son of King Robert II and Constance of Provence; associated with the throne and crowned at Rheims 1027; s his father 20 July 1031; m (1) 1043 Matilda (d 1044), niece of Emperor Conrad II; m (2) Rheims 19 May 1051 Anne, Regent of France 1060–1067 (b 1036; m (2) Raoul II, Count of Crespy and of Valois; d after 1076), dau of Yaroslav I, Prince of Kiev, and Ingigerd (Irene) of Sweden; 3 sons, 1 dau; d Vitry-en-Brie 4 August 1060; bur St Denis

Philip I 1060–1108

b before 23 May 1052, eldest son of King Henry I; associated with the throne and crowned at Rheims 23 May 1059; s his father 4 August 1060; m (1) 1071 (repudiated 1091) Bertha (b ca 1055; d Montreuil-sur-Mer 1094), dau of Florence I, Count of Holland, and Gertrude of Saxony; 4 sons, 1 dau; m (2) 15 May 1092 Bertrade (d Fontevrault 14 February 1117), formerly wife of Fulk IV, Count of Anjou, and dau of Simon I, Count of Montfort, and Agnes of Evreux; 2 sons, 2 daus; d Melun-sur-Seine 29 July 1108; bur Monastery of St Benoît-sur-Loire

Louis VI the Fat 1108–1137

b Paris 1081, eldest son of King Philip I and Bertha of Holland; associated with the throne before 25 December 1100; s his father and was crowned at Orleans 3 August 1108; m (1) 1104 (repudiated 1107) Lucienne, dau of Guy I, Sire de Rochefort, and Elisabeth of Crécy-en-Valois; m (2) Paris 3 August 1115 Adelaide (b ca 1100; m (2) Matthew I, Sire de Montmorency; d 18 November 1154; bur Montmartre), dau of Humbert II of Savoy, Count of Maurienne, and Gisela of Burgundy; 7 sons, 1 dau; d Paris 1 August 1137; bur St Denis

Louis VII the Young 1137–1180

b ca 1120, 2nd but eldest surviving son of King Louis VI; associated with the throne after the death of his elder brother Philip and crowned at Rheims 25 October 1131; s his father 1 August 1137 and was recrowned at Bourges 25 December 1137; m (1) Bordeaux 22 July 1137 (m annulled on grounds of consanguinity 1152) Eleanor, Duchess of Aquitaine (b Bordeaux or Belin ca 1122; m (2) 18 May 1152 Henry II, King of England; d Poitiers 31 March 1204; bur Fontevrault), dau of William VIII, Duke of Aquitaine, and Aënor of Chatellerault; 2 daus; m (2) Orleans 1154 Constance (b ca 1134; d 4 October 1160; bur St Denis), dau of Alfonso VII, King of Castile and Leon, and Berengaria of Barcelona; 2 daus; m (3) 13 November 1160 Adèle (b ca 1140; d Paris 4 June 1206; bur Pontigny), dau of Theobald IV, Count of Champagne, and Matilda of Carinthia; 1 son, 2 daus; d Paris 18 September 1180; bur Abbey of Barbeaux, Melun

Philip II Augustus 1180–1223

b Gonesse, nr Paris, 21 or 22 August 1165, only son of King Louis VII and his 3rd wife Alice of Champagne; associated with the throne and crowned at Rheims 1 November 1179; s his father 18 September 1180; m (1) Bapaume 28 April 1180 Isabelle (b Valenciennes April 1170; d Paris 15 March 1190; bur Notre-Dame, Paris), dau of Baldwin VIII, Count of Hainaut, and Margaret of Flanders; 1 son and twin sons who d at birth; m (2) Amiens 14 August 1193 (repudiated 5 November 1193) Ingeborg (b 1175; d Corbeil 29 July 1236), dau of Valdemar I, King of Denmark, and Sophie of Polotsk; m (3) 1 June

1196 (repudiated 1200) Agnes (*d* Poissy 29 July 1201), dau of Berthold VI, Duke of Meran, and Agnes of Wettin-Rochlitz; 1 son, 1 dau; *d* Mantes 14 July 1223; *bur* St Denis

---

LOUIS VIII THE LION   1223–1226

b Paris 5 September 1187, eldest son of King Philip II and Isabelle of Hainaut; *s* his father 14 July 1223; crowned at Rheims 6 August 1223; *m* nr Pont-Audemer, Normandy, 23 May 1200 Blanche, Queen Regent of France 1226–1234 (*b* Palencia before 4 March 1188; *d* Paris 27 November 1252; *bur* Abbey of Maubuisson, which she founded), dau of Alfonso VIII, King of Castile, and Eleanor of England; 11 sons, 3 daus; *d* Montpensier 8 November 1226; *bur* St Denis

---

ST LOUIS IX   1226–1270

b Poissy 25 April 1214, 4th but eldest surviving son of King Louis VIII; *s* his father 8 November 1226; crowned at Rheims 29 November 1226; *m* Sens 27 May 1234 Margaret (*b* St Maime, nr Forçalquier 1221; *d* Paris 21 December 1295; *bur* St Denis), dau of Raymond Berengar IV, Count of Provence, and Beatrice of Savoy; 6 sons, 5 daus; *d* Carthage 25 August 1270; *bur* St Denis; canonized 1297

PHILIP III THE BOLD   1270–1285

b Poissy 1 May 1245, 2nd but eldest surviving son of King Louis IX; *s* his father 25 August 1270; crowned at Rheims 15 August 1271; *m* (1) Clermont-en-Auvergne 28 May 1262 Isabelle (*b* 1243; *d* Cosenza 28 January 1271; *bur* there), dau of James I, King of Aragon, and his second wife Yolande of Hungary; 4 sons; *m* (2) Vincennes 21 August 1274 Marie (*b* Liège *ca* 1260; *d* Murel 12 January 1322), dau of Henry III, Duke of Brabant, and Alice of Burgundy; 1 son, 2 daus; *d* Perpignan 5 October 1285; *bur* St Denis (entrails at Narbonne Cathedral)

PHILIP IV THE FAIR   1285–1314

b Fontainebleau 1268, 2nd but eldest surviving son of King Philip II; *s* his father 5 October 1285; crowned at Rheims 6 January 1286; *m* 16 August 1284 Jeanne I, Queen of Navarre (*b* 1271; *d* 2 April 1304), only dau of Henry I, King of Navarre, and Blanche of Artois; 4 sons, 3 daus; *d* Fontainebleau 29 November 1314; *bur* St Denis

---

LOUIS X THE QUARRELSOME   1314–1316

b Paris 4 October 1289, eldest son of King Philip IV; *s* his mother as King of Navarre 2 April 1304 and was crowned at Pamplona 1307; *s* his father as King of France 29 November 1314; crowned at St Denis 29 August 1315; *m* (1) 23 September 1305 (*m* annulled), Margaret (*b* 1290; *d* Château Gaillard 14 August 1315), dau of Robert II, Duke of Burgundy, and Agnes of France (youngest dau of King Louis IX); 1 dau; *m* (2) 19 August 1315 Clémence (*b* February 1293; *d* 12 October

1328), dau of Charles I Martel, King of Hungary, and Clemence of Habsburg; 1 son; *d* Vincennes 5 June 1316; *bur* St Denis

---

JOHN I   1316

b (posthumously) The Louvre 15 November 1316, only son of King Louis X and his second wife Clémence of Hungary; *s* to the throne at birth; *d* aged five days 20 November 1316; *bur* St Denis

---

PHILIP V THE TALL   1316–1322

b Lyons 1293/4, 2nd son of King Philip IV; *cr* Count of Poitou; Regent of France 5 June to 20 November 1316; *s* his nephew King John I 20 November 1316; crowned at Rheims 9 January 1317; *m* June 1307 Jeanne (*b* 1294; *d* 21 January 1329), dau of Otho IV, Count of Burgundy, and Mahaut of Artois; 1 son (*d* young), 4 daus; *d* Longchamp 3 January 1322; *bur* St Denis

---

CHARLES IV THE FAIR   1322–1328

b ca 1295, 3rd son of King Philip IV; *cr* Count of La Marche; *s* his brother King Philip V 3 January 1322; crowned at Rheims 21 February 1322; *m* (1) by April 1307 (*m* annulled 1322) Blanche (*b* 1296; *d* Maubuisson by 5 April 1326), dau of Otho IV, Count of Burgundy, and Mahaut of Artois; 1 son, 1 dau (both *d* young); *m* (2) 21 September 1322 Marie (*b* 1305; *d* 25 March 1324), dau of Henry VII (of Luxembourg), Holy Roman Emperor, and Margaret of Brabant; 1 son (*d* in infancy); *m* (3) 5 August 1325 Jeanne (*b* 1310; *d* 4 March 1371), dau of Louis of France, Count of Evreux (yst son of King Philip III), and Margaret of Artois; 3 daus; *d* Vincennes 1 February 1328; *bur* St Denis (entrails at Maubuisson)

The origins of the Capetians have been the subject of much controversy and the first ancestor of whom we can be certain is Robert the Strong, Count of Tours, Marquis of Anjou and Duke of France, who rose to a position of great importance and died in 866. It seems most probable that he was descended from one Lambert, who was an official at the court of King Dagobert I about 630; but genealogists have also sought to derive him from the Saxon hero Wittekind, from the Welfs of Bavaria, from Nebelong, Count of Madrie, and even from Charlemagne or some other scion of the Carolingians.

Robert's son Eudes was elected King of the West Franks in 888 and reigned until his death in 898. Eudes's brother Robert, Count of Paris, was similarly elected King in 922 in rivalry to the ineffective Charles the Simple, but was killed in battle at Soissons in June 923. Robert's son-in-law Raoul of Burgundy, the husband of his daughter Emma, was then elected King in July 923 and soon thereafter succeeded in capturing Charles the Simple and imprisoning him at Péronne until his death in 929. Raoul reigned until his death in 935, then Charles the Simple's son Louis IV was brought back from exile in England and set on the throne by Hugh the Great, Count of Paris, the son of Robert I and brother-in-law of

Raoul. Hugh was the real ruler of France until his death in June 956.

Hugh the Great's son, Hugh Capet, who succeeded him as Duke of France and Count of Paris, derived his nickname from the cape (*cappa*), which he wore as a lay abbot, and was content to serve the Carolingian monarchs as his father had done until fate took a hand and Louis V was thrown from his horse and killed while hunting, leaving no heir. Adalberon, Archbishop of Rheims, appointed Hugh Regent and influenced the council of nobles which met at Senlis to elect him to fill the vacant throne.

Very little is known about Hugh. He appears to have been less forceful than his immediate ancestors and to have had a pious and peaceful disposition. After a reign of nine years, he died of smallpox in October 996 and was succeeded by his son Robert II, whom he had already associated with him on the throne, beginning a custom which was to be continued by his successors for several centuries.

Robert II is distinguished by the sobriquet of 'the Pious' and is said by his eulogistic biographer, the monk Helgald of Fleury-sur-Loire, to have been tall, handsome and of regal bearing, as well as being 'gentle, graceful and . . . well-versed in literature'. His father had arranged a marriage for him with Rozala (also called Susanna), the widow of the Count of Flanders and the daughter of Berengar, King of Italy, but she was much older than Robert and they did not get on together, so he repudiated her but refused to return her dowry, which included the important fortified town of Montreuil-sur-Mer overlooking the Channel. Rid of Rozala, Robert married another widow, Bertha of Burgundy, who was more to his liking although already the mother of five children by her first husband the Count of Blois. Her only child by Robert died at birth and as the Pope had excommunicated the King for contracting a marriage within the prohibited degrees, they agreed to part in 1000 and the excommunication was lifted. Robert's third and last wife, Constance of Provence, was a terrible woman. She gave birth to four sons and two daughters, so the succession was well assured, but as the sons grew up she encouraged them to rebel against their father and fomented trouble between them as well. The eldest son, Hugh, died at the age of eighteen after being associated in the kingdom with his father. Robert then wished to designate his second son Henry as his successor, but Queen Constance preferred the third son Robert, later to receive the Duchy of Burgundy. The King had his way, however, and Henry was crowned in 1027. Four years later Robert died and Henry succeeded as sole ruler.

Henry I's reign saw the burning of Paris and a famine of seven years' duration. The King appears to have been something of a nonentity and is chiefly remembered for the novelty of his second marriage. His first wife, Matilda, niece of the Emperor Conrad II, bore one daughter who died young and died herself very soon after. Henry, anxious to avoid a marriage within the prohibited degrees of kindred and affinity, determined to find his next bride from far afield and in 1051 married Anne, daughter of Yaroslav I, Great Prince of Kiev, who duly bore him three sons. The eldest, Philip, was crowned as associate King at the age of seven in May 1059. Although only fifty-two Henry apparently suffered from premature senility, being described as 'old and wretched'. He obtained a potion which he hoped would restore his health and prolong his life from a doctor in Chartres, but apparently disobeyed the instructions to take it without water and died the next day. Philip succeeded at the age of eight. Queen Anne refused the regency which was undertaken by King Henry's brother-in-law Baldwin V, Count of Flanders. She was soon after abducted by Count Raoul de Crépy and eventually became his second wife.

Nothing good is said of King Philip I, whose gluttony rendered him obese. His matrimonial affairs caused a great scandal. His first wife, Bertha of Holland, had borne him several children, of whom Louis and Constance survived, when Philip fell in love with Bertrade de Montfort, the wife of Fulk IV, Count of Anjou. In 1092 he repudiated Bertha and managed to find a Bishop willing to marry him to Bertrade. When the news reached Rome, the King was ordered to give her up. He refused and was excommunicated. He still persisted in living with Bertrade and treating her as Queen and the Pope then placed an interdict on the kingdom, closing all the churches and prohibiting the administration of the sacraments. Finally Philip gave in and ceased living with Bertrade in 1104. He died of malaria in July 1108. On his deathbed he said that he was unworthy to be buried with his ancestors at St Denis and requested that he should be buried in the monastery of St Benoît-sur-Loire instead. His tomb was discovered there in 1830. Bertrade, 'still young and beautiful', took the veil at Fontevrault after the King's death and died there in 1117.

Louis VI, who in accordance with established custom had been designated successor (though not crowned) in 1100, was as gross and gluttonous as his father and has gone down in history as 'the Fat'. More is known about him than his predecessors thanks to the writings of his friend and mentor Suger, Abbot of St Denis. In spite of his size, Louis was an energetic King and and in the course of a long reign of twenty-nine years did much to curb the growing power of the feudal nobility, many of whom had become semi-independent of the French crown. He was also skilful in his foreign policy and a deeply religious man. Louis was married twice: first, to Lucienne of Rochefort, whom he repudiated after three years of childless marriage; second, to Adelaide of Savoy, who gave him eight children. The eldest son, Philip, was designated successor in the customary way, but was killed while boar hunting in 1131, so the next son Louis took his place. In 1137 his father arranged a splendid marriage for him with the heiress of the Duchy of Aquitaine, Eleanor, and the marriage took place at Bordeaux on 22 July. During the festivities the King was taken severely ill with dysentery, which had long plagued him. He returned to Paris as speedily as possible and there had himself laid on a bed of cinders in the form of a cross, whereon he died, at the age of fifty-six.

Louis VII 'the Young' and his high-spirited young wife were crowned at Bourges on Christmas Day. Two daughters were born to them in the early years of their marriage, but no more children followed and it would appear that Eleanor, amorous

King Charles V of France (third from left) entertaining
the Emperor Charles IV (second from left) and his son
Wenceslas, King of the Romans, with the Archbishop of
Rheims and two other Bishops: a manuscript in the
Bibliothèque Nationale, Paris.

Jean Fouquet's portrait of King Charles VII of France conveys much of the King's melancholy, introspective character.

King Francis I of France, by Titian, a splendid portrait of this swashbuckling Renaissance Prince which gives a strong impression of his larger-than-life character.

Fontainebleau, a favourite French royal residence.

*Louis XIV of France in all the splendour of majesty, looking as if he
has just uttered those memorable words, 'L'état c'est moi'.
This painting is by Rigaud.*

by nature, found Louis an unsatisfactory husband. In 1148 the couple went to the Holy Land to take part in the Crusade and Eleanor's behaviour scandalized everybody. Not only did she disport herself immodestly with her dashing young uncle Raymond of Poitiers, Prince of Antioch, but she also entertained a passion for a handsome Moorish slave and is credited with having had an affair with Saladin, too, although on the face of it, it seems unlikely. In 1149 the King and Queen returned to France, where the King's father's faithful old friend Suger had been acting as Regent, and Louis determined on ending his marriage. The usual grounds of consanguinity were cited and after a somewhat lengthy process the marriage was annulled in March 1152. Eleanor lost no time in finding herself another husband in the person of Henry of Anjou, who two years later succeeded as Henry II, King of England, so she became a Queen again.

Louis himself did not remarry for nearly two years. His second wife was Constance of Castile, who bore him two more daughters and died at the birth of the younger in 1160. Anxious for a son, Louis married a third wife only one month after Constance's death. The new Queen, Adèle of Champagne, bore the desired heir, Philip Augustus, five years later in August 1165 and his birth was followed by that of two more daughters. The long reign of Louis VII ended in September 1180, when he died after suffering a series of strokes.

The new King, Philip II Augustus, was a boy of fifteen. His second name was derived from the fact that he was born in August. He was deemed of age to reign and is described by a contemporary as 'a handsome strapping man, with a pleasant face, warm, with a high colour and a temperament disposed to good food, wine and women ... generous to his friends and mean to those who displeased him'. He had been married, a few months before his accession, to Isabelle of Hainaut, who brought him Amiens and Artois as her dowry. She gave birth to the future Louis VIII in 1187, but died in March 1190 after giving birth to male twins who did not survive. Three years later Philip married Ingeborg of Denmark, but for some strange reason which has never come to light, conceived a strong aversion to the eighteen-year-old girl on the wedding day. It is not known if the marriage was consummated, but Philip sought and obtained an annulment within three months and the unfortunate Ingeborg was despatched to a nunnery. Philip now fell in love, perhaps for the first time in his life, with Agnes of Meran, the sixteen-year-old daughter of a powerful German noble, and married her in June 1196. She bore him a daughter and a son, but the Pope, who had refused to ratify the annulment of Philip's marriage to Ingeborg, excommunicated the King and then took the further step of placing an interdict on the kingdom. This last move forced Philip to part from Agnes in September 1200 and reinstate Ingeborg as Queen. Agnes died at Poissy in the following year.

Apart from his matrimonial entanglements, Philip's long reign of forty-three years was a successful one. He went crusading with Richard I of England (the son of his father's first wife by her second husband), with whom he subsequently fought, and regained Normandy, Anjou, Maine, Poitou and Touraine for the French crown. Philip died of malaria at the

age of fifty-eight, leaving a secure and greatly enlarged kingdom to his son Louis VIII.

The short reign of Louis VIII, nicknamed 'the Lion', and the first Capetian not to be crowned in his father's lifetime, lasted a little over three years. Before his accession he had led quite an adventurous life, for the English Barons had called him in to lead them in their struggle against King John and he took possession of London in the summer of 1216. In October, however, John, who had been forced to fly into East Anglia, died and there was a revulsion of feeling in favour of his young son Henry III, with whom the Barons felt they had no quarrel. Louis was defeated by Henry's supporters at Lincoln and abandoned his attempt to gain the English crown, withdrawing to France in the following year.

Louis VIII's reign was occupied in putting down the Albigensian heresy in Languedoc. The King took a personal role in the procedure and the heretics were massacred in vast numbers, women and children suffering with the rest. While returning home Louis was struck down with dysentery at Montpensier and medical opinion held that he 'would be cured by using a woman'. A suitable virgin was procured, unknown to the King, and sent to his room to effect the cure, but he would have none of it, saying, 'I will not commit mortal sin for whatever reason', and gave instructions that the girl was to be honourably married. Having done so, he died on 8 November 1226, aged thirty-nine. He had been a faithful husband to his wife, Blanche of Castile, to whom he was greatly attached, and she bore fourteen children, the youngest posthumously in March 1227. The eldest surviving son succeeded his father as Louis IX at the age of twelve, and Queen Blanche assumed the regency and reigned skilfully and energetically for nearly ten years, during which she had to contend with sundry uprisings led by Philip Hurepel, the son of Philip II and Agnes of Meran, and the Duke of Brittany.

Louis was content to leave affairs in his mother's hands until he was twenty-one, by which time he had been married to Margaret of Provence, the eldest of the four beautiful daughters of Raymond Berengar V, Count of Provence, all of whom were to become Queens. Like his father, Louis was a man of strict moral principles and although he loved his wife and fathered eleven children by her, always insisted that they should abstain from marital relations during the seasons of Advent and Lent and it is recorded that if 'he found himself moved by carnal desire on account of the proximity of his wife ... he would get out of bed and walk around the room until his rebellious flesh was quiescent'. Louis also affected a very plain style of dress which did not always please the Queen. In appearance he was tall, thin and slightly stooping, with long fair hair, somewhat irregular features and a pleasing, kindly expression.

In 1248 the King, accompanied by the Queen, set out for the Holy Land to lead the Seventh Crusade, and again assigned France to his mother's regency, which she was to exercise until her death in 1252. In the course of the Crusade, Queen Margaret gave birth to her sixth child and fourth son at Damietta while her husband was in Arab captivity, from which he had to be ransomed. The royal couple were in Acre when the news of Queen Blanche's death arrived and Louis determined to set out for home. Margaret must have received the news of her mother-in-law's death with relief, for relations between the two Queens had always been strained, Blanche being a typically possessive mother who resented the time the King spent with his wife.

Back home, Louis effected many internal reforms and gave many more instances of his piety and goodness. He drew up a code of conduct for his eldest son and continually exhorted his children to eschew all evil and avarice. The failure of the Crusade had left him with the desire to return to the Holy Land as soon as possible, but it was not until 1270 that he was able to do so. His youngest brother Charles, who had become King of Sicily, persuaded him to sail first to Carthage and subdue the infidels there. Plague was raging in the city and the King caught it soon after his arrival. Like his ancestor King Louis VI, he died lying on a bed of ashes on 25 August 1270. Only twenty-seven years after his death he was canonized by Pope Boniface VIII. A modern author has written that his 'title to sainthood can be summed up in one word, integrity – the quality on which he set so much value and which he possessed in a superlative degree'.

By comparison with his father, Philip III the Bold appears an insignificant figure, but he was a conscientious ruler and greatly respected for his wisdom. He had accompanied his father on his last Crusade and brought his body back to France, travelling overland through Italy. In the course of the journey Philip's wife, Isabelle of Aragon, fell from her horse and died of her injuries at Cosenza at the end of January 1271, having never set foot in France as Queen. Three years later the King married again and his choice fell on Marie of Brabant, of whom he had heard good reports. The new Queen was only eighteen and Philip soon came to love her dearly, much to the annoyance of his chamberlain Pierre de la Broce, who felt that his influence over the King was being undermined. In 1276 Philip's eldest son Louis, aged nine, died suddenly after a mysterious illness. Pierre put it about that he had been poisoned by his stepmother and for a time things looked very black for Marie until her brother the Duke of Brabant sent a knight from his court to prove her innocence by combat in the approved style of those days. She was completely vindicated and her accuser was hanged. After a reign of fifteen years Philip III died of malaria at Perpignan in October 1285, aged only forty. Marie of Brabant, who had given him three children in addition to the four sons borne by Isabelle, survived for many years and died in the reign of her step-grandson Philip V in 1321.

Philip III was succeeded by his second son Philip IV, described as 'the most handsome man in the world, tall, [and] well-proportioned'. He has, however, gained a bad reputation from his heavy taxes, his devaluation of the currency, his persecution of the Jews and the Knights Templar, and the moral laxity of his court exemplified in the loose conduct of his daughters-in-law. In spite of all this, he was popular with the people and on the credit side it must be admitted that he vastly expanded the royal domain, gaining several territories by purchase, and increased the efficiency of the central

The monumental effigy of King Philip IV of France in the Abbey of St Denis.

administration. He was the first King to summon the three estates of the realm to take a part in the government.

A year before his accession Philip married Jeanne (I), Queen of Navarre, and became King of that country in her name, France and Navarre thus becoming united under one ruler for the first time. The royal pair had seven children, of whom three sons and one daughter grew to maturity. Queen Jeanne died in 1305 and the last decade of Philip the Fair's reign was shaken by the scandal surrounding the conduct of his three daughters-in-law. These girls were themselves all Capetians, Margaret the wife of Louis being the daughter of the Duke of Burgundy, while Jeanne and Blanche, the wives of Philip and Charles, were both daughters of the Count of Burgundy-Franche-Comté. They were all extremely flirtatious and soon involved themselves in more serious affairs, of which their husbands remained (or affected to remain) ignorant. Their conduct was revealed by Philip's daughter, Isabelle, Queen of England, 'the She-wolf of France', whose own conduct later was to be equally scandalous, and an inquiry was initiated. It found that the ladies did have lovers, two of whom were identified as the brothers Philippe and Gautier d'Aulnay, who confessed under torture. The Princesses were imprisoned and two admitted their guilt. Margaret, the wife of Louis, had a daughter Jeanne, whose paternity was questioned. Her marriage was annulled and she was imprisoned in Château Gaillard where she died in 1315, virtually starved to death. Jeanne, the wife of Philip, the second brother, strongly protested her innocence and her husband believed her and took her back after her release from prison. The marriage of Blanche, wife of the youngest brother Charles, was also annulled on the grounds that her mother had been Charles's godmother and she ended her days as a nun at Maubuisson in 1326. As for the d'Aulnay brothers, they were publicly flayed alive, castrated and finally beheaded. The scandals no doubt served to hasten Philip the Fair's death. He suffered a stroke and died at Fontainebleau in November 1314, aged forty-six.

Philip's eldest son Louis X, known as 'the Quarrelsome' or 'the Headstrong' from his participation in the rioting and street fights which followed his father's death, was destined to reign for only eighteen months. In 1315 he took a second wife in the person of Clémence of Hungary, who made her state entry into Paris on 19 August 1315 and was crowned with him at Rheims ten days later. The following May, when the Queen was pregnant, Louis became overheated while playing a game of indoor tennis at Vincennes and quenched his thirst with a draught of chilled wine. He developed a high fever, pulmonary complications set in, and within a week he was dead from pneumonia at the age of twenty-six.

Since the Queen was pregnant Louis X's death was followed by an interregnum, during which his brother Philip acted as Regent. On the night of 14/15 November 1316, Clémence gave birth to a son, who was baptized John and is one of the very few people to have been born a King (Alfonso XIII of Spain was another, as we have seen). The little King only survived five days. His death was attributed to the evil Mahaut of Artois, mother of the two discredited Franche-Comté Princesses, who is said to have stuck a pin into him. Others said that the real King had been stolen away and a dead baby substituted in his place. Years later a false John I was to claim the crown with support from Italy, but was soon routed.

On the baby King's death the Regent was proclaimed as Philip V and was crowned with his rehabilitated wife Jeanne in January 1317. To justify his right of succession he called a meeting of the Estates-General to endorse the Salic Law and declare that 'a woman should not succeed to the throne of France', thus successfully excluding Louis X's daughter Jeanne, whose legitimacy was doubtful anyway. Apart from his height, little is known of Philip's personal appearance. When still only twenty-eight he fell ill with dysentery, which had proved fatal to several of his ancestors, and died at Longchamp in January 1322 after a reign of five years. Queen Jeanne, who survived until 1329, had borne him one son, Louis, who died young, and four daughters. The three eldest had advantageous marriages arranged for them by their father while still children, the fourth became a nun.

Philip V was succeeded by his brother Charles IV, the youngest son of Philip the Fair, who was distinguished by the same sobriquet as his father. His first act was to obtain the annulment of his marriage to Blanche of Burgundy, still languishing in Château Gaillard and, still as morally unstable as ever, having had a child by one of her gaolers. This done,

and Blanche despatched to her nunnery, Charles married Marie of Luxembourg, daughter of the Holy Roman Emperor Henry VII, in September 1322. Two years later she died of puerperal fever after giving birth to a stillborn child, and in August 1325 Charles married for the third time. His new wife was his cousin Jeanne of Evreux and the necessary dispensation was obtained. Two daughters were born in due course and the Queen was pregnant again when Charles succumbed to a mysterious illness and died at Vincennes on 1 February 1328. He appointed his cousin, Philip, Count of Valois, to act as Regent, the situation being the same as it had been on the death of Louis X some twelve years before. Two months later Queen Jeanne gave birth to another girl and the Regent ascended the throne as Philip VI, inaugurating the collateral line of Valois. Navarre now separated again from the French crown and passed to Louis X's daughter Jeanne, the wife of Philip of Evreux.

The House of Valois

Philip VI   1328–1350

b 1293, eldest son of Charles of France, Count of Valois (4th son of King Philip III), and his first wife Margaret of Naples; *s* his father as Count of Valois 1325; Regent of France 1 February to 1 April 1328, when he became King on Charles IV's posthumous child proving to be a daughter; crowned at Rheims 29 May 1328; *m* (1) July 1313 Jeanne (*b* 1293; *d* 12 September 1348), dau of Robert II, Duke of Burgundy, and Agnes of France; 6 sons, 2 daus; *m* (2) 29 January 1349 Blanche (*b* 1331; *d* 5 October 1398; *bur* St Denis), dau of Philip III, King of Navarre, Count of Evreux, and Jeanne II, Queen of Navarre (dau of King Louis X); 1 dau; *d* Nogent-le-Roi 22 August 1350; *bur* St Denis (entrails in Church of the Jacobins, Paris; heart at Château de Bourgfontaine, Valois)

John II the Good   1350–1364

b Gue-de-Maulny, nr Le Mans, 26 April, 1319, 2nd but eldest surviving son of King Philip VI; *s* his father 22 August 1350; crowned at Rheims 26 September 1350; *m* (1) 28 July 1332 Bonne of Luxembourg (*b* 20 May 1315; *d* 11 September 1349), dau of John the Blind, King of Bohemia, and his 1st wife Elizabeth of Bohemia; 4 sons, 7 daus; *m* (2) 19 February 1350 Jeanne (*b* 8 May 1326; *d* 29 September 1361), dau of William IX de La Tour d'Auvergne, Count of Boulogne, and Margaret of Evreux; 1 son, 2 daus; *d* imprisoned in the Palace of the Savoy, London 8 April 1364; *bur* St Denis

Charles V the Wise   1364–1380

b Vincennes 21 January 1337, eldest son of King John II; the first heir apparent to bear the title of Dauphin; Regent of France during his father's captivity in England 1360–64; *s* his father 8 April 1364; crowned at Rheims 19 May 1364; *m* Vincennes 8 April 1350 Jeanne (*b* Vincennes 3 February 1338; *d* 6 February 1377), dau of Peter I, Duke of Bourbon, and Isabelle of Valois; 3 sons, 5 daus; *d* Beauté-sur-

Marne, nr Vincennes, 16 September 1380; *bur* St Denis (heart at Notre-Dame, Rouen)

CHARLES VI THE MAD   1380–1422

---

b Paris 3 December 1368, 2nd but eldest surviving son of King Charles V; *s* his father 16 September 1380; crowned at Rheims 4 November 1380; *m* Amiens 17 July 1385 Isabeau (*b* Ingolstadt 1371; *d* Paris 24 September 1435; *bur* St Denis), dau of Stephen III, Duke of Bavaria-Ingolstadt, and Thaddaea Visconti; 6 sons, 6 daus; *d* Hôtel de St Pol, Paris, 22 October 1422; *bur* St Denis

---

CHARLES VII THE VICTORIOUS   1422–1461

---

b Hôtel de St Pol, Paris 22 February 1403, 5th but eldest surviving son of King Charles VI; Regent of France 24 June 1418 to 22 October 1422, when he *s* his father; crowned at Rheims 17 July 1429; *m* Bourges 2 July 1422 Marie (*b* Angers 14 October 1404; *d* Abbey of Châteliers, Poitou 29 November 1463), dau of Louis II, Duke of Anjou, King of Naples, and Yolande of Aragon; 5 sons, 9 daus; *d* Mehun-sur-Yèvre, nr Bourges, 22 July 1461; *bur* St Denis

---

LOUIS XI   1461–1483

---

b Bourges 3 July 1423, eldest son of King Charles VII; *s* his father 22 July 1461; crowned at Rheims 15 August 1461; *m* (1) Tours 24 June 1436 Margaret (*b* Linlithgow, Scotland 1424; *d* Châlons 16 August 1445), dau of James I, King of Scots, and Joan Beaufort; *m* (2) 14 February 1457 Charlotte (*b* Chambéry *ca* 1445; *d* Paris 1 December 1483), dau of Amadeus VIII, Duke of Savoy, and Anne of Cyprus; 4 sons, 3 daus; *d* Plessis-les-Tours 30 August 1483; *bur* Notre-Dame de Cléry, Montils

---

CHARLES VIII   1483–1498

---

b Amboise 30 June 1470, 3rd but only surviving son of King Louis XI; *s* his father 30 August 1483; crowned at Rheims 14 May 1484; *m* 6 December 1491 Anne, Duchess of Brittany (*b* Rennes 25 January 1476; *m* (2) King Louis XII; *d* Blois 9 January 1514), dau of Francis II, Duke of Brittany, and Margaret of Foix; 3 sons, 1 dau (all *d* in infancy); *d* Amboise 7 April 1498; *bur* St Denis

---

Philip VI was no less a Capetian than any of his predecessors but as the first ruler of the collateral line of Valois he is often spoken of as if he had initiated a completely new dynasty. As the male heir of his predecessor his right to succeed was indisputable, the Salic Law being accepted, but he was challenged by King Edward III of England, whose mother Isabelle was the sister of the last three Kings and the pursuit of Edward's claim was to embroil the two countries in the Hundred Years' War.

Philip loved luxury and display and spent an inordinate amount on his coronation and the celebrations for the marriage of his son John to Bonne of Luxembourg in 1332. However, the war with England did not go well for him and he suffered the ignominy of the destruction of his fleet at the naval battle of Sluys in 1340. Still worse was the battle of Crécy in August 1346, in which Philip fought in person, where he had two horses killed under him, and saw his ally the blind King John of Bohemia, who was also his son's father-in-law, killed while fighting bravely. Philip only escaped from the battlefield with the utmost difficulty and managed to make his way to Broyes, where he called upon the Châtelain to open the gates, shouting 'I am the unfortunate King of France'. The next year Edward besieged Calais and a three-year truce was signed. In 1348 the Black Death carried off Philip's Queen Jeanne of Burgundy and the following year his son John's wife Bonne. Philip arranged a new marriage for his son with Blanche of Evreux, the daughter of the King of Navarre and through her mother the granddaughter of Louis X. When she arrived at the French court, Philip fell in love with her himself and decided to marry her, although many years her senior. Another bride was found for John in the person of Jeanne of Boulogne, whom he accepted without demur. Philip wore himself out in his attempts to satisfy his new wife and prove his vigour and within a year sickened and died at Nogent-le-Roi in August 1350 at the age of fifty-seven.

John II, who has earned the sobriquet of 'the Good', is certainly one of the more complex French Kings; he is also one of the most unfortunate. John's weaknesses were a love of splendour inherited from his father and a tendency to surround himself with favourites, giving rise to rumours (almost certainly unfounded) of his being a homosexual. On the credit side, he was chivalrous and extremely courageous. The war with England had been renewed and John fought in person, as his father had done. The Black Prince was leading the English forces and at the battle of Poitiers in 1356 John was taken prisoner and borne off in triumph to London. His son Charles managed to escape and become Lieutenant-General of the Kingdom. John was kept in honourable captivity in England and although confined to the Tower of London had every possible comfort. He was naturally eager to regain his freedom and return home and in April 1360 agreed to sign the shameful treaty of Brétigny, whereby England was to retain all the territory captured in France with other additions, and a ransom of three million écus in gold was to be paid within six years, two of John's sons being retained as hostages against its payment. Returned to Paris and the first instalment of the ransom paid, John plunged into a round of festivities to celebrate his return in spite of the dire straits in which the country was languishing. In 1363 one of John's hostage sons escaped and returned to France. John's chivalrous nature came to the fore and against all advice he determined to go to London himself to take the young man's place. He arrived in January 1364 and was received with great honour and lodged in the Savoy Palace, but within two months he had fallen ill, doubtless a victim of the English winter, and he died in April, aged forty-five. Edward III arranged a magnificent funeral service for him and his body was returned to France for burial at St Denis.

Charles V was already an experienced ruler when he succeeded his father, having acted as Lieutenant-General of the Realm during the latter's periods of captivity in England. As heir to the throne he had been the first to bear the title of Dauphin, derived from the Dauphiné region which his grandfather Philip VI had purchased in 1349. Charles was a cultured man with scholarly tastes and no great liking for warlike pursuits. He was of a slight and delicate build and his health may have been undermined by an early attempt to poison him made by a jealous cousin. Christine de Pisan, a poet residing at the court, has left a flattering description of Charles, referring to his beautiful chestnut eyes, his pale skin, his even temper and his pleasant voice, among other things.

Charles had been married at the age of thirteen to the plump and slightly unstable Jeanne of Bourbon. In the early years of their marriage he preferred the company of his mistress Biette Cassinel, but after his coronation he decided that it was unseemly to indulge in extra-marital relationships and remained faithful to the Queen. She bore him nine children, but only three survived infancy. Jeanne died at the birth of her youngest child in February 1377, leaving her husband so grief-stricken that he only survived her a little over two years, racked with gout in his hands and feet, and finally succumbed to kidney failure in September 1380 at the early age of forty-three.

Charles's son and successor, Charles VI, has gone down in history as Charles the Mad, and we now know that his madness was a symptom of porphyria, the 'royal malady', which can perhaps be traced back as far as Alfred the Great of England and afflicted many of Charles's descendants, the most notable being King George III of Great Britain. Charles's father's condition may well have been attributable to the same cause and as his mother, too, had exhibited signs of instability, poor Charles VI probably inherited the disease in good measure. At the time of his accession, Charles had not completed his twelfth year and his uncles the Dukes of Anjou, Berry, Burgundy and Bourbon undertook the government on his behalf and, to put it bluntly, made a mess of things by imposing such severe taxes that they provoked a civil war which had to be put down in 1382. The young King had not yet shown any signs of madness and appeared to be both handsome and athletic. In 1385 a marriage was arranged for him with the half-German half-Italian Princess Isabeau, daughter of Duke Stephen of Bavaria. The marriage was to prove a disaster both for Charles and for France. The King fell instantly in love with his bride when he met her at Amiens. The wedding ceremony was performed at once and Froissart commented, 'You can be sure they had great pleasure together that night'.

At first the marriage went well; the Queen soon learnt French and under her influence the court again became a lively place with much feasting and other celebrations. Charles's first attack of insanity occurred in August 1392 when he was leading a punitive expedition against Pierre de Craon, who had attacked and wounded the Constable de Clisson. While on the road an aged man clad in rags rushed from some bushes and seized the bridle of the King's horse, crying out

that he had been betrayed. Charles at once turned on his own men and killed four with his battleaxe before he could be overcome and pinioned. Doctors were called in and, recalling the strange behaviour of the King's mother, they shook their heads and declared his derangement to be hereditary. However, Charles recovered in a short while and was full of remorse when he heard how he had killed his faithful followers. In the following January there was a ball at the Hôtel de St Pol in Paris. The King and some of his boon companions dressed themselves as 'wild men' in feathers and cotton rags and sought to enliven the evening with an improvised dance. Charles's brother, Louis, Duke of Orleans, in order to see them better, seized a torch and, waving it too near them, accidentally set their costumes on fire, transforming them into fireballs. Pandemonium reigned for several minutes, but the King's aunt, the Duchess of Berry, with great presence of mind threw her cloak over him and extinguished the flames before he had been harmed. Shortly afterwards Charles suffered another attack and imagined he was made of glass and about to break. The attacks became more and more frequent and of longer duration. Sadly, the poor King was conscious of their onset and wept copiously when he felt them coming on. He no longer slept with the Queen, who, a highly sexed woman, found consolation in the arms of her brother-in-law the Duke of Orleans and after he had been assassinated, indulged her near nymphomaniac passions with whoever she fancied. During Charles's lucid periods they did occasionally come together again and several more children were born to Isabeau, although their paternity is an open question. To tend for the King a young woman, Odette de Champdivers, was provided and she looked after him with tender devotion, even bearing him a daughter.

Charles's incapacity naturally led to many disorders in the kingdom, not least being the renewal of England's claims on France after a truce of twenty-five years. Charles's daughter Isabelle had become the child bride of Richard II of England in 1396, but in 1399 he was deposed and the throne was usurped by his cousin Henry of Bolingbroke. It was Bolingbroke's son, Henry V, who renewed the war, supported by Burgundy, and on 25 October 1415 won the decisive battle of Agincourt. Queen Isabeau played a treacherous role throughout, siding with the Burgundians, who had taken Paris and eventually signing the treaty of Troyes on 22 May 1420. By this treaty her daughter Catherine was to be married to Henry V, who on the death of Charles was to be acknowledged as the rightful King of France. Her son, the Dauphin Charles, had escaped to lead the resistance. Henry V died of dysentery in August 1422 and his father-in-law survived him only two months, dying in October at the age of fifty-three. Henry's infant son Henry VI was proclaimed King of both England and France and his uncle the Duke of Bedford was appointed Regent.

The Dauphin Charles was at Mehun-sur-Yevre when he received news of his father's death. His first thought was to proceed to Rheims to be crowned as the legitimate King, but it was in English hands and his attempts to force his way there were easily defeated by the English troops, who jestingly referred to Charles as the 'King of Bourges', that being the only city of any size still in his hands. The situation seemed hopeless and Charles lapsed into a state of hypochondria, beset with doubts as to his legitimacy when he considered his mother's notorious reputation. His portrait by Fouquet depicts a man with a gloomy, pessimistic countenance, obviously much troubled within himself.

In 1429 a seeming miracle occurred. Charles had moved from Bourges to Chinon and there, in February, a girl dressed in man's clothes and calling herself Joan of Arc, demanded audience of the King and said she would lead him to victory having been sent by God. Joan was only seventeen and was ostensibly a peasant girl from Domrémy in Lorraine, but an intriguing theory propounded in recent years has attempted to prove that she was really Charles's half-sister, the offspring of Queen Isabeau by the Duke of Orleans. Whatever the truth might be, Joan successfully led Charles's troops, took Orleans and pressed on to Rheims where Charles was finally crowned by the Archbishop of Chartres on 17 July 1429. Joan went on with the intention of besieging Paris, but at Compiègne was captured by the Burgundians who sold her to the English. She was handed over to the ecclesiastical authorities to be tried for heresy and for wearing male attire but managed to defend herself so well that she was sentenced only to life imprisonment. The English soldiers who had charge of her made so many attempts on her virtue that she resumed male costume giving the church cause to declare her a lapsed heretic and condemn her to death without a further hearing. She was handed over to the civil authorities and burnt at the stake in Rouen on 30 May 1431. The King she had saved made no attempt to save her but later initiated a rehabilitation trial to clear her reputation. She was canonized in 1920.

Charles had been betrothed in 1414 to Marie of Anjou, who two years later came to Paris to live under the care of his mother Queen Isabeau. That lady was hardly a suitable guardian for a young girl and when King Charles VI, during one of his lucid spells, learned of the arrangement he had Marie removed from the Queen's care in May 1417. After the Burgundian occupation of Paris and the escape of the Dauphin, Marie was left behind for several months until she was rescued by the Duke of Brittany and her brother the Duke of Anjou and finally reunited with the Dauphin. Their marriage was concluded at Bourges in 1422 shortly before the death of Charles VI. Their eldest son Louis was born in the Archiepiscopal Palace at Bourges in July 1423 and his birth was followed by that of four more sons and nine daughters. Marie was a plain woman with a large rather sharp nose and to her bitter disappointment she was to lose the King's affections in 1443 to a beautiful young rival Agnes Sorel, known as the 'Dame de Beauté' from the residence Charles bestowed upon her. Agnes reigned over the court almost as Queen and bore Charles three daughters, Marie, Charlotte and Jeanne, who were all provided with rich husbands in due course. The favourite's reign was to be but short, however, for in 1449 she died of dysentery when accompanying the King to Normandy. Charles never forgot her.

Apart from the successful end to the Hundred Years' War, Charles's reign witnessed many important governmental reforms. Charles had always been sickly and was generally tubercular. Towards the end of his life he suffered from an ulcerated leg and the final cause of his death was a necrosis of the lower jaw which rendered eating impossible. He died in July 1461, aged fifty-eight, and was accorded a magnificent funeral at St Denis.

Louis XI, who succeeded his father at the age of thirty-eight, is one of the least attractive monarchs to have reigned in any country. He has been described as 'a bad subject, a bad King, a dangerous enemy, a treacherous ally, and a hopelessly disappointing son'. His appearance was completely unprepossessing with a sly, shifty expression. He was parsimonious in the extreme and dressed plainly in shabby clothes, the most distinctive being a black hat hung about with religious charms and medals, for he was superstitious to a degree. He had no natural dignity and preferred the company of his doctor and his barber to all others. Finally, he possessed a streak of sadistic cruelty and enjoyed locking his prisoners into iron cages and visiting them as though they were animals in a zoo.

In 1436, when he was still Dauphin, his father arranged a marriage for him with the charming Scottish Princess Margaret, daughter of King James I. As the bride and bridegroom were both still children, she lived with her mother-in-law Queen Marie, but in spite of the kind treatment she received from both the King and the Queen, Margaret was not happy in France. Her unhappiness grew when Louis took a dislike to her and said that he had been tricked into the marriage by his father before he was old enough to have any say in the matter. Continuing disagreements with his father caused Louis to withdraw from court and retire into the Dauphiné, while Margaret remained in Paris. In August 1445 she accompanied the King on a pilgrimage to Notre-Dame de l'Epine near Châlons. It was a very hot day and on her return to the Château she sat in a draughty gallery to cool down, developed a chill and within ten days was dead from inflammation of the lungs.

Louis determined on choosing his next wife for himself. His primary aim was to secure a large dowry and he accordingly began negotiations with the Duke of Savoy to obtain the hand of his daughter Charlotte, who was still a very young child. The dowry was not quite as big as Louis had desired but he found it a good source of income nevertheless. He never developed any great feeling for Charlotte, although she bore him seven children, and she resided mostly apart from him at Amboise or Tours. Unlike most of the French Kings, Louis does not appear to have been highly sexed. He did, however, have one mistress, Marguerite de Sassenage, who gave him two daughters, one of whom was destined to become the grandmother of Diane de Poitiers, the powerful favourite of King Henry II.

For all his faults, Louis was a good statesman and diplomat. He also travelled endlessly and restlessly about the kingdom, perfecting the governmental system begun by Charles V and laying the foundation of royal absolutism which was to endure until the Revolution in 1789. It was doubtless Louis's abstemious way of life which caused him to live longer than any of his predecessors. He was the first Capetian King to celebrate his sixtieth birthday, but shortly thereafter he suffered a series of strokes and died at Plessis-les-Tours in August 1483.

Louis XI's only surviving son, who succeeded him as Charles VIII, was only thirteen years old so the regency passed into the hands of his very able elder sister Anne, known as 'Madame la Grande', and her husband Pierre de Bourbon, Sire de Beaujeu, until 1491, in which year Charles was married to Anne of Brittany, the heiress of that duchy. There is a very unflattering description of Charles at about this time, written by the Venetian Ambassador, who says he was 'small and ill-shaped ... has an ugly face, with large white eyes – better formed for seeing evil than good. His hooked nose is larger and longer than it should be and his gross lips are always open. He has a nervous habit of twitching his hands, which are far from beautiful, and his speech is slow'. The description the Ambassador gave of the seventeen-year-old Queen is only slightly less unflattering: 'She too is thin and has an obvious limp despite wearing high heels. She has dark hair, a pretty face, and is, for her age, very wily. Once she has set her mind on something she will get it by any means, for she is jealous of and greedy for the King beyond reason, so much so that since becoming his wife there have been few nights that she has not slept with him – with such success that she is now eight months pregnant.' The 'success' was shortlived unfortunately, as the child, a boy, and two subsequent boys and one girl born to Charles and Anne all died in infancy.

In 1495 Charles undertook a military expedition to Italy to claim the kingdom of Naples to which he had inherited a rather tenuous right through his grandmother Marie of Anjou. His troops met with little resistance and after a triumphal march through Italy, he entered Naples on 22 February 1495. The sovereigns of Europe became alarmed at his success and with the blessing of the Pope a Holy League was formed to protect Italy from foreign aggression and Charles was forced to return to France in the summer. While in Italy he had imbibed an enthusiasm for Italian art and the new learning and introduced the Renaissance into France.

In April 1498 Charles was staying at his birthplace and favourite residence, the Château of Amboise. On the eve of Palm Sunday he played a game of real tennis in the moat, watched by the Queen. On returning they passed through a disused and slightly derelict part of the Château and the King, although not tall, violently struck his head against the low lintel of a stone doorway. An hour or so later he suddenly lost consciousness and was put to bed, where he died about nine hours later. He left no direct heir and the crown passed to his father's second cousin, the Duke of Orleans.

The House of Valois-Orleans

Louis XII   1498–1515

b Blois 27 June 1462, only son of Charles, Duke of Orleans (great-grandson of King Charles V), and his third wife Marie of Cleves; *s* his father as Duke of Orleans 4 January 1465; *s* his second cousin once removed King Charles VIII 7 April 1498; crowned Rheims 27 May 1498; *m* (1) 8 September 1476 (*m* annulled 1498) Jeanne (*b* 23 April 1464; *d* Bourges 4 February 1505; canonized as St Jeanne of France 1950), yst dau of King Louis XI; *m* (2) 8 January 1499 Anne, Duchess of Brittany (*b* Rennes 25 January 1476; *d* Blois 9 January 1514), widow of King Charles VIII; 4 sons (all stillborn or *d* in infancy), 2 daus; *m* (3) Abbeville 9 October 1514 Mary, crowned as Queen Consort St Denis 5 November 1514 (*b* Richmond Palace 18 March 1496; *m* (2) Paris 3 March, Greenwich 13 May 1515, Charles Brandon, 1st Duke of Suffolk; *d* Westhorpe, Suffolk 25 June 1533), third dau of Henry VII, King of England, and Elizabeth of York; *d* Palais du Tournelles, Paris 1 January 1515; *bur* St Denis

Francis I   1515–1547

b Cognac 12 September 1494, only son of Charles of Orleans, Count of Angoulême (first cousin of King Louis XII), and Louise of Savoy; *s* his first cousin once removed King Louis XII 1 January 1515; crowned Rheims 25 January 1515; *m* (1) 18 May 1514 Claude, crowned as Queen Consort 1517 (*b* Romorantin 13 October 1499; *d* Bourges 26 July 1524), elder dau of King Louis XII and Anne of Brittany; 3 sons, 4 daus; *m* (2) Mont-de-Marsan 8 July 1530 Eleanor (*b* Brussels 24 November 1498; *d* Talavera 18 February 1558), widow of Manuel I, King of Portugal, and eldest dau of Philip I, titular King of Castile, and Juana, Queen of Castile; no issue; *d* Rambouillet 31 March 1547; *bur* St Denis

Henry II   1547–1559

b St Germain-en-Laye 31 March 1519, 2nd but eldest surviving son of King Francis I; *s* his father 31 March 1547; crowned Rheims 26 July 1547; *m* Marseilles 28 October 1533 Catherine (*b* Florence 13 April 1519; *d* Paris 5 January 1589), only dau of Lorenzo de'Medici, Duke of Urbino, and Madeleine de la Tour d'Auvergne; 5 sons, 5 daus; *d* Paris 10 July 1559; *bur* St Denis

Francis II   1559–1560

b Fontainebleau 19 January 1544, eldest son of King Henry II; *s* his father 10 July 1559; crowned Rheims 8 September 1559; *m* Paris 24 April 1558 Mary, Queen of Scots (*b* Linlithgow 7 December 1542; *m* (2) Edinburgh 29 July 1565 Henry Stuart, Lord Darnley (*d* 10 February 1567); *m* (3) Edinburgh 15 May 1567 James Hepburn, 4th Earl of Bothwell (*d* 14 April 1578); *d* (beheaded) Fotheringay 8 February 1587), only dau of James V, King of Scots, and his second wife Marie of Guise; no issue; *d* Orleans 5 December 1560; *bur* St Denis

CHARLES IX	1560–1574

b St Germain-en-Laye 27 June 1550, 3rd but 2nd surviving son of King Henry II; *s* his brother King Francis II 5 December 1560; crowned Rheims 15 May 1561; *m* Paris 26 November 1570 Elizabeth (*b* Vienna 5 June 1554; *d* Vienna 22 January 1592), 2nd dau of Maximilian II, Holy Roman Emperor, and Maria of Austria; 1 dau; *d* Château de Vincennes 30 May 1574; *bur* St Denis

HENRY III	1574–1589

b Fontainebleau 19 September 1551, 4th son of King Henry II; elected King of Poland 11 April 1573; crowned Cracow 21 February 1574; *s* his brother King Charles IX as King of France 30 May 1574; left Poland 18 June 1574; crowned King of France Rheims 13 February 1575; declared by the Polish Diet to have vacated the Polish throne 12 May 1575; *m* 15 February 1575 Louise (*b* 30 April 1553; *d* 29 January 1601), dau of Nicholas of Lorraine-Vaudemont, Duke of Mercoeur, and Margaret of Egmont; no issue; *d* (assassinated) St Cloud 2 August 1589; *bur* St Denis

With the accession of Louis XII the throne again passed to a collateral line. Louis was the grandson of Charles VI's brother Louis, Duke of Orleans, who was notorious for his love affair with his sister-in-law Queen Isabeau and had been murdered in Paris by the Burgundians. At the age of fourteen he had been forced into marriage with Louis XI's crippled daughter Jeanne. The marriage had never been consummated and the first thought of the new King was to rid himself of his unwanted wife. An annulment was obtained without difficulty and Jeanne, a sweet and saintly character, retired to Bourges to govern the duchy of Berry and found a religious order for women, the 'Annonciades'. She died in 1505 and was canonized by Pope Pius XII in 1950.

The way was now paved for Louis to marry Anne of Brittany, the widow of his predecessor, and so ensure that Brittany was retained by the French crown. He appears to have genuinely loved Anne, and she him, and although their sons all died in infancy, two daughter survived.

Like his predecessor, Louis became involved in Italian affairs, having claims on the duchy of Milan through his grandmother Valentina Visconti. He drove out Lodovico Sforza and annexed the duchy in 1500. In the following year he allied himself with Ferdinand of Aragon to conquer the kingdom of Naples, but they soon fell out and the Holy League was re-formed to drive the French out of Italy, which was finally accomplished in 1513.

In January 1514 Anne of Brittany died of a severe attack of gallstones, two weeks short of her thirty-eighth birthday. Louis, gazing on her as she lay in her coffin, cried out, 'Go make the vault big enough for us two. Before the year is out I shall be with her, to keep her company'. His words came true, but before they did so he had acquired another wife.

It was for political reasons in the first place that Louis agreed to marry Henry VIII of England's sister Mary, but when he discovered the eighteen-year-old bride was charming, beautiful and vivacious, his enthusiasm for the match knew no bounds. Louis was fifty-two, considered quite elderly in those days, and according to a contemporary 'reported that he had performed marvels' on his wedding night. 'At least, that is what he said for he was not very virile', is the wry comment. The marriage took place at Abbeville and after Mary's coronation at St Denis she made her state entry into Paris, where feasting and dancing continued for several weeks until the King, having exhausted himself in his efforts to be a good husband, fell ill and died rather suddenly on New Year's Day 1515. The Parisians said that the King of England had 'sent a mare [Mary] to the King of France to take him quickly and gently to heaven or hell'. Louis was laid beside Anne as he had predicted.

Louis had no son and there was no question of his young widow being pregnant so the crown passed without delay to the male heir, Francis, Count of Angoulême, the son of Louis XII's first cousin and the husband of his elder daughter Claude. As for Mary Tudor, she consoled herself very speedily with one of her English gentlemen, Charles Brandon, later Duke of Suffolk, with whom she had long been in love. They were married secretly before she left Paris and again in England after she had overcome her brother Henry's wrath at her impetuous conduct. She thus faded out of French history, to live happily ever after we hope.

Francis I is one of those larger-than-life characters, resembling his contemporary Henry VIII of England in many ways. When he was born there seemed to be little prospect that he would ever ascend the throne. His father died before he was two years old and Francis and his only sister Margaret, to whom he was devoted all his life, were carefully brought up by their ambitious mother Louise of Savoy, who lived to see both her children occupying thrones, for Margaret was to marry Henry II, King of Navarre, as her second husband and herself become the grandmother of the great Henry IV.

Francis had a look of Mephistopheles about him with his dark hair, pointed beard, enormous nose and large dark eyes. He loved magnificent clothes and display of every kind and was a perfect Renaissance gentleman. His mother had negotiated his marriage to Claude of France, which took place four months after the death of Anne of Brittany, Claude's mother, who had bitterly opposed it, she and Louise being inveterate enemies. Francis and Claude were happy together in spite of his many infidelities and she bore seven children before she died prematurely in July 1524, aged twenty-four.

The events of Francis's reign, his meeting with Henry VIII on the Field of the Cloth of Gold and his dealings with the Emperor Charles V, do not concern us here. His patronage of Benvenuto Cellini, who designed a magnificent golden seal for him, is noteworthy. Also noteworthy are his many mistresses, among them Françoise de Foix, Dame de Chateaubriant, and Anne de Heilly de Pisseleu, Duchess of Etampes, who both exercised great influence at court. The first of these two ladies entertained other lovers besides the King and on one occasion concealed one of them behind an arrangement of leaves in a fireplace when she heard the King coming. Francis doubtless had his suspicions for after he had made love to her he urinated copiously into the fireplace before taking his leave.

In 1530 Francis made a second marriage for political reasons with Charles V's sister Eleanor, the widowed Queen of Portugal. She was in her early thirties and not unattractive, but has hardly made her mark among the Queens of France, being quiet and self-effacing. There were no children of the marriage and one wonders if Francis had already contracted the syphilis which was to be the probable cause of his death. He died in March 1547 at the age of fifty-two, his end hastened by the news of the death of his old friend Henry VIII of England.

Francis's first son, also called Francis, had died at the age of nineteen in 1536, so it was the second, Henry, who succeeded his father. Henry was one of those dull louts, completely uncultured and interested only in jousting, tennis and other physical exercises. He was, moreover, completely dominated by the two women in his life, his wife Catherine de'Medici, and his mistress Diane de Poitiers. He had been married at fourteen to the Florentine Catherine, who was the same age, and she was destined to become one of France's most interesting and most sinister Queens. The marriage was mysteriously childless for over ten years, then Catherine bore

ten children in quick succession, almost annually, ending with twin girls, who did not survive, in 1556. Of the rest, four sons and three daughters grew to maturity. When Henry was twenty-nine he fell madly in love with Diane de Poitiers, a married woman of forty-eight. He created her Duchess of Valentinois and she gained and maintained a complete ascendancy over him. In spite of her age, she was far more attractive than the Queen, who was plump and dumpy with a sensual mouth, receding chin and a high forehead framed in curly auburn hair.

Henry's reign was marked by the great growth in power of the house of Guise led by Francis, Duke of Guise, and Charles, Cardinal of Lorraine. The reformed religion was also spreading from Germany and a persecution of French Protestants began. War was pursued with Charles V and ended with the peace of Cateau-Cambrésis signed on 3 April 1559. To celebrate the treaty Henry ordered a round of tournaments in which he himself took part. At one of these on 30 June 1559 the lance of his opponent splintered and a piece of it pierced the King in the eye. The crude surgery of the day only served to aggravate the condition and after ten days of agony he died at the early age of forty on 10 July in the Palais du Tournelles.

Henry's eldest son and successor Francis II was already fifteen and deemed old enough to rule without a regency. He

A full-length portrait of King Henry II of France by François Clouet. The picture hangs in the Uffizi Gallery, Florence.

A splendid portrait of Catherine de'Medici, the powerful Queen Mother of France. By an unknown artist, it hangs in the Palazzo Riccardi, Florence.

was delicate and lacking in spirit and is chiefly remembered as the first husband of Mary, Queen of Scots, to whom he had been married since April 1558. They were greatly attached to each other and Mary, a healthy sensuous girl of great charm, sapped the King's feeble strength still further. She was also more than a match for her scheming mother-in-law Queen Catherine, who hoped to rule through her son. Since Mary had already been anointed and crowned as Queen of Scots it was considered beneath her dignity to be crowned again as a mere Queen Consort of France so she watched her husband's coronation from a tribune in the Cathedral. The persecution of the Protestants continued throughout Francis's short reign and the King and Queen are said to have amused themselves by viewing the hanged corpses of the victims from the battlements of the Château d'Amboise. In November 1560 Francis became seriously ill with headaches and fainting fits and from the description of his symptoms it is clear that he had meningitis. His surgeons carried out an horrific operation of trepanning but could do nothing to save him and he continued screaming unceasingly until death came to him on 5 December 1560. He was just over one month short of completing his seventeenth year.

Francis and Mary had no child and the heir to the throne was his brother Charles who was only ten years old. Queen Catherine demanded and obtained the regency and the senior Prince of the Blood, Antoine de Bourbon, Duke of Vendôme, and husband of the Queen of Navarre, was appointed Lieutenant of the Realm.

The religious wars now began in real earnest. It is estimated that the Protestant faith had been espoused by between two-fifths and one half of the French nobility, augmented by the rising middle class. Only Paris and the north-east of France remained staunchly Catholic. The Huguenots, as the Protestants were called, took up arms to ensure their freedom of worship, and despite several defeats were granted their aim on surrendering four of their fortresses, including La Rochelle. In August 1572, however, the celebrations following the marriage of Charles IX's sister Margaret to Henry of Navarre, the son of Antoine, provided the occasion for a massacre of the Protestants in Paris and throughout the provinces. Henry, himself a Protestant, only saved his life by feigning conversion and the Massacre of St Bartholomew as it is known took a terrible toll, upwards of 15,000 being killed. Catholics were warned to distinguish themselves by wearing a white armband to avoid being slaughtered. It is to Charles IX's everlasting shame that he agreed to the massacre at his mother's bidding. His own gentle wife, Elizabeth of Austria, was horrified by the deed and upbraided him in no uncertain terms and the memory of the horror he had unleashed and his sense of remorse were to remain with him for the rest of his life.

Charles was almost as sickly as his brother Francis had been and succumbed to tuberculosis on 30 May 1574. In his last days he produced a constant bloody sweat and in his delirium fancied that he was surrounded by the blood of those he had ordered to be slain.

Charles's only legitimate child was a girl and he was succeeded by his next brother Henry, who had been elected King of Poland the previous year. Their mother, whose favourite son Henry was, contrived to send a speedy message to inform him of his brother's death and he fled from Poland by night to take up his French inheritance. He was crowned at Rheims on 13 February 1575 and two days later married the charming Louise de Vaudemont, whom he is said to have met and admired in Lorraine in the course of his journey to Poland in 1573.

Henry III is an enigma. He was cultured, well educated, politically astute and physically brave on the one hand; on the other he was extremely effeminate, loving rich clothes, jewels and earrings and delighting in giving entertainments in which he appeared dressed as a woman. He surrounded himself with handsome young male favourites, his *mignons*, whose haughty behaviour alienated many of his subjects. In spite of this, he was on excellent terms with his wife although their prayers and pilgrimages to be vouchsafed a son came to naught. Like his elder brothers he was delicate and of very slight build. His last remaining brother, the Duke of Alençon, was almost as foppish as Henry and is best remembered as the unsuccessful suitor of Queen Elizabeth I of England. The Duke died while campaigning in the Netherlands in June 1584, and in the event of Henry himself dying without having a son the next heir to the throne was his brother-in-law Henry of Navarre, who had again reverted to Protestantism.

Another religious war broke out in 1587 following the news of the execution of Henry's former sister-in-law Mary, Queen of Scots. It was called the War of the Three Henrys, they being Henry III, Henry of Navarre and Henry, Duke of Guise. The Catholic party triumphed and formed a League of Sixteen under the leadership of the Duke of Guise. Its avowed intent was to depose the King, who could not be persuaded to bar Henry of Navarre from the succession, and set Guise on the throne. In May 1588 Guise entered Paris and an insurrection known as the Day of the Barricades forced the King to flee to Blois and summon the States-General to meet there. The lack of support he received made him decide that the only course was to have Guise, who had attended the assembly, eliminated and on 23 December 1588 he was cut down by the King's bodyguard in a room of the Château. Henry came with his ailing mother to view the body of his rival. 'He is greater in death than he was in life,' he said. 'It is not enough to cut,' said Queen Catherine, 'now you must also sew.' She died twelve days later on 5 January 1589, in her seventieth year.

The Duke of Guise's brother, the Duke of Mayenne, at once set out to avenge him. Henry of Navarre's uncle the Cardinal de Bourbon was proclaimed King as Charles X and Henry III was excommunicated by the Pope for the murder of the Cardinal de Lorraine, another brother of Guise and Mayenne. Henry was thus forced to seek the aid of his brother-in-law Henry of Navarre. They met at Plessis-les-Tours in April 1589 and decided to lay siege to Paris, setting up their quarters at St Cloud. The members of the League saw their position was hopeless and in a last desperate attempt to gain an advantage induced a mad monk, Jacques Clément, to assassinate the King. He obtained an audience and, on the pretext of presenting a petition to Henry, stabbed him in the stomach.

The assassin was immediately flung to his death from the window. Henry lingered until the next day before dying of his wound. His last words to Henry of Navarre were: 'My brother, I know well that it is for you to possess the right which I have worked for to keep that which God has given you.' He further exhorted him to change his faith and charged all his officers to acknowledge him as his lawful successor. So the crown of France passed from the Valois to the Bourbons.

The House of Bourbon

HENRY IV THE GREAT   1589–1610

b Pau, Béarn 14 December 1553, 2nd but eldest surviving son of Antoine de Bourbon, 2nd Duke of Vendôme, and Jeanne III (d'Albret), Queen of Navarre; s his father as 3rd Duke of Vendôme 17 November 1562 and his mother as titular King (Henry III) of Navarre 9 June 1572; Governor of Guienne 1576; s King Henry III as King of France 1 August 1589; crowned Chartres 27 February 1594; m (1) Paris 18 August 1572 (m annulled 1599) Margaret (b St Germain-en-Laye 14 May 1553; d Paris 27 March 1615; bur St Denis), 3rd dau of King Henry II; no issue; m (2) proxy Florence 7 October, in person Lyons 17 December 1600, Marie, crowned as Queen Consort St Denis 13 May 1610, Queen Regent of France 1610–17 (b Florence 26 April 1575; d Cologne 4 July 1642; bur St Peter's Church, Cologne), dau of Francis I (de'Medici), Grand Duke of Tuscany, and Johanna of Austria; 3 sons, 3 daus; d (assassinated) Paris 14 May 1610; bur St Denis

LOUIS XIII THE JUST   1610–1643

b Fontainebleau 27 September 1601, eldest son of King Henry IV; s his father 14 May 1610; crowned Rheims 17 October 1610; m proxy Burgos 18 October, in person Bordeaux 24 November 1615, Anne, Queen Regent of France 1643–51 (b Valladolid 22 September 1601; d Paris 20 January 1666; bur St Denis), eldest dau of Philip III, King of Spain, and Margarita of Austria; 2 sons; d St Germain-en-Laye 14 May 1643; bur St Denis

LOUIS XIV THE GREAT   1643–1715

b St Germain-en-Laye 5 September 1638, elder son of King Louis XIII; s his father 14 May 1643; crowned Rheims 7 June 1654; m (1) proxy Fuenterrabia 3 June, in person St Jean-de-Luz 9 June 1660, his double 1st cousin, Marie Thérèse (b Madrid 20 September 1638; d Versailles 30 July 1683; bur St Denis), eldest dau of Philip IV, King of Spain, and his first wife Elisabeth of France (eldest dau of King Henry IV); 3 sons, 3 daus; m (2) (secretly) Versailles ca 12 June 1684 Françoise, Marquise de Maintenon et du Parc (b Niort 27 November 1635; d St Cyr 15 April 1719; bur St Cyr), widow of Paul Scarron and dau of Constantin d'Aubigné, Baron de Surimau, and his 2nd wife Jeanne de Cardillac; d Versailles 1 September 1715; bur St Denis

LOUIS XV THE WELL-LOVED   1715–1774

b Versailles 15 February 1710, 3rd and yst but only surviving son of Louis, Duke of Burgundy and (1711–12) Dauphin of France (eldest son of Louis, Dauphin of France, eldest and only surviving son of King Louis XIV), and Marie Adélaïde of Savoy; s his great-grandfather 1 September 1715; crowned Rheims 25 October 1722; m proxy Strasbourg 15 August, in person Fontainebleau 5 September 1725, Marie (b Poznan 23 June 1703; d Versailles 24 June 1768; bur St Denis), dau of Stanislas I (Leszczynski), King of Poland, later Duke of Lorraine and Bar, and Catherine Opalinska; 2 sons, 8 daus; d Versailles 10 May 1774; bur St Denis

LOUIS XVI   1774–1793

b Versailles 23 August 1754, 3rd but eldest surviving son of Louis, Dauphin of France (elder and only surviving son of King Louis XV), and his second wife Maria Josepha of Saxony; s his grandfather 10 May 1774; crowned Rheims 11 June 1775; m proxy Vienna 19 April, in person Versailles 16 May 1770, Marie Antoinette (b Vienna 2 November 1755; d (guillotined) Paris 16 October 1793; bur Cemetery of the Madeleine, transferred to St Denis 1815), yst dau of Francis I, Holy Roman Emperor, and Maria Theresa, Queen of Hungary and Bohemia, Archduchess of Austria; 2 sons, 2 daus; d (guillotined) Paris 21 January 1793; bur Cemetery of the Madeleine, transferred St Denis 1815

LOUIS XVII   1793–1795

b Versailles 27 March 1785, yr but only surviving son of King Louis XVI; theoretically succeeded his father 21 January 1793, but never reigned; said to have d in prison in the Temple, Paris, 8 June 1795; bur Cemetery of St Marguerite

LOUIS XVIII   (1795) 1814–1824

b Versailles 17 November 1755, 4th son of Louis, Dauphin of France (elder and only surviving son of King Louis XV), and his second wife Maria Josepha of Saxony; proclaimed King of France and Navarre (in exile) at Mühlheim, Baden, 16 June 1795 after receiving the report of the death of his nephew King Louis XVII; restored April 1814; again in exile March–June 1815; m proxy Turin 21 April, in person Versailles 14 May 1771, Marie Josephine (b Turin 2 September 1753; d Hartwell, nr Aylesbury, Buckinghamshire, 13 November 1810; bur Westminster Abbey, transferred Cagliari 1811), 2nd dau of Victor Amadeus III, King of Sardinia, and Maria Antonietta of Spain; no issue; d Tuileries, Paris 16 September 1824; bur St Denis

CHARLES X   1824–1830

b Versailles 9 October 1757, 5th and yst son of Louis, Dauphin of France (elder and only surviving son of King Louis XV), and his second wife Maria Josepha of Saxony; s his brother King Louis XVIII 16 September 1824; crowned Rheims 29 May 1825; abdicated 2

August 1830 (confirmed 27 November 1830); *m* proxy Moncalieri 24 October, in person Versailles 16 November 1773, Marie Thérèse (*b* Turin 31 January 1756; *d* Graz 2 June 1805; *bur* Graz, transferred St Denis 1814), 3rd dau of Victor Amadeus III, King of Sardinia, and Maria Antonietta of Spain; 2 sons, 2 daus; *d* Schloss Graffenberg, Gorizia, 6 November 1836; *bur* Castagnavizza, nr Gorizia

Henry IV, King of France and Navarre. A superb portrait of le vert galant at the height of his glory.

Henry IV, the first King of the House of Bourbon, derived his claim to the throne through his descent from Robert, Count of Clermont, the youngest son of St Louis, but was also his predecessor's second cousin (as the grandson of Francis I's sister Margaret) and brother-in-law (as the husband of another Margaret, daughter of Henry II). He was without a doubt to become one of France's greatest and best-loved Kings and as a popular folk hero the subject of many affectionate anecdotes. Henry began his reign by having to overcome the Catholic League and renounce the Protestant faith, giving rise to his famous remark that 'Paris is worth a mass'. Once established on his throne, he proved a wise and benevolent ruler and set about the work of reconstruction required after the devastating forty years of the Religious Wars. In appearance, Henry was well built and moderately handsome, with a large nose, ruddy complexion, and sporting a large square beard. In his portraits he has a somewhat cynical but kindly expression which one sees again in the portraits of his grandson King Charles II of England. He was, however, careless about personal hygiene and often had a rank goatlike smell about him. In spite of this he was highly successful with the ladies and is reputed to have

had fifty-six mistresses, by several of whom he fathered large families of bastards whom he lovingly acknowledged and ennobled. His marriage to Margaret of Valois was not a happy one as they were quite unsuited temperamentally although they remained good friends. Queen Margot, as she was known, resembled her mother Queen Catherine in appearance, and was almost as sensual as Henry, taking many lovers. The couple were childless and Henry was anxious to obtain an annulment of the marriage in order to marry his most famous mistress Gabrielle d'Estrées and legitimate her children, but the suit was a protracted affair and before it was over and to Henry's great grief Gabrielle died suddenly in April 1599. He then contemplated marriage to another of his mistresses, Henriette Catherine de Balzac d'Entragues, and even wrote to her father promising to marry her should she bear him a son. However, his chief minister the Duc de Sully had other ideas for him and when the desired annulment had been achieved, arranged a marriage with the Florentine Marie de'Medici, a distant relation of Queen Catherine. Known as 'the fat banker', the new Queen was far from attractive but she did her duty by Henry and produced many children. At the same time he maintained his ménage with Henriette, who also presented him with children, as did several other ladies subsequently. All the children, legitimate and illegitimate, were brought up together.

In 1610 Henry was in his fifty-seventh year and, although in excellent health and as vigorous as ever, foresaw the possibility of a regency in the future as his eldest legitimate son and heir, the Dauphin Louis, was only eight. He therefore determined on having Queen Marie crowned so that her position would be unassailable. The last coronation of a Queen of France took place at St Denis on 13 May 1610. The next day the King set out in his coach, with several companions but no guards, to visit Sully, who was lying ill at the Arsenal. The coach was held up when a pig and a handcart blocked the way at the corner of the rue de la Ferronerie, giving the opportunity for a crazed religious fanatic, François Ravaillac, to rush up to the coach, which had open sides, and stab the King twice with a dagger. The King's aorta was severed and Henry died almost immediately without speaking. The coach returned with all speed to the Louvre, where a post mortem revealed that Henry's organs were in a very healthy state and he might well have lived another twenty years. Ravaillac suffered for his crime after a hasty trial and his true motivation was never made clear.

The regency of Queen Marie which lasted effectively until 1617 was a bad time for France. The Queen replaced Sully by the Italian Concini, the husband of her foster-sister Leonora Galigaï. The move was unpopular with the Princes of the Blood and the nobility who formed a league to oppose the crown. Concini placated them by granting pensions which beggared the treasury and a States General had to be summoned in 1614 to look into the matter. Louis officially came of age that year but it was not until 1617 that the arrest and murder of Concini and the banishment of the Queen Mother to Blois enabled him to assume the government.

Relations between the fat, indolent and stupid Marie and

her son had always been bad and there seems to have been no natural affection between them. He had been a morose and backward child, probably because of a speech impediment caused by the fact that he had to have the frenum of his tongue cut before he could speak at all. His daily doings for the first twenty-six years of his life were minutely chronicled by his physician Jean Héroard so that more is known about his childhood and young manhood than that of any previous King. His portrait by Pourbus painted when he was fifteen depicts a rather plump but not unattractive boy. As he grew older he became thinner and anxious looking. He did not retain power in his own hands for very long, entrusting all affairs of state to his favourite the Duke of Luynes, after whose death in 1621 they passed into the able hands of Cardinal Richelieu. At first a favourite of the Queen Mother, who had regained her position of power, Richelieu completely supplanted her in 1624 and remained in control until his death in 1642.

For political reasons, Marie and Concini had negotiated the King's marriage to Anne of Austria in November 1615 when both parties were fourteen. Louis does not appear to have been a very physical person and strenuously resisted the attempts made by his mother to get him to consummate the marriage, although he claimed that he had 'performed twice' on his wedding night. Anne was seemingly no keener than he was and for twenty years they led separate lives. There were rumours of the King's homosexuality and the Queen's affair with the Duke of Buckingham, but both are unsubstantiated. At last, on a stormy night in December 1637 the King, who had been hunting, was forced to seek shelter at the Queen's

Louis XIV as a child: a contemporary painting showing him wearing the Order of the Holy Ghost, the principal French Order of Knighthood founded by Henry III in 1578 and superseding that of St Michael founded by Louis XI.

residence. They slept together for the first time in many years and the result was the birth of the future Louis XIV in September 1638. Two years later the Queen conceived again and her second son Philip, later the Duke of Orleans, was born.

Louis had always been delicate and in May 1643 he died of tuberculosis, aged forty-one, leaving the throne to his elder son Louis, destined to become France's best-remembered King.

Louis XIV was in his fifth year when he ascended the throne under the regency of his mother Anne of Austria. The real power was in the hands of Cardinal Mazarin, the apt pupil of Richelieu. Although a Cardinal he was reputed to be the lover of the Queen Mother. He practised nepotism on a large scale and his many nieces (nicknamed the 'Mazarinettes') were brought to France from their native Italy and married off to rich and noble husbands. One of them, Marie Mancini, became the first love of the King himself and at one time even seemed likely to become Queen.

Louis XIV was the most prominent figure on the European stage throughout his long reign of seventy-two years. He was the personification of kingship, 'Le Roi Soleil', surrounded by his satellites. It is impossible to do justice to him within the limitations of a book such as this. Dignified, gracious, exquisitely polite, he was endowed with the taste which constructed the vast and magnificent Palace of Versailles, a

Louis XIII with allegorical figures representing France and Navarre: a portrait by Simon Vouet at Versailles.

monument to absolute monarchy which all contemporary European sovereigns strove to imitate.

Louis was married for political reasons to his cousin Marie Thérèse of Austria, the daughter of King Philip IV of Spain. She was dull and rather plain and it is doubtful if he ever loved her, although he always treated her with the utmost consideration and respect as he did all women. She bore six children, of whom only one survived infancy. There is a legend that one of her children, a daughter, was born black, the explanation given being that the Queen had been 'frightened' by a black page who had jumped out from behind a curtain during the early stages of her pregnancy. This child, it is said, did not die but was taken away to be brought up in a convent, a dead child being substituted in its place. The King's sister-in-law the Duchess of Orleans, known as Liselotte, whose very outspoken letters give us an entertaining account of court life, utterly refuted the story.

Louis is well known for his many mistresses. The two best remembered are Louise de la Vallière, who retired from court to become a nun after giving the King five children; and Françoise Athénais de Rochechouart-Mortemart, Marquise de Montespan, a frighteningly sinister woman who dabbled in witchcraft and practised the black arts in order to bind the King to her even more closely. She gave him eight children. All Louis's surviving natural children were recognized by him, legitimated, and well provided for.

Queen Marie Thérèse died in 1683, her death it is said

being the only trouble she ever caused the King. The following year Louis made a surprising second marriage which took place in secret and was never openly acknowledged although the whole court knew about it. The lady was already forty-eight, three years older than the King, and had been governess to his children by Madame de Montespan. Madame Françoise Scarron, *née* d'Aubigné, belonged to a family of minor nobility. In 1688 the King created her Marquise de Maintenon et du Parc, and it is as Madame de Maintenon that she is best known. Although never Queen in name, she enjoyed all the privileges of a Queen of France, remaining seated in the presence of the Princes of the Blood and being treated in every respect as the King's wife. She was deeply religious and influenced the King's mind into more religious ways of thought in his latter years. Louis preserved his virility well into his old age and when Madame de Maintenon was over seventy she used to complain that she found her husband's insistence on intercourse every night very fatiguing.

Louis lived so long that he survived his son, Louis, 'le Grand Dauphin', a gross man of somewhat unpleasant habits who once had his ears boxed by his aunt the Duchess of Orleans when he made a fist with his hand in the seat of a chair she was just about to sit on. He had been married to the very ugly and grumbling Bavarian Princess Marie Anne Christine Victoire (always known in cumbersome style by these four names). She gave him three sons and died unlamented in 1690. A year or two later the Dauphin emulated his father by

Louis XIV with three generations of his descendants. The Grand Dauphin is lolling on the back of his father's chair and the Duke of Burgandy stands on the right. The baby is not the future Louis XV, but one of his elder brothers who died young. It would have been nice if it had been Madame de Maintenon holding the leading-strings, but it is the Duchesse de Ventadour, the official gouvernante. Busts of Henry IV and Louis XIII look down on the scene and one nosy little dog is just bustling around the corner to see what the other is yapping about.

contracting a secret marriage with Marie-Emilie Joly de Choin, a lady-in-waiting to his half-sister the Princess of Conti. If the Duchess of Orleans is to be believed, the lady was no beauty, 'was of very small stature; had very short legs, large rolling eyes, a round face, a short turned-up nose, and a large mouth filled with decayed teeth'. There were no children of this union and in April 1711 the Dauphin fell ill with smallpox and died at the Château de Meudon, aged forty-nine. His eldest son Louis, Duke of Burgundy, who was married to the enchanting Princess Marie Adélaïde of Savoy, succeeded as Dauphin, but like his father succumbed to smallpox in less than a year, dying at Versailles in February 1712, six days after his wife had died of the same disease. They had had three sons, but the eldest had died in 1705, so that the second now became Dauphin at the age of five but only held the title for a few days before smallpox carried him off, too, leaving the youngest son, a two year old, as the heir of his great-grandfather.

Louis XIV's robust health remained unimpaired until within a year of his death, when physical and mental weakness began to overcome him. He suffered from prolonged attacks of gout and constipation and lost his hitherto hearty appetite. Eventually his gouty legs became ulcerated and gangrenous and he died after two agonising weeks on 1 September 1715, four days before his seventy-seventh birthday. His last words were: 'O God, help me. Haste Thou to succour me.' Madame de Maintenon, who was at his bedside when he died, retired to her religious foundation of St Louis at St Cyr and died there in April 1719.

Louis XV succeeded his great-grandfather at the age of five. As his uncle Philip had become King of Spain and his other uncle Charles, Duke of Berry, had died as the result of a fall from his horse while hunting in the previous year, the regency passed to the next senior Prince of the Blood, Philip, Duke of Orleans, grandson of Louis XIII, and son of the outspoken Duchess we have already met. He was also married to one of the legitimated daughters of Louis XIV and Madame de Montespan. The Regent was intelligent and cultured, although dissolute in his private life. He was greatly influenced by Cardinal Dubois and in 1718 backed the Scottish banker John Law who had floated companies to promote the French colonies in Africa and America. The outcome was a financial collapse in 1720, ruining many people.

Louis XV came of age in February 1723 and asked the former Regent to continue in office as his chief minister. Orleans died suddenly while visiting his mistress the Duchess of Falari on 2 December and Louis replaced him by the Duke of Bourbon, another Prince of the Blood. The young King was extremely handsome and the Persian ambassador said he 'was like Adonis reborn, of noble bearing, of a splendid height, his limbs ideally proportioned; from his almond-shaped eyes a gentle look would captivate all those who approached him'. He had been affianced at an early age to his cousin the Infanta Mariana Victoria of Spain (later to become Queen of Portugal), but she was still too young for marriage and, Louis being fifteen, it was felt desirable that he should marry at

A pastel study of Louis XV by Maurice Quentin de la Tour in the Musée de St Quentin.

Queen Marie Leszczynska standing before a bust of her husband Louis XV and pretending to be arranging flowers. The little dog is surely a descendant of the one in the picture of Louis XIV and his descendants. This beautiful portrait by C van Loo is at Versailles.

once. The chosen bride, almost seven years his senior, was Marie Leszczynska, whose father had been elected King of Poland and after occupying that throne twice for short periods, had been recompensed by being made reigning Duke of Lorraine and Bar for life. Louis was instructed in the part he had to play as a bridegroom by being shown explicit diagrams and learnt the lesson so well that he had ten children by the Queen by the time he was twenty-seven. Queen Marie has left little impression on history. She was modest, shy and retiring and in spite of the age difference, Louis was completely satisfied with her until she made the firm decision after the birth of her tenth child to discontinue marital relations for the sake of her health. It was from this point that the King began his pursuit of other ladies for which he is best remembered today.

He has been credited with a vast number of natural children, but he only recognized one and the claims of most of the others can be disproved or at least remain unsubstantiated. In fact Louis took steps to ensure that he was not burdened with a large progeny, for it has recently been discovered that he ordered condoms by the gross from England, where they were made from the gut of small animals. His best-known mistress was Madame de Pompadour, who held sway for nineteen years until her death in 1764 and provided the King with a constant flow of young girls to satisfy his needs and make amends for her own frigidity. Four years after Madame de Pompadour's death a new favourite rose in the person of Madame du Barry, a rather common, vulgar woman, who was loathed by the King's daughters and most of the court but managed to retain her hold until Louis died.

Louis was also greatly attached to his four unmarried daughters, Mesdames Adélaïde, Victoire, Sophie and Louise. The youngest found a religious vocation and became a Carmelite nun, but the other three remained at court and earned a reputation for being rather fast and dashing. There were some ugly rumours of incestuous relationships with their father and Madame Adélaïde was even credited with having had a child by him, but the whole thing can be proved a malicious rumour put about by the leaders of the unrest which was growing throughout the country. During Louis XV's reign France was involved in the War of the Polish Succession followed closely by the War of the Austrian Succession, in the course of which Louis led his army, at the battle of Fontenoy in 1745, being the last King of France to do so in person.

Queen Marie died in June 1768. In 1747 she had had to accept as her daughter-in-law Marie Josèphe of Saxony, the daughter of her own father's successful rival for the throne of Poland, but the girl behaved with such tact that the Queen was completely won over. Marie Josèphe had she lived would have made an excellent Queen and with her concern for people's well-being might well have delayed the Revolution. But it was not to be, for the Dauphin died of consumption in 1765 and the Dauphine followed him eighteen months later in March 1767. Three of her sons were to sit on the throne. Louis XV was taken ill with a high fever while staying with Madame du Barry at the Grand Trianon. He returned to Versailles on his doctor's advice and in a few days smallpox

Louis XVI: a fine engraving by Benri from a portrait by Collet.

developed, carrying him off on 10 May 1774.

The new King was Louis XVI, the eldest surviving son of the late Dauphin and consequently Louis XV's grandson. He was a solemn, solid young man with a bull-neck and bulging eyes, taking after his Saxon mother. His tastes were simple and he liked nothing better than working as a locksmith and hunting. He had been well educated and was blessed with a very beautiful young Queen, the legendary Marie Antoinette of Austria, and the beginning of the new reign seemed full of brilliant promise. The King's marriage to the Austrian Archduchess had taken place in 1770, when he was in his sixteenth and she in her fifteenth year, but it had still not been consummated when they ascended the throne. The reason for this was a physical disability. The King loved the Queen dearly but he suffered from a medical condition (phimosis) which made full intercourse impossible. The remedy was circumcision, but Louis feared the knife and it took a visit from his brother-in-law the Emperor Joseph II to persuade him at last to undergo the necessary surgery. Once this had been done, all went well and the royal couple's first child, a daughter, was born in December 1778, to be followed in due course by two boys and another girl.

The Palace of Versailles, painted by
J B Martin in 1722. This gives a good
impression of the vast complex of buildings
erected by Louis XIV of France.

Louis XVI of France and his family, a
charming group.

Albert I, King of the Belgians, on horseback.

Queen Juliana of the Netherlands: a photographic study of the former Queen wearing some of the magnificent jewellery which formed part of the dowry of Grand Duchess Anna Pavlovna of Russia when she married the future King William II.

Queen Beatrix of the Netherlands with her husband Prince Claus and their three sons, Prince William Alexander, Prince Constantine and Prince (Johan) Friso.

Frederiksborg Castle, from a painting by P C Skorgaard in 1891. Frederiksborg was a favourite residence of the Danish Kings.

Marie Antoinette was a thoughtless, empty-headed creature and a great pleasure-lover. Her extravagances, her love of playing shepherdess with the Princess de Lamballe and her other ladies at the Petit Trianon and her seeming indifference to the poverty of the people which was rife, all served to render her unpopular. As the true daughter of her mother the Empress Maria Theresa, she was not afraid to meddle in politics and dictate to the King, who adored her and was persuaded to dismiss his chief minister Turgot at her behest. It is not within the scope of this book to recount the events leading to the Revolution of 1789. On 5 May that year the King was compelled to summon a States General, the first since 1616, with the object of establishing a constitutional monarchy to replace the old royal absolutism. The King and Queen were desperately worried at the time by the health of their elder son, the seven-year-old Dauphin, who died on 4 June. On 14 July the storming of the Bastille took place and the commander of the National Guard compelled the King to don the red, white and blue tricolour. On 4 August the National Assembly abolished all feudal rights and the privileges of the nobility. Louis was haled as the 'Restorer of French Liberty' on 13 August and all might have gone well had he not attempted to gather his forces at Versailles with the probable intention of attempting a coup. Getting wind of this, a large mob marched from Paris to Versailles on 6 October and dragged the King and Queen back to Paris, where they were confined in the Tuileries. On 9 November the Assembly proclaimed Louis 'by the Grace of God and the constitutional law of the State, King of the French', but he and his family remained virtual prisoners. On the anniversary of the storming of the Bastille, 14 July 1790, the King was forced to attend a festival celebration on the Champ de Mars and swear an oath to the Constitution.

After another year Louis could stand the situation no longer and determined on making a bid to escape. On the night of 20–21 June 1791, he, the Queen, their surviving son and daughter, and his sister Madame Elisabeth, left the Tuileries in a large coach and set off towards freedom. The news of their flight was soon made known and a force despatched after them with a warrant for the King's arrest. The party was apprehended at Varennes and brought back to Paris where they were again imprisoned in the Tuileries and the Assembly suspended the King from exercising his constitutional powers. They decided, however, to retain him as King and after amending the Constitution restored his powers when he agreed to swear a new oath to it in September.

Not long afterwards the Constituent Assembly was dissolved and replaced by a Legislative Assembly of entirely new men. The royal powers were again suspended in August 1792 and the King and his family were removed to the Temple prison after the Tuileries had been pillaged by the mob. The Legislative Assembly gave place in its turn to a National Convention, whose first act was to declare royalty abolished on 21 September 1792. Not content with this, they sought a way to rid themselves of the King for good and the discovery that he had been carrying on a correspondence with emigrés provided the excuse to try him for treason to the state. The

trial lasted for several weeks, but its outcome was a foregone conclusion and on 20 January 1793, Louis was condemned to death, his kinsman the Duke of Orleans being one of those who voted for the death penalty. The next day he bade farewell to the Queen, his children and his sister and was taken in a tumbril to the Place de la Concorde, where he died bravely on the guillotine. 'Frenchmen, I die innocent', he said to the crowd, 'and I pray to God that my blood will not fall upon my people.'

Back at the Temple as soon as the drum rolls told them that Louis XVI was dead, the Queen and her sister-in-law stood the seven-year-old Dauphin on a chair and curtseyed to their new King Louis XVII. Louis XVI's brother, the Count of Provence, had managed to escape in 1791 and was at Hamm in Westphalia when he received the news of his brother's death. He at once proclaimed his nephew King and assumed the regency in his name, being recognized by Great Britain, Sardinia, Spain, Austria, Prussia and Russia.

In Paris the Convention decided to get rid of the Queen, too, and a horrible charge of incest with her little son was concocted against her. The innocent child, who was now eight, was made to say things which he could not understand and Marie Antoinette, whose regal dignity and bearing never deserted her, was inevitably found guilty and sentenced to death, suffering as her husband had done on 16 October 1793. Her sister-in-law Madame Elisabeth suffered the same fate in the following May and Louis XVII was separated from his sister and put into the care of a sinister couple named Simon. It was

An amusing aquatint after Rosenberg of King Louis XVIII.

alleged that he died in the Temple on 8 June 1795, but there was a strong suspicion that another boy was substituted for him and in years to come there were to be many pretenders claiming to be the 'little Dauphin'. The descendants of some of them still maintain claims to the French throne today. Louis XVI's sole surviving child, Marie Thérèse, was finally released and allowed to join her uncle. Her life was a tragic one and we shall hear of her again.

When the Count of Provence heard of his nephew's death he at once proclaimed himself King as Louis XVIII. He greatly resembled his brother Louis XVI although grosser and heavier. He, too, had been well educated and loved literature and poetry. He was married in his fifteenth year in 1771 to Marie Josephine of Savoy, two years his senior. She was alarmingly ugly with black beetle brows and it is almost certain that the marriage was never consummated. The Count of Provence, as he then was, probably suffered from the same physical defect as Louis XVI, but never took the trouble to have it corrected as his brother had done. He did have a mistress, but contented himself with the rather bizarre habit of taking snuff from her bare back. There were also romantic attachments to handsome young men. The neglected Josephine consoled herself with strong drink and girls.

After effecting his escape from Paris in 1791, Louis had become something of a wanderer, moving from Brussels to Koblenz, to Hamm, to Verona, to Blankenburg, to Mitau, to Warsaw, back to Mitau, and finally to England in 1808, where he settled down at Hartwell House, near Aylesbury, living very comfortably and enjoying the patronage of the English court, which of course recognized him as King of France. Queen Josephine, who accompanied him in spite of their indifference to each other, died at Hartwell in November 1810 and was accorded a funeral and temporary resting place in Westminster Abbey before her body was returned to her native Italy.

In April 1814 the victory of the Allies brought about Louis's restoration. He landed at Calais on 24 April and entered Paris on 3 May. While asserting that he ruled by divine right, he bowed to pressure put upon him to grant a charter setting up a constitutional monarchy based on that of Great Britain. The treaty of Paris signed on 30 May was extremely favourable to France. The boundaries of 1792 were restored plus Avignon, Savoy, Venaissin and other territories which had not been French possessions in 1789; Britain restored the French colonies overseas, with the exception of Tobago, St Lucia and Mauritius; all claims for war indemnity were set aside; and France undertook to abolish the slave trade. The Congress of Vienna was set up in September 1814 to remodel Europe, but its deliberations were interrupted in March 1815 when news of Napoleon's escape from exile in Elba were received. French troops were despatched against him but they defected at Auxerre opening up the way to Paris for the former Emperor. Louis was again obliged to flee during the night of 19–20 March and set up a provisional government at Ghent. The defeat of Napoleon at Waterloo in June brought the King back to Paris again. He made his re-entry on 8 July and thereafter reigned uninterruptedly until his death. Because his size and

affliction with gout made all movement cumbersome for him, the King decided to forego the rite of coronation, the first King of France to do so. Louis died at the age of sixty-eight on 16 September 1824 after prolonged suffering almost identical to that undergone by Louis XIV.

Charles X: one of the series of portraits painted by Sir Thomas Lawrence for the Prince Regent after the end of the Napoleonic Wars.

Charles X was a very different man from his two elder brothers. Tall, slim, handsome and debonair, he had, as Count of Artois, led a life devoted to pleasure in the days before the Revolution. He was married at sixteen to Marie Thérèse of Savoy, eighteen months older than himself and almost as ugly as her sister the wife of Louis XVIII. He managed to do his duty by her and she produced four children in due course. The two girls both died young, but two sturdy boys survived. Charles had the sex drive lacking in his elder brothers and compensated for his wife's lack of charm by conducting a number of amours, being particularly partial to actresses. In 1784 he began an affair with Madame de Polastron, a sister-in-law of Marie Antoinette's favourite the Duchess de Polignac, and she was to accompany him into exile and retain a great influence over him for the next twenty years.

Charles's complete hostility to any reform had caused Louis XVI to suggest that he should leave France, which he did in July 1789, a few days after the storming of the Bastille. He first went to his father-in-law's court at Turin and later joined his brother the Count of Provence at Koblenz and then at Hamm, eventually establishing himself in London. His wife, Marie

Thérèse, did not accompany him and died at Klagenfurth in Carinthia in June 1805. The same year saw the death of Madame de Polastron in London. On her deathbed she made Charles swear to amend his ways and draw closer to God and thenceforth he became a different man, leading a strictly moral life and practising religion to a point bordering on bigotry.

Of Charles's two sons, the elder, Louis, Duke of Angoulême, married his cousin Marie Thérèse, the only surviving daughter of Louis XVI and Marie Antoinette. The harsh treatment she had received as a girl in prison in Paris was said to have rendered her sterile, so there were no children of the marriage which was not a terribly happy one. There is even a story that she was not the true daughter of Louis and his Queen, but an illegitimate daughter of Louis, born as the result of a 'test' of his virility, who took the place of her half-sister who went into voluntary exile wishing only to lead a quiet, peaceful life. A mysterious lady known as '*Die Dunkelgräfin*' (the obscure countess), lived for many years under the protection of the Duke of Saxe-Hildburghausen and was never seen in public unveiled. She is alleged to have been the real Marie Thérèse. It is a mystery on a par with those of the man in the iron mask, Kaspar Hauser, and the lost Dauphin.

Charles's younger son, Charles Ferdinand, Duke of Berry, was an attractive young man of great promise. While in England he formed a liaison with a girl of respectable family named Amy Brown. It was later claimed that he had married her at Kensington in 1804, but no evidence was forthcoming. Several children were born to Amy, but only two daughters were acknowledged by the Duke and ennobled by Louis XVIII in 1820. (The elder was the great-great-grandmother of Anne-Aymone Sauvage de Brantes, the wife of Valéry Giscard d'Estaing, recently President of the French Republic.) Berry was married in 1816 to the delightful Princess Caroline of Naples with whom he was very happy. Their first two children, a girl and then a boy, died at birth, but in 1819 a healthy girl was born. In February 1820 the Duchess was again pregnant when the couple attended a performance at the Paris Opera House. On leaving the Duke was stabbed by a deranged fanatic named Louvel. He was carried back into the Opera House and died a few hours later cradled in his wife's arms. The future of France hung on the outcome of Caroline's pregnancy and on 28 September 1820 she gave birth to a son to the unspeakable joy of the King and her father-in-law.

The child, '*l'enfant du miracle*', who received Dieudonné (Godgiven) as one of his baptismal names, was destined never to reign. Charles X was determined to show the world that he reigned by divine right. No one better than he exemplified the well known maxim that the Bourbons 'had learnt nothing and forgotten nothing'. He arranged every meticulous detail of his coronation at Rheims, which took place with great pomp and all the traditional ceremonies on 29 May 1825. It was to be the last coronation of a King of France. The King, who was popular at first, soon alienated the goodwill of his subjects by imposing a tight censorship on the press, compensating returned emigrés and favouring the church.

In July 1830, acting on the advice of his chief minister Polignac, the King illegally dissolved the newly elected Chamber of Deputies, refusing to accept government by the opposition who had gained a majority. He ordered new elections to take place in September, but his high-handed conduct cost him his throne. A revolt broke out on 28 July and once again Paris saw barricades in the streets. The King had hoped that the recent conquest of Algeria would have boosted his popularity, but it was not so and on 2 August he and his elder son were forced to abdicate their rights in favour of the little duke of Bordeaux, son of the murdered Berry. The child, theoretically Henry V, never reigned and went into exile with the rest of the royal family. His heroic mother conducted a campaign on his behalf in the Vendée, but it came to naught when she fell in love with Ettore Lucchesi-Palli, an Italian nobleman, and became pregnant by him, thus completely alienating herself from the royal family. She married Ettore the following year and lived happily with him for many years, producing a large second family. Charles X was assigned the Palace of Holyroodhouse in Edinburgh as a residence by the British crown, but he found the Scottish climate trying and in 1832 moved to Prague, where he stayed until 1836, when he moved to Schloss Graffenberg at Gorizia. He had not been there long when he contracted cholera and died on 6 November 1836, aged seventy-nine. It is one of those curious coincidences of history that the direct line of the Capetians, the direct line of the Valois and the direct line of the Bourbons all ended with the reigns of three brothers in succession.

The House of Bourbon-Orleans

LOUIS PHILIPPE I 1830–1848

---

b Palais Royal, Paris, 6 October 1773, eldest son of Louis Philippe, Duke of Orleans, and Louise Marie Adélaïde of Bourbon-Penthièvre; styled Duke of Valois 1773–85, Duke of Chartres 1785–93; *s* his father as Duke of Orleans 6 November 1793; granted qualification of Royal Highness by King Charles X 21 September 1824; appointed Lieutenant-General of the Realm by the Chambers 31 July (confirmed 1 August) 1830; proclaimed King of the French 7 August 1830; took the oath at Chartres 9 August 1830; abdicated 24 February 1848; *m* Palermo 25 November 1809 Marie Amélie (*b* Caserta 26 April 1782; *d* Claremont House, Esher, Surrey, 24 March 1866, *bur* Weybridge, transferred to Dreux 1876), 6th dau of Ferdinand I, King of the Two Sicilies, and Maria Carolina of Austria (sister of Queen Marie Antoinette); 6 sons, 4 daus; *d* Claremont House, Esher, Surrey, 26 August 1850; *bur* Weybridge, transferred to Dreux 1876.

On 7 August 1830 the Chamber of Deputies voted for a continuation of the monarchy under the Duke of Orleans, who had been appointed Lieutenant-General of the Realm with Charles X's approval on 31 July. He was to reign not as King of France and Navarre, but as King of the French, the title which had been borne for a short while by Louis XVI as constitutional sovereign. Louis Philippe was nearly fifty-seven and had a pear-shaped face surrounded by a mass of dark curly hair and side whiskers. He was a godsend to cartoonists.

As the son of the Duke of Orleans who had voted for the death of Louis XVI and later suffered on the scaffold himself, Louis Philippe had led a hazardous and adventurous early life. He was educated by his father's mistress, the celebrated bluestocking Madame de Genlis, and served in the army until his commanding officer Dumouriez defected to the Austrians. Being unwilling to serve in a foreign army, he went to Switzerland and for a time found employment as a schoolmaster. His virtual desertion from the army was a contributory cause to his father's downfall and execution and the arrest of his two younger brothers, who were imprisoned at Marseilles under conditions of great hardship. From Switzerland he went to Hamburg, thence to Lapland, and then to America, where his brothers joined him after their release. In 1800 they joined the French emigrés in London. Their sufferings in prison had ruined the health of the brothers. Antoine, Duke of Montpensier, died near Windsor in 1807 and as the youngest brother, the Count of Beaujolais, was also suffering from tuberculosis, Louis Philippe accompanied him to Malta in a vain attempt to regain his health. Beaujolais died there in May 1808 and Louis Philippe was invited to visit Sicily as the guest of King Ferdinand. He fell in love with the King's daughter Marie Amélie and they were married after some parental opposition. The couple were well suited and remained devoted to one another throughout a long married life, being blessed with ten children.

After the restoration of the monarchy in 1814 the Duke and Duchess of Orleans and their family returned to France, but they were not popular with Louis XVIII, who obliged them to live in England for two years. They returned to France in 1817. Charles X was fond of his cousin and the family was fully restored to favour during his reign. Louis Philippe's attitude during the Revolution of 1830 is a puzzling one. He was charged by Charles X to proclaim the little Duke of Bordeaux King, but did nothing about it and, as we have seen, disloyally allowed the Chamber to elect him King instead.

In spite of being dubbed 'the citizen King', Louis Philippe aspired to authoritarian rule as much as any of his predecessors and there were various conspiracies to overthrow his government and several assassination attempts which proved abortive. The King's greatest assets were his charmingly sympathetic and gracious Queen and their five handsome and dashing sons, the Duke of Orleans, the Duke of Nemours, the Prince of Joinville, the Duke of Aumâle and the Duke of Montpensier, who all distinguished themselves in different ways. The Prince of Joinville, who served in the French navy, was sent to St Helena to bring the body of Napoleon back to France for reburial at Les Invalides in 1840; the Duke of Aumâle was a noted historian; and the Duke of Montpensier became the husband of the Infanta Luisa Fernanda, sister of Queen Isabel II of Spain. Louis Philippe's eldest daughter became the first Queen of the Belgians, and the youngest, Clementine, married to Prince Augustus of Saxe-Coburg and Gotha, was destined to become the mother of the first King of Bulgaria in modern times. The King's eldest son, Ferdinand, Duke of Orleans, was married to

Queen Victoria and Prince Albert visiting Louis Philippe and Queen Marie Amélie at Château d'Eu in 1845. This group was painted by Winterhalter and includes many members of the French royal family.

Princess Hélène of Mecklenburg-Schwerin in 1837, but lost his life in a carriage accident in 1842, leaving two young sons.

Although the first half of the reign was politically unstable, the monarchy seemed to be well established until the close of 1847, when the opposition demanded electoral reforms which the chief minister Guizot refused to consider. The banning of a dinner to be held by the reform movement on 21 February 1848 provoked a slight riot which soon grew into a formidable insurrection. The King offered to change the ministry and yield to popular demands, but things had gone too far and his abdication in favour of his nine-year-old grandson and namesake on 24 February came too late. The King and Queen were obliged to make an ignominious flight from Paris in a hackney carriage under the pseudonyms of Mr and Mrs William Smith. They eventually reached the coast, took ship for England and landed at Newhaven on 3 March 1848. Their son-in-law the King of the Belgians put his house Claremont at their disposal and the royal pair lived there for the rest of their lives, the King dying in 1850 and the Queen in 1866.

French legitimists discounted the reign of Louis Philippe, regarding the Duke of Bordeaux as the rightful King Henry V. When he died childless in 1883, however, the majority of his followers accepted Louis Philippe's grandson as his successor and styled him King Philip VII. The present claimant to the French throne is the eighty-year-old Count of Paris – King Henry VI to his followers – who in 1987 took part with the President of the French Republic in celebrations marking the millennium of the succession of his ancestor Hugh Capet.

Belgium and Holland

The Kings of the Belgians

LEOPOLD I   1831–1865

b Coburg 16 December 1790, 3rd surviving son of Francis, Duke of Saxe-Coburg-Saalfeld, and Augusta Reuss-Ebersdorf; elected King of the Belgians 4 June 1831, accepted the throne conditionally 26 June and definitively 12 July 1831; entered Brussels and took the oath to the Constitution 21 July 1831; *m* (1) Carlton House, London, 2 May 1816 Charlotte Augusta (*b* Carlton House 7 January 1796; *d* Claremont House, Esher, Surrey, 6 November 1817; *bur* St George's Chapel, Windsor), only child of George, Prince Regent of Great Britain (later King George IV), and Caroline of Brunswick; 1 son (stillborn); *m* (2) Compiègne 9 August 1832 Louise Marie (*b* Palermo 3 April 1812; *d* Ostende 11 October 1850; *bur* Laeken), eldest dau of Louis Philippe I, King of the French, and Marie Amélie of Bourbon-Two Sicilies; 3 sons, 1 dau; *d* Laeken 10 December 1865; *bur* Laeken

LEOPOLD II   1865–1909

b Brussels 9 April 1835, 3rd but eldest surviving son of King Leopold I and 2nd son by his 2nd wife; *s* his father 10 December 1865; took the oath to the Constitution 17 December 1865; Sovereign of the Free State of the Congo 1 August 1885 (ceded to Belgium 1908); *m* (1) Brussels 22 August 1853 Marie Henriette (*b* Pesth 23 August 1836; *d* Spa 19 September 1902; *bur* Laeken), yst dau of Archduke Joseph of Austria, Palatine of Hungary, and his 3rd wife Marie Dorothea of Württemberg; 1 son, 3 daus; *m* (2) Laeken 12 December 1909 Blanche, entitled Baroness de Vaughan (*b* Bucharest, Roumania, 13 May 1883; *m* (2) Arronville, Seine et Oise, France, 13 August 1910 (*m diss* 1913) Antoine Emmanuel Durrieux (*d* 1917); *d* Cambo, Pyrénées Atlantique 12 February 1948), dau of Jules Delacroix and Catherine Joséphine Sébille; 2 sons (born before marriage); *d* Laeken 17 December 1909; *bur* Laeken

ALBERT I   1909–1934

b Brussels 8 April 1875, yr but only surviving son of Philip, Count of Flanders (yst son of King Leopold I), and Marie of Hohenzollern-Sigmaringen; *s* his uncle King Leopold II 17 December 1909; took the oath to the Constitution 23 December 1909; *m* Munich 2 October 1900 Elisabeth (*b* Possenhofen 25 July 1876; *d* Château de Stuyvenberg 23 November 1965; *bur* Laeken), dau of Charles Theodore, Duke in Bavaria, and his 2nd wife Maria Josepha of Bragança; 2 sons, 1 dau; *k* in a mountaineering accident Marche-les-Dames, nr Namur, 17 February 1934; *bur* Laeken

LEOPOLD III   1934–1951

b Brussels 3 November 1901, elder son of King Albert I; *s* his father 17 February 1934; took the oath to the Constitution 23 February 1934; abdicated 17 July 1951; *m* (1) Stockholm 4 November (civil) and

Brussels 10 November (religious) 1926 Astrid (*b* Stockholm 17 November 1905; *k* in a motor accident Küssnacht, Switzerland, 29 August 1935; *bur* Laeken), yst dau of Prince Carl of Sweden, Duke of Västergötland, and Ingeborg of Denmark; 2 sons, 1 dau; *m* (2) Laeken 11 September (religious) and 6 December (civil) 1941 Mary Liliane, entitled Princess of Belgium (*b* Highbury, London, 28 November 1916), dau of Henri Baels, Governor of West Flanders, and Anne Marie de Visscher; 1 son, 2 daus; *d* Woluwé-Saint-Lambert, nr Brussels, 25 September 1983; *bur* Laeken

BAUDOUIN I   1951–

b Château de Stuyvenberg 7 September 1930, eldest son of King Leopold III; Prince Royal and Lieutenant-General of the Kingdom 11 August 1950; *s* his father on his abdication and took the oath to the Constitution 17 July 1951; *m* Brussels 15 December 1960 Fabiola (*b* Madrid 11 June 1928), dau of Don Gonzalo de Mora y Fernández, 2nd Conde de Mora, 4th Marqués de Casa Riera, and Doña Blanca de Aragón y Carrillo de Albornoz.

In August 1830 the southern and Catholic portion of the kingdom of the Netherlands revolted against the rule of the Protestant House of Orange and united with the former

Leopold I: this portrait by Sir Thomas Lawrence shows the future King of the Belgians in Garter robes as he appeared at the coronation of his father-in-law King George IV in 1821.

sovereign bishopric of Liège to form the modern country of Belgium. A provisional government was set up in September and independence was proclaimed on 4 October. On 10 November the Belgian National Congress declared the House of Orange deposed and voted for a constitutional hereditary monarchy to replace it, the monarch to be elected. Their first choice fell on the Duke of Nemours, second son of Louis Philippe, King of the French, but the British government headed by Lord Palmerston was against this and brought pressure to bear on Louis Philippe to reject his son's election. On 4 June the National Congress made a second choice of Prince Leopold of Saxe-Coburg, a German Prince who had been destined to become the consort of a future Queen of England until the death of his young wife Princess Charlotte in childbirth in 1817. Leopold had stayed on in England after his wife's death, was popular with the royal family and acted as mentor to his widowed sister the Duchess of Kent, carefully guiding the early education of his niece Victoria, heiress presumptive to the crown which would have been Charlotte's. His life was comfortable if somewhat boring and although a scandal was circulated about his relationship with a young German girl, Caroline Bauer, it seems to have been largely trumped up, much in the manner of modern press sensationalism. Leopold became something of a valetudinarian, wearing wigs and treble-soled boots to keep himself warm and dry, and the devastating good looks which had captivated Charlotte soon turned to a rather forbidding expression accentuated by the early loss of his teeth and the uneasy fit of a false set.

This, then, was the man who was offered and accepted the new crown of Belgium in June 1831. He was an astute politician and spent the early part of his reign consolidating the kingdom. The clerical-liberal coalition which had ruled since independence gave way to a party system in 1847 and the King's skilful diplomacy won the admiration of all Europe. He was largely instrumental in bringing about the marriages of his two nephews Albert and Ferdinand to Queen Victoria and to Queen Maria da Gloria of Portugal and imparted sound advice to all his many relations with whom he managed to keep up a voluminous correspondence. Leopold had genuinely loved Princess Charlotte and it was only from a sense of duty that he married again. His second wife, over twenty years his junior, was Louise Marie of Orleans, daughter of Louis Philippe, King of the French, and sister of the Duke of Nemours who had been the first choice for the Belgian throne. The marriage was not unhappy, however, and Queen Louise bore three sons and a daughter before dying at the age of thirty-eight. Rather touchingly, she named her daughter Charlotte after her husband's first wife. The girl was to have a tragic history as Empress of Mexico, eventually sinking into irrecoverable madness and surviving long after the First World War. Leopold also had an affair with one Arcadie Claret, who bore him two sons (one before and one after the death of Queen Louise), who were obligingly created Barons von Eppinghoven by his nephew Duke Ernest II of Saxe-Coburg.

Although King of a Catholic country, Leopold remained a staunch Lutheran and his tomb in the centre of the royal tombhouse at Laeken was unconsecrated. When he died, in December 1865, he was sincerely loved by his subjects and respected throughout Europe for his statesmanship.

Queen Louise Marie of the Belgians with her son the Duke of Brabant, later King Leopold II, a portrait by Winterhalter.

King Leopold I of the Belgians, a photograph taken towards the end of his life.

Leopold's son and successor, Leopold II, while inheriting his father's ability, energy and strong will, was a very different type of man with a cunning, avaricious streak in his makeup. At the age of eighteen, while still Duke of Brabant, he had been married to the seventeen-year-old Archduchess Marie Henriette of Austria, a girl of little charm. She bore two daughters and a son who died at the age of nine in 1869. Following this child's death the couple, who were incompatible in every way, made one more attempt to get an heir, but another girl was born in 1872 and thereafter the King and Queen lived mostly apart.

Leopold had travelled widely in his youth and his keenness to make money had inspired him with the idea of gaining a rich colony as his personal property rather than that of the country. He accordingly founded the Association Internationale du Congo, providing the entire capital himself, and called on the aid of H M Stanley, the explorer. As a result, a large territory in central Africa was acquired as the Congo Free State, and Leopold was proclaimed its sovereign in August 1885. The development of the new state occupied all Leopold's energy and the natives were exploited and wickedly ill-treated in the pursuit of his aim, to such an extent that the King was obliged to cede the Congo to Belgium in 1908 to avoid an international outcry. By this time, however, he had amassed his fortune.

Leopold's three daughters were large, plain, horse-featured girls. Louise, the eldest, was pushed into an unhappy marriage at the age of seventeen with Prince Philip of Saxe-Coburg, fourteen years her senior. After thirty years of marriage they were divorced in 1906 and the Princess, mentally deranged, lived on until 1924. The second daughter, Stephanie, made an equally unhappy marriage with the Austrian Crown Prince Rudolf, who died tragically at Mayerling in 1889. Eleven years later she found a measure of happiness in a second marriage to a Hungarian nobleman. Only Leopold's youngest daughter, Clementine, was to find real happiness. She fell madly in love with Prince Victor Napoleon, who reciprocated her feelings, but King Leopold would not countenance the marriage of his daughter to an upstart Bonaparte. The Princess waited patiently and finally married her Prince a year after her father's death in 1910. She was then thirty-eight and he forty-eight and they lived happily together until the Prince's death in 1926, having two children, of whom the son is the present head of the Imperial House of Bonaparte. Princess Clementine died at Nice in 1955.

King Leopold II, with his long white beard and bright eyes, presented the appearance of a wily old fox. He spent much time in the south of France in the pursuit of young women. In the last years of his life he became greatly infatuated with Blanche Delacroix and eagerly accepted the paternity of the sons she bore in 1906 and 1907, although there is some reason to believe that their real father was Monsieur Durrieux, whom Blanche married within a year of the King's death. In December 1909 Leopold fell ill and an operation was advised by his physicians. In view of his age and general health the outcome was doubtful and Leopold decided to 'make an honest woman' of Blanche. Accordingly they were married in a 'marriage of conscience', that is to say a religious marriage only, without the civil ceremony required by Belgian law to validate it. The marriage was solemnized in the King's bedroom, he wearing his nightshirt and dressing-gown,

and when it was over Leopold presented the bride to his attendants with the words, 'Gentlemen, meet my widow'. For the rest of her life Blanche was to bear the title of Baroness de Vaughan, though it seems she was never formally so created. Leopold is said to have chosen it to avenge an old grudge against Cardinal Vaughan, Archbishop of Westminster, who had criticized his behaviour in the Congo, but who was already long since dead. Leopold survived his second marriage by five days.

Albert I, who succeeded his uncle at the age of thirty-four, was a very different man from his predecessor. Tall, good-looking and popular, he was married to Duchess Elisabeth in Bavaria, who, although not exactly a beauty, had a distinctive appearance and was a talented violinist as well as being artistic in other ways. The couple had only been on the throne a little over four years when the First World War broke out. The King took personal command of the army and fought bravely against the German invaders, while the Queen helped nurse the wounded in field hospitals. The little country suffered very badly, but when the war was over the royal couple took a lead in rebuilding the ruins and restoring prosperity. Both liked a very simple lifestyle and the Queen's politics veered so much to the left that she was dubbed 'the Red Queen' in later years, when she even visited Soviet Russia. King Albert's hobby was rock-climbing and it was

King Leopold III of the Belgians.

while engaged in this that he met with a fatal accident in the Ardennes on 17 February 1934.

Leopold III, who succeeded thus unexpectedly at the age of thirty-two and had been partly educated in England at Eton, was good-looking like his father and was, moreover, married to the very beautiful Swedish Princess Astrid, whom the Belgians had come to adore. Eighteen months later, however, tragedy was to strike again. The King and Queen were on holiday in Switzerland and, while motoring in an open car with the King at the wheel, skidded and left the road, hitting a tree. The Queen, who was expecting her fourth child, was flung out and killed instantly while the King suffered broken ribs and other injuries. The death of his young wife and the possible guilt aroused thereby had a profound effect on the King, who became serious and introspective and lived only for his children and his work.

At the outbreak of the Second World War in September 1939 Belgium was again invaded by the Germans and after eighteen days Leopold, finding the situation desperate, capitulated and requested an armistice. Belgium was occupied and the King held prisoner in his own palace. Much controversy has raged about Leopold's action and the French Prime Minister, Paul Reynaud, sought to vilify him to cover his own grave derelictions. The King had a champion, however, in Admiral Sir Roger Keyes (later 1st Baron Keyes), who was stationed at the Belgian headquarters and was able to state categorically that the King had no option but to surrender. However, a violent campaign of feeling against Leopold was conducted both in Belgium and among his former allies. At home, matters were not helped when in September 1941 Leopold married the twenty-five-year-old governess of his children, which was regarded as an outrage to the memory of the adored Queen Astrid. It was announced that the King's second wife, a commoner by birth, would not take the title of Queen but would be known as Princess de Rethy. There was no formal creation of this title, however, and after the war the position was regularized and the King's wife was declared a Princess of Belgium and a Royal Highness and was thereafter referred to as Princess Liliane. The marriage was a happy one and gave Leopold three more children.

Before the war was over Leopold and his family were removed from Laeken and imprisoned in Germany, where they were liberated by the American army in May 1945. Feeling in Belgium still ran high and the King was unable to return home for five years, his brother Prince Charles acting as Regent. In 1950 a plebiscite resulted in a majority vote for the King's return. His arrival was followed by riots stirred up by left-wing agitators and Leopold realized that the only course open to him was to resign in favour of his eldest son Baudouin, first as Lieutenant-General of the Kingdom in August 1950, then as King in July 1951. The rest of Leopold's life was spent quietly living on his estate near Brussels and making frequent visits to the south of France, where he played much golf. He was surrounded by the love and affection of his family and went to his grave in 1983 without ever having made any personal attempt to explain or justify his conduct. It is now widely accepted that his actions were honourable.

King Baudouin I, a serious, bespectacled young man, was only nineteen when he became Prince Royal and Lieutenant-General of the Kingdom, and still only twenty when he took the oath to the Constitution as King on his father's abdication in July 1951. He had always been close to his father, sharing his deportation and imprisonment in Germany and later his five years of exile in Switzerland, returning to Brussels with the rest of the royal family in 1950.

In 1960 King Baudouin fell in love with a Spanish noblewoman, Doña Fabiola de Mora y Aragón, two years older than himself. She was slight, dark and attractive and the marriage, which took place in December 1960, has been a happy one although to the great grief of both childless, the Queen suffering several miscarriages. Queen Fabiola has won the hearts of the Belgians and is almost as greatly loved as her mother-in-law Queen Astrid was. The King and Queen lead a very simple life at Laeken and are always ready to join in the joys and sorrows of their subjects. They were, for example, among the first on the scene following the Zeebrugge ferry disaster in 1987, offering comfort and sympathy to the survivors and the bereaved.

The heir to the Belgian throne is King Baudouin's brother, Prince Albert, Prince of Liège, who married Donna Paola Ruffo di Calabria and has two sons and one daughter.

The Napoleonic Kingdom of Holland

LOUIS I   1806–1810

---

b Ajaccio, Corsica, 2 September 1778, 5th son of Charles Bonaparte and Marie Laetitia Ramolino; French Prince and Grand Constable of the French Empire on its proclamation by his brother Emperor Napoleon I 18 May 1804; King of Holland 5 June 1806; abdicated in favour of his eldest surviving son 1 July 1810; *m* Paris 4 January 1802 Hortense (*b* Paris 10 April 1783; *d* Château de Arenenberg, Canton of Thurgau, Switzerland, 5 October 1837; *bur* Church of Rueil-Malmaison), only dau of Alexandre, Vicomte de Beauharnais, and Joséphine de Tascher de La Pagerie (later first wife of Emperor Napoleon I); 3 sons; *d* Leghorn 25 July 1846; *bur* St Leu

---

LOUIS II   1–9 JULY 1810

---

b Paris 11 October 1804, 2nd son of King Louis I; *s* his brother Napoleon as Prince Royal of Holland 5 May 1807; Grand Duke of Berg and Cleves 3 March 1809 to 1 December 1813; nominal King of Holland from his father's abdication 1 July 1810 until Holland was united to the French Empire 9 July 1810; *m* Brussels 23 July 1826 his first cousin, Charlotte (*b* Paris 31 October 1802; *d* Sarzana 2 March 1839), yst dau of Joseph, King of Spain, and Julie Clary; no issue; *d* Forli 17 March 1831

The Kings of the Netherlands

WILLIAM I   1815–1840

b Oraniensaal 24 August 1772, 2nd but eldest surviving son of William V, Prince of Orange and Nassau-Dietz, Stadhouder of the United Provinces of the Netherlands, and Wilhelmina of Prussia; *s* his father as Prince of Orange and Nassau-Dietz 9 April 1806; Sovereign Prince of Fulda and Corvey 29 August 1802 to 7 July 1807; Hereditary Sovereign Prince of the Netherlands 6 December 1813; inaugurated in the Nieuwe Kerk, Amsterdam, 30 March 1814; King of the Netherlands and Duke (from 9 June 1815 Grand Duke) of Luxembourg 16 March 1815; abdicated 7 October 1840; *m* (1) Berlin 1 October 1791 Wilhelmina (*b* Potsdam 18 November 1774; *d* The Hague 12 October 1837), 3rd dau of Frederick William II, King of Prussia, and 2nd dau by his 2nd wife Frederica of Hesse-Darmstadt; 2 sons, 2 daus; *m* (2) Berlin 17 February 1841 Henrietta (*b* Maastricht 28 February 1792; *d* Schloss Rahr, nr Aachen, 26 October 1864), dau of Ferdinand, Count d'Oultremont de Wégimont, and Johanna Susanna Hartsinck; *d* Berlin 12 December 1843

WILLIAM II   1840–1849

b The Hague 6 December 1792, elder son of King William I; *s* his father on his abdication 7 October 1840; *m* St Petersburg 21 February 1816 Anna (*b* St Petersburg 18 January 1795; *d* The Hague 1 March 1865), yst dau of Paul I, Emperor of Russia, and his 2nd wife Maria Feodorovna (Sophia Dorothea) of Württemberg; 4 sons, 1 dau; *d* Tilburg 17 March 1849

WILLIAM III   1849–1890

b Brussels 19 February 1817, eldest son of King William II; *s* his father 17 March 1849; *m* (1) Stuttgart 18 June 1839 Sophie (*b* Stuttgart 17 June 1818; *d* Het Loo, Apeldoorn, 3 June 1877), 2nd dau of William I, King of Württemberg, and his 2nd wife Grand Duchess Catherine Pavlovna of Russia; 3 sons; *m* (2) Arolsen 7 January 1879 Emma, Queen Regent of the Netherlands 8 December 1890 to 31 August 1898 (*b* Arolsen 2 August 1858; *d* The Hague 20 March 1934), 4th dau of George Victor, Prince of Waldeck and Pyrmont, and Helene of Nassau; 1 dau; *d* Het Loo 23 November 1890

WILHELMINA   1890–1948

b The Hague 31 August 1880, only dau of King William III; *s* her father 23 November 1890; inaugurated in the Nieuwe Kerk, Amsterdam, 31 August 1898; abdicated 4 September 1948; *m* The Hague 7 February 1901, Duke Henry of Mecklenburg, naturalized in the Netherlands and created Prince of the Netherlands 6 February 1901 (*b* Schwerin 19 April 1876; *d* The Hague 3 July 1934), yst son of Frederick Francis II, Grand Duke of Mecklenburg-Schwerin, and his 3rd wife Marie of Schwarzburg-Rudolstadt; 1 dau; *d* Het Loo 28 November 1962

JULIANA   1948–1980

b The Hague 30 April 1909, only child of Queen Wilhelmina; Princess Regent of the Netherlands,14 October to 1 December 1947 and 14 May to 30 August 1948; *s* her mother on her abdication 4 September, and was inaugurated in the Nieuwe Kerk, Amsterdam, 6 September 1948; abdicated 30 April 1980; *m* The Hague 7 January 1937 Prince Bernhard of Lippe-Biesterfeld, naturalized in the Netherlands 24 November 1936 and created Prince of the Netherlands 7 January 1937 (*b* Jena 29 June 1911), elder son of Prince Bernhard of Lippe and Armgard von Cramm; 4 daus

BEATRIX   1980–

b Soestdijk Palace 31 January 1938, eldest dau of Queen Juliana; *s* her mother on her abdication and was inaugurated in the Nieuwe Kerk, Amsterdam, 30 April 1980; *m* Amsterdam 10 March 1966 Claus von Amsberg, naturalized in the Netherlands and created Prince of the Netherlands, Jonkheer van Amsberg, 16 February 1966 (*b* Dotzingen, nr Hitzacker an der Elbe, 6 September 1926), son of Claus von Amsberg and Baroness Gosta von dem Bussche-Haddenhausen; 3 sons

The kingdom of the Netherlands was one of the new European states which came into being following the Napoleonic Wars. Its nucleus, the County of Holland, had been ruled by a line of Counts since 922 and had passed by marriage to the Dukes of Burgundy and from them to the Spanish Habsburgs, whose oppressive rule and religious persecution led to a revolution under the leadership of William 'the Silent', Prince of Orange, who was elected Stadhouder of Holland and Zeeland. After his assassination at Delft in 1584 his descendants continued to govern the Netherlands and their office was eventually made hereditary. William III, Prince of Orange, became King William III of England in 1689 and on his death without issue in 1702 was succeeded as Stadhouder by his kinsman Jan Willem Friso, Prince of Nassau Dietz. He was followed by his son William IV, who married Anne, Princess Royal, the eldest daughter of King George II of Great Britain. Their son William V was driven out by the French in 1795, when the Batavian Republic was proclaimed and lasted until 1805. Napoleon, Emperor of the French, then imposed a new constitution and appointed a Grand Pensionary of Holland to administer the government until the following year when he created the kingdom of Holland with his brother Louis as King.

Louis was a conscientious and well-meaning young man and soon showed that he was prepared to put the interests of his new subjects before those of his brother the Emperor, particularly in the matter of trading with Britain which was an essential part of the country's livelihood. This naturally displeased Napoleon who expected his brothers and other occupants of the satellite thrones he had created to place his interests before all else. Louis was continually being called to heel. To add to his troubles he had a very flighty wife in the person of Queen Hortense, Napoleon's stepdaughter and the daughter of the Empress Joséphine. She preferred to remain in Paris, where she conducted a number of scandalous love affairs, most notably with the Comte de Flahault, an illegitimate son of Talleyrand by an alleged illegitimate daughter of Louis XV. The result of this affair was the Duc de Morny, who was later to play a prominent part in the reign of his half-brother Napoleon III. Eventually Napoleon demanded that Louis should abdicate, which he did on 1 July 1810. There was a feeble attempt to continue the kingdom with his five-year-old son reigning as Louis II, but eight days later Napoleon decreed Holland to be reunited to the French Empire.

The Stadhouder William V, after spending some years of his exile in England as a guest of the government, residing first at Kew and then at Hampton Court, later went to Germany and died at Brunswick in 1806. His eldest son, who succeeded him as William VI, Prince of Orange, had been driven by ambition to throw in his lot with Napoleon and when the secularization of the ecclesiastical states of the Holy Roman Empire began was rewarded by being made Sovereign Prince of Fulda and Corvey in 1802, but he was deprived of this principality by the treaty of Tilsit in July 1807. Thereafter, William decided to court the allies with a view to regaining his family's position in the Netherlands. In 1809 he sent his sixteen-year-old son, yet another William, to England to study at Oxford and later to serve under Wellington in the Peninsular War. Young William was of unprepossessing appearance with a broad face, bulging eyes and a big mouth which earned him the nickname of 'the Young Frog'. However, his personality at that time was not unpleasing and he gained a lot of support, particularly from Lord Bathurst, the Secretary of State for War. He paid court to the Regent's daughter Princess Charlotte but she found him rather boring so nothing came of that.

At the end of 1813 after Napoleon's defeat at Leipzig liberated the Netherlands, the provisional government under Gijsbrecht Karel van Hogendorp invited William VI to return as Hereditary Sovereign Prince rather than Stadhouder as before. The provisions of the Congress of Vienna published on 8 June 1815 created the kingdom of the Netherlands consisting of the former Republic of Holland, the Austrian Netherlands (Belgium) and Luxembourg. William had already been proclaimed King of the Netherlands and Duke of Luxembourg on 16 March and he now changed the latter title to Grand Duke. The Battle of Waterloo was fought in the territory of the new kingdom and its King was graciously to reward the victorious Duke of Wellington with the title of Prince of Waterloo. The King's son the Prince of Orange fought in the campaign but was somewhat disgruntled when Wellington ordered him to return to headquarters just as he was getting into the swing of things at the Duchess of Richmond's famous ball in Brussels. He was quite severely wounded in the battle. William I suited the Dutch very well, but the Belgians found his attempts to foist the Dutch language upon them and his interference in ecclesiastical affairs oppressive (he being a strict Protestant and they Catholic). Consequently a revolt in 1830 resulted in Belgium gaining independence.

Queen Wilhelmina, William's wife, died in 1837 and he at once began to think of a way in which he could marry his mistress Countess Henrietta d'Oultremont, a lady of mature years and a Roman Catholic. Added to this difficulty the country was beset with financial embarrassments causing great popular

King William II of the Netherlands as Prince of Orange. This portrait, after Copley, was painted when the young Prince was acting as ADC to Wellington during the Peninsular War.

discontent and the King's stern opposition to any reform was making him personally very unpopular. His solution was to abdicate in favour of the Prince of Orange on 7 October 1840. He assumed the title of King William Frederick, Count of Nassau, and retired to Berlin where he married his Countess the following February, and died, enormously rich, in December 1843.

William II was in his late forties when he ascended the throne on his father's abdication. After his rejection by Princess Charlotte he had married one of the many sisters of Emperor Alexander I of Russia. She brought a huge dowry both in money and in jewels. William II was more liberal than his father and in October 1848 approved a revised constitution limiting his own powers and increasing those of parliament. The King died rather suddenly the following March and was succeeded by his eldest son.

William III was thirty-two when he became King. He was both liberal minded and benevolent and his reign saw many developments and reforms. He had been married at the age of twenty-two to the highly intellectual and cultured Princess Sophie of Württemberg and they had three sons. The middle son died as a child, but the eldest and the youngest grew up leading unruly and disordered lives with frequent visits to Paris. Queen Sophie died in 1877 and her eldest son died unmarried in Paris two years later. The last remaining son, Prince Alexander, was also unmarried and was so worn out by his debaucheries that it was evident he could not live very long, although only in his twenty-eighth year. There was nothing for it but for King William to marry again in the hope of providing more heirs to the throne. He was over sixty and his own morals were not beyond reproach, a large number of bastards being attributed to him. He scoured the courts of Europe and finally settled on the twenty-year-old Princess Emma of Waldeck and Pyrmont, whose father reigned over a tiny principality from his toy town capital of Arolsen. His daughters were all homely in appearance, to put it as kindly as possible, but all made good marriages; Marie, a year older than Emma, married the Crown Prince of Württemberg, and Helena, a little over two years younger, married Queen Victoria's youngest son the Duke of Albany.

What Emma thought of her elderly husband, with the reputation of a roué, is unknown, but the year after her marriage she gave birth to a daughter, her only child. Alexander, Prince of Orange, died in June 1884 and his half-sister Wilhelmina became heiress presumptive. William III himself died in November 1890 and his ten-year-old daughter ascended the throne with Queen Emma as Regent.

Emma's regency was extremely efficient and she handed over to Wilhelmina when she came of age in 1898. The Queen had the bloom of youth about her, but like her mother was certainly no beauty. She had been well educated and made a round of visits to various courts. In England the septuagenarian Queen Victoria had greeted her with the words, 'We are both Queens, my dear, so we may say what we like to each other'.

The question of the Queen's marriage soon arose, the next heir to the throne being the Grand Duke of Saxe-Weimar whose mother was the only sister of King William III. The bridegroom selected was Duke Henry of Mecklenburg, youngest son of the Grand Duke Frederick Francis II of Mecklenburg-Schwerin. The marriage took place in February 1901, the bridegroom being naturalized and created Prince of the Netherlands with the qualification of Royal Highness. For several anxious years there were no children and the Queen suffered at least one miscarriage, but in 1909 a healthy girl was born and christened Juliana after the mother of William the Silent (the famous Prince of Orange in the sixteenth century). Prince Henry made little mark in his adopted country and as his wife grew plainer and plainer he soon sought diversion elsewhere and produced several illegitimate offspring. In 1934 Queen Wilhelmina lost her mother Queen Emma in March and her husband Prince Henry in July. She adopted white mourning and white was used for all the funeral draperies. The custom has been followed by the Dutch royal family ever since.

During the German occupation of Holland in the Second

Queen Wilhelmina of the Netherlands and her consort Prince Henry, formerly Duke Henry of Mecklenburg. This must be the most flattering picture of the Queen ever taken, but does little for the Prince.

Queen Wilhelmina of the Netherlands in later life, the revered mother of her people.

Soestdijk Palace, one of the principal residences of the Dutch royal family and the birthplace of Queen Beatrix.

World War, Queen Wilhelmina headed a government in exile in London and became the symbol of resistance for the Dutch people. She returned as soon as the country had been liberated and was received with wild enthusiasm. However, the next few years were to involve the Queen in difficulties with her government regarding the policy to be adopted over the Dutch colonies in the East Indies, now seeking their independence. She finally resolved to abdicate in favour of her only child Princess Juliana, to whom she had already twice delegated the regency, and did so on 4 September 1948, assuming the title of Princess and retiring into private life, where she occupied herself in writing her memoirs entitled 'Lonely but Not Alone'. She died in November 1962.

Queen Juliana's reign, which lasted until she, too, abdicated in April 1980, weathered several crises, notably the affair of the faith-healer consulted by the Queen regarding the poor eyesight of her youngest daughter and the Lockheed scandal in which the Queen's husband was involved. It is still too early for any assessment or conclusions to be drawn from these affairs.

Queen Juliana had been carefully educated for her role and graduated with a law degree from Leyden University. Only a little less plain than her mother and grandmother, she married a plain Prince in 1937. Prince Bernhard of Lippe-Biesterfeld was naturalized as his father-in-law had been and entitled Prince of the Netherlands. The marriage produced four daughters but no son, so when Queen Juliana emulated her mother and abdicated on 30 April 1980, she was succeeded by her eldest daughter.

Queen Beatrix enjoys the same popularity as her mother and grandmother before her and like them has married a German husband, Prince Claus, whose health has given rise to some anxiety since his wife's accession although he now appears to be better. In 1990 the kingdom of the Netherlands will have seen a hundred years of Queens, but the line of female succession will be broken in the next generation for Queen Beatrix has three sons and her sister Princess Margriet who is next in line after them has four sons.

SCANDINAVIA

DENMARK

The purported early history of Denmark is recounted in the Norse sagas and the writings of Saxo Grammaticus, Snorre Sturlasson, Svend Aageson and other early chroniclers. We may discount the stories of the eponymous founder King Dan Mykillati and of King Skjold, from whom the reigning family became known as the Skjoldunger, as largely, if not completely, unhistorical. Equally unhistorical is the story of Amled, on whom Shakespeare based his Hamlet. Although some later Kings can be accepted with certainty, it is not until we reach Gorm the Old that the real history of Denmark begins. Gorm, who is the ancestor of every subsequent Danish monarch, was a pagan with a built-in hatred of Christianity, but his wife Thyra, who won herself the epithet of Danebod (Comfort of the Danes), was a Christian and greatly renowned as the constructor of a great earthwork, the Danevirke. Gorm is said to have died of grief on receiving the news of the death of his elder son Canute Dana-ast while on a raiding expedition to Ireland, and was succeeded about 936 by his younger son Harold Bluetooth, who constructed a great burial mound for his parents at Jellinge in Jutland. Harold, who became a Christian, conquered Norway and did much to consolidate his kingdom before dying at Jomsborg in 986. His son Sweyn conquered England and died still flushed with victory in 1014, leaving a large inheritance to his son Canute the Great, who is chiefly remembered in England for getting his feet wet when he ordered the tide to turn as an object lesson to his flattering courtiers who had told him that he could command the waves. Canute re-conquered Norway, but his dominions split up again soon after his death and Denmark eventually passed to the son of Canute's half-sister Estrid, who ascended the throne as Sweyn II in 1047 and reigned until his death on 28 April 1074. The reigns of his successors were marked by the rise of the church and periods of civil war. King Canute IV was murdered in Odense Cathedral by some nobles who resented the imposition of tithes in 1086. He was later canonized and became Denmark's patron saint.

King Valdemar I the Great conquered the Wends in 1169 and had his seven-year-old son Canute acknowledged and crowned as his successor on 25 June 1170. He was fortunate in having as his friend and adviser Absalon, Bishop of Roskilde, a great warrior priest, who after Valdemar's death in 1182 continued to be the mainstay of his successor Canute VI, defeating the Pomeranians on his behalf. Canute died childless in 1202 and was succeeded by his brother Valdemar II the Victorious, who conquered Esthonia and extended Denmark's boundaries to the Eider. He also codified the ancient laws of Denmark.

On his death Valdemar was succeeded by his son, the twenty-five-year-old Eric Plough-penny, so named from his unpopular imposition of a tax on all ploughs. His oppression of the church and the peasantry soon rendered him unpopular and he became involved in differences with his brother Abel, who had married Mechtild, the daughter of Count Adolph IV of Holstein, and had become administrator of the country for his young brothers-in-law. The brothers warred on and off for several years and Eric was finally induced to visit Abel in Schleswig, whence he was taken out to sea and decapitated in rather mysterious circumstances in 1250. Abel denied being implicated but it was widely said that he 'was only Abel by name but in reality a Cain'.

Abel ascended the throne but only reigned for two years, being killed by a wheelwright when attempting to escape after being defeated in battle by the Frisians. His sons were passed over in the succession and his brother Christopher became King, being crowned on Christmas Day 1252. Christopher died suddenly on 29 May 1259, supposedly poisoned, and was succeeded by his ten-year-old son Eric Klipping, whose mother Margaret of Pomerania acted as Regent. She was known as 'Black Greta' from her swarthy complexion and also as 'the horse-breaker', being an intrepid horsewoman. The crown was contested by the son of King Abel and fighting took place for several years. Eric Klipping was declared of age on his fifteenth birthday, but Queen Margaret continued to exercise a strong influence until her death at Rostock in December 1282.

Four years later the King's attempts to curb the growing power of the nobility gave rise to a conspiracy against him and he was murdered while sleeping on a heap of straw after a day's hunting. Eric's son and successor Eric Maendved was only twelve years old and his mother Agnes of Brandenburg became Regent with Duke Valdemar, a grandson of King Abel. Eric reigned until 1319. His fourteen children all died before him and he was succeeded by his brother Christopher II, a weak king who fled the country in 1326, when the throne was declared vacant. An interregnum of fourteen years followed during which the royal power was exercised by Duke Valdemar of Schleswig, a descendant of King Abel, who did not however assume the title of King. In 1340 Christopher II's son Valdemar Atterdag was restored to the throne after marrying the sister of Duke Valdemar. He is styled Valdemar III or Valdemar IV, depending on whether one includes King Valdemar II's son Valdemar, who was co-ruler with his father until his early death in 1231.

Valdemar was a very able ruler, consolidating the royal power and dealing successfully with his neighbours. His only surviving child Margaret married King Haakon VI of Norway and on Valdemar's death on 24 October 1375, Margaret's son Olaf was elected King of Denmark in May 1376 with his mother as Regent. In 1380 he succeeded his father as King of Norway also, but he died at the age of seventeen and his mother now reigned alone. In 1389 she was elected 'Lady and Mistress' of Sweden also and thus united under her personal rule all three Scandinavian kingdoms. She selected her great-nephew Eric of Pomerania (who later married Philippa, daughter of King Henry IV of England) to rule in 1396 and in the following year instigated the Union of Kalmar to declare the three kingdoms perpetually united, but it was to prove a shortlived and virtually unworkable union. Margaret, a woman of outstanding ability and despotic disposition, whose subjects referred to her as 'the lady King', retained power in her own hands until her sudden death on 28 October 1412. Eric of Pomerania's reign aroused discontent and in 1439 he left Denmark and his nephew Christopher of Bavaria was appointed Regent and in 1440 elected King in Eric's place. Christopher III, a man of good intentions, successfully put down a revolt in Jutland and died suddenly at Helsingborg at the age of thirty-three on 6 January 1448. He had no children by his wife Dorothea of Brandenburg, who was destined to become the wife of his successor.

The House of Oldenburg

CHRISTIAN I   1448–1481

b February 1426, son of Dietrich II, Count of Oldenburg and Delmenhorst, and Hedwig, dau of Gerard VI, Count of Holstein; *s* his father as Count of Oldenburg and Delmenhorst 22 January 1440; elected King of Denmark 20 August 1448; crowned at Copenhagen 28 October 1449; elected King of Norway 20 July 1450; elected King of Sweden and crowned at Uppsala 3 July 1457; *s* his maternal uncle Duke Adolph VIII as Duke of Schleswig and Count of Holstein (created a Duchy 1474) 1459; ceded Oldenburg and Delmenhorst to his brother Gerard 1460; *m* Copenhagen 28 October 1449 Dorothea (*b* 1430; *d* Kalundborg 10 November 1495), widow of King Christopher III, dau of John (the Alchemist), Margrave of Brandenburg-Kulmbach, and Barbara of Saxe-Wittenberg; 4 sons, 1 dau; *d* Copenhagen 21 May 1481

HANS   1481–1513

b 8 July 1455, 3rd but eldest surviving son of King Christian I; elected successor to his father May 1481; proclaimed King of Denmark and Norway at Halmstad 1483; King of Sweden 1497; deposed as King of Sweden 1501; *m* 6 September 1478 Christina (*b* 25 December 1461; *d* 8 December 1521; *bur* Odense), elder dau of Ernest, Elector of Saxony, and Elizabeth of Bavaria; 4 sons, 1 dau; *d* 20 February 1513; *bur* Odense

CHRISTIAN II   1513–1523

b Nyborg 2 July 1481, 3rd but eldest surviving son of King Hans; Viceroy of Norway 1506–12; *s* his father as King of Denmark and Norway 20 February 1513; King of Sweden April 1520; crowned at Stockholm 4 November 1520; deposed in all three kingdoms 20 January 1523; *m* Oslo 12 August 1515 Isabella (*b* Ghent 18 July 1501; *d* Lierre, Belgium, 19 January 1526), 2nd dau of Philip I and Juana, King and Queen of Castile; 4 sons, 2 daus; *d* Kalundborg 25 January 1559

FREDERICK I   1523–1533

b 7 October 1471, 4th and yst son of King Christian I; King of Denmark and Norway on the deposition of his nephew King Christian II January 1523; *m* (1) Stendal 10 April 1502 Anna (*b* Berlin 27 August 1487; *d* Kiel 3 May 1514), 2nd dau of John Cicero, Elector of Brandenburg, and Margaret of Saxony; 1 son, 1 dau; *m* (2) Keil 9 October 1518 Sophie (*b* 1498; *d* Keil 13 May 1568), dau of Bogislaw X, Duke of Pomerania, and Anna of Poland; 3 sons, 3 daus; *d* Gottorp 10 April 1533

CHRISTIAN III   1533–1559

b Gottorp 12 August 1503, eldest son of King Frederick I; received the Duchies of Schleswig and Holstein from his father 1523; *s* his father as King of Denmark and Norway April 1533; *m* Lauenburg 29 October 1525 Dorothea (*b* 9 July 1511; *d* Sonderburg 7 October 1571), 2nd dau of Magnus II, Duke of Saxe-Lauenburg, and Catherine of Brunswick-Wolfenbüttel; 3 sons, 2 daus; *d* Coldingen 1 January 1559

FREDERICK II   1559–1588

b Haderslevhus 1 July 1534, eldest son of King Christian III; *s* his father as King of Denmark and Norway 1 January 1559; *m* Copenhagen 20 July 1572 Sophie (*b* Wismar 4 September 1557; *d* Nyköbing 4 October 1631), dau of Ulrich III, Duke of Mecklenburg-Güstrow, and Elizabeth of Denmark (dau of King Frederick I and his 2nd wife Sophie of Pomerania); 3 sons, 4 daus; *d* Antvorslev Castle 4 April 1588; *bur* Roskilde Cathedral

CHRISTIAN IV   1588–1648

b Frederiksborg 12 April 1577, eldest son of King Frederick II; elected successor to the throne at Viborg 14 June 1584; *s* his father as King of Denmark and Norway 4 April 1588; *m* (1) 27 November 1597 Anne Catherine (*b* 26 June 1575; *d* 29 March 1612), dau of Joachim Frederick, Elector of Brandenburg, and his 1st wife Catherine of Brandenburg-Küstrin; 5 sons, 2 daus; *m* (2) 31 December 1615 (*m diss* 1630) Christine, entitled Countess of Schleswig-Holstein (*b* 6 July 1598; *d* Odense 19 April 1658), dau of Ludvig Munk and Ellen Marsvin; 1 son, 5 daus; *d* Copenhagen 28 February 1648

FREDERICK III   1648–1670

b Hadersleben 18 March 1609, 4th but eldest surviving son of King Christian IV; elected successor to his father April 1648; monarchy declared hereditary 1661; *m* Glückstadt 1 October 1643 Sophia Amelia (*b* Herzberg 24 March 1628; *d* Copenhagen 20 February 1685), 2nd dau of Duke George of Brunswick-Lüneburg, and Anna Eleonora of Hesse-Darmstadt; 3 sons, 5 daus; *d* Copenhagen 9 February 1670

CHRISTIAN V   1670–1699

b Flensborg 15 April 1646, eldest son of King Frederick III; *s* his father 9 February 1670; *m* proxy Cassel 14 May, in person Copenhagen 25 June 1667, Charlotte Amelia (*b* Cassel 27 April 1650; *d* Copenhagen 27 March 1714), eldest dau of William VI, Landgrave of Hesse-Cassel, and Hedwig Sophie of Brandenburg; 5 sons, 3 daus; *d* 25 August 1699

FREDERICK IV   1699–1730

b Copenhagen 21 October 1671, eldest son of King Christian V; *s* his father 25 August 1699; *m* (1) 5 December 1695 Louise (*b* 28 August 1667; *d* 15 March 1721), 7th dau of Gustav Adolph, Duke of Mecklenburg-Güstrow, and Magdalena Sibylla of Holstein-Gottorp; 4 sons, 1 dau; *m* (2) 4 April 1721 Anna Sophie (*b* 16 April 1693; *d* Klausholm 7 January 1743), dau of Count Konrad von Reventlow and his 2nd wife Sophie Amalie Haha til Seekamp; 2 sons, 1 dau; *d* Copenhagen 12 October 1730

CHRISTIAN VI   1730–1746

b Copenhagen 10 December 1699, 2nd but eldest surviving son of King Frederick IV; *s* his father 12 October 1730; *m* 7 August 1721 Sophie Magdalene (*b* 28 November 1700; *d* Christiansborg 27 May 1770), 4th dau of Margrave Christian Heinrich of Brandenburg-Kulmbach and Countess Sophie Christiane von Wolfstein; 1 son, 2 daus; *d* Copenhagen 6 August 1746

FREDERICK V   1746–1766

b Copenhagen 31 March 1723, only son of King Christian VI; *s* his father 6 August 1746; crowned at Frederiksborg 4 September 1747; *m* (1) proxy Hanover 10 November, in person Christiansborg 11 December 1743 Louisa (*b* London 18 December 1724; *d* Christiansborg 19 December 1751), 5th and yst dau of George II, King of Great Britain, and Caroline of Brandenburg-Ansbach; 2 sons, 3 daus; *m* (2) Frederiksborg 8 July 1752 Juliana Maria (*b* Wolfenbüttel 4 September 1729; *d* Fredensborg 10 October 1796), 6th and yst dau of Ferdinand Albert II, Duke of Brunswick-Wolfenbüttel, and Antoinette Amelia of Brunswick-Wolfenbüttel; 1 son; *d* Christiansborg 14 January 1766

CHRISTIAN VII   1766–1808

b Copenhagen 29 January 1749, 2nd but eldest surviving son of King Frederick V; *s* his father 14 January 1766; crowned at Christiansborg 1 May 1767; placed under his son's regency from 14 April 1784; *m* proxy London 1 October, in person Christiansborg 8 November 1766 (*m* diss 6 April 1772) his 1st cousin Caroline Matilda (*b* London 11 July 1751; *d* Celle 10 May 1775; *bur* Celle), 4th and yst dau of Frederick, Prince of Wales, and Augusta of Saxe-Gotha; 1 son, 1 dau; *d* Rendsborg 13 March 1808

FREDERICK VI   1808–1839

b Christiansborg 28 January 1768, only son of King Christian VII; assumed the government as Regent 14 April 1784; *s* his father 13 March 1808; ceded the kingdom of Norway to Sweden 14 January 1814; crowned at Frederiksborg 31 July 1815; *m* Gottorp 31 July 1790 his 1st cousin Marie (*b* Hanau 28 October 1767; *d* Amalienborg 21 March 1852), eldest dau of Landgrave Charles of Hesse-Cassel and Louise of Denmark (dau of King Frederick V); 2 sons, 6 daus; *d* Amalienborg 3 December 1839

CHRISTIAN VIII   1839–1848

b Christiansborg 18 September 1786, eldest son of Hereditary Prince Frederick (son of King Frederick V and Juliana Maria of Brunswick-Wolfenbüttel) and Sophia Frederica of Mecklenburg-Schwerin; elected King of Norway 17 May 1814; abdicated 15 August 1814; *s* his cousin King Frederick VI as King of Denmark 9 December 1839; crowned at Frederiksborg 28 June 1840 (the last Danish King to be crowned); *m* (1) Ludwigslust 21 June 1806 (*m* diss 1810) Charlotte (*b* Ludwigslust 4 December 1784; *d* Rome 13 July 1840), yr surviving dau of Frederick Francis I, Grand Duke of Mecklenburg-Schwerin, and Louise of Saxe-Gotha; 2 sons; *m* (2) Augustenburg 22 May 1815 Caroline (*b* Copenhagen 22 June 1796; *d* Amalienborg 9 March 1881), only dau of Frederick Christian, Duke of Schleswig-Holstein-Sonderburg-Augustenburg, and Louise Augusta of Denmark (dau of King Christian VII); no issue; *d* Amalienborg 20 January 1848

FREDERICK VII   1848–1863

b Amalienborg 6 October 1808, yr but only surviving son of King Christian VIII; *s* his father 20 January 1848; *m* (1) Copenhagen 1 November 1828 (*m* diss 1837) Wilhelmine (*b* Kiel 18 January 1808; *d* Glücksburg 30 May 1891), yst dau of King Frederick VI; no issue; *m* (2) Neustrelitz 10 June 1841 (*m* diss 1846) Caroline (*b* Neustrelitz 10 January 1821; *d* Neustrelitz 1 June 1876), yr dau of George, Grand Duke of Mecklenburg-Strelitz, and Marie of Hesse-Cassel; no issue; *m* (3) (morganatically) Frederiksborg 7 August 1850 Louise Rasmussen, *cr* Countess Danner (*b* Copenhagen 21 April 1815; *d* Cannes 6 March 1874), natural dau of G L Koppen and Juliane Caroline Rasmussen; no issue; *d* Glücksburg 15 November 1863

CHRISTIAN IX   1863–1906

b Gottorp 8 April 1818, 4th son of William, Duke of Schleswig-Holstein-Sonderburg-Glücksburg, and Louise of Hesse-Cassel; granted the title of Prince of Denmark 31 July 1853; granted the qualification of Royal Highness 1858; *s* his kinsman King Frederick VII 15 November 1863; *m* Copenhagen 26 May 1842 Louise (*b* Cassel 7 September 1817; *d* Bernstorff 29 September 1898), 3rd dau of Landgrave William of Hesse-Cassel, and Charlotte of Denmark (sister of King Christian VIII); 3 sons, 3 daus; *d* Amalienborg 29 January 1906; *bur* Roskilde

FREDERICK VIII	1906–1912

b Copenhagen 3 June 1843, eldest son of King Christian IX; *s* his father 29 January 1906; *m* Stockholm 28 July 1869 Louise (*b* Stockholm 31 October 1851; *d* Amalienborg 20 March 1926), only dau of Carl XV, King of Sweden and Norway, and Louise of the Netherlands; 4 sons, 4 daus; *d* Hamburg 14 May 1912; *bur* Roskilde

CHRISTIAN X	1912–1947

b Charlottenlund 26 September 1870, eldest son of King Frederick VIII; *s* his father 14 May 1912; *m* Cannes 26 April 1898 Alexandrine (*b* Schwerin 24 December 1879; *d* Copenhagen 28 December 1952), elder dau of Frederick Francis III, Grand Duke of Mecklenburg-Schwerin, and Grand Duchess Anastasia Mikhailovna of Russia; 2 sons; *d* Amalienborg 20 April 1947; *bur* Roskilde

FREDERICK IX	1947–1972

b Sorgenfri 11 March 1899, elder son of King Christian X; *s* his father 20 April 1947; *m* Stockholm 24 May 1935 Ingrid (*b* Stockholm 28 March 1910), dau of Gustav VI Adolph, King of Sweden, and his 1st wife Margaret of Great Britain; 3 daus; *d* Copenhagen 14 January 1972; *bur* Roskilde

MARGRETHE II	1972–

b Copenhagen 16 April 1940, eldest dau of King Frederick IX; *s* her father 14 January 1972; *m* Copenhagen 10 June 1967 Henri de Laborde de Monpezat, *cr* Prince of Denmark with the qualification of Royal Highness 10 June 1967 (*b* Talence, Gironde, France, 11 June 1934), son of André de Laborde de Monpezat and Renée Yvonne Doursenot; 2 sons

King Christian I of Denmark and his wife Dorothea of Brandenburg: a painting on panel at Frederiksborg Castle.

The sudden death of King Christopher III left the united northern thrones with no obvious heir. Duke Adolph VIII of Schleswig was approached but claimed that he was too old (at forty-seven!) to undertake the burden of sovereignty and proposed instead that his sister's son Count Christian of Oldenburg should be elected. Christian was a handsome young man of twenty-two and his claim to the throne was based on his descent from a daughter of King Eric Klipping. Duly elected, he celebrated his coronation and his marriage to Queen Dorothea, the widow of King Christopher, on the same day in October 1449.

King Christian I was Denmark's Renaissance Prince and a model of chivalry. He had to do quite a lot of fighting in Sweden, which he lost in 1464, but succeeded in strengthening the royal authority in Denmark. Denmark was an elective monarchy in theory, though in practice the reigning monarch's son was usually designated as his successor. After Christian I's death in 1481 his son Hans had to wait two years until his

election was ratified by the Council of State and he was proclaimed King of Denmark and Norway. He was unable to assert his rights to Sweden until 1497 and then only maintained his rule there until 1501. Hans was a man of simple habits and a somewhat melancholy disposition. His wife Christina of Saxony heroically held Stockholm for eight months when it was besieged by her husband's enemies and after its fall remained in prison for six months before she was allowed to rejoin the King in Denmark. Hans died as the result of a fall from his horse in February 1513 and was succeeded by his son Christian II, who had already been named as heir to the three northern thrones.

The new King was thirty-two and had hitherto resisted all attempts to make him marry, being completely in thrall to his mistress Dyveke, a Dutch girl he had met at Bergen in 1507 or 1509 when acting as Viceroy of Norway. In 1515 the Council arranged his marriage to Isabella of Austria, a sister of the future Emperor Charles V. The bride was no beauty, possessing the famous 'Habsburg lip', and arrived in Denmark in a very sorry state prostrated by seasickness. It was not to be expected that Christian would ever fall in love with her, but he treated her with respect and fathered several children by her. His regard for Dyveke continued undiminished until she died suddenly in 1517 under suspicious circumstances. Christian believed, probably quite truly, that she had been poisoned by Torben Oxe, the governor of Copenhagen Castle, and had him executed in spite of pleas from the Queen and the nobility to spare him. The King now gave full reign to his hatred of the nobility and clergy and

Queen Christina of Sweden as a child, a charmingly naïve portrait by J H Elbfas.

Carl X Gustav, King of Sweden, a very unflattering portrait by A Wuchters.

King Carl XI of Sweden on horseback: in this heroic canvas by D K Ehrenstrahl it is not surprising if it had to maintain that pose that the horse should be frothing at the mouth.

King Gustav IV Adolph of Sweden and Queen Frederica, a charming portrait of the young sovereigns by J Forsslun.

William II, German Emperor and King of Prussia in 1903, by Nicol J Watson.

began to promote ordinary citizens to fill positions of power. His chief adviser was Dyveke's mother Sigbrit, an extremely capable woman who took charge of the country's finances with great success, but was naturally resented by the nobility who referred to her as 'the foul-mouthed Dutch sorceress who has bewitched the King'.

Christian now prepared a campaign to assert his rights in Sweden. He eventually succeeded and was crowned at Stockholm in November 1520. The coronation was followed by mass executions which became known as the Stockholm Massacre. The King returned to Denmark in September 1521 and began a programme of sweeping reforms directed at curbing the power of the nobility and bettering the lot of the lower classes. Christian II's tragedy is that he could have been a great and enlightened ruler under happier circumstances. By 1523 Sweden was in revolt again, war with Lübeck broke out, and Jutland rose against Christian, renouncing its allegiance and offering the crown to his uncle Frederick. In April Christian left the country to seek help abroad. He made an attempt to regain his kingdom in October 1531, but his fleet was scattered off the Norwegian coast and he himself captured and kept in solitary confinement for the rest of his life, first in the Blue Tower at Copenhagen, then at Kalundborg, where he died in January 1559.

This portrait of King Christian III of Denmark by Jost Verheiden hangs at Frederiksborg Castle.

Frederick I was in his fifty-second year when his nephew's deposition made him King. He allied himself with the nobility and showed favour to the Lutherans, who were making great strides in superseding the Catholic faith in Denmark, but he was not a popular King with either the nobility or the people and died unmourned in April 1533.

Frederick's son, Christian III, was a zealous Lutheran and had been present at the Diet of Worms in 1521 when Luther made a deep impression on him. Although Lutheranism had taken strong hold in almost all the Danish towns, the countryside remained Catholic as did most of the nobility and clergy, who strenuously opposed Christian's succession and would have preferred his half-brother Hans. However, the local Diet at Viborg proclaimed Christian King and after a campaign known as the Counts' War, Christian triumphed with the aid of German mercenaries and began a ruthless spoliation of the church, and the establishment of Lutheranism as the state religion. The King possessed many good qualities and left the country in a far more prosperous state than he had found it. His right to the throne was contested by the daughters of Christian II, encouraged by their uncle Charles V, but they dropped their claim after the treaty of Speier was concluded with the Emperor in 1544, whereby Denmark granted the Netherlands free right of entry to all harbours in Denmark and Norway on payment of harbour dues. At the same time the imprisonment of the former King Christian II was greatly ameliorated with the result that in 1546 he renounced all right to the Danish throne for himself and his descendants. Strangely enough, the two Christians both died in January 1559, the death of Christian III preceding that of Christian II by twenty-eight days.

Christian III's son Frederick II had already been elected heir presumptive in 1536 at the Diet of Copenhagen. He lacked his father's wisdom and was rather a man of impulse. His wish to marry his mother's lady-in-waiting Anna Hardenberg alienated him from his father during the last few years of Christian's reign and Frederick declined to attend his father's deathbed. His attachment to Anna lasted for several years, but eventually he married Sophie of Mecklenburg in 1572.

In 1560 Frederick backed an abortive attempt to set up his brother Magnus as King of Livonia, which involved him in a period of war until 1570. It was followed by a period of peace which lasted until the end of the reign in 1588. Frederick was a great patron of learning and Tycho Brahe, the astronomer, was one of his protégés. Frederick died at the age of fifty-three in April 1588, his life probably shortened by his drinking habits, and was succeeded by his eleven-year-old son Christian, whose reign of nearly sixty years was to be the longest in Danish history.

Christian IV had been elected successor to the throne in 1584. He had been brought up partly by his maternal grandparents in Mecklenburg and then by carefully chosen tutors. On his accession his mother Queen Sophie became Regent with four Councillors appointed to assist her. She was a shrewd woman and apart from demanding the right to superintend her son's upbringing and arrange the marriages of her daughters, she insisted on the payment of her marriage jointure, which she invested so well that she was able to leave Christian IV a large fortune when she died in 1631. Another of

Christian IV, Denmark's most memorable King, depicted by Peter Isaacsz. Note the open-style crown, still in use in Denmark in Christian's time.

enemies of their half-siblings the children of Christine.

During the period of recovery after the treaty of Lübeck Christian's attempts to retrieve his fortunes met with little success because of his inconsistent nature and in 1643 he became involved in another war with Sweden resulting in the loss of some territory and a temporary weakening of the royal power. Christian fell ill while at Frederiksborg in February 1648 and had himself carried back to Copenhagen in a litter. He died a week later at Rosenborg Castle attended by his favourite daughter (by Christine Munk) Leonora Christina, whose husband Corfits Ulfeld played a prominent role in Danish affairs until his downfall in the succeeding reign. Christian's original heir, Prince Christian, died seven months before his father after a lifetime of debauchery. He had been married to Magdalena Sibylla of Saxony, but there were no children and no other heir to the throne had been designated before Christian IV died so that two months elapsed before the Council of State, headed by Corfits Ulfeld, elected his next surviving son as his successor.

Frederick III was thirty-nine years old when elected, an austere and scholarly man, married to the pleasure-loving Sophia Amelia of Brunswick-Lüneburg, who had a strong dislike for the sober Danish nobility and particularly for her husband's half-sister Leonora Christina. The court soon split into two factions, one headed by the King and Queen and supported by Hannibal Sehested (married to another daughter of Christine Munk), the other by the Ulfelds. At the beginning of his reign Frederick was

An equestrian portrait of King Frederick III of Denmark painted by Wolfgang Heimback in 1660.

her coups was the marriage of her second daughter Anna to James VI, King of Scots, later James I of England, in 1589.

Christian was declared of age in 1596 and the following year married Anne Catherine of Brandenburg. Christian had an impressive appearance, tall, well-made if a little portly, with piercing brown eyes, a large nose and a goatee beard. He was athletic, interested in art and music, and possessed a keen sense of duty. On the debit side, he had inherited his father's addiction to drink and gave himself up to frivolous pursuits lacking in refinement. Christian IV was a great builder and Copenhagen was greatly embellished during the early years of his reign. Later, Denmark was involved in the Thirty Years' War, but concluded the treaty of Lübeck in May 1629, whereby its lost lands were restored. After the death of Queen Anne Catherine in 1612, Christian married his mistress Christine Munk, by whom he had a large family both before and after the marriage. Although she was not acknowledged as Queen and only bore the title of Countess of Schleswig-Holstein, Christine wielded great influence. In 1628, however, she was discovered misconducting herself with a German officer from the Rhineland and Christian finally divorced her in 1630, when she retired to her estates in Jutland. The King had also conducted an intrigue with Vibeke Kruse, who had been one of Christine's maids, and she too had presented him with a family, destined to become the inveterate forced to sign a humiliating charter greatly curtailing the royal power. A trumped-up charge against the Ulfelds, accusing them of plotting to kill the King, brought about their downfall, and although they were acquitted of that charge, an enquiry into the management of the country's finances forced them to leave Denmark.

A war with Sweden from 1657 to 1660 was followed by the proclamation of Denmark as an hereditary monarchy with the King as an absolute monarch. Corfits Ulfeld had returned to Denmark after the war, and in 1663 obtained permission to travel abroad for health reasons. While doing so, he approached the Elector of Brandenburg and offered to help him obtain the Danish throne. The Elector reported the matter to Copenhagen and Ulfeld was tried for high treason in his absence. He was sentenced to death with confiscation of property, but managed to evade capture and lived in disguise until his death at Neuburg in 1664. His wife Leonora Christina was confined in the Blue Tower at Copenhagen for twenty-two years and only released after the death of Queen Sophia Amelia. She wrote a touching account of her imprisonment.

Frederick III's last years were given up to mysticism and magical experiments in which he was assisted by the Italian alchemist Francesco Borri for whom he constructed a laboratory in Copenhagen Castle. One of Frederick's younger sons became the husband of Queen Anne of England.

Christian V was the first Danish King to ascend the throne by hereditary right and not by election. Twenty-four years old, he was completely unintellectual and interested only in riding and hunting. Nevertheless, he possessed a strong sense of duty allied to an exaggerated idea of the importance of his royal role. He was married to Charlotte Amelia of Hesse-Cassel, a gentle inoffensive lady, but publicly insulted her by introducing his mistress Sophie Amalie Moth, the sixteen-year-old daughter of his former tutor, into the court and ennobling her as Countess of Samsøe. The King was popular with the people but alienated the old nobility by swelling their ranks with a number of newly created Counts and Barons from the middle classes and decreeing that estates with no heirs fell to the crown. In this, as in most other matters, Christian was led by his Chancellor Griffenfeld, the son of a wine merchant named Schumacher, who rose to a position of supreme power and was one of the first twenty members of the new Order of Dannebrog instituted in 1671. Griffenfeld suffered a spectacular fall from power in 1676 after his secret negotiations for an alliance with France had come to light and the King yielded to the clamour of the many enemies the Chancellor had made, only commuting the death penalty to life imprisonment. It was a bad day for the Danish monarchy. Christian V assumed the office of Prime Minister himself, but in reality the government was led by Count Frederick Ahlefeldt and the court became a hotbed of intrigue between him, the Queen and the King's mistress during the pursuit of a fruitless war with Sweden lasting until 1679. The last twenty years of the reign were peaceful but unprogressive and the King was killed in a hunting accident in August 1699, aged fifty-three.

Frederick IV, who succeeded his father, had been badly educated but was full of good intentions and an indefatigable worker. He had shown that he had a mind of his own by choosing his own wife when travelling abroad rather than submitting to an arranged marriage in the customary way. His bride was Princess Louise of Mecklenburg-Güstrow, but once having chosen her he was unable to remain faithful to her for very long and took mistresses with whom he went through forms of bigamous marriage to salve his conscience. The first twenty years of the reign saw Denmark involved in the Northern War which established a balance between Denmark and Sweden and ended with the peace of Frederiksborg on 3 July 1720. In home affairs, the King perfected royal absolutism and gave much attention to education, establishing 240 new schools, and religion, sending missionaries to Lapland, Greenland and the Danish East Indies. Less than a month after the death of the Queen in March 1721, Frederick married Anna Sophie Reventlow, whom he had already married bigamously in 1712, and in the face of some opposition made her Queen. In 1728 two-fifths of Copenhagen was destroyed by fire and Frederick died two years later on 12 October 1730.

The momentous reign of Frederick IV was followed by that of his feeble son Christian VI. As was only to be expected, he had no love for his stepmother Queen Anna Sophie, but she wisely took a meek line and flung herself upon his mercy so that although she was deprived of most of her inheritance under the late King's will, she was allowed to retire to her estate at Klausholm and live there in comfort until her death in 1743. Christian VI was characterized by his extreme piety which was fully shared by his wife Sophie Magdalene of Brandenburg-Kulmbach, a plain and insignificant German Princess. Their sole

Christian VII, King of Denmark, by Nathaniel Dance. The weakness of the King's character is apparent in this portrait.

worldly pursuit was shooting game. The King died in his forty-seventh year in August 1746 and was succeeded by his only son Frederick V, a young man of twenty-three who had married Princess Louisa of Great Britain, daughter of King George II.

The new King and Queen were as popular as their predecessors had been unpopular. The Queen, especially, was loved for her grace and gentleness, but unfortunately she died in December 1751 and the following year Frederick married the unpleasant Juliana Maria of Brunswick-Wolfenbüttel, who never gained his affections. He died in his forties, as his father had done, but unlike his father worn out by a dissolute life. The name of his first wife was on his lips as he died.

The new King, Christian VII, was just coming up to his seventeenth birthday. It was generally agreed that he was intelligent and endowed with a pleasing personality, but he had been subjected to the harsh regime of a brutal governor. Unfortunately, he seems to have inherited the terrible 'royal malady', porphyria, from his Hanoverian mother and his mental capacities were greatly impaired thereby. In November 1766 he married his first cousin, Caroline Matilda, the attractive and vivacious youngest sister of King George III of Great Britain, but he neglected her shamefully while indulging in 'every form of gaiety and dissipation', including playing leading roles at the Court Theatre. However, he acquitted himself well on a tour of European courts he made in 1768.

On his return he fell under the growing influence of his physician, Johann Friedrich Struensee, a German and a radical free thinker, who in 1770 became Master of Requests and Minister of the Royal Cabinet with almost unlimited powers. He was also reputed to have become the lover of the Queen, who had found her marriage far from satisfactory, and may well have been the father of her daughter Louise Augusta, born in July 1771. The affair soon became known and a court revolution was organized to bring about Struensee's fall. Its principal instigator was the Queen Dowager Juliana Maria, eager to discredit the Queen and promote the interests of her own son Prince Frederick. Early in the morning of 17 January 1772 following a ball at the Royal Theatre, the King was awakened and induced to sign the orders for the arrest of the Queen, Struensee and his henchman Brandt. The Queen, protesting vigorously, was conveyed under escort to Kronborg Castle. Struensee, on hearing of the Queen's arrest, confessed his relationship with her and the wretched girl (she was still only twenty) was compelled to admit to it as well. Struensee was hastily brought to trial and condemned to death, his right hand being severed first and his body broken on the wheel before his final beheading. Brandt suffered the same fate. The marriage of the King and Queen was declared dissolved and Caroline Matilda, parted forcibly from her children, was, through the intervention of her brother George III, conveyed by a British warship to his Hanoverian dominions and lodged in the castle at Celle, where her great-grandmother Sophia Dorothea had ended her days. Her dowry was restored to her and she was able to live in comfort, but she felt the separation from her children so keenly that she died in May 1775, before completing her twenty-fourth year. At the end she protested her innocence, claiming that she had been forced to sign the confession of adultery.

For the next twelve years the effective rulers of Denmark were the Queen Dowager Juliana Maria, Prince Frederick and their favourite Ove Höegh-Guldberg. In 1784 Christian VII's son Crown Prince Frederick came of age at sixteen and at his first meeting of the Council on 14 April staged a coup by submitting a document bearing his father's signature, dissolving the cabinet and appointing four new ministers. The Queen Dowager was compelled to retire to Fredensborg and the administration passed from Guldberg into the hands of Count Andreas Peter Bernstorff, an enlightened statesman. Christian VII was never formally deposed and remained the nominal ruler, kept under close restraint, until his death in 1808, when the Crown Prince whose regency had seen the abolition of serfdom and the slave trade in the Danish West Indies and a greater tolerance in the treatment of the Jewish community, ascended the throne as Frederick VI. Mistakenly he threw in his lot with Napoleon and ruined the country's economy thereby, also losing Norway, which had been united to the Danish crown since 1450. Frederick's wife, Marie of Hesse-Cassel, bore him eight children, but only two daughters survived infancy. He also had a long-standing liaison with a dockyard labourer's daughter, Bente Mortensdatter Andersen, who assumed the grander-sounding name of Frederica Julia Benedicta Dannemand and rather oddly was granted the rank of a Colonel's wife. She gave the King four children.

Frederick VI died after a long illness on 3 December 1839, having reigned as Regent and King for fifty-five years. He enjoyed great personal popularity in spite of the vicissitudes of his reign and was much regretted by the people. As he had no surviving son the crown passed to the son of Prince Frederick and grandson of Queen Juliana Maria. Christian VIII had had a brief tenure of the throne of Norway for five months in 1814 and was fifty-three when he became King of Denmark. He and his second wife Caroline were crowned at Frederiksborg on 28 June 1840 and it was to be the last Danish coronation. The King was a highly cultured man and his short reign saw a flowering of art and

A watercolour sketch of the unfortunate Queen Caroline Matilda of Denmark with her son the future King Frederick VI, painted in 1771. Note the little Prince's toy wheelbarrow in the background.

literature. Hans Christian Andersen was writing his fairy stories at this time. A number of administrative reforms came to fruition in Christian's reign and he was on the point of framing a liberal constitution when he died in January 1848.

Frederick VII was the only surviving child of Christian VIII's first marriage to a Princess of Mecklenburg. His parents' marriage had been dissolved when he was only two years old and he did not acquire a stepmother for another five years, so he may be said to have had a childhood deprived of mother love. At the age of twenty he was thrust into marriage with the younger surviving daughter of King Frederick VI, but it was not a success and the marriage was ended by divorce in 1837. Four years later Frederick married again, but this marriage was equally unsuccessful and of even shorter duration, ending in 1846, two years before he became King. Frederick then went to live in Fünen and while there fell in love with Louise Rasmussen, an opera dancer of very humble origin. She was plump and far from attractive, but then so was Frederick. After his accession he established her in the Palace as his mistress and in 1850 he actually married her morganatically, giving her the title of Countess Danner. Although the royal family and most of the court regarded her with disapproval, she probably exercised a good influence on Frederick.

Frederick had granted the liberal constitution his father had planned ten days after his accession, but by rejecting a plan to divide Schleswig with Prussia paved the way for the war which was to lose the Duchies to Prussia in the next reign. Since Frederick was childless and his state of health, undermined by his addiction to strong drink, rendered it unlikely that he would survive for very long, the question of the succession presented some problems, since there were no male heirs apart from Frederick's uncle Prince Ferdinand, who was also childless. Eventually it was agreed that the crown should pass to Prince Christian of Schleswig-Holstein-Sonderburg-Glücksburg, a great-grandson in the female line of King Frederick V. The death of Prince Ferdinand in June 1863 was followed by that of the King in November and Prince Christian duly ascended the throne as Christian IX.

Christian IX was to become one of Denmark's most popular and greatly loved Kings although at the outset of his reign the 'Schleswig-Holstein Question' involving Denmark in war with Prussia and Austria rendered him extremely unpopular for a time. Christian became known as the 'Father-in-Law' of Europe as a result of his children's marriages. He and Queen Louise, who was to incur the censure of Queen Victoria for a discreet use of make-up which her daughter Alexandra far exceeded and managed to get away with without comment, had three sons and three daughters. The second son, William, was elected King of Greece even before his father ascended the Danish throne, while the eldest daughter, Alexandra, married the Prince of Wales, later King Edward VII, the second, Dagmar, married Emperor Alexander III of Russia, and the youngest, Thyra, married the Duke of Cumberland, son and heir of the dispossessed King George V of Hanover. King Christian and Queen Louise were the hosts at great gatherings of their children, grandchildren and great-grandchildren held annually at Fredensborg. Queen Louise died in 1898, having been the first woman to receive the Order

King Frederick VIII of Denmark: a portrait by Otto Backe made in 1911, the year before the King's death.

of the Elephant, Denmark's premier order of knighthood, conferred on her by her husband on the occasion of their golden wedding. King Christian remained hale and hearty to the last, dying at the age of eighty-seven in January 1906 after less than a day's illness.

Frederick VIII was already in his sixty-third year when he succeeded his father and reigned for only six years. In May 1912 he was returning to Denmark after taking a cure and stayed overnight in Hamburg. In the evening he apparently left the hotel in which he was staying without informing his attendants. Alarmed by his prolonged absence, they informed the police and the King was finally found dead in a public morgue, having collapsed with a heart attack and died in the street with no identification on him. Later stories were to circulate that he had died in a brothel, but they cannot be confirmed any more than they can be denied. The circumstances of King Frederick VIII's death made such an impression on the late Queen Louise of Sweden (wife of King Gustav VI Adolph) that she always carried in her handbag a card on which she had written, 'I am the Queen of Sweden'. Had she ever been involved in a street accident, one can well imagine the disbelieving smiles which might have played on the faces of whoever found such a message.

Frederick VIII's second son Charles had been elected King of

Denmark on marriage and is Chancellor of the Royal Danish Orders and a Danish Admiral and General. The royal couple have two sons and the heir to the throne is Prince Frederick, who was born in May 1968.

King Christian X of Denmark.

Queen Margrethe II of Denmark and her husband Prince Henrik. This was the first official photograph of the royal couple taken after the Queen's accession in 1972. She wears a black dress in mourning for her father King Frederick IX.

Norway in 1905 and his eldest son now succeeded to the Danish throne as Christian X. Tall and of majestic bearing, King Christian had a long reign which encompassed the two World Wars, during the second of which Denmark was under German occupation. The King went for a daily ride through the streets of Copenhagen and was a great inspiration to his people. When the Jews were required to wear a yellow patch on their sleeves, King Christian did so too. From 1918 to 1944 King Christian was also King of Iceland until it was declared a Republic. He died in April 1947, his health having been broken during the war years.

King Frederick IX who succeeded his father was a real sailor King even to the extent of being heavily tattooed. He was also intensely fond of music and would often conduct the Danish State Orchestra. He married Princess Ingrid of Sweden, who both as Queen and Queen Mother, enjoyed and continues to enjoy great popularity. They had three daughters and no son, so in 1953 the law of succession was altered to allow their eldest daughter to succeed to the throne. King Frederick died after a short illness in January 1972 and was succeeded by his eldest daughter Queen Margrethe II.

Queen Margrethe is one of the three reigning Queens of Europe today and is at least a head and shoulders taller than her co-monarchs Queen Elizabeth II and Queen Beatrix of the Netherlands. She is married to a Frenchman, Henri de Laborde de Monpezat, who received the title of Prince Henrik of

NORWAY

The early history of Norway, like that of Denmark, is related in the Norse sagas, a blend of fact and fiction, which begin to become more reliable with the accounts of Halfdan the Black, King of Westfold, and his son Harald the Fairhaired who subjugated many petty kingdoms and gradually brought the whole of Norway under one rule. Harald died about 936 after making a division of his lands among his many sons (at least twenty are recorded) with the usual disastrous results. One of the younger sons, Eric Bloodaxe, murdered seven of his half-brothers and reigned despotically until he was driven out by his youngest half-brother Haakon I in about 945. Haakon fell in battle some fifteen years later and was followed by Eric's son Harald II Greycloak, whose attempts to introduce Christianity resulted in his murder in about 965. A period of anarchy followed until 995 when Olav Tryggvesson, a great-grandson of Harald the

Fairhaired, obtained the throne and reunited the country. A great warrior, he led raiding parties to England and was finally killed in a sea battle with the Swedes and the Danes on 9 September 1000. An interregnum of fifteen years followed, during which Norway was the prey of a number of squabbling Jarls, as the great nobles were entitled.

In 1015 the twenty-year-old Olav II obtained the throne. He was a great-great-grandson of Harald the Fairhaired and his father, grandfather and great-grandfather had been under-Kings in Westfold. Olav had been brought up in England at the court of King Ethelred the Unready and on his return to Norway set about establishing Christianity, even by force of arms where necessary. His powerful rule alienated his Jarls, who felt their own power threatened, and they conspired against him with Canute the Great of Denmark, driving him out in 1028. Olav was killed fighting to regain his kingdom on 29 July 1030. He was later canonized and became Norway's patron saint. On Canute's death in 1035, Olav's eleven-year-old son Magnus was restored to his father's throne. From 1046 he shared it with his father's half-brother Harald III Hardraade ('the hard in council'), who became sole ruler when Magnus was killed in battle on 25 October 1047.

Harald III is best known for his invasion of England, where he was defeated and slain by King Harold II at Stamford Bridge on 23 September 1066. He had married a Russian wife, Elizabeth, whose three sisters became Queen of Poland, Queen of Hungary and Queen of France, thus forging an early inter-dynastic connection between the reigning families of Europe. It was their sons, Magnus II and Olav III who succeeded to the throne jointly, reigning together until Magnus died in 1069 and Olav became sole King. Olav the Peaceful was succeeded in 1093 by his natural son Magnus III Barefoot, who reigned ten years before being killed in battle on 24 August 1103. His wife, a Princess of Sweden, was childless and the throne was shared by his three natural sons, Eystein I, Sigurd I the Crusader, and Olav IV. By 1122 Sigurd had become the sole ruler, and when he died on 26 March 1130 he was succeeded jointly by his natural son Magnus IV and Harald IV, another alleged natural son of Magnus III. In 1135 Harald deposed and blinded Magnus and then reigned alone until his death on 14 December 1136, when his sons Inge I the Hunchback, Sigurd II and Eystein II shared the throne. Only Inge was legitimate and he managed to outlive his two half-brothers and become sole ruler, dying in 1161. Sigurd II's natural son Haakon II then reigned for a year and was succeeded by Magnus V, a son of Erling Skakke who had married King Sigurd II's widow Christina, herself the daughter (for once legitimate) of King Sigurd I. Magnus V reigned until 1184 when he was killed by Sverre, another natural son of Sigurd II.

Sverre had been a priest in the Faröes and this experience probably gave him the determination to curb the power of the Bishops which led to his excommunication. When he died in February or March 1202 he was succeeded by Haakon III, the son of his first wife Astrid. After barely two years on the throne Haakon was poisoned by his stepmother Margaret of Sweden. He was followed by Inge II, a maternal grandson of Sigurd II, until 1217, when Haakon's posthumous natural son Haakon IV ascended the throne. He was the best ruler Norway had had for many years, restoring order, promoting maritime trade and acquiring Greenland and Iceland. When he died in December 1263 he left a stable kingdom to his son Magnus VI the Law Mender. Magnus was succeeded in 1280 by his son Eric II, who married first, in 1281, Margaret, daughter of King Alexander III of Scotland. She died in childbirth in 1283, leaving a daughter Margaret, who in 1286 succeeded her maternal grandfather on the Scottish throne. In September 1290 the little girl, who is known to history as 'the Maid of Norway', died of seasickness in Orkney while on her voyage to Scotland. In 1293, Eric, who had put in a claim for the Scottish crown as his daughter's heir, took another Scottish wife, Isabella Bruce, sister of the eventual successful competitor Robert Bruce. This marriage, too, produced but one daughter and when Eric died in 1299 he was succeeded by his brother Haakon V, who encouraged the merchants of the Hanseatic League with far-reaching and disastrous effects.

Like his brother and predecessor, Haakon only had daughters and it was the three-year-son of his elder daughter Ingeborg who succeeded him as Magnus VII when he died on 8 May 1319. In the same year Magnus succeeded his paternal uncle, Birger, as King of Sweden. Magnus came of age in 1333 and in 1335 married Blanche, daughter of John, Count of Namur, and they had two sons Eric and Haakon. As these grew up they were both to have an unsatisfactory relationship with their parents. Magnus was greatly under the influence of his Queen, a highly ambitious woman, and the licentiousness of his court brought him into ill-repute with his senators. In 1343 Magnus associated Haakon with him on the throne of Norway, resigning the kingdom to him completely in 1355. The following year Magnus's elder son Eric forced Magnus to accept him as co-ruler in Sweden. Later we shall see what befell Eric at his mother's hands. Magnus was imprisoned in Stockholm for six years, but eventually liberated when his other son Haakon paid a heavy ransom. He returned to Norway and lived there quietly for several years until making a sea voyage to the islands off Bergen when a violent storm arose and his ship was lost with all on board on 1 December 1374.

Haakon VI reigned until his death on 1 May 1380. He was married to the masterful Margaret of Denmark and their only son Olav V (now reckoned Olav IV, the son of King Magnus III being usually omitted in the enumeration of Norwegian sovereigns), who had already been King of Denmark since 1376 in succession to his maternal grandfather, now became King of Norway also under his mother's regency. As we have seen she united all three northern kingdoms at Kalmar in 1397.

Norway remained united to the kingdom of Denmark until 14 January 1814, when King Frederick VI ceded it to Sweden. There was a bid for independence when the Storthing (the Norwegian parliament) elected the former Danish Viceroy, Prince Christian Frederick (later King Christian VIII of Denmark) King on 17 May 1814, but he renounced the throne on 7 October 1814 and the Storthing accepted King Carl XIII of Sweden as King of Norway. On 7 June 1905 a serious disagreement with the policies pursued by King Oscar II led the Storthing to present an address to the throne declaring the union with Sweden dissolved and on 18 November Prince Charles of Denmark was elected King of Norway.

The House of Oldenburg

HAAKON VII	1905–1957

b Charlottenlund 3 August 1872, 2nd son of King Frederick VIII of Denmark; elected King of Norway 18 November 1905; crowned Trondheim Cathedral 22 June 1906; *m* Buckingham Palace, London, 22 July 1896 Maud (*b* Marlborough House, London, 26 November 1869; *d* London 20 November 1938), yst dau of Edward VII, King of Great Britain and Ireland, Emperor of India, and Alexandra of Denmark; 1 son; *d* Oslo 21 September 1957

OLAV V	1957–

b Appleton House, Sandringham, Norfolk, 2 July 1903, only son of King Haakon VII; Regent of Norway from 30 June 1955; *s* his father 21 September 1957; *m* Oslo 21 March 1929 Märtha (*b* Stockholm 28 March 1901; *d* Oslo 5 April 1954), 2nd dau of Prince Carl of Sweden, Duke of Västergötland, and Ingeborg of Denmark; 1 son, 2 daus

For the first thirty-three years of his life there was very little prospect that Prince Charles of Denmark would ever wear a crown. As the second son of the then Crown Prince of Denmark, he seemed scarcely eligible when he married his cousin Princess Maud of Wales at Buckingham Palace in 1896. His only recommendation, apart from his royal birth, was his height and his handsome appearance which contrasted greatly

The late Crown Princess Märtha of Norway, wife of King Olav V, a photograph taken in 1939.

King Haakon VII and Queen Maud of Norway in their coronation robes in June 1906. It was the last coronation to take place in Scandinavia.

with that of his bride who was distinctly plain and pop-eyed and who in later life was to apply cosmetics so heavily that she presents a clown-like appearance in most photographs. The couple spent a lot of their early married life in England and it was at Sandringham that their only child, christened Alexander but later renamed Olav, was born in 1903. In November 1905 the Norwegian parliament (or Storthing) effected a bloodless revolution, severed the union with Sweden, and offered the throne to Prince Charles of Denmark, who accepted it.

To please his new subjects, Prince Charles adopted the style of King Haakon VII. He and Queen Maud were crowned in Trondheim Cathedral in June 1906. In a curious ceremony blending the religious and the secular, the crown was actually placed on the King's head by the Prime Minister. King Haakon soon identified himself heart and soul with his people and in the course of a long reign of over fifty years became greatly loved. In the First World War he managed, in common with the other two northern monarchies, to maintain a strict neutrality, and hoped to be able to do the same when the Second World War broke out in 1939, in spite of German depredations on Norway's merchant fleet. In April 1940 Germany invaded Norway and the King and members of the government moved to Tromsö in the far north, shortly afterwards going to England. There a government in exile was set up and the King worked tirelessly in the allied cause, keeping in touch with the resistance movement at home. He returned to a tumultuous welcome when Norway was liberated in 1945. Ten years later, tired and ageing, the King appointed his son Regent after suffering a bad fall and fracturing his femur. King Haakon VII died on 21 September 1957, aged eighty-five.

The Crown Prince who succeeded his father as King Olav V was already a much-loved figure. Unfortunately he was a widower, his wife Princess Märtha of Sweden, a sister of the adored Queen Astrid of Belgium, having died in 1954, so Norway was to have no Queen (Queen Maud had died in 1938).

The Norwegian monarchy is perhaps the least stylish of the existing European monarchies. Norway has no titled nobility; the King's two daughters both married commoners and retired into private life, one living in South America; and Crown Prince

King Olav V of Norway as Crown Prince (a portrait study by Karsh of Ottawa).

Harald has also married a commoner, the charming Crown Princess Sonja. King Olav, now well into his eighties, is a frequent visitor to England, the land of his birth. He makes a special point of attending the British Legion Festival of Remembrance at the Royal Albert Hall every November and of being present at the Cenotaph Ceremony in Whitehall the following morning. Long may he continue to do so!

SWEDEN

The first dynasty to rise to a position of pre-eminence among the many small Iron Age kingdoms in Sweden was that of the Ynglinga, who held sway in Uppsala and whose legendary deeds are recounted in the sagas. About the same time as Gorm the Old was consolidating the kingdom of Denmark, the brothers Olof and Eric were reigning together in Uppsala, having succeeded their father Bjorn the Old. Olof died quite soon, leaving Eric as sole ruler. He was of warlike disposition and conquered Finland, Esthonia and Livonia, earning the name of Eric the Victorious. Eric's wife, aptly named Sigrid the Haughty, was a proud beauty and eventually he could stand her no longer and they separated after she had borne him a son and a daughter. She later married Sweyn Forkbeard, King of Denmark and by

conquest of England, and became the stepmother of our King Canute.

Eric died about 995 and was succeeded by his only son Olof, whom he had proclaimed as his successor and paraded before his army when he was only two years old. From this fact Olof was known as Olof Skötkonung (Olof Lap-King). He was converted to Christianity and baptized in 1001. Olof had a son Emund and a daughter Astrid by his concubine Edla and as his Queen, also called Astrid, could not stand them, they were sent away from court to be brought up. Later Queen Astrid gave birth to a daughter Ingegerd, afterwards married to Yaroslav I, Great Prince of Kiev, by whom she was the mother of Queen Anne of France among others. Finally, Queen Astrid gave birth to a son

Anund Jacob, who succeeded his father in 1021 or 1022. As Anund Jacob only had a daughter he was succeeded on his death in 1050 by his elder half-brother Emund the Old. Emund's only son fell in battle and when Emund died in 1060 he was succeeded by his son-in-law Stenkil Ragnvaldsson, whose grandfather Ulf had been a brother of Queen Sigrid the Haughty. Stenkil died in 1066 and a period of anarchy ensued until 1078 when his sons Inge I and Halstan secured the throne and reigned jointly until 1099 when Halstan died.

Inge, 'a tall and strong man like his father Stenkil', reigned alone until 1081 when he was driven out by his wife's brother, Blot Sven, who usurped the throne until 1083, when Inge managed to trap and kill him and regain the throne. He reigned until his death in 1112, completing the extirpation of paganism by burning the great temple at Uppsala, and was succeeded by his nephews Philip and Inge II, the sons of Halstan. Neither had children and on Inge II's death in 1130, Magnus, son of King Niels of Denmark by Inge I's daughter Margaret, was elected to fill the vacant throne. He was unable to establish his rule and was killed in 1134. Sverker I, son of Kol and grandson of Blot Sven then became King. He was 'of a very mild and pious character' and founded many monasteries. His second wife, Richeza, was a daughter of King Boleslaw III of Poland.

For a hundred years after Sverker's death in 1156 the throne was held alternately by members of the rival houses of Sverker and Eric. Sverker's immediate successor was his cousin Eric IX (so numbered by later reckoning), the son of one Jedvard by Cecilia, daughter of Blot Sven. Eric has been the subject of many legends. He attempted to convert Finland and gained a great reputation for holiness. In 1160 he was murdered at Uppsala by a party of Danes. A spring of clear water is said to have gushed forth on the spot where his blood was shed. He was later canonized and became Sweden's patron saint. His bones still rest inside his magnificent shrine in Uppsala Cathedral. The noble family of Bonde, which was to produce King Carl VIII, claims descent from Eric's brother Ivar. Eric was succeeded by Carl VII, the son of Sverker I. (Here it must be stated that Carls I–VI do not exist. They were figments of the enthusiastic imagination of an early chronicler, but the enumeration once established was allowed to continue. There is similar confusion over the earlier Erics.) Carl VII was surprised and murdered by St Eric's son Canute in 1167. Canute prudently associated Carl's son Sverker in the sovereignty and thus contrived to die peacefully in his bed in 1196. Sverker II succeeded and lived on good terms with Canute's sons for several years until seeds of suspicion were sown in his mind and he murdered three of them in November 1205. Eric, the eldest son, managed to escape to Norway. King Sverker was, we are told, 'a very handsome, eloquent, and valiant man', but he aroused animosity by exempting the clergy from all taxes. Eric returned from Norway in a bid to gain the throne and Sverker was finally defeated and killed on 17 July 1210.

Eric X was the first Swedish King to be crowned, or at any rate of whose coronation a record exists. The ceremony took place at Uppsala and was performed by the Archbishop in the presence of the other Bishops and nobles of the kingdom. Eric died a natural death in 1216 and was succeeded by King Sverker II's son Johan I, the last of the Sverker line, who died on 10 March 1222. Eric

X's six-year-old son then succeeded as Eric XI. He grew up a mild-tempered man with a lisp and a limp. In 1229 he lost the throne to a usurper set up by the powerful Folkung family, who reigned as Canute II the Long until Eric returned with Danish help and defeated and killed him in 1234. Thereafter Eric reigned in peace until his death, supposedly from poison, on 2 February 1250. He was the last of the Eric line. The noble Swedish families of Sparre and Oxenstjerna descend from his sister Märtha.

After Eric's death the government was assumed immediately by his brother-in-law the powerful Birger Jarl in the name of his son Valdemar, whose mother was Eric's sister Ingeborg. Birger Jarl was Sweden's greatest statesman of the Middle Ages and founded the city of Stockholm. Valdemar was only seven years old and his father had him crowned in Linköping Cathedral in 1251 to assure his title to the crown. In the following year Birger's mother, Ingrid Ylfva, died and in order to fulfil a prophecy that her family would remain in power as long as her head was up, Birger had her buried upright within a pillar at Bjelbo Church. Birger strengthened his family's position by a series of judicious marriages. His first wife Princess Ingeborg died in 1254 and in 1261 he married Mechthild of Holstein, the Dowager Queen of Denmark, widow of King Abel. A year previously he had arranged the marriage of King Valdemar to King Abel's niece Sophia. His eldest daughter was married to a Norwegian Prince and the youngest to the German Prince of Anhalt-Zerbst. Birger Jarl died in 1266. Apart from King Valdemar he left three other sons, Magnus, Duke of Södermanland, Bengt, Duke of Finland, and Eric, Duke of Småland, the first Dukes created in Sweden.

King Valdemar was greatly addicted to pleasure and his consort Queen Sophia did not get on with her brothers-in-law, to whom she gave disparaging nicknames which they greatly resented. The Queen went to visit her family in Denmark and returned with her sister Jutta, who had been a nun and Prioress of Roskilde, but had tired of the monastic life and returned to the court. She was very young and beautiful and King Valdemar fell in love with her. To Queen Sophia's great chagrin Jutta gave birth to the King's son in 1273. The whole country was horrified at the enormity committed by the King with his sister-in-law, a professed nun, and he was obliged to go to Rome to seek a pardon from the Pope. On his return civil war broke out and Valdemar was captured and forced to surrender half the kingdom to his brother Magnus in 1275. Three years later he attempted to regain that which he had lost but instead lost all and was imprisoned at Nyköping Castle, where he died on 26 December 1302. Queen Sophia died in 1286.

Magnus Ladulås (Lockbarn) enacted many new laws and was loved by the peasants who gave him his sobriquet because they felt he had made their livelihood safer. King Magnus died on 18 December 1290 and was carried to Stockholm for burial in the Franciscan Church there. He had had the foresight to have his son Birger declared his heir, although only a child. The regency was undertaken by Thorgils Knutsson, who among other things arranged the King's marriage with Princess Märtha of Denmark in 1298 and that of Birger's sister Ingeborg with King Eric Menved of Denmark in 1296. Both marriages were celebrated with great splendour. A few years later King Birger became involved in war with his brothers Eric and Valdemar. There was a temporary reconciliation in 1305, but trouble started again in 1306, and continued in an on-and-off state until 1319, when King Birger was finally deposed and replaced by his nephew Magnus, the only son of Eric, Duke of Södermanland, who had died imprisoned by Birger in 1318. Birger's innocent son Magnus, aged twenty, was made to suffer for his father's offences and executed in October 1320. The news of his death caused that of his hapless father on 31 May 1321. Queen Märtha lived on until 1341.

Magnus Smek was only three years old when placed on the throne by the partisans of his father and uncle Valdemar in 1319. We have already encountered Magnus as King of Norway and there is really very little more to be said about him here, except that he was finally deposed and imprisoned in 1364, after two periods of co-rulership with his sons Eric XII and Haakon. Eric XII was actually murdered by his own mother Blanche of Namur, thirsty for power herself, who lured her son and daughter-in-law to spend Christmas 1359 with her and poisoned them both. The young Queen Beatrix died at once after being delivered of stillborn male twins, but Eric lingered for several days and was able to gasp out with his last breath, 'She who gave me life, has also deprived me of it'. Magnus Smek's younger son Haakon has also been mentioned already as King of Norway and husband of the famous Queen Margaret who united the three Scandinavian crowns at Kalmar in 1389. He was away in Norway in 1364 when King Magnus was overthrown in a coup engineered by the nobles who set up Albert of Mecklenburg as their puppet. Albert was the son of Magnus's sister Euphemia, who had married Duke Albert I of Mecklenburg.

Once on the Swedish throne, Albert began to resent the restrictions imposed upon him by the nobles and filled his magnificent court with Germans of every description. He delighted in being entertained by singers and dancers who were so lavishly rewarded that he had to impose crippling new taxes. Eventually matters reached a point where another coup was effected by the nobles, Albert was driven out and the crown of Sweden was offered to the redoubtable Queen Margaret, already the ruler of Denmark and Norway. We have had occasion to refer to the union of Kalmar more than once. It was always uneasy. In 1397 Margaret took as her co-ruler her great-nephew Eric of Pomerania. Strangely enough he was also the great-nephew of the deposed King Albert, whose brother Duke Henry of Mecklenburg had married Margaret's sister Ingeborg. Eric XIII was the son of their daughter Marie, who married Duke Wartislaw VII of Pomerania. He succeeded as sole ruler of the three kingdoms when Queen Margaret died suddenly of plague in October 1412. The former King Albert had died in March the same year.

Eric's sole reign came as something of a relief after the harsh and tyrannical rule of Queen Margaret. He made several improvements in the administration of justice and improved the lot of the downtrodden peasantry, but pursued an indecisive war in Holstein for a matter of thirty years. Eric's Queen was Philippa, the daughter of King Henry IV of England, whom he married in 1406 when she was twelve. Philippa, 'a mild and gentle lady', proved an excellent Queen and acted as Regent when Eric undertook a pilgrimage to Jerusalem. After many childless years the Queen at last gave birth to a stillborn son. Broken in health she retired to the Convent of Vadstena and died there on 5 January 1430. After her death things went badly for Eric and in 1435 he was obliged to leave Sweden in the hands of Engelbrekt Engelbrektsson as Administrator. Engelbrekt was killed on 3 May 1436 and was followed as Administrator by Carl Knutsson Bonde, a handsome young man of noble descent. Meanwhile, King Eric was living in Denmark and fast alienating his Danish subjects by his debaucheries. One of his many mistresses even went so far as to have her seal inscribed 'Dorothea, King Eric's Concubine'. In 1438 the people could stand it no longer and he was deposed in favour of his nephew Christopher, the son of his sister Catherine, who had married John, Count Palatine of Neumarkt. Eric retired into obscurity and continued to lead a dissolute life until his death in 1459.

Christopher lost no time in writing to the Swedish Senate and proposing himself as King. He also flattered the Administrator Carl Knutsson and overcame his opposition so that eventually in 1440 he was elected King of Sweden and made his entry into Stockholm. After a reign in Sweden of eight years, Christopher died suddenly on 6 January 1448. He left no heirs and once again the nobles assembled to elect a King. The successful candidate was the former Administrator Carl Knutsson Bonde, who now became King Carl VIII and was duly crowned with his wife at Uppsala Cathedral. Immensely popular at first, Carl soon lost favour with both nobles and people. With the former because he reserved all the provincial revenues for himself; with the latter because of his extravagance and display. At one feast he is said to have displayed fourteen hundred silver dishes as well as many other articles of gold and silver plate. At last an uprising dethroned him in 1457 and he fled to Danzig. The Archbishop of Uppsala had been instrumental in Carl's deposition and now invited Christian I of Denmark to take the Swedish throne also. Christian came to Sweden and was crowned at Uppsala on 29 July 1457. He reigned uneasily until 1464 when he was driven out and Carl was invited to return. His restoration lasted but a year and he was forced into exile again by the King-making Archbishop, who attempted to rule Sweden himself with an iron hand. When the Archbishop died in 1466 Carl regained the throne again and this time reigned until his death in May 1470 at the age of sixty-two. On his deathbed he nominated his half-nephew Sten Sture as Administrator, warning him not to strive for the royal office which he said had ruined his own happiness and cost him his life.

Sten Sture the Elder ruled Sweden as Administrator until 1497, when the Danish King Hans, son of Christian I, was called to the throne by the Senate. In Sweden he is reckoned as King Johan II. His rule in Sweden only lasted until 1501, when he was driven out and Sten Sture was re-appointed Administrator. Sten died at Jönköping on 13 December 1503 and was succeeded as Administrator by Svante Sture, who came from a different family of Stures. His rule lasted until his sudden death on 2 January 1512, when his son Sten Sture the Younger took over and remained in power until his death from wounds received in battle with the Danes in February 1520. Sten's heroic wife Christina

Gyllenstjerna made a brave attempt to hold Stockholm but the might of the Danish army prevailed and Christian II entered the city in triumph and was crowned on 4 November 1520. His reign was to be short and disastrous. The story of the massacre at Stockholm has already been told. The struggle for Swedish independence was begun under the leadership of Gustav Ericsson Vasa and ended when Christian was deposed and Gustav elected King in his place in June 1523.

GUSTAV I VASA	1523–1560

---

b Lindholmen, Uppland 12 May 1496, son of Eric Johansson Vasa of Rydboholm, and Cecilia Månsdotter of Eka; appointed Administrator of Sweden 24 August 1521; elected King 6 June 1523; crowned Uppsala 12 January 1528; *m* (1) Stockholm 24 September 1531 Catherine (*b* 1513; *d* Stockholm 23 September 1535), dau of Magnus I, Duke of Saxe-Lauenburg, and Catherine of Brunswick-Wolfenbüttel; 1 son; *m* (2) Uppsala 1 October 1536 Margaret (*b* 1 January 1514; *d* Tynnelsö 26 August 1551; *bur* Uppsala Cathedral), dau of Eric Abrahamsson Leijonhufvud and Ebba Vasa; 5 sons, 5 daus; *m* (3) Vadstena 22 August 1552 Catherine (*b* 22 July 1536; *d* 13 December 1621), dau of Gustav Olofsson Stenbock, Governor of West Gothland, and Brita Leijonhufvud (sister of Queen Margaret); no issue; *d* Stockholm 29 September 1560; *bur* Uppsala Cathedral

---

ERIC XIV	1560–1568

---

b Stockholm 13 December 1533, eldest son of King Gustav I; *s* his father 29 September 1560; crowned Uppsala 29 June 1561; deposed 29 September 1568; *m* Stockholm 4 July 1568 Karin Månsdotter, crowned Queen Consort at Stockholm 5 July 1568 (*b* 6 November 1550; *d* Ljuxala 13 September 1612; *bur* Åbo Cathedral), dau of Magnus (Måns), corporal in the Royal Life Guards; 4 sons, 1 dau; *d* Örby 26 February 1577; *bur* Västerås

---

JOHAN III	1568–1592

---

b Stockholm 21 December 1537, 2nd son of King Gustav I and eldest son by his 2nd wife; *s* on the deposition of his half-brother King Eric XIV 29 September 1568; confirmed in his title by the Riksdag 25 January 1569; crowned Uppsala July 1569; *m* (1) 4 October 1562 Catharina Jagellonica (*b* Cracow 1626; *d* Stockholm 16 November 1583; *bur* Uppsala Cathedral), yst dau of Sigismund I, King of Poland, and his 2nd wife Bona Sforza; 1 son, 2 daus; *m* (2) Västerås 21 February 1585 Gunilla (*b* 25 June 1568; *d* 25 June 1597), dau of Johan Axelsson Bielke and Margaretha Posse; 1 son; *d* Stockholm 17 November 1592; *bur* Uppsala Cathedral

---

SIGISMUND	1592–1599

---

b Gripsholm 20 June 1566; elected King of Poland (as Sigismund III) 19 August 1587; crowned Cracow 28 December 1587; *s* his father as King of Sweden 17 November 1592; crowned Uppsala 19 February 1594; deposed as King of Sweden 1599; *m* (1) Cracow 31 May 1592 Anna (*b* Graz 16 August 1573; *d* Cracow 10 February 1598), eldest dau of Archduke Charles of Austria and Maria of Bavaria; 2 sons, 3 daus; *m* (2) Cracow 11 December 1605 Constance (*b* Graz 24 December 1588; *d* Cracow 10 July 1631), sister of his 1st wife and 8th dau of Archduke Charles of Austria; 5 sons, 2 daus; *d* Cracow 30 April 1632

CARL IX	1599–1611

---

b Stockholm 4 October 1550, 6th and yst son of King Gustav I; *s* as Administrator on the deposition of his nephew King Sigismund 1599; proclaimed King March 1604; crowned Uppsala 1607; *m* (1) Heidelberg 11 May 1579 Anna Maria (*b* Heidelberg 24 July 1561; *d* Eskilstuna 29 July 1589), eldest dau of Ludwig VI, Elector Palatine, and his 1st wife Elisabeth of Hesse; 2 sons, 4 daus; *m* (2) 27 August 1592 Christina (*b* 13 April 1573; *d* 8 December 1625), 2nd dau of Adolph, Duke of Holstein-Gottorp, and Christina of Hesse; 2 sons, 2 daus; *d* Nyköping 30 October 1611; *bur* Stregnaes

---

GUSTAV II ADOLPH	1611–1632

---

b Stockholm 9 December 1594, 3rd but eldest surviving son of King Carl IX and elder son by his 2nd wife Christina of Holstein-Gottorp; *s* his father 30 October 1611; crowned Uppsala 1617; *m* 5 November 1620 Maria Eleonora, crowned Queen Consort Stockholm 28 November 1620 (*b* 11 November 1599; *d* 28 March 1655), 2nd dau of John Sigismund, Elector of Brandenburg, and Anna of Prussia; 2 daus; *d* Lützen 16 November 1632; *bur* Stockholm

---

CHRISTINA	1632–1654

---

b Stockholm 8 December 1626, yr but only surviving dau of King Gustav II Adolph; *s* her father 16 November 1632; crowned Stockholm 20 October 1650; abdicated 6 June 1654; *d unm* Rome 19 April 1689

CARL X GUSTAV	1654–1660

---

b Nyköping 18 November 1622, 2nd but eldest surviving son of Count Palatine Johan Casimir of Zweibrücken, and Catherine of Sweden (dau of King Carl IX and his 1st wife); *s* his cousin Queen Christina on her abdication 6 June 1654; crowned Uppsala 16 June 1654; *m* Stockholm 24 October 1654 Hedwig Eleonora (*b* Gottorp 23 October 1636; *d* Stockholm 24 November 1715), 4th dau of Frederick III, Duke of Holstein-Gottorp, and Maria Elisabeth of Saxony; 1 son; *d* Göteborg 23 February 1660

CARL XI	1660–1697

---

b Stockholm 4 December 1655, only son of King Carl X Gustav; *s* his father 23 February 1660; crowned Uppsala 1675; *m* Skottorp, nr Helsingborg, 16 May 1680 Ulrika Eleonora (*b* Copenhagen 11 September 1656; *d* Karlberg Castle, nr Stockholm, 15 August 1693), 4th dau of Frederick III, King of Denmark and Norway, and Sophia Amelia of Brunswick-Lüneburg; 5 sons, 2 daus; *d* Stockholm 15 April 1697; *bur* Stockholm

CARL XII   1697–1718

b Stockholm 27 June 1682, eldest and only surviving son of King Carl XI; *s* his father 15 April 1697; crowned Stockholm 1697; *d unm* Frederikshald, Norway, 11 December 1718; *bur* Stockholm

ULRIKA ELEONORA   1719–1720

b Stockholm 2 February 1688, yr dau of King Carl XI; elected successor to her brother King Carl XII 23 January 1719; crowned Uppsala 17 March 1719; abdicated in favour of her husband 26 March 1720; *m* Stockholm 15 April 1715 Frederick I, Landgrave of Hesse-Cassel; *d* Stockholm 5 December 1741; *bur* Stockholm

FREDERICK I   1720–1751

b Cassel 8 May 1676, son of Charles, Landgrave of Hesse-Cassel, and Maria Amelia of Courland; *s* his 2nd wife as King of Sweden on her abdication 26 March 1720; crowned Stockholm 3 May 1720; *s* his father as Landgrave of Hesse-Cassel 23 March 1730; *m* (1) Berlin 31 May 1700 Louise (*b* Berlin 29 September 1680; *d* Cassel 23 December 1705), dau of Frederick I, King in Prussia, and his 1st wife Elisabeth Henriette of Hesse-Cassel; no issue; *m* (2) Stockholm 15 April 1715 Ulrika Eleonora, Queen of Sweden; no issue; *d* Stockholm 5 April 1751; *bur* Stockholm

ADOLPH FREDERICK   1751–1771

b Gottorp 14 May 1710, 2nd son of Christian August, Duke of Holstein-Gottorp, and Albertina Frederica of Baden-Durlach; Prince Bishop of Lübeck 16 September 1727; elected heir to the Swedish throne 4 July 1743; resigned the bishopric of Lübeck 29 October 1750; *s* King Frederick I as King of Sweden 5 April 1751; crowned Stockholm 26 November 1751; *m* Drottningholm 29 August 1744 Louisa Ulrika (*b* Berlin 24 July 1720; *d* Svartsjö Castle, Lake Mälaren 16 July 1782), 6th dau of Frederick William I, King of Prussia, and Sophia Dorothea of Hanover; 3 sons, 1 dau; *d* Stockholm 12 April 1771; *bur* Stockholm

GUSTAV III   1771–1792

b Stockholm 24 January 1746, eldest son of King Adolph Frederick; *s* his father 12 April 1771; crowned Stockholm 29 June 1772; *m* Copenhagen 1 October 1766 Sophia Magdalena (*b* Christiansborg Castle, Copenhagen, 3 July 1746; *d* Ulriksdal Castle 21 August 1813), eldest dau of Frederick V, King of Denmark, and his 1st wife Louise of Great Britain; 2 sons; *d* (assassinated) Stockholm 29 March 1792; *bur* Stockholm

GUSTAV IV ADOLPH   1792–1809

b Stockholm 1 November 1778, elder and only surviving son of King Gustav III; *s* his father 29 March 1792 under the regency of his uncle Prince Carl, Duke of Södermanland until 1796; crowned St Olai Church, Norrköping 3 April 1800; deposed 13 March and abdicated 29 March 1809; *m* Stockholm 31 October 1797 (*m* diss 1812) Frederica (*b* Karlsruhe 12 March 1781; *d* Lausanne, Switzerland, 25 September 1826), 4th dau of Charles, Hereditary Prince of Baden, and Amelia Frederica of Hesse-Darmstadt; 2 sons, 3 daus; *d* St Gallen, Switzerland, 7 February 1837

CARL XIII   1809–1818

b Stockholm 7 October 1748, 2nd son of King Adolph Frederick; Regent of Sweden for his nephew King Gustav IV Adolph 1792–96; Protector of the Realm 13 March 1809; elected King 3 June 1809; crowned Stockholm 6 June 1809; elected King of Norway 4 November 1814; *m* Stockholm 7 July 1774 Charlotte (*b* Eutin 22 March 1759; *d* Rosersberg Castle, Uppland, 20 June 1818), yr dau of Frederick Augustus, Duke of Oldenburg and Delmenhorst (brother of King Adolph Frederick), and Frederica of Hesse-Cassel; 1 son, 1 dau (both *d* in infancy); *d* Stockholm 5 February 1818; *bur* Stockholm

CARL XIV JOHAN   1818–1844

b (Jean Baptiste Jules Bernadotte) Pau, Béarn, 26 January 1763, 3rd and yst son of Henri Bernadotte, Procurator to the Seneschal of Pau, and Jeanne de Saint-Jean; General in the French army 1794; Marshal of the French Empire 19 May 1804; Prince of Ponte Corvo 5 June 1806; elected Crown Prince of Sweden 21 August 1810; adopted by King Carl XIII and assumed the name of Carl Johan 5 November 1810; *s* as King of Sweden and Norway 5 February 1818; crowned King of Sweden Stockholm 11 May 1818, and King of Norway Trondheim 7 September 1818; *m* Sceaux 17 August 1798 Désirée (Desideria), crowned Queen Consort of Sweden Stockholm 21 August 1829 (*b* Marseilles 9 November 1777; *d* Stockholm 17 December 1860; *bur* Riddareholms-kyrkan, Stockholm), dau of François Clary of Marseilles, and his 2nd wife Françoise Rose Somis; 1 son; *d* Stockholm 8 March 1844; *bur* Riddareholmskyrkan, Stockholm

OSCAR I   1844–1859

b Paris 4 July 1799, only son of King Carl XIV Johan; *s* his father 8 March 1844; crowned King of Sweden Stockholm 28 September 1844; declared incapable of governing 25 September 1857; *m* proxy Munich 22 May, in person Stockholm 19 June 1823, Joséphine (*b* Milan 14 March 1807; *d* Stockholm 7 June 1876), eldest dau of Eugène de Beauharnais, 1st Duke of Leuchtenberg, and Augusta of Bavaria; 4 sons, 1 dau; *d* Stockholm 8 July 1859; *bur* Riddareholmskyrkan, Stockholm

CARL XV   1859–1872

b Stockholm 3 May 1826, eldest son of King Oscar I; Regent for his father 25 September 1857; *s* his father 8 July 1859; crowned King of

Sweden Stockholm 3 May 1860 and King of Norway Trondheim 5 August 1860; *m* Stockholm 19 June 1850 Louise (*b* The Hague 5 August 1828; *d* Stockholm 30 March 1871; *bur* Riddareholmskyrkan, Stockholm), elder dau of Prince Frederick of the Netherlands and Louise of Prussia; 1 son, 1 dau; *d* Malmö 19 August 1872; *bur* Riddareholmskyrkan, Stockholm

---

OSCAR II   1872–1907

---

b Stockholm 21 January 1829, 3rd son of King Oscar I; *s* his brother King Carl XV 19 August 1872; crowned King of Sweden Stockholm 12 May 1873, and King of Norway Trondheim 18 July 1873; renounced the throne of Norway 7 June 1905; *m* Biebrich 6 June 1857 Sophie (*b* Biebrich 9 July 1836; *d* Stockholm 30 December 1913), yst dau of William, Duke of Nassau, and his 2nd wife Pauline of Württemberg; 4 sons; *d* Stockholm 8 December 1907; *bur* Riddareholmskyrkan, Stockholm

---

GUSTAV V   1907–1950

---

b Drottningholm 16 June 1858, eldest son of King Oscar II; *s* his father 8 December 1907; *m* Karlsruhe 20 September 1881 Victoria (*b* Karlsruhe 7 August 1862; *d* Rome 4 April 1930; *bur* Riddareholmskyrkan, Stockholm), only dau of Frederick I, Grand Duke of Baden, and Louise of Prussia; 3 sons; *d* Drottningholm 29 October 1950; *bur* Riddareholms-kyrkan, Stockholm

---

GUSTAV VI ADOLPH   1950–1973

---

b Stockholm 11 November 1882, eldest son of King Gustav V; *s* his father 29 October 1950; *m* (1) Windsor 15 June 1905 Margaret (*b* Bagshot Park 15 January 1882; *d* Stockholm 1 May 1920), elder dau of Arthur, Duke of Connaught (3rd son of Queen Victoria of Great Britain), and Louise Margaret of Prussia; 4 sons, 1 dau; *m* (2) London 3 November 1923 Lady Louise Mountbatten (*b* Schloss Heiligenberg 13 July 1889; *d* Stockholm 7 March 1965), yr dau of Louis Alexander Mountbatten, 1st Marquess of Milford Haven (formerly Prince Louis of Battenberg), and Victoria Alberta of Hesse; 1 dau (stillborn); *d* Helsingborg 15 September 1973; *bur* Royal Cemetery in Haga Castle Park

---

CARL XVI GUSTAV   1973–

---

b Haga Castle 30 April 1946, only son of Prince Gustav Adolph, Duke of Västerbotten (eldest son of King Gustav VI Adolph), and Sibylla of Saxe-Coburg and Gotha; *s* his grandfather King Gustav VI Adolph 15 September 1973; *m* Stockholm 19 June 1976 Silvia Renate (*b* Heidelberg 23 December 1943), dau of Walther Sommerlath and Alice de Toledo; 1 son, 2 daus

A nineteenth-century Swedish historian has provided us with a pen portrait of Gustav Vasa which can hardly be bettered: 'a tall and well-made man, somewhat above six feet high. He had a firm and full body without spot or blemish, strong arms, delicate legs, small and beautiful hands and feet. His hair of a light yellow, combed down and cut straight across his eyebrows; forehead of a middle height, with two perpendicular lines between the eyes, which were blue and piercing; his nose straight, and not long; red lips, and roses on his cheeks, even in his old age. His beard in younger years was brown and parted, a hand-breadth long, and cut straight across; in later years growing at will, till it at last reached his waist, and became hoary like his hair'. This kingly figure, who was elected to replace the tyrant Christian II on the Swedish throne, was to prove himself a born ruler. In the course of his thirty-seven years' reign he established Sweden's independence from Denmark, restored the economy by breaking the power of the Hanseatic League, and paved the way for the Reformation by the confiscation of church lands. He ruled with a firm hand and could be harsh when occasion required.

Gustav married three times. His first marriage to Catherine of Saxe-Lauenburg, a 'mild and beautiful' German Princess and a Lutheran, was contracted largely because Gustav wished to avoid allying himself too closely to any Swedish noble family. The marriage was not a success, however. There was one son, Eric, and Queen Catherine died suddenly in 1535. A year later Gustav married again. This time his choice fell on a Swedish lady, Margaret Leijonhufvud, who made him an excellent wife in every way and bore ten children. Her death in August 1551 was a great blow to Gustav, but within a year he had fallen in love with Margaret's sixteen-year-old niece Catherine Stenbock, who was induced to give up the young man to whom she was engaged and accept the ageing King. There was some clerical opposition to the marriage but Gustav chose to ignore it and the wedding took place at Vadstena in August 1552 with the Bishop of Lindköping officiating, the Archbishop of Uppsala having refused to do so. In spite of all the circumstances and the great disparity in age, the marriage was not unhappy and Catherine set out to be a good wife. King Gustav died after a long illness on 29 September 1560. His burial did not take place until December, when a solemn procession conveyed his coffin and those of his first two Queens from Stockholm to Uppsala. Queen Catherine was not to join them for another sixty-one years.

Gustav's only son by his first marriage succeeded him as King Eric XIV. He is described by the same historian who described his father as 'in height somewhat shorter than his father; perfectly well formed, and perhaps handsomer. He had light hair, arched eyebrows, large blue eyes, a roman nose, beautiful mouth, his skin fair and fresh, mustachios and beard auburn, the latter divided into two points six inches long. In suppleness, strength and agility in all manner of bodily exercises he had not his equal'.

Eric loved splendour and his coronation was the most magnificent display hitherto seen in Sweden. A completely new set of regalia was constructed and King Eric's crown, used at many subsequent coronations, is still on display in the Royal Treasury at Stockholm. Eric was also the first Swedish King to be styled 'Majesty'. In the early years of his reign he made overtures for the hand of Queen Elizabeth of England, Mary, Queen of Scots, Princess Renée of Lorraine, and Princess Christina of Hesse, but all negotiations fell through. Eric was far from leading

An eighteenth-century engraving of the Royal Palace in Stockholm.

a celibate life, however, and his mistress during the first years of his reign was a beautiful Stockholm girl named Agda, who bore him two children. She was superseded in the King's affections by Karin Månsdotter, who was said to have started out in life as a nut-seller in Stockholm market and later to have been taken into the household of Eric's half-sister Elizabeth.

Eric had a great dread of the powerful Sture family, fearing probably quite unreasonably that they were plotting to seize the throne. In May 1567 he had three members of the family imprisoned and murdered with several of their relations. He was immediately filled with remorse and hid himself for a couple of days, then re-emerged and in an attempt to make amends arranged a magnificent funeral for the victims in Uppsala Cathedral. He then retired to Svartsjö Castle, where a ridiculous scene was enacted between Eric and his half-brother Johan, who had also been imprisoned but was now released. The two brothers kept falling at each other's feet in tears, Eric calling Johan his Lord and his Sovereign and Johan replying that it was Eric who was King and he but a poor prisoner imploring for mercy. At length the Queen Dowager Catherine Stenbock intervened and called upon them to control themselves. Shortly afterwards Johan went to live in Arboga. In his diary Eric noted above the year 1567: 'The most unfortunate year for King Eric.'

It has been claimed that Eric was mentally deranged and he certainly exhibited signs of schizophrenia in his alternating moods of murderous frenzy and abject repentance. His ambitious half-brothers were only too eager to take advantage of the situation to further their own advancement to the throne and Eric provided them with a final excuse to rebel in 1568. On 4 July he publicly married and crowned Karin Månsdotter, declaring her sons to be heirs to the throne. The King's half-brothers, Johan, Magnus and Carl, rose in rebellion and

marched on Stockholm, made Eric prisoner and proclaimed Johan King in his place. Eric was brought to trial for his misdeeds in January 1569, formally deposed and sentenced to life imprisonment. For several years he was moved from place to place, his imprisonment varying in severity. For much of the time his wife, who never wavered in her loyalty to him, was allowed to join him and their youngest child was born in captivity. As long as Eric lived, however, Johan feared plots to restore him and finally determined he must die. A poison was prepared, either opium or mercury, and given to Eric mixed in pea soup. He died in agony on 26 February 1577, aged forty-three, and the public announcement of his death gave out that he had died following a long illness. He was buried at Västerås with scant ceremony. Queen Karin was treated with the generosity occasioned by remorse, being granted lands and an income enabling her to live in comfort with her daughter Sigrid, who married twice into noble families. Two of Karin's sons died young, another, Gustav, died in Russia in 1607. Karin herself died in 1612 and was buried in Åbo Cathedral, where a monument was erected to her memory.

The fratricide Johan III involved Sweden in the Livonian War whereby she was to acquire Esthonia. His first wife was Catharina Jagellonica, the daughter of Sigismund I and sister of Sigismund II, Kings of Poland. Her only son, also named Sigismund, was elected King of Poland as Sigismund III in 1587 in succession to Stephen Bathory, the husband of his mother's sister Anna. In November 1592 Sigismund succeeded his father as King of Sweden also. He had been educated by the Jesuits and did all he could to restore Catholicism to Sweden, which he seldom visited. This resulted in his deposition in 1599, when his uncle Carl, the youngest son of Gustav I, assumed power although he did not actually take the title of King until 1604.

Sigismund, King of both Sweden and Poland. This equestrian portrait is part of the fine collection of royal portraits at Gripsholm Castle.

Gustav II Adolph, King of Sweden, wearing some very fancy pants. The royal regalia on the table include the Key of State, an item peculiar to Sweden.

Carl IX was a coarse, uncultured man, whose reign was virtually a reign of terror. He was practically a Calvinist by religion, although Sweden was officially Lutheran and the Swedish church was unique among the Lutheran churches in having maintained the Apostolic Succession and episcopal government. He also had aspirations to gain the Russian throne and marched on Moscow during the so-called Time of Troubles in that country. Sigismund made several unsuccessful attempts to regain the Swedish throne and was to continue to do so into the next reign. Carl died unlamented in October 1611, aged sixty-one, and was succeeded by his son Gustav II Adolph, the first of Sweden's two great warrior Kings.

Popularly known as the 'Lion of the North', Gustav II Adolph was a brilliant military tactician and is generally regarded as the champion of Protestantism. He was engaged in defensive wars against the Imperial forces and his cousin Sigismund of Poland, who still sought to regain the Swedish throne. This involved him in the Thirty Years' War and resulted in Sweden becoming a world power and dominating northern Europe. At home many governmental reforms were carried out with the aid of Gustav's very able minister Axel Oxenstierna.

Gustav married Maria Eleonora of Brandenburg in 1620.

Their first child Christina was born in 1623 and died in 1624. In December 1626 the Queen gave birth to another daughter also named Christina. The child was born covered in hair and at first was thought to be a boy and a certain sexual ambivalence was to remain throughout her life. No further children followed and on 16 November 1632 the great King fell in battle at Lützen and the six-year-old Christina became Queen.

During the Queen's minority Axel Oxenstierna acted as Regent. When Christina came of age and took over in December 1644 the complexities of her strange character soon became apparent. She had received a good education in masculine style, was cultured and a great patron of the arts. At the same time she lavished estates on her favourites, badly depleting the treasury. All efforts to persuade her to marry met with strenuous opposition on her part, although she was reputed to be in love with Magnus De la Gardie. It seems likely that she was frigid and possibly suffered from some physical defect of which she alone was aware. The dubiety as to her sex at birth would seem to point to this. The business of government soon became burdensome to Christina and at the age of twenty-seven she determined on abdicating in favour of her cousin and heir Prince Carl of Pfalz-Zweibrücken, who was also a rejected suitor.

Stupinigi, near Turin, a favourite residence of the House of Savoy.

Victor Amadeus II, Duke of Savoy, who became the first King of Sardinia in 1718. This heroically posed portrait is in the Basilica of La Superga, near Turin.

Charles Albert, King of Sardinia, an equestrian portrait
by Vernet in the Turin Gallery.

King Victor Emmanuel II of Italy. This portait of il re galantuomo by Gerolamo Induno hangs in the Museo del Risorgimento at Milan.

The Norman Count Roger II being crowned by Christ as first King of Sicily: a contemporary mosaic at Palermo. The King's robes and crown closely resemble those of the Byzantine Emperors.

King Charles of Naples visiting
Pope Benedict XIV in the coffee
house of the Quirinale Palace at
Rome. This crowded canvas by
Pannini is in the Capodimonte
Palace at Naples.

A delightful family group by
Angelica Kauffmann depicting
King Ferdinand IV of Naples,
Queen Maria Carolina and six of
their many children. The
likenesses of the King and Queen
are highly idealized, both being far
stouter and plainer.

The abdication took place at Uppsala.

In the ten years of her personal rule Christina created seventeen Counts, forty-six Barons and four hundred and twenty-eight untitled nobles, providing them all with generous grants from the crown revenues, so that her decision to abdicate came as something of a relief to her government. After her abdication she wandered about the courts of Europe for several years, often dressing in male attire and calling herself Count Dohna. She made a spectacular conversion to the Roman Catholic church, taking the additional name of Alexandra in honour of her godfather Pope Alexander VII. During a visit to France in 1657 she ordered the murder of her major-domo Monaldischi for reasons which have never become clear. She made two visits to Sweden in 1660 and 1667, hoping in vain to be reinstated, and finally settled in Rome where she became the patron of Scarlatti, Corelli and Bernini, collected Venetian paintings and became something of a social attraction. She died there on 19 April 1689, having outlived her successor on the Swedish throne by nearly thirty years.

Carl X Gustav, who succeeded to the throne on Christina's abdication, was the son of Count Palatine Johan Casimir of Zweibrücken and Princess Catherine, the eldest surviving daughter of King Carl IX. He had been declared heir presumptive by the Riksdag (the Swedish parliament) in 1650 and a special crown and hat (now exhibited in the Royal Treasury) were made for him to wear at Christina's coronation. He was an unprepossessing individual and involved Sweden in the First Northern War by declaring war on Poland in 1655 on the pretext that the Polish King John Casimir, a son of Sigismund III, had refused to recognize him. He found an ally in the Elector of Brandenburg and their combined forces invaded Poland and gained a great victory at Warsaw in 1656. Russia, Denmark and the Empire then joined forces against Sweden and Brandenburg changed sides when Poland agreed to recognize the Elector's sovereignty over East Prussia, so the Swedes were driven out of Poland in 1657. Undeterred, Carl invaded Denmark in 1658 but failed to take Copenhagen. His short, warlike reign ended with his death on 13 February 1660 at the early age of thirty-seven. His marriage to Hedwig Eleonora of Holstein-Gottorp produced but one son, who succeeded his father as Carl XI at the age of four, his mother and five others forming a regency.

The reign of Carl XI was less warlike than that of his father and he established absolutism, getting the Riksdag to pass a law providing for the fiefs of all nobles dying without direct heirs to revert to the crown. By this and other means he managed to reduce the national debt quite dramatically. On his death in April 1697, Carl XI was succeeded by his only surviving son Carl XII, the second of Sweden's great warrior Kings. Carl XII was a military genius. He was nearly fifteen at his accession and at once declared himself of age. The whole of his reign was taken up with the Great Northern War in which Russia, Poland and Denmark challenged Sweden's supremacy in the Baltic. Carl's forces swept all before them until he was checked by the Russians at the battle of Poltava on 8 July 1709, when the Swedish army was broken up and a large part made prisoner. Carl spent five years in Moldavia, reforming Sweden's government and finances

Carl XII, Sweden's second great warrior King. This portrait by David Krafft is in the Gripsholm Castle collection.

from a distance, and finally made his way home through Hungary and Germany heavily disguised.

On 11 December 1718 Carl was killed by a musket shot in the head while leading a military expedition in Norway. He had never married and there was no clear heir to the throne, but his youngest sister Ulrika Eleonora was elected Queen by the Riksdag on agreeing to allow a constitution to be drawn up providing for joint rule by the sovereign and the council when the Riksdag was not in session. This accorded so ill with the new Queen's despotic character that she abdicated after fifteen months in favour of her husband Landgrave Frederick of Hesse-Cassel. Frederick I proved a very capable constitutional monarch. Under his rule the country's economy, ruined by Carl XII's wars, was restored once again and the Northern War was brought to a successful close. Two political parties, the Hats and the Caps, came to the fore and alternated in power throughout the eighteenth century.

Frederick I and Ulrika Eleonora had no children and in 1743 Adolph Frederick of Holstein-Gottorp, a great-grandson of Carl X Gustav's sister was elected Crown Prince, succeeding to the throne on Frederick's death in 1751. Adolph Frederick is said to have 'looked gracious even from behind'. His election had been backed by the Hats in a conciliatory move towards Russia, whose Empress Elizabeth had once been betrothed to Adolph Frederick's brother, who died young. The sentimental Empress still entertained warm feelings for her dead fiancé's family and in due course was to marry off her nephew and heir to the insignificant little Princess Sophie of Anhalt-Zerbst, whose mother Johanna Elizabeth was Adolph Frederick's sister. That little Princess was in the fullness of time to become Catherine the Great of Russia.

King Adolph Frederick was an amiable creature and allowed himself to be completely dominated by his wife Louisa Ulrika, the masterful sister of Frederick the Great of Prussia. He was extremely fond of the little buns which form part of the traditional Lenten fare in Sweden and died very suddenly after partaking of a supper consisting of those buns accompanied by sauerkraut, oysters, lobster and champagne on 12 April 1771, a month short of his sixty-first birthday.

Gustav III, who succeeded his father at the age of twenty-five, was Sweden's most cultured and artistic King. When his father died he was on a visit to Louis XV at Versailles and he returned to Sweden filled with ideas inspired by the elegance of the French court. His reign has been called Sweden's 'Golden Age'. At its start the Caps were in the ascendant but on 19 August 1772 Gustav staged a military coup by which he restored absolute government to his own person. He soon showed himself to be an 'enlightened despot' of the type so much admired in the late eighteenth century, abolishing all forms of torture, improving the lot of the poor and proclaiming religious toleration and the freedom of the press.

Gustav's domestic life was not happy. He had been married at the age of twenty to Princess Sophia Magdalena of Denmark, but he was a homosexual and the marriage remained unconsummated for eleven years. At last, in November 1778, the Queen gave birth to a son and some four years later to another. There were rumours that the King was not their father, but he never denied paternity or treated his wife with less than deference. The younger boy survived seven months only, but the elder flourished. On 16 March 1792 Gustav attended a masked ball at the Royal Theatre in Stockholm. There he was approached by an assassin, Captain Jacob af Ankarström, and mortally wounded by a pistol shot. He lingered for thirteen days and died on 29 March, aged forty-six. The heir to the throne, Gustav IV Adolph, was only thirteen so his uncle Prince Carl, Duke of Södermanland acted as Regent until he came of age in 1796.

Gustav IV Adolph was an unsatisfactory King in every way. At a time when Sweden was isolated and threatened by the advancing power of Napoleon, he stubbornly refused to co-operate with his army and maintained an anti-French stand which led an officers' coup to depose him in 1809 and, passing over his ten-year-old son, to offer the throne to his uncle the former Regent. The rest of Gustav's life was lived out in exile and loneliness. His marriage was dissolved in 1812 and he died in Switzerland in 1837.

The new King Carl XIII was elderly, disagreeable and childless, so an heir to the Swedish throne had to be found. The first choice was Prince Christian August of Schleswig-Holstein-Sonderburg-Augustenburg, a forty-one-year-old bachelor who was duly adopted and changed his name to Carl August in January 1810. Four months later he died suddenly of a paralytic stroke while riding on Kvidinge Hed in Skåne, brought on it is said by imbibing too freely a considerable quantity of beer. Little time was lost in selecting another heir. The dashing Marshal Bernadotte, Prince of Ponte Corvo, had made a favourable impression in Sweden by his humanitarian treatment of the Swedish prisoners he had taken when the French army had defeated the Swedish army in Pomerania in 1807. It was resolved to offer him the succession, Napoleon agreed, and the election took place on 21 August 1810, the formal adoption by the old King following on 5 November, when the new Crown Prince assumed the name of Carl Johan. Carl XIII, who may almost be regarded as a 'stop-gap' King, died in February 1818 and the Crown Prince ascended the throne as Carl XIV Johan. He was the best looking King Sweden had had for a long time and in the course of his twenty-six years' reign gained great popularity with all his subjects although he never mastered Swedish. His Queen, Désirée, had once been courted by Napoleon, whose brother Joseph was married to her sister Julie. Her father, François Clary, was a silk merchant in Marseilles and Désirée (called Desideria in Sweden) found it difficult to adapt to the chilly northern climate and it was several years before she could be persuaded to venture to Stockholm to be crowned, eleven years after her husband. There was only one child of the marriage, Oscar, and he succeeded his father in March 1844. Queen Désirée, reconciled at last to life in Stockholm, lived on to see her eighty-third birthday. A month later she was suddenly taken ill at the theatre, returned hastily to the Royal Palace, and died on the stairs before she could reach her apartments.

Oscar I was a skilled diplomat and sought a close alliance with Denmark. His reign saw the construction of the Swedish railways as a national concern. He had maintained the Napoleonic connection by his marriage to Joséphine of Leuchtenberg, whose father Eugène was son of the Empress Joséphine and stepson of Napoleon. In September 1857 the King's ill-health led to the Crown Prince Carl being appointed Regent and when Oscar I died two years later, he became King as Carl XV.

Carl had to cope with the growth of Liberalism and the growth of Norwegian Nationalism in the course of his thirteen-year reign. A new Constitution was granted in December 1864, framed by the Liberal Prime Minister Louis de Geer. Carl was married to Princess Louise of the Netherlands, who died in 1871. Their only son died as a child in 1854, so when Carl died in August 1872 he was succeeded by his brother Oscar II.

Oscar II was the last King of Sweden to be crowned. An imposing, white-bearded man, he was a talented writer and musician and among other things wrote the libretto for an opera which was performed in Stockholm. His long reign terminated with the separation of Norway from Sweden in which the King finally acquiesced on 7 June 1905. His rather plain Queen, Sophie of Nassau, gave him four sons, the youngest of whom, Prince Eugen, became a very distinguished artist, a number of whose works hang in the National Gallery in Stockholm. King Oscar II died in December 1907 at the age of seventy-eight and was succeeded by his eldest son Gustav V.

Gustav V, a tall, spare man of austere appearance, managed to

The bridal group of Crown Prince Gustav Adolph of Sweden (later King Gustav VI Adolph) and Princess Margaret of Connaught at Windsor Castle on 15 June 1905. The bridesmaid on the extreme left is Princess Ena of Battenberg (later Queen Victoria Eugenia of Spain).

Gustav VI Adolph, King of Sweden.

King Gustav V of Sweden.

keep Sweden neutral in both World Wars. His wife, Victoria of Baden, a formidably unattractive woman who added to her lack of attraction by paying scant heed to personal hygiene, was regarded by legitimists as the *de jure* Queen of Sweden, being the lineal representative of King Gustav IV Adolph, who had been deposed in 1809. Since she thus brought the blood of the Vasas and Holstein-Gottorps back into the royal line, perhaps her shortcomings can be overlooked. The marriage produced three sons, but was not a happy one. The Queen spent most of her time in Capri or Rome, where she died in 1930. The famous tall-story teller Axel Munthe was her personal physician and, it was rumoured, her lover.

King Gustav V was a keen and above-average tennis-player until well into his eighties. The only breath of scandal to touch him was a rather sordid attempt at blackmail by a former valet who was successfully bought off by the Crown Prince. The King died at the age of ninety-two in October 1950. He lived long enough to see his great-grandson who is now King of Sweden.

Gustav VI Adolph, who succeeded his father at the age of sixty-seven, was nevertheless to reign for nearly twenty-three years and prove one of Sweden's most popular Kings. It was often said that if Sweden were to exchange its monarchy for a republic the King would be elected the first President. Gustav VI Adolph was the last King to exercise constitutional power, the last vestiges of which were removed by the Constitution of 1975, which provided for the Swedish monarch to be the Head of State with no political influence or right to appoint or dismiss cabinet ministers. The duties of the monarch thus became purely ceremonial. The King was a renowned archaeologist and possessed an expert knowledge of Chinese porcelain. Both his wives were British, the first a granddaughter, the second a great-granddaughter of Queen Victoria. His first wife, Princess Margaret of Connaught, was allegedly unhappy in Sweden. She had four sons and one daughter and died very suddenly of a throat infection on 1 May 1920, aged thirty-eight. There were rumours, probably unfounded, that she had committed suicide. In November 1923 the Crown Prince, as he then was, married again. His second wife was Lady Louise Mountbatten, formerly Princess of Battenberg. The marriage was a supremely happy one although the only child, a daughter, was stillborn. Both as Crown Princess and Queen, Louise enjoyed great popularity in Sweden and was a loving and loved stepmother and stepgrandmother. She died in March 1965. King Gustav VI Adolph lived to celebrate his ninetieth birthday in 1972 and died on 15 September 1973. His eldest son, also named Gustav Adolph, had been killed in an air crash near Copenhagen in January 1947, so the King was succeeded by his grandson, King Carl XVI Gustav, who was then twenty-seven. King Carl Gustav enjoys great personal popularity which was enhanced by his marriage in June 1976 to Silvia Renate Sommerlath, a young German lady. The King and Queen have one son and two daughters.

On 1 January 1980 the law of succession was altered to provide for the succession of the eldest child regardless of sex, so the heir to the throne is the monarchs' elder daughter Crown Princess Victoria, Duchess of Västergötland, who was born on 14 July 1977.

FINLAND

Finland was conquered by Eric the Victorious in the tenth century and again came under Swedish rule in the thirteenth century, being governed by Dukes appointed by the Swedish crown until 1561 and then by Governors and Governor-Generals until it was ceded to Russia by the treaty of Friedrichsham on 17 September 1809. The Russian Emperors assumed the title of Grand Duke of Finland. The country proclaimed its independence on 6 December 1917 and a monarchical form of government was decided upon, Dr Pehr Evind Svinhufvud being appointed Regent in May 1918 pending the election of a King. On 9 October 1918 Landgrave Frederick Charles of Hesse, a brother-in-law of the German Emperor William II, was elected King and accepted the throne. The following month the Armistice followed by the abdication of the German Emperor caused him to withdraw his acceptance. Marshal Baron Carl Gustav Emil Mannerheim succeeded Dr Svinhufvud as Regent in November 1918 and remained in office until a Republic was proclaimed on 25 July 1919 and Dr Kaarlo Juho Stahlberg became the first President. Frederick Charles, the King who never was, died on 28 May 1940.

GERMANY

Although the medieval Holy Roman Emperors are often referred to as Kings of Germany or German Kings, this is really a misnomer. The correct appellation of the Emperor Elect until he received Imperial Coronation was King of the Romans and although these Kings often ruled over German lands they cannot correctly be described as Kings of Germany. Therefore it is not until the establishment of the kingdom of Prussia in 1701 that there was a German King reigning over German land. The other German kingdoms of Bavaria, Hanover, Saxony and Württemberg were established a little over a hundred years later. The ephemeral Napoleonic kingdom of Westphalia must also be included.

The German empire in 1914.

PRUSSIA

FREDERICK I   1701–1713

---

b Königsberg 11 July 1657, 3rd but eldest surviving son of Frederick William, Elector of Brandenburg, and his first wife Louise Henrietta of Orange; *s* his father as (Frederick III) Elector and Margrave of Brandenburg and Duke of Prussia 29 April 1688; assumed the title of King in Prussia and was crowned Königsberg 18 January 1701; *m* (1) Potsdam 23 August 1679 Elizabeth Henrietta (*b* Cassel 8 November 1661; *d* Cöln au der Spree 27 June 1683), yst dau of William VI, Landgrave of Hesse-Cassel, and Hedwig Sophie of Brandenburg; 1 dau; *m* (2) Herrenhausen 8 October 1684 Sophia Charlotte (*b* Schloss Iburg, nr Osnabrück 20 October 1668; *d* Hanover 1 February 1705; *bur* Berlin Cathedral), only dau of Ernest Augustus, Elector of Hanover, and Sophia of the Palatinate; 3 sons; *m* (3) Berlin 28 November 1708

Sophia Louise (*b* 16 May 1685; *d* Grabow 29 July 1735), only dau of Frederick, Duke of Mecklenburg-Grabow, and Christine Wilhelmine of Hesse-Homburg; no issue; *d* Berlin 25 February 1713

FREDERICK WILLIAM I   1713–1740

b Berlin 14 August 1688, yst and only surviving son of King Frederick I; *s* his father 25 February 1713; *m* proxy Hanover 14 November, in person Berlin 28 November 1706, Sophia Dorothea (*b* Hanover 26 March 1687; *d* Monbijou, nr Berlin, 28 June 1757), only dau of George I, King of Great Britain and Ireland, and Sophia Dorothea of Celle; 7 sons, 7 daus; *d* Berlin 31 May 1740; *bur* Potsdam

FREDERICK II THE GREAT   1740–1786

b Berlin 24 January 1712, 3rd but eldest surviving son of King Frederick William I; *s* his father 31 May 1740; *m* Schloss Salzdalum, nr Wolfenbüttel, 12 June 1733 Elizabeth Christine (*b* Wolfenbüttel 8 November 1715; *d* Berlin 13 January 1797), eldest dau of Ferdinand Albert, Duke of Brunswick-Wolfenbüttel, and Antoinette Amelia of Brunswick-Wolfenbüttel; no issue; *d* Potsdam 17 August 1786

FREDERICK WILLIAM II   1786–1797

b Berlin 25 September 1744, eldest son of Prince Augustus William of Prussia (5th son of King Frederick William I) and Louise Amelia of Brunswick-Wolfenbüttel; *s* his uncle King Frederick II 17 August 1786; *m* (1) Charlottenburg 14 July 1765 (divorced 1769) Elizabeth Christine (*b* Wolfenbüttel 8 November 1746; *d* Stettin 18 February 1840), 4th dau of Charles I, Duke of Brunswick-Wolfenbüttel, and Philippine Charlotte of Prussia (dau of King Frederick William I); 1 dau; *m* (2) Charlottenburg 14 July 1769 Frederica Louise (*b* Prenzlau 16 October 1751; *d* Berlin 25 February 1805), 2nd dau of Ludwig IX, Landgrave of Hesse-Darmstadt, and Caroline of Zweibrucken; 5 sons, 3 daus; *d* Marmorpalais, Potsdam, 16 December 1797

FREDERICK WILLIAM III   1797–1840

b Potsdam 3 August 1770, eldest son of King Frederick William II; *s* his father 16 December 1797; *m* (1) Berlin 24 December 1793 Louise (*b* Hanover 10 March 1776; *d* Hohenzieritz 19 July 1810; *bur* Potsdam), 4th dau of Charles, Grand Duke of Mecklenburg-Strelitz, and his first wife Frederica of Hesse-Darmstadt; 5 sons, 5 daus; *m* (2) Charlottenburg 9 November 1824 Auguste, *cr* Princess of Liegnitz and Countess of Hohenzollern (*b* 30 August 1800; *d* Homburg 5 June 1873; *bur* Potsdam), dau of Count Ferdinand von Harrach, and his first wife Johanna von Rayski; no issue; *d* Berlin 7 June 1840; *bur* Potsdam

FREDERICK WILLIAM IV   1840–1861

b Berlin 15 October 1795, eldest son of King Frederick William III; *s* his father 7 June 1840; *m* Berlin 29 November 1823 Elizabeth (*b* Munich 13 November 1801; *d* Dresden 14 December 1873), 4th dau of Maximilian I Joseph, King of Bavaria, and his second wife Caroline of Baden; no issue; *d* Sans Souci 2 January 1861

WILLIAM I   1861–1888

b Berlin 22 March 1797, 2nd son of King Frederick William III; Regent of Prussia 1858; *s* his brother King Frederick William IV 2 January 1861; crowned Königsberg 18 October 1861; proclaimed German Emperor 8 January 1871; *m* Berlin 11 June 1829, Augusta (*b* Weimar 30 September 1811; *d* Berlin 7 January 1890; *bur* Charlottenburg), yr dau of Charles Frederick, Grand Duke of Saxe-Weimar-Eisenach, and Grand Duchess Maria Pavlovna of Russia; 1 son, 1 dau; *d* Berlin 9 March 1888; *bur* Charlottenburg

FREDERICK III   MARCH–JUNE 1888

b Neues Palais, Potsdam 18 October 1831, only son of Emperor and King William I; *s* his father 9 March 1888; *m* London 25 January 1858 Victoria, Princess Royal of Great Britain and Ireland (*b* Buckingham Palace, London, 21 November 1840; *d* Friedrichshof, nr Kronberg, Taunus, 5 August 1901; *bur* Friedenskirche, Potsdam), eldest dau of Victoria, Queen of Great Britain and Ireland, Empress of India, and Prince Albert of Saxe-Coburg and Gotha; 4 sons, 4 daus; *d* Neues Palais, Potsdam, 15 June 1888; *bur* Friedenskirche, Potsdam

WILLIAM II   1888–1918

b Berlin 27 January 1859, eldest son of Emperor and King Frederick III; *s* his father 15 June 1888; abdicated 28 November 1918; *m* (1) Berlin 27 February 1881 Augusta Victoria (*b* Dolzig 22 October 1858; *d* Haus Doorn, Netherlands, 11 April 1921), eldest dau of Frederick, Duke of Schleswig-Holstein-Sonderburg-Augustenburg, and Adelaide of Hohenlohe-Langenburg; 6 sons, 1 dau; *m* (2) Haus Doorn 5 November 1922 Hermine (*b* Greiz 17 December 1887; *d* Frankfurt an der Oder 7 August 1947), widow of Prince John George of Schoenaich-Carolath, and 4th dau of Prince Heinrich XXII Reuss (Elder Line) and Ida of Schaumburg-Lippe; no issue; *d* Haus Doorn 4 June 1941

The kingdom of Prussia, the first among the modern German kingdoms, was largely the creation of the House of Hohenzollern. A line of petty counts tracing their descent from Frederick I of Zollern, who died in 1125, they obtained the Burggraviate of Nuremberg through the marriage of Count Frederick III to its heiress Sophie about 1192. On Frederick's death his possessions were divided between his sons and Conrad, probably the younger, received Nuremberg and the counties of Raats and Abensberg. In 1363 Burggrave Frederick V obtained recognition as a Prince of the Empire and in 1417 his son and successor Frederick VI was invested as Elector and Margrave of Brandenburg at the Council of Constance, starting a new enumeration as Frederick I. Elector George William obtained the Duchy of Prussia from the King of Poland in 1618 and his son Frederick William, known as 'the Great Elector', freed Prussia from feudal subjection to Poland, conquered Pomerania, joined the league against Louis XIV and successfully defeated the

Swedes when they invaded Prussia in 1674. He gave protection to French Huguenot refugees, thereby gaining some 20,000 useful new citizens greatly needed in north Germany, and encouraged agricultural improvements. He also founded the library at Berlin and a university at Duisburg and on his death in 1688 left his son Frederick a greatly enlarged state and a well-filled treasury.

Frederick was a weedy little man, asthmatic and unimpressive in appearance, but not lacking in character. He entered into the alliance against France, seized Bonn and other towns, and supplied the Emperor with troops to fight against the Turks. He obtained Liegnitz, Brieg and Wohlau from the Emperor in exchange for other territories and in 1701, as a reward for supporting Austria in the War of the Spanish Succession, obtained the title of King which he had long coveted. The title he took was King in Prussia (altered to King of Prussia in 1742) and he almost exhausted his treasury in the lavish display he put on for his coronation at Königsberg, where he placed the crown on his head with his own hands. He was determined to make his court a splendid one modelled on that of Versailles and built three new palaces, the Berlin Schloss, Charlottenburg, and the town palace at Potsdam. Apart from this, Frederick did not neglect the arts and sciences, founding the University of Halle and the Berlin Academies of Painting and Sciences.

Frederick's first wife, a Princess of Hesse-Cassel, died early leaving one daughter. His second wife Sophia Charlotte was the only sister of George I of England. He loved her dearly although he took a mistress because he thought it the correct thing for a monarch to do. The Queen died in 1705 and three years later Frederick married again. His new wife, Princess Sophia Louise of Mecklenburg, was to be the unwitting cause of his death in 1713. She had become schizophrenic and during periodic fits of violence had to be kept under restraint. The King was in failing health and was slumbering in his chair when the Queen evaded her attendants and rushed to his apartments clad in her white nightdress and with her long hair streaming about her shoulders. She burst through a glass door and flung herself upon the King who awoke terrified imagining that she was the White Lady, the Hohenzollerns' hereditary harbinger of doom. He fell into a fever and died six weeks later at the age of fifty-five. The Queen was returned to the care of her widowed mother in Grabow and died there in 1735, ignorant to the last of the fatal role she had played.

Frederick's son and successor Frederick William I was almost the complete opposite of his father. He had frugal tastes, simple habits and no appreciation whatsoever of the arts or literature. Of coarse appearance, fat and bloated, his chief delight was in drinking and smoking with his small band of close friends, discussing military matters and laying the foundations of Prussian militarism and Prussian bureaucracy. He was married to his first cousin Sophia Dorothea, the only daughter of King George I of Great Britain. She bore him fourteen children and in a strange way he was devoted to her, although she for her part seems to have been devoid of any human affection, even for her children. Frederick William bullied his children unmercifully, especially his eldest surviving son and heir Fritz, whom he treated with great severity. Poor Fritz had intellectual tastes which were

Frederick the Great, King of Prussia, a fine engraving of the warrior King in later life.

anathema to his father and worse still developed a romantic attachment for a handsome young Lieutenant Katte. The couple planned to run away together, but the King had them apprehended and brought back to Berlin, where Fritz was flung into prison and Katte court-martialled and by the King's express command beheaded beneath the Prince's prison window. Before Katte died he called out, 'Death for so sweet a Prince is sweet!' Frederick William was quite prepared to have his son beheaded, too, but only just forebore. In an attempt to avoid any further entanglement he forced Fritz to marry a Princess of Brunswick-Wolfenbüttel. She was an amiable girl and Fritz always treated her with the greatest respect although the marriage was almost certainly never consummated and they lived apart after he became King.

Frederick William's passion for building up the Prussian army led him to have his agents scour Europe to find the tallest men to enrol in his dragoons. When he died in 1740 he left a full treasury and a standing army of 66,000 men.

Frederick II, known to history as 'the Great', was in both appearance and temperament like his grandfather Frederick I. He was twenty-eight at his succession and his interests were without exception things which his father had considered effeminate and despicable: poetry, flute-playing, literary discussion, and an interest in art. He soon showed, however, that he was a soldier too and laid claim to Silesia, which he invaded and wrested from Austria. As a ruler, Frederick was more enlightened

Sans Souci, Frederick the Great's favourite palace at Potsdam, where he died.

than his father, relaxing censorship and granting freedom of worship. He considered the German language boorish and preferred to speak and write French, carrying on a correspondence with French writers and savants such as Maupertuis and Voltaire. The King's lifestyle was austere and his preferred residence was Sans Souci, a secluded mansion. Although married, he lived as a bachelor and ladies were seldom seen at his court, which was the occasion of some scandal. Frederick's inclinations were almost certainly homosexual but it is doubtful if his relationships ever became physical. The Queen, who was herself something of a bluestocking and also wrote books in French, was quite content with the arrangement and spent half her generous income on works of charity. Frederick has been the subject of many anecdotes, some surely apocryphal. He was admired and feared by his fellow rulers. His death was the result of a chill caught during a military review held in a rainstorm. He died at his beloved Sans Souci on 17 August 1786, aged seventy-four.

Frederick was succeeded by his nephew, Frederick William II, a very different type of man, indolent, pleasure-loving and grossly sensual. He was also handsome, though somewhat stout, and a generous patron of the arts, particularly music. His first marriage to Elizabeth Christine of Brunswick ended in divorce in 1769 but his second marriage to Frederica of Hesse-Darmstadt was more successful, although Frederick William neglected her shamefully for his mistresses, with two of whom he even contracted bigamous marriages. The mistress who exercised the greatest influence over him was Wilhelmine Enke, a trumpeter's daughter, whom he created Countess von Lichtenau. All these ladies presented the King with families. Frederick William's reign depleted the treasury and saw Prussia's involvement in a war against revolutionary France. The extra territory gained by the partitioning of Poland in 1793 and 1795 did nothing to help the general decline. The King died in December 1797, worn out by his debaucheries at the age of fifty-three, and was succeeded by his eldest son.

Frederick William III was twenty-seven when he became King, a good-looking, well-intentioned, but hesitant young man. It took him some time to decide to commit himself to the allied cause against Napoleon, but he was finally forced into it by military pressure from the Prussian army and the influence of his strong-minded Queen, Louise of Mecklenburg-Strelitz, whose beauty and goodness have become legendary. The Prussians were defeated at Jena in 1806 and the King and Queen were forced to seek refuge with their ally the Emperor Alexander I of Russia. The treaty of Tilsit concluded on 9 July 1807 deprived Prussia of much territory, all that west of the Elbe being ceded to France and all that gained from Poland in the previous reign being ceded to Russia. Queen Louise was a tower of strength and encouraged the reorganization of the army, but unfortunately she died in July 1810, leaving the weak King to cope on his own. He was forced to join Napoleon in the Russian campaign but changed sides when it ended disastrously and, to the great relief of his people, became the faithful follower of Emperor Alexander, who generally exercised an almost hypnotic influence over all who came in contact with him. After the successful outcome of the Napoleonic Wars, Prussia began to rebuild, the lost territories were restored and even extended and the reforms of the army and the state by von Scharnhorst and von Stein were effected, in spite of the King's covert hostility. Openly, Frederick William played the role of constitutional monarch, although distrusting all forms of liberalism.

Frederick William III, King of Prussia: a portrait painted by Sir Thomas Lawrence to commemorate the visit of the allied sovereigns to London at the end of the Napoleonic Wars.

Queen Louise of Prussia, by Peter Eduard Stroehling. A pensive study of the Queen who fascinated both Napoleon and the Emperor Alexander of Russia.

In 1824 Frederick William III contracted a second marriage with Countess Auguste von Harrach. Although his new bride, who was only twenty-four, belonged to a family conceded equality of birth with the reigning families, the marriage was treated as a morganatic one and she received the title of Princess of Liegnitz. There were no children and the Princess, whose conduct was always irreproachable, was favourably treated by the royal family.

Frederick William III died in June 1840 and was succeeded by his eldest son, King Frederick William IV, who was in his forty-fifth year and had been married since 1823 to Elizabeth of Bavaria, by whom he had no children, although the marriage was a happy one. The new King had been carefully educated and had a love of culture and art. He was more liberal minded than his father, but underneath his amiable exterior lay a deep-rooted sense of his own importance as the recipient of a God-given trust. The revolutionary movements which beset Europe in 1848 led to the granting of a new Constitution and in the move to create a new German Empire, Frederick William was offered the Imperial Crown which he refused saying that he would never 'stoop to pick up a crown out of the gutter'. In 1857 the King suffered two paralytic strokes and became mentally deranged so that his brother and heir Prince William took over the government and was formally recognized as Regent on 7 October

1858. Frederick William IV died on 2 January 1861 and the Regent succeeded as King William I.

The new King was staunchly conservative and after a struggle with his parliament which almost ended in his abdication in favour of his only son, he appointed Prince Otto von Bismarck Minister-President. Bismarck was the real ruler of Prussia for the rest of the reign. He engineered a series of wars calculated to further Prussia's domination of Germany and on the termination of the Franco-Prussian War, King William was persuaded with some difficulty to accept the title which his brother had refused and was accordingly proclaimed German Emperor at Versailles on 8 January 1871. The new Emperor was already nearly seventy-four and was to enjoy his new dignity for many years. He was a kindly, benevolent figure with massive white whiskers, while his wife, the Empress Augusta, who kept up a friendly correspondence with Queen Victoria over many years, presented a somewhat bizarre appearance with her red wig and wheelchair. The Emperor had almost completed his ninety-first year when he died in March 1888.

The second German Emperor was a tragic figure. Frederick III, known to his family as 'Fritz', was a fine-looking man, tall, broad-shouldered and bearded and esteemed for his goodness and his liberal views. As a young man visiting England with his parents he had won the heart of the Princess Royal, Queen

Frederick III, German Emperor and King of Prussia, with his wife Victoria (behind him) and, on the steps in ascending order, their daughters Margaret, Victoria and Sophie.

Victoria's eldest daughter, and they were married in 1858 when 'Vicky' was just seventeen. The marriage was to be a supremely happy one for both of them, although the Princess never became popular in Germany being far too aggressively English and outspoken. She kept up a voluminous correspondence with her mother, pouring her heart out about the shortcomings of the Prussian court. The Crown Prince and Crown Princess both had a strong dislike of Bismarck, who reciprocated their feelings. Unfortunately, in 1887 the Crown Prince fell ill with cancer of the throat, a condition which was wrongly diagnosed for some time. The poor man suffered untold agonies at the hands of his physicians as one treatment after another was advised, tried and rejected. By the time he succeeded his father he was a doomed man with but a matter of weeks to live, only able to breathe and feed through tubes inserted in an open wound in his throat. Only his strong constitution and determination made him live as long as he did. His reign lasted just over three months and he died on 15 June 1888, aged fifty-six. His death was a tragedy not just for Germany but for the world.

William II, who succeeded to the thrones of the German Empire and of Prussia at the age of twenty-nine was the first and favourite grandchild of Queen Victoria. It has well been said that he was 'too moody to rule'. His complex character is almost impossible to assess and opinions about him are still widely divided. Was he 'Kaiser Bill', the war-mongering Prussian militarist determined on conquering Europe; or was he the quiet, tea-drinking, English country squire manqué? Maybe we shall never know. The animosity against him engendered by the First World War mellowed considerably during his long years of exile and when the Second World War broke out he scribbled a pencilled note to his cousin Queen Mary expressing his sorrow that war should have broken out again 'between our two dear countries'. Mark Bence-Jones provided the best epitaph for the Emperor when he wrote: 'Before he died, there were many among his former enemies who wished that he was still reigning in Berlin, instead of the vulgar maniac who had taken his place.'

Today the head of the Royal House of Prussia is His Imperial and Royal Highness Prince Louis Ferdinand, Emperor William II's grandson. A widower, now in his eighties, he lives in modest style near Bremen.

BAVARIA

The House of Wittelsbach

MAXIMILIAN I JOSEPH	**1805–1825**

b Mannheim 27 May 1756, son of Frederick Michael, Count Palatine of Zweibrücken-Birkenfeld, and Franziska, Countess Palatine of Sulzbach; *s* his brother Charles as Duke of Zweibrücken 1 April 1795; *s* his kinsman Elector Charles Theodore as Elector of Bavaria and Elector Palatine 16 February 1799; assumed the title of King of Bavaria 26 December 1805; *m* (1) Darmstadt 30 September 1785 Augusta (*b* Darmstadt 14 April 1765; *d* Rohrbach-am-Neckar, nr Heidelberg, 30 March 1796), yst dau of Prince George of Hesse-Darmstadt and Louise of Leiningen-Dachsburg-Heidesheim; 2 sons, 3 daus; *m* (2) Karlsruhe 9 March 1797 Caroline (*b* Karlsruhe 13 July 1776; *d* Munich 13 November 1841; *bur* Theatinerkirche, Munich), 2nd dau of Charles, Hereditary Prince of Baden, and Amelia of Hesse-Darmstadt; 2 sons, 6 daus; *d* Schloss Nymphenburg 12/13 October 1825; *bur* Theatinerkirche

LUDWIG I	**1825–1848**

b Strassburg 25 August 1786, eldest son of King Maximilian I Joseph; *s* his father 12/13 October 1825; abdicated in favour of his eldest son 20 March 1848; *m* Munich 12 October 1810 Therese (*b* Hildburghausen 8 July 1792; *d* Munich 26 October 1854; *bur* Church of St Boniface, Munich), 4th dau of Frederick, Duke of Saxe-Hildburghausen, and Charlotte of Mecklenburg-Strelitz; 4 sons, 5 daus; *d* Nice 29 February 1868; *bur* Church of St Boniface, Munich

MAXIMILIAN II	**1848–1864**

b Munich 28 November 1811, eldest son of King Ludwig I; *s* his father on his abdication 20 March 1848; *m* proxy Berlin 5 October, in person Munich 12 October 1842, Marie (*b* Berlin 15 October 1825; *d* Schloss

Hohenschwangau 17 May 1889; *bur* Theatinerkirche), yst dau of Prince William of Prussia and Maria Anna of Hesse-Homburg; 2 sons; *d* Munich 10 March 1864; *bur* Theatinerkirche

---

LUDWIG II   1864–1886

---

b Schloss Nymphenburg 25 August 1845, elder son of King Maximilian II; *s* his father 10 March 1864; placed under the regency of his uncle Prince Luitpold 10 June 1886; *d* (drowned) Starnbergersee, nr Schloss Berg, 13 June 1886; *bur* St Michael's Church, Munich

---

OTTO I   1886–1913

---

b Munich 27 April 1848, yr son of King Maximilian II; *s* his brother King Ludwig II 13 June 1886 but reigned entirely under the regencies of Prince Luitpold and Prince Ludwig; replaced as King by the latter 5 November 1913; *d* Schloss Fürstenried, nr Munich, 11 October 1916; *bur* St Michael's Church, Munich

---

LUDWIG III   1913–1918

---

b Munich 7 January 1845, eldest son of Prince Regent Luitpold (3rd son of King Ludwig I) and Archduchess Augusta of Austria-Tuscany; *s* his father as Prince Regent of Bavaria 12 December 1912; proclaimed King, replacing King Otto, 5 November 1913; deposed by the revolution of 7/8 November 1918; *m* Vienna 20 February 1868 Maria Theresa (*b* Brünn 2 July 1849; *d* Schloss Wildenwart 3 February 1919; *bur* Dom Church, Munich), only dau of Archduke Ferdinand of Austria-Este, Prince of Modena, and Archduchess Elizabeth of Austria; 4 sons, 9 daus; *d* Sárvár, Hungary, 18 October 1921; *bur* Dom Church, Munich

The House of Wittelsbach, which has reigned over the south German state of Bavaria and the Rhenish Palatinate as Dukes, Electors and finally Kings for many centuries, is one of the most brilliant, colourful, wayward, talented and eccentric families in Europe. It was not until 1805 that the Elector Max Joseph, having sided with Napoleon, was rewarded with the title of King and a considerable increase in territory. Less than a month after he had been proclaimed King, Maximilian gave his eldest daughter in marriage to Napoleon's stepson Eugène de Beauharnais, a charming man who was to become greatly loved by his father-in-law and to end life as Premier Hereditary Peer of Bavaria. Maximilian, with the aid of his very able Minister Montgelas, made his kingdom one of the most prosperous and liberal states in Germany and second to Prussia in importance. His first wife, Augusta of Hesse-Darmstadt, died before he became King, leaving several children. His second wife, Caroline of Baden, made an admirable Queen, and of her six daughters (including two sets of twins), three became Queens and one the mother of Emperor Franz Joseph of Austria. King Max, as he was popularly known, died in 1825, passing on a very stable throne to his eldest son Ludwig.

King Ludwig I has had almost as much written about him as

A silver gulden of King Ludwig I of Bavaria struck in 1838.

his grandson and namesake King Ludwig II. Good-looking in a somewhat leonine way, he was a cultured patron of the arts and added many fine buildings in the classical style and broad vistas to the elegant city of Munich. He was, however, a reactionary, jealous of his royal prerogatives, although not above walking alone through the streets of Munich in old, threadbare clothes. His parsimony was a byword and he is said to have banned onions from being served at his table because they were too highly priced. Married to the rather dull Therese of Saxe-Hildburghausen, he was a good husband and a devoted father, but, like many other men, over susceptible to a pretty face. His downfall was his infatuation for the Anglo-Irish adventuress Lola Montez (born Maria Rosanna Gilbert), a former dancer, who gained a great ascendancy over him. She was regarded as a dangerous radical and feeling against her ran so high that rioting broke out in Munich and the King was compelled to abdicate on 20 March 1848. He lived on for another twenty years, outliving his son and successor and dying at Nice in February 1868 at the age of eighty-one.

Ludwig's eldest son succeeded to the throne on his father's abdication. A mild, rather colourless man, he was a great patron of the arts and built the fairy-tale Castle of Hohenschwangau. He married Princess Marie of Prussia who has been blamed for carrying the defective gene responsible for the mental deterioration of their two sons. In 1864 Maximilian, on his doctors' advice, went to spend the winter in Italy, but the blowing-up of the Schleswig-Holstein question made him insist on returning to Munich where he soon fell victim to the harsh winter and died on 10 March 1864, aged fifty-two. He was succeeded by his elder son.

King Ludwig II, the 'Dream King', has become his country's greatest asset in the years since his death, doing more for Bavaria's tourist trade than any other individual, living or dead. He began his reign at nineteen, full of promise, a young Adonis

King Ludwig II of Bavaria: the young King's dashing good looks and air of romantic idealism are very apparent in this photograph taken early in his reign.

King Ludwig III and Queen Maria Theresa of Bavaria.

loved and adored by all his subjects. He had little aptitude for governing, however, and lived in a romantic fantasy world of his own. He had become an ardent devotee of Wagner's music at the age of sixteen and immediately after his accession wrote to him offering his patronage. He built the theatre at Bayreuth for Wagner and made huge sums of money available for the production of his operas. Ludwig is best remembered for the fantastic castles and palaces designed in different tastes to suit his moods. The grandest is Neuschwanstein, a medieval castle in Disneyland style; next the island palace of Herrenchiemsee, a Versailles in miniature which was never finished; lastly the baroque pavilion of Linderhof. These creations nearly bankrupted Bavaria but have proved a godsend today, being visited by thousands of tourists annually.

King Ludwig II was definitely not the marrying kind, as the saying goes. For a time, however, he formed a romantic attachment for his cousin Elizabeth, Empress of Austria. Since she was married and unattainable he became engaged to her sister Sophie and preparations for the wedding were well under way when Ludwig suddenly broke the engagement. The jilted Sophie later married the Duke of Alençon and tragically lost her life many years later when she was burnt to death while attending a large charity bazaar in Paris.

After breaking off his engagement Ludwig's eccentricities became more apparent. He paid no attention to affairs of state and passed his time as a recluse, only driving out at night for coach or sleigh rides surrounded by torchbearing outriders. He became infatuated with a handsome young actor upon whom he lavished expensive gifts of jewellery. Gradually, the King lost his looks and became fat and bloated with a mouthful of blackened, decaying teeth. The young Adonis was no more. Ludwig's only brother and heir presumptive Prince Otto, once even handsomer than he and known for his happy disposition which had earned him the nickname of 'The Merry Otto', became mentally deranged in 1871 and had to be kept under severe restraint. The government began to entertain fears that the King was going the same way and appointed Dr Bernhard von Gudden to report on his mental condition in 1886. A diagnosis was made without examining the King and he was duly pronounced insane. A commission of doctors, headed by von Gudden, was sent to Neuschwanstein to take Ludwig into custody and he was removed to Schloss Berg, some twenty miles south of Munich. The day after his arrival the King and Dr von Gudden went for a walk in the castle grounds. They did not return at the expected time and on a search being made the bodies of both men were found drowned in Lake Starnberg. It was generally believed that

Linderhof, one of King Ludwig II's architectural creations.

An eighteenth-century engraving of the Nymphenburg Palace, which remains almost unaltered today.

the King had intended suicide and his doctor had been drowned in an attempt to restrain him, but the truth will never be known.

The demented Prince Otto was proclaimed King in spite of his sad condition and his uncle Prince Luitpold was appointed Regent. Luitpold was Regent for twenty-five years and eventually became a much-loved figure with his long white beard and patriarchal appearance. He died at the age of ninety-one in 1912 and was succeeded as Regent by his son Ludwig. On 5 November 1913 Ludwig decided that the time had come for him to take the royal title and he proclaimed himself King Ludwig III although Otto was still living and did not die until 1916. Ludwig III had married Archduchess Maria Theresa of Austria-Este, who as the lineal representative of King Charles I of England, was regarded by a small band of die-hard British legitimists as 'Queen Mary IV and III'. The King and Queen had a large family and enjoyed a reasonable popularity until the end of the First World War, when a Communist uprising in Munich drove them from the throne two days before the Armistice was signed. The Queen was ailing and died three months later at one of the family properties, Schloss Wildenwart. King Ludwig eventually found refuge in Hungary where he died in October 1921. After his death his son Crown Prince Rupprecht was allowed to return to Munich and take up residence in the Nymphenburg Palace. He was King in all but name and very much loved by the Bavarians. When he died at the age of eighty-six in August 1955 his funeral was conducted as that of a reigning monarch. Crown Prince Rupprecht's son Albert is the present head of the Bavarian Royal House. Twice widowed and now in his eighties, he lives at the Nymphenburg Palace as his ancestors have done for many centuries and enjoys a popularity almost as great as that of his father.

HANOVER

ERNEST AUGUSTUS 1837–1851

---

b London 5 June 1771, 5th son of George III, King of Great Britain and Hanover, and Charlotte of Mecklenburg-Strelitz; *cr* Duke of Cumberland and Teviotdale and Earl of Armagh 24 April 1799; Deputy Elector of Hanover 1813; Field Marshal in the British Army 1813; *s* his brother King William IV as King of Hanover 20 June 1837; *m* Neustrelitz 29 May, and Carlton House, London, 29 August 1815, Frederica (*b* Hanover 2 March 1778; *d* there 29 June 1841; *bur* Herrenhausen), widow of Prince Frederick William of Solms-Braunfels and previously of Prince Louis of Prussia, and 5th dau of Charles, Grand Duke of Mecklenburg-Strelitz, and his first wife Frederica of Hesse-Darmstadt; 1 son, 1 stillborn dau; *d* Herrenhausen 18 November 1851; *bur* Herrenhausen

---

GEORGE V 1851–1866

---

b Berlin 27 May 1819, only son of King Ernest Augustus; *s* his father 18 November 1851; deposed when Hanover was annexed by Prussia 20

September 1866; *m* Hanover 18 February 1843 Marie (*b* Hildburghausen 14 April 1818; *d* Gmunden, Austria, 9 January 1907; *bur* Gmunden), eldest dau of Joseph, Duke of Saxe-Altenburg, and Amelia of Württemberg; 1 son, 2 daus; *d* Paris 12 June 1878; *bur* St George's Chapel, Windsor

---

The House of Guelf, which obtained the Duchy of Brunswick in the twelfth century, was of Italian origin, sharing the same line of ancestry as the House of Este. Its various German possessions were acquired through a series of marriages with heiresses. In common with most other German reigning families, it failed to establish the law of primogeniture early, and the consequent divisions and subdivisions greatly weakened its power. By the seventeenth century only two lines, Brunswick-Wolfenbüttel and Brunswick-Lüneburg, remained. Duke Ernest Augustus of the latter line was raised to the dignity of Elector of Hanover by the Emperor in March 1692. He married Princess Sophia of the Palatinate, upon whom and upon whose heirs the succession to the throne of Great Britain was settled by Act of Parliament. Their eldest son, the Elector George Louis, succeeded to the British throne as King George I on the death of Queen Anne in 1714. A hundred years later King George III assumed the title of King of Hanover on 12 October 1814. Hanover remained united to.the British crown until 1837 when King William IV died. As women were barred from the Hanoverian succession he was succeeded in that country by his brother Ernest Augustus, Duke of Cumberland.

King Ernest Augustus has always received a very bad press in Britain and has generally been represented as the wickedest of Queen Victoria's 'wicked uncles'. He was certainly of fearsome appearance, having lost an eye at the battle of Tournai in 1794, and something of a martinet. Moreover, he had been involved in several unsavoury scandals including the mysterious murder of his valet Sellis and an alleged incestuous relationship with his sister Princess Sophia, resulting in the birth of a child. He had remained a bachelor until the age of forty-four when he fell in love with his first cousin, the thirty-seven-year-old Princess Frederica of Mecklenburg-Strelitz. The Princess had a 'past', having been married twice already and gained the reputation of being somewhat loose in her ways. Her aunt Queen Charlotte heartily disapproved of the match and refused to be present or to receive her new daughter-in-law. In spite of this the marriage was a happy one. The Duchess of Cumberland gave birth to a stillborn daughter in January 1817 and possibly to another in April 1818 (accounts are conflicting) and finally to a son George in May 1819.

As King of Hanover, all Ernest Augustus's good qualities came to the fore. He believed in paternalistic rule and did much to improve the lot of his subjects, who were delighted to have their own King living in their midst after years of being governed by Viceroys. Needless to say, the King had no time for liberalism and dealt very firmly with a revolutionary mob which demanded concessions in the troublesome year of 1848. Queen Frederica died in 1841 and the old King's last years were considerably brightened by the pleasure he took in seeing his three young grandchildren playing around him. He died in November 1851, aged eighty.

King George V, who succeeded his father, had the great misfortune of being blind, having lost his sight as a boy in an accident with a swinging bunch of keys. He was able to overcome his disability to a large extent. Unfortunately he sided with Austria in the war of 1866 and as a result Hanover was annexed by Prussia. King George went into exile at Gmunden in Austria and died while on a visit to Paris in June 1878. His body was brought to England for burial in St George's Chapel, Windsor.

The blind King had married Princess Marie of Saxe-Altenburg and their only son (they also had two daughters), Ernest Augustus, one of the ugliest men imaginable, reverted to the title of Duke of Cumberland. He married Princess Thyra of Denmark, the youngest sister of Queen Alexandra and the Empress Marie of Russia, and their son, another Ernest Augustus, actually became reigning Duke of Brunswick in 1913 following his marriage to Princess Victoria Louise of Prussia, Emperor William II's only daughter. His sovereignty was short lived, however, and he abdicated in November 1918 along with all the other German rulers. His grandson, yet another Ernest Augustus, is the present representative of the Royal House. Born in 1954, he has been married since 1981 to a Swiss girl, Chantal Hochuli, and they have two sons.

SAXONY

The House of Wettin

FREDERICK AUGUSTUS I   1806–1827

b Dresden 23 December 1750, eldest son of Frederick Christian, Elector of Saxony, and Maria Antonia of Bavaria; *s* his father as Elector 17 December 1763, under the regency of his uncle Prince Xaver until 13 September 1768; assumed the title of King of Saxony 11 December 1806; Grand Duke of Warsaw 8 July 1807 to 1 June 1813; in exile 1813–15; restored 1815; *m* proxy Mannheim 17 January, in person Dresden 29 January 1769, Amelia (*b* Mannheim 10 May 1752; *d* Dresden 15 November 1828), dau of Frederick Michael, Count Palatine of Zweibrücken-Birkenfeld-Bischweiler, and Franziska, Countess Palatine of Sulzbach; 1 dau; *d* Dresden 5 May 1827

ANTHONY I   1827–1836

b Dresden 27 December 1755, 4th son of Frederick Christian, Elector of Saxony; *s* his brother King Frederick Augustus I 5 May 1827; appointed his nephew and heir presumptive Prince Frederick Augustus co-Regent 13 September 1830; *m* (1) proxy Turin 29 September, in person Dresden 24 October 1781, Charlotte (*b* Turin 17 January 1764; *d* Dresden 28 December 1782), yst dau of Victor Amadeus III, King of Sardinia, and Maria Antonietta of Spain; no issue; *m* (2) proxy Florence 8 September, in person Dresden 18 October 1787, Theresa (*b* Florence 14 January 1767; *d* Leipzig 7 November 1827), eldest dau of Leopold II, Holy Roman Emperor, and Maria Louisa of Spain; 1 son, 3 daus (all died in infancy); *d* Pillnitz 6 June 1836

FREDERICK AUGUSTUS II   1836–1854

b Dresden 18 May 1797, eldest son of Prince Maximilian of Saxony (5th and yst son of Elector Frederick Christian) and his 1st wife Caroline of Bourbon-Parma; appointed co-Regent by his uncle King Anthony 13 September 1830 and *s* him as King 6 June 1836; *m* (1) proxy Vienna 26 September, in person Dresden 7 October 1819, Caroline (*b* Vienna 8 April 1801; *d* Dresden 22 May 1832), 7th dau of Francis I, Emperor of Austria, and his 2nd wife Maria Theresa of Bourbon-Two Sicilies; no issue; *m* (2) Dresden 24 April 1833 Marie (*b* Munich 27 January 1805; *d* Wachwitz 13 September 1877), 7th dau of Maximilian I Joseph, King of Bavaria, and his 2nd wife Caroline of Baden; no issue; *d* Brennbüchel, Tyrol, 9 August 1854

JOHN I   1854–1873

b Dresden 12 December 1801, 3rd and yst son of Prince Maximilian of Saxony; *s* his brother King Frederick Augustus II 9 August 1854; *m* proxy Munich 10 November, in person Dresden 21 November 1822, Amelia (*b* Munich 13 November 1801; *d* Dresden 8 November 1877), 5th dau of Maximilian I Joseph, King of Bavaria, and his 2nd wife Caroline of Baden; 3 sons, 6 daus; *d* Pillnitz 29 October 1873

ALBERT I   1873–1902

b Dresden 23 April 1828, eldest son of King John I; *s* his father 29 October 1873; *m* Dresden 18 June 1853 Caroline (Carola) (*b* Schönbrunn 5 August 1833; *d* Dresden 15 December 1907), only dau of Prince Gustav Vasa and Louise of Baden; no issue; *d* Schloss Sibyllenort 19 June 1902

GEORGE I   1902–1904

b Pillnitz 8 August 1832, 3rd and yst son of King John I; *s* his brother King Albert I 19 June 1902; *m* Lisbon 11 May 1859 Maria Anna (*b* Lisbon 21 July 1843; *d* Dresden 5 February 1884), 2nd dau of Maria II da Gloria, Queen of Portugal and the Algarves, and her 2nd husband Ferdinand of Saxe-Coburg and Gotha; 4 sons, 4 daus; *d* Pillnitz 15 October 1904

FREDERICK AUGUSTUS III   1904–1918

b Dresden 25 May 1865, eldest son of King George I; *s* his father 15 October 1904; abdicated 13 November 1918; *m* Vienna 21 November 1891 (*m* diss Dresden 11 February 1903) Louise (*b* Salzburg 2 September 1870; *d* Brussels 23 March 1947), dau of Ferdinand IV, Grand Duke of Tuscany, and his 2nd wife Alicia of Bourbon-Parma; 3 sons, 4 daus; *d* Sibyllenort 18 February 1932

The House of Wettin can be traced back to Burkhard, Count in the Grabfeld, who died in 908. His descendant Frederick the Warlike received the Duchy of Saxe-Wittenberg and the Electoral dignity in 1423. The brothers Ernest and Albert divided their lands in 1485, founding the Ernestine and Albertine lines of the family. Ernest's son Frederick the Wise made Saxony the most powerful state of the Empire and fostered the Protestant Reformation. Elector John Frederick the Magnanimous got involved in the war of the League of Schmalkaldern and was captured by Emperor Charles V who forced him to cede the Electoral dignity to the junior Albertine line, although he was allowed to retain certain territories and the title of Duke. His descendants broke up into the various Saxon Duchies (Saxe-Coburg, Saxe-Altenburg, Saxe-Meiningen, Saxe-Weimar and so on).

Elector Frederick Augustus I reverted to Catholicism in order to secure his election to the throne of Poland in 1697. His son Frederick Augustus II was also elected King of Poland in 1733. When he died in October 1763 he was succeeded in the Electorate of Saxony by his son Frederick Christian who only reigned for three months and was succeeded on his death in December 1763 by his eldest son Frederick Augustus III, who was to become the first King of Saxony.

Frederick Augustus came of age in 1768 and showed himself to be a conscientious ruler, eager to reduce taxation, earning the sobriquet of 'the Just'. He was studious to preserve Saxony's neutrality during the struggles between Austria and Prussia and refused the crown of Poland in 1791. He was compelled to take part in the war against France until 1796. Later he remained neutral during the war between France and Austria in 1805, but joined Prussia against France in 1806. After the battle of Jena he concluded a peace treaty with Napoleon at Posen, assumed the title of King and joined the Confederation of the Rhine on 11 December 1806. After the treaty of Tilsit the following July, Frederick Augustus received the Grand Duchy of Warsaw from Napoleon, with whom he soon became on fairly friendly terms, entertaining him at Dresden on several occasions, and supplying Saxon troops to fight in his campaigns. At the battle of Leipzig, however, the Saxons deserted to the allies and Frederick Augustus was taken prisoner on 19 October 1813. He did not regain his freedom until after the Congress of Vienna, which compelled him to cede three-fifths of his kingdom (the northern part) to Prussia. He returned to Dresden in 1815 and was received with enthusiasm by the people. The rest of his reign was passed in recovering from the ravages wrought by the Napoleonic Wars and effecting various administrative and judicial reforms. The King was a great patron of art and science with a personal interest in botany which led him to lay out the beautiful park at Schloss Pillnitz. Frederick Augustus married a sister of the first King of Bavaria. Their only child was a daughter, who died unmarried at the age of eighty, so the King was succeeded by his brother Anthony.

King Anthony lost his second wife a few months after his accession. Their four children had all died in infancy and his heir was his next brother Maximilian. In 1830 there was a rising in Dresden which prompted the King to proclaim Maximilian's son Frederick Augustus as co-Regent on 13 September (Maximilian having already waived his rights of succession). Frederick Augustus thus became the effective ruler and succeeded as King Frederick Augustus II on Anthony's death in 1836. An enlightened liberal, he was a popular ruler and, apart from a speedily repressed insurrection at Dresden in May 1849, reigned in peace and tranquillity until his death in a carriage accident in the Austrian Tyrol in August 1854. Frederick Augustus II was interested in botany like his uncle and published a learned book on the subject with a long German title in 1837. He had married twice but there were no children from either marriage and he was succeeded by his brother John. King John of Saxony, who joined the North German Confederation in 1866, was a very learned man and translated and annotated the works of Dante. He died in October 1873 and was succeeded by his eldest son Albert. Albert had distinguished himself as a General and commanded the Saxon army on the Austrian side in 1866. The Prussian victory led to a short occupation of Saxony and the payment of an indemnity, but in 1870 Saxony sided with Prussia in the Franco-Prussian War. King Albert's military days were over by the time he became King and he was noted for his benevolence. His equally amiable Queen, Carola, was the only daughter of Prince Gustav Vasa, son of the deposed King Gustav IV Adolph of Sweden, and a small band of Swedish legitimists regarded her as the rightful Queen of Sweden. The couple had no children and King Albert was succeeded on his death in June 1902 by his brother Prince George.

King George was a very different type of man. A widower for eighteen years, he had been eagerly awaiting his succession and could scarcely restrain his delight in being King at last. The place of first lady of the land should have been taken by his attractive young daughter-in-law, Crown Princess Louise, a Princess of Tuscany, but instead the King's unmarried daughter Princess Mathilde ruled the roost. Large, red-faced, mannish and extremely disagreeable, Princess Mathilde was nevertheless quite a talented artist, producing vast heroic canvases depicting historical and religious subjects. She bullied her sister-in-law unmercifully and made her most unhappy. In 1903 there was a great scandal which shook Europe when the Crown Princess, pregnant with her seventh child, fled from Dresden and joined her lover, an Italian pianist and composer named Enrico Toselli. Her marriage was immediately dissolved, but the daughter to whom she gave birth at Lindau in Bavaria in May was acknowledged by the Crown Prince and sent back to Dresden to be brought up by the royal family. Louise received the title of Countess of Montignoso and in 1907 married Toselli, by whom she had one son. They separated in 1912 and Louise died in Brussels in July 1947.

King George, after waiting so long and so impatiently for the throne, only lived two years to enjoy it. He died in October 1904 and was succeeded by the Crown Prince.

King Frederick Augustus III, the last King of Saxony, was a homely, good-natured man, speaking with a broad Saxon accent which was almost incomprehensible to some of his fellow Germans. He never remarried after his wife's desertion. The Saxon monarchy came to an end on 13 November 1918, when the King abdicated along with the other German rulers. He had been extremely popular and when making a train journey a few

Joseph Bonaparte, Napoleon's elder brother, who occupied the throne of Naples for a few years before being transferred to that of Spain, seen here with one of his daughters.

Joachim Murat, Napoleon's brother-in-law, looking very splendid as King of Naples. This portrait by F P Gerard is in the Collegio Spalletti at Ravenna.

The throne room of the royal Palace at Caserta, Naples.

*John Sobieski, the great warrior King of Poland, who saved
Europe from the Turkish menace at the end of the
seventeenth century.*

Queen Geraldine of the Albanians signing copies of her authorized biography in London in August 1987. The Queen's charm, which has inspired Albanian monarchists for half a century, is very apparent in this photograph.

The Greek royal family in 1987: (left to right) Crown Prince Paul, Princess Alexia, King Constantine with Princess Theodora in front, Queen Anne-Marie holding Prince Philip, and Prince Nicholas.

A silver two-thirds tharler of King Anthony of Saxony showing the King with a fine head of hair. It was minted in 1827.

King Albert of Saxony, a distinguished General.

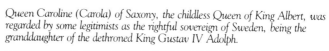

King John of Saxony, a charming photograph of the scholarly, benevolent King.

Queen Caroline (Carola) of Saxony, the childless Queen of King Albert, was regarded by some legitimists as the rightful sovereign of Sweden, being the granddaughter of the dethroned King Gustav IV Adolph.

A silver two marks piece of the last King of Saxony, Frederick Augustus III, minted in 1907.

years later was greeted at a station by a cheering crowd begging him to show himself to them at the window of his carriage. This prompted him to call out, with a broad grin: 'Well, I must say, you *are* a fine set of Republicans!'

King Frederick Augustus III died on 18 February 1932, aged sixty-six. His eldest son had become a priest so he was succeeded as head of the Royal House by his second son, Frederick Christian, who assumed the old family title of Margrave of Meissen. He died in 1968 and the representation passed to his elder son Maria Emanuel, born in 1926, who is married but has no children.

WÜRTTEMBERG

FREDERICK I   (1797) 1805–1816

b Treptow 6 November 1754, eldest son of Frederick Eugene, Duke of Württemberg, and Frederica of Brandenburg-Schwedt; *s* his father as Duke of Württemberg 22 December 1797; assumed the title of Elector of Württemberg 25 February (proclaimed 27 April) 1803; assumed the title of King of Württemberg (proclaimed 1 January 1806) 26 December 1805; *m* (1) Brunswick 15 October 1780 Augusta (*b* Brunswick 3 December 1764; *d* Lohde, nr Reval, Esthonia, 27 September 1788), eldest dau of Charles II, Duke of Brunswick, and Augusta of Great Britain (sister of King George III); 2 sons, 2 daus; *m* (2) London 18 May 1797 Charlotte, Princess Royal of Great Britain and Ireland (*b* London 29 September 1766; *d* Ludwigsburg 6 October 1828), eldest dau of George III, King of Great Britain and Ireland, and Charlotte of Mecklenburg-Strelitz; 1 dau (stillborn); *d* Stuttgart 30 October 1816

WILLIAM I   1816–1864

b Lübben 27 September 1781, elder son of King Frederick I; *s* his father 30 October 1816; *m* (1) Munich 8 June 1808 (*m* diss 1814) Charlotte (*b* Mannheim 8 February 1792; *d* Vienna 9 February 1873), 3rd dau of Maximilian I Joseph, King of Bavaria, and his 1st wife Augusta of Hesse-Darmstadt; no issue; *m* (2) St Petersburg 24 January 1816 Catherine (*b* St Petersburg 21 May 1788; *d* Stuttgart 9 January 1819), widow of Duke George of Oldenburg, and 4th dau of Paul I, Emperor of Russia, and his 2nd wife Maria Feodorovna (Sophia Dorothea) of Württemberg (sister of King Frederick I); 2 daus; *m* (3) Stuttgart 15 April 1820 Pauline (*b* Riga 4 September 1800; *d* Stuttgart 10 March 1873), 3rd dau of Duke Ludwig of Württemberg (brother of King Frederick I), and his 2nd wife Henriette of Nassau-Weilburg; 1 son, 2 daus; *d* Schloss Rosenstein, nr Stuttgart, 25 June 1864

CHARLES I   1864–1891

b Stuttgart 6 March 1823, only son of King William I; *s* his father 25 June 1864; *m* St Petersburg 13 July 1846 Olga (*b* St Petersburg 11 September 1822; *d* Friedrichshafen 30 October 1892), 3rd dau of Nicholas I, Emperor of Russia, and Alexandra Feodorovna (Charlotte) of Prussia; no issue; *d* Stuttgart 6 October 1891

WILLIAM II   1891–1918

b Stuttgart 25 February 1848, only son of Prince Frederick of Württemberg (eldest son of Prince Paul, yr son of King Frederick I), and Catherine of Württemberg (3rd dau of King William I); *s* his uncle King Charles I 6 October 1891; abdicated 29 November 1918; *m* (1) Arolsen 15 February 1877 Marie (*b* Arolsen 23 May 1857; *d* Ludwigsburg 30 April 1882), 3rd dau of George Victor, Prince of Waldeck and Pyrmont, and Helene of Nassau; 1 son, 2 daus (1 stillborn); *m* (2) Bückeburg 8 April 1886 Charlotte (*b* Ratibořitz 10 October 1864; *d* Schloss Bebenhausen 16 July 1946), eldest dau of Prince William of Schaumburg-Lippe, and Bathildis of Anhalt; no issue; *d* Schloss Bebenhausen 2 October 1921

The House of Württemberg took its name from an ancient castle on the Rotenberg, near Stuttgart. On 31 July 1485 Count Eberhard the Bearded received the title of Duke from the Emperor. Duke Frederick II served in the Prussian and Russian armies before succeeding his father, Duke Frederick Eugene, in 1797 and for a time acted as Governor of Finland. In 1800 the Duchy was occupied by the French and the Duke fled to Vienna, but in 1801 he concluded a private treaty, ceding Montbéliard to France and receiving Ellwangen in exchange two years later. In 1803 he was proclaimed Elector and received nine Imperial towns. He had a meeting with Napoleon in 1805 and after supplying him with a large auxiliary force received the title of King. He joined the Confederation of the Rhine, took part in the Congress of Erfurt, and provided a contingent for the disastrous Russian campaign. In 1813 he changed sides and went over to the Allies, where his standing was helped by the fact that he was brother-in-law of the Prince Regent. After the fall of

A silver gulden of King William I of Württemberg struck in 1843.

Charles I, King of Württemberg.

Napoleon, Frederick attended the Congress of Vienna and on returning home offered a new Constitution to the Württemberg parliament which was rejected. He was in the midst of preparing another when he died suddenly in October 1816.

King Frederick was twice married. His first wife, Augusta of Brunswick, accompanied him to Russia where she became involved in an intrigue (so it was rumoured) with the Grand Duke Paul, the heir apparent. His mother Catherine the Great put an end to the affair by banishing the young Princess to the Castle of Lohde on the Baltic, where she was reported to have died two years later. Her husband and children had been sent home to Württemberg without her. Shortly before he succeeded his father, Frederick married again. His second wife, who was first cousin to his first wife, was the Princess Royal, eldest daughter of King George III of Great Britain. She was already over thirty and quite prepared to marry almost any suitor who offered. Frederick was enormously fat and cannot have been very appealing, but the marriage turned out quite happily although the only child was stillborn. After Frederick had become King his mother-in-law Queen Charlotte became very incensed at his assumption of the title, as Napoleon's henchman, and refused to address her daughter as Queen when writing to her so that her letters had to be sent to the Prince Regent to be properly redirected. Matters were not helped when the younger Charlotte tactlessly began a letter to her mother 'My dear Mama and Sister', sister being the usual salutation between Queens when addressing each other formally. Württemberg's first Queen grew to be almost as amply proportioned as her husband as can be seen in her later portraits.

Frederick was succeeded by his elder son William I who enjoyed a long and peaceful reign although obliged to grant a new liberal Constitution in that year of revolutions, 1848. He married three times. His first marriage to Princess Charlotte Augusta of Bavaria was childless and unhappy and ended in divorce in 1814. Two years later the Princess was to make a far grander marriage when, renamed Caroline Augusta, she became the fourth wife of Emperor Francis I of Austria, with whom she lived quite happily in spite of an age difference of twenty-four years. William's second wife was Grand Duchess Catherine of Russia, the favourite sister of Emperor Alexander I. She only survived the marriage three years and died in January 1819, leaving William two daughters. His third and last wife was another first cousin, Pauline of Württemberg, who produced a son and two daughters.

William I died in June 1864 and was succeeded by his only son Charles. King Charles, as the German Crown Princess wrote to her mother Queen Victoria, 'was very peculiar and difficult to manage and had the funniest caprices – in fact was not always "all there" '. His court, which was very stiff and formal, was noted for its family feuds and Princess May of Teck (later our Queen Mary) commented when staying with her Württemberg relations, 'they would all drive me wild in a week *if I had* to live there'. King Charles married a Russian Grand Duchess Olga, a niece of his father's second wife and his own second cousin. There were no children and when King Charles died in 1891 he was succeeded by his nephew Prince William, the only son of his sister Catherine who had married her cousin Prince Frederick,

A magnificent portrait by Winterhalter of Queen Olga of Württemberg, the wife of King Charles I.

King William II of Württemberg, who abdicated in 1918.

whose father Prince Paul was the younger son of King Frederick I. It was his male descent, of course, which entitled Prince William to the throne.

King William II was a man of culture and refinement and also renowned as a judge of horseflesh and the keeper of a first-class stud. His first wife, Marie, a sister of Queen Emma of the Netherlands and of the Duchess of Albany, died in childbirth in April 1882 after being delivered of her third child, a stillborn daughter. Her only son, Ulrich, had died at the age of five months in 1880, and only her daughter Pauline survived. William's second wife, whom he married in 1886, was the very plain Princess Charlotte of Schaumburg-Lippe. There were no children of the marriage, but the couple suited each other very well and as King and Queen led a very simple life. The late Duke of Windsor drew a very touching portrait of them in his memoirs, referring to the time he stayed with them shortly before the First World War:

Onkel Willie and Tante Charlotte were sympathetic and easygoing. Their ample figures betrayed the justice they did to their four full meals a day ... After an enormous lunch, almost every fine afternoon the King and Queen took a leisurely drive through the suburbs of Stuttgart in an open victoria, and sometimes I was summoned to drive with them. Under the influence of the warm sun and the gentle motion of the carriage, Onkel Willie would quickly fall asleep, only to be constantly aroused by a swift jab of the Queen's elbow to acknowledge the salute of one of his soldiers, the precise salutation of a stolid Württemberger, or to straighten the Homburg hat that kept sliding rakishly to one side of his head. This process had been going on for so many years that, when Onkel Willie got that dig into his well-padded ribs, he was able to straighten his hat in his sleep.

When at the end of the First World War the German monarchies were swept away in the wake of the Armistice, King William II of Württemberg was the last German sovereign to abdicate, on 29 November 1918, one day after Emperor William II. The line of Kings of Württemberg descended from King Frederick I died with William II in October 1921. He was succeeded as head of the Royal House by his kinsman Duke Albert, who descended from one of the younger brothers of King

Frederick I. The present representative is Albert's grandson Duke Carl, born in 1936, who is married to Princess Diane of France, the fourth daughter of the Count of Paris, pretender to the French throne. They have six children.

WESTPHALIA

HIERONYMUS NAPOLEON	1807–1813

b (Jérôme Bonaparte) Ajaccio, Corsica, 15 November 1784, 6th and yst son of Charles Marie Bonaparte and Marie Laetitia Ramolino; recognized as French Prince and Imperial Highness by his brother Emperor Napoleon I 24 September 1806; King of Westphalia 8 July 1807; left his kingdom 26 October 1813; *cr* Prince of Montfort by his father-in-law King Frederick I of Württemberg 31 July 1816; Governor-General of the Invalides and Marshal of France 1850; Heir Presumptive of the Second Empire from 18 December 1852 until the birth of the Prince Imperial 16 March 1856; *m* (1) Baltimore, Maryland, USA, 24 December 1803 (*m* annulled by Imperial Decree 2 March 1805 and religiously 6 October 1806) Elizabeth (*b* Baltimore 6 February 1785; *d* Baltimore 4 April 1879), dau of William Patterson and Dorcas Spear; 1 son; *m* (2) proxy Stuttgart 12 August, in person Paris 22 August (civil) and 23 August (religious) 1807, Catherine (*b* St Petersburg 21 February 1783; *d* Villa Monrepos, nr Lausanne, Switzerland, 28 November 1835), eldest dau of Frederick I, King of Württemberg, and his 1st wife Augusta of Brunswick; 2 sons, 1 dau; *m* (3) Florence (?) 1840, Paris 19 January 1853 (civil), Giustina (*b* Florence 27 November 1811; *d* Florence 30 January 1903), widow of Marchese Luigi Bartolini-Baldelli, and dau of Count Bernardo Pecori-Suárez (later Pecori-Giraldi) and his 2nd wife Giulia Sirigatti; *d* Paris 24 June 1860; *bur* Notre-Dame des Invalides

The puppet kingdom of Westphalia was created by Napoleon in 1807 for his youngest brother Jérôme. It consisted of the greater part of Hesse-Cassel, the whole of Brunswick and parts of , Prussia, Hanover and Saxony. Jérôme ascended his newly created throne as Hieronymus Napoleon.

Jérôme, probably the least talented and certainly the most dissolute of Napoleon's brothers, had blotted his copybook in 1803, when he was serving in the French navy, by falling in love with and marrying a young Bostonian, Elizabeth Patterson. She was a girl of perfectly good family but not good enough for her new brother-in-law who was on the eve of proclaiming himself Emperor and wished to keep the unmarried members of his family free to contract grand alliances with the old royal families of Europe. For this reason Jérôme was excluded from membership of the Imperial family when the Empire was proclaimed on 18 May 1804. Jérôme returned to Europe in 1805 and Elizabeth, now pregnant, followed him with her father but was prevented from landing in France on Napoleon's orders. She went to England instead and gave birth to a son at Camberwell on 7 July 1805. Meanwhile it had not taken Napoleon long to persuade his faithless brother to agree to an annulment of the marriage by pointing out the glittering prospects which awaited him. In September 1806 Jérôme was admitted to membership of the Imperial family and in the following July received the kingdom of Westphalia and in August the hand of Princess Catherine of Württemberg.

As a ruler Jérôme made little or no mark, being merely a satellite of his brother, and after the battle of Leipzig fled the country on 26 October 1813. Queen Catherine had had no children as a reigning Queen, but in exile at Trieste she gave birth to three, two sons and a daughter. She died in November 1835 and on an unknown date in 1840 the feckless Jérôme contracted a third marriage with the Florentine heiress Giustina Bartolini-Baldelli, who was over twenty-five years his junior. He got her money and she may be said to have got a raw deal as she was never openly acknowledged as his wife or rewarded with any title, although he did marry her in accordance with French civil law in January 1853. When the Second Empire was proclaimed by Jérôme's nephew Napoleon III, he became Heir Presumptive until the birth of the Prince Imperial, and was created a Marshal of France. He died full of years if not of honour on 24 June 1860.

Jérôme's American family died out in the male line in 1945. His only surviving son by Catherine became the representative of the Imperial House on the death of the Prince Imperial in Zululand in 1879 and was the grandfather of the present representative, Prince Louis Napoleon.

ITALY

In 476 the Roman army chose the Barbarian officer Odoacer as leader and he defeated the Patrician Orestes at Pavia and dethroned his son Romulus Augustulus, the last Roman Emperor of the West. Odoacer became ruler of all Italy and made Ravenna his capital, obtaining the title of Patrician from the Eastern Emperor Zeno, although he did not assume the Imperial dignity. He proved a good ruler, but in 489 Italy was invaded by the Ostrogoths under their King Theodoric, who took Rome and treacherously murdered Odoacer on 15 March 493, a few days after concluding a treaty with him whereby they had agreed to rule jointly.

Theodoric died in 526 and was succeeded by his eleven-year-old grandson Athalaric, the son of his daughter Amalasuntha, who ruled as Regent in his name. In spite of his mother's care, Athalaric grew up a wayward youth and died as a result of his debauchery in 534. Amalasuntha then selected her cousin Theodahad, a son of Theodoric's sister, to be her husband and reign with her, but he murdered her the following year, only to be assassinated in his turn in 536, when the throne was usurped by Witigis, of uncertain provenance. Four Kings reigned after him and in 553 Italy passed into the possession of the Eastern or Byzantine Empire for a short period until 568, when the Germanic Lombards invaded from the north and established a kingdom which lasted until 774, when the last King, Desiderius, was deposed by his son-in-law the Emperor Charlemagne. Carolingian Kings ruled Italy as tributaries of the Emperor until 887 and were followed by a period of anarchy during which Kings of rival dynasties reigned for short periods. In 951 the Holy Roman Emperor Otto I was called in to restore order by Adelaide, the widow of King Lothario II, and Italy was completely absorbed into the Holy Roman Empire. In the following centuries it split up into a number of small states, the only kingdoms being those of Naples and Sicily in the south and later that of Sardinia.

Following the incursion of the French under Napoleon, Lombardy, Emilia and the Marches were formed into the Cisalpine Republic on 29 June 1797 with Napoleon as President. It was renamed the Italian Republic in January 1802 and on 17 March 1805 became the kingdom of Italy with Venetia added to its territory. Napoleon was proclaimed King and on 26 May 1805 was crowned with the ancient Iron Crown of Lombardy, alleged to have been fashioned from a nail of the true cross. Napoleon appointed his stepson Eugène de Beauharnais to act as Viceroy of Italy on 7 April 1805 and he filled the office with great ability earning much popularity. Napoleon abdicated the thrones of both France and Italy on 11 April 1814 and the Congress of Vienna formed Lombardy and Venetia into the Lombardo-Venetian kingdom and gave it to the Emperor Francis of Austria, Napoleon's father-in-law. Italy was not to be united in a single kingdom until 1861.

SARDINIA

The House of Savoy

VICTOR AMADEUS II	(1675) 1718–1730

b Turin 14 May 1666, only son of Charles Emmanuel II, Duke of Savoy, and his 2nd wife Marie Jeanne Baptiste of Savoy-Nemours; *s* his father as Duke of Savoy 12 June 1675, under the regency of his mother until 1684; proclaimed King of Sicily 22 September 1713; crowned Palermo 24 December 1713; proclaimed King of Sardinia (in exchange for Sicily) 2 August 1718; abdicated 3 September 1730; *m* (1) proxy Versailles 10 April, in person Chambéry 6 May 1684, Anne Marie (*b* St Cloud 27 August 1669; *d* Turin 26 August 1728; *bur* La Superga), 3rd dau of Philippe of France, Duke of Orleans, and his 1st wife Henrietta Anne of England; 5 sons, 5 daus; *m* (2) Turin 12 August 1729 Anna Teresa, *cr* Marchesa di Spigno (*b* 1678; *d* 12/13 April 1769), widow of Ignatio Francesco Novarina, Conte di San Sebastian, and dau of Francesco Maurizio Canali, Conte di Cumiana, Marchese di San Tomaso; no issue; *d* Moncalieri 31 October 1732; *bur* La Superga

CHARLES EMMANUEL III	1730–1773

b Turin 27 April 1701, 3rd but eldest suriving son of King Victor Amadeus I; *s* his father on his abdication 3 September 1730; *m* (1) proxy 16 February, in person Vercelli 15 March 1722, Anne Christine Louise (*b* Sulzbach 5 February 1704; *d* Turin 12 March 1723; *bur* Turin Cathedral, transferred La Superga 1786), 5th and yst dau of Theodore, Count Palatine in Sulzbach, and Maria Eleonora of Hesse-Rheinfels-Rotenburg; 1 son; *m* (2) proxy Rotenburg 23 July, in person Thonon, Lake Geneva, 20 August 1724 Polyxene Christine (*b* Langenschwalbach 21 September 1706; *d* Turin 13 January 1735; *bur* Turin Cathedral, transferred La Superga 1786), eldest dau of Ernest Leopold, Landgrave of Hesse-Rheinfels-Rotenburg, and Eleonora Maria Anna of Löwenstein-Wertheim-Rochefort; 4 sons, 3 daus; *m* (3) Chambéry 1 April 1737 Elizabeth Theresa (*b* Lunéville 15 October 1711; *d* Turin 3 July 1741; *bur* Turin Cathedral, transferred La Superga 1786), 7th and yst dau of Leopold Joseph Charles, Duke of Lorraine and Bar, and Elizabeth Charlotte of Orleans; 2 sons, 1 dau; *d* Turin 20 February 1773; *bur* La Superga

VICTOR AMADEUS III	1773–1796

b Turin 26 June 1726, 2nd but eldest surviving son of King Charles Emmanuel III, and eldest son by his 2nd wife; *s* his father 20 February 1773; *m* Oulx 31 May 1750 Maria Antonietta (*b* Seville 17 November 1729; *d* Moncalieri 19 September 1785; *bur* La Superga), yst dau of Philip V, King of Spain, and his 2nd wife Elizabeth Farnese; 6 sons, 6 daus; *d* Moncalieri 16 October 1796; *bur* La Superga

CHARLES EMMANUEL IV	1796–1802

b Turin 24 May 1751, eldest son of King Victor Amadeus III; *s* his father 16 October 1796; abdicated in favour of his brother Victor Emmanuel 4 June 1802; *m* proxy Versailles 21 August, in person Chambéry 6 September 1775, Clotilde (*b* Versailles 23 September 1759; *d* Naples 7 March 1802; declared Venerable by Pope Pius VII 10 April 1808), 4th dau of Louis, Dauphin of France (son of Louis XV, King of France and Navarre), and his 2nd wife Maria Josepha of Saxony; no issue; *d* Rome 6 October 1819; *bur* Church of the Gesù, Rome

VICTOR EMMANUEL I	1802–1821

b Turin 24 July 1759, 3rd son of King Victor Amadeus III; *s* his brother King Charles Emmanuel IV on his abdication 4 June 1802; abdicated in favour of his brother Charles Felix 13 March 1821; *m* proxy 23 April, in person Turin 25 April 1789, Maria Theresa (*b* Milan 1 November 1773; *d* Genoa 29 March 1832), eldest dau of Ferdinand, Duke of Modena, Archduke of Austria, and Maria Beatrice, Duchess of Massa and Princess of Carrara; 1 son (*d* young), 6 daus; *d* Moncalieri 10 January 1824; *bur* La Superga

CHARLES FELIX	1821–1831

b Turin 6 April 1765, 5th son of King Victor Amadeus III; *s* his brother King Victor Emmanuel I on his abdication 13 March 1821; *m* Palermo 6 April 1807 Maria Christina (*b* Caserta 17 January 1779; *d* Savona 11 March 1849), 5th dau of Ferdinand I, King of the Two Sicilies, and Maria Caroline of Austria; no issue; *d* Turin 27 April 1831; *bur* Hautecombe

CHARLES ALBERT	1831–1849

b Paris 29 October 1798, only son of Charles Emmanuel of Savoy, Prince of Carignano, and Maria of Saxony; *s* his kinsman King Charles Felix 27 April 1831; abdicated in favour of his son Victor Emmanuel 23 March 1849; *m* Florence 30 September 1817 Maria Theresa (*b* Vienna 21 March 1801; *d* Turin 12 January 1855), yst dau of Ferdinand III, Grand Duke of Tuscany, and his 1st wife Louisa of Bourbon-Two Sicilies; 2 sons, 1 dau; *d* Oporto, Portugal, 28 July 1849

VICTOR EMMANUEL II	1849–1878

Became the first King of united Italy (*see hereafter*)

The House of Savoy first appeared on the European stage in 1003 when Humbert (or Umberto) of the White Hands is mentioned as Count of Salmourenc in the Viennois. His origins are shrouded in mystery and have been the subject of many theories, but it seems most likely that he was of Teutonic origin. He acquired many lands, including Savoy, before his death in 1047

or 1048 and his descendants added to the family's possessions by marrying heiresses and other means. Count Amadeus VIII of Savoy was raised to the rank of Duke by the Emperor Sigismund in 1417. He later abdicated and was elected Pope, taking the name of Felix V. The election by the Council was irregular, however, and he is regarded as an antipope. He renounced the Papacy in 1448 and lived in honourable retirement until his death in 1451. His son, Duke Louis, married Anna de Lusignan, through whom the family eventually acquired rights to the kingdom of Cyprus and the titular kingdoms of Jerusalem and Armenia. However, it was not until 1713 that the Dukes of Savoy became *de facto* Kings. In that year the treaty of Utrecht awarded the Duchy of Montferrat to Savoy and Duke Victor Amadeus II received the kingdom of Sicily, which the powers made him exchange for Sardinia in 1718. Victor Amadeus abdicated in favour of his son Charles Emmanuel in 1730 and retired to Chambéry with his morganatic second wife the Marchesa di Spigno. Her ambitions persuaded him to attempt to regain the crown, but his son had him placed under arrest and confined at Moncalieri, where he died in 1732.

Charles Emmanuel III was a soldier by nature and sided with France against Austria in the War of the Polish Succession. His victory at Guastalla in 1734 was rewarded with the Duchy of Milan, but he was compelled to relinquish it by the treaty of Vienna in 1736, retaining only Novara and Tortona. He later took Maria Theresa's side in the War of the Austrian Succession and gained further territory for himself at the treaty of Aix-la-Chapelle in 1748.

Charles Emmanuel III died in February 1773 and was succeeded by his son Victor Amadeus III, a weak and incapable ruler, whose reign was a period of decadence and extravagance. In the aftermath of the French Revolution, Sardinia took up arms against the French Republic and was ignominiously defeated, Savoy becoming a French province. The King died in 1796 and was succeeded by his eldest son Charles Emmanuel IV.

Within two months of Charles Emmanuel's succession, Piedmont was overrun by French troops and the King and the royal family were obliged to take refuge in Sardinia. During Napoleon's absence in Egypt, Charles Emmanuel landed at Leghorn in an attempt to regain his mainland possessions, but Napoleon returned and defeated him at Marengo. Charles Emmanuel was a deeply religious man and had married the equally religious Princess Clotilde of France, a sister of Louis XVI. They had no children and the Queen died at Naples in March 1802. Three months later the King abdicated in favour of his brother Victor Emmanuel I and went to Rome to enter the Religious Society of Jesus (the Jesuits). He lived to see Queen Clotilde declared Venerable by Pope Pius VII in 1808 and died in 1819.

Victor Emmanuel I remained in Sardinia until the Congress of Vienna restored Piedmont and his other mainland territories, plus Genoa, in June 1815. Differences with his government led him to abdicate in his turn in 1821. His only son had died young, so he was succeeded by his brother Charles Felix, who reigned for ten years and died childless in April 1831. The succession now passed to the collateral branch of the Princes of Carignano, descended from a younger son of Duke Charles

Emmanuel I of Savoy, who died in 1630.

The new King, Charles Albert, was thirty-two years old and a staunch champion of legitimacy and absolutism, which made him hated by the liberals. In 1848, however, he unexpectedly granted a Constitution and then waged war on Austria in an attempt to gain the Lombardo-Venetian kingdom. His army was defeated by the octogenarian Marshal Radetzky (of the march fame) at the battles of Custozza and Novara and as a result Charles Albert abdicated in favour of his son Victor Emmanuel in March 1849. He died in Portugal a few months later. Victor Emmanuel II was to fulfil his father's dream and bring about the unification of Italy.

UNITED ITALY

VICTOR EMMANUEL II   (1849) 1861–1878

---

b Turin 14 March 1820, elder son of King Charles Albert of Sardinia; s as King of Sardinia on his father's abdication 23 March 1849; proclaimed King of Italy 17 March 1861; m (1) Stupinigi 12 April 1842 Adelaide (b Milan 3 June 1822; d Turin 20 January 1855), yr dau of Archduke Rainer of Austria and Elizabeth of Savoy-Carignano (sister of King Charles Albert); 6 sons, 2 daus; m (2) (morganatically) Rome 2 November 1869 Rosa, cr Countess di Mirafiori e Fontanafredda 11 April 1859 (b Moncalvo, Montferrat, 3 June 1833; d Pisa 27 December 1885), dau of Giovanni Battista Vercellana and Luisa Albera; 1 son, 1 dau; d Rome 9 January 1878

UMBERTO I   1878–1900

---

b Turin 14 March 1844, eldest son of King Victor Emmanuel II; s his father 9 January 1878; m Turin 22 April 1868 Margherita (b Turin 20 November 1851; d Bordighera 4 January 1926), only dau of Prince Ferdinand of Savoy, Duke of Genoa (2nd son of King Charles Albert), and Elizabeth of Saxony; 1 son; d (assassinated) Monza 29 July 1900

VICTOR EMMANUEL III   1900–1946

---

b Naples 11 November 1869, only child of King Umberto I; s his father 29 July 1900; proclaimed Emperor of Ethiopia 9 May 1936 and King of Albania 16 April 1939; renounced those thrones 3 September 1943; abdicated in favour of his only son 9 May 1946; m Rome 24 October 1896 Elena (b Cetinje 8 January 1873; d Montpellier 28 November 1952), 5th dau of Nicholas I, King of Montenegro, and Milena Vukotić; 1 son, 4 daus; d Alexandria, Egypt, 28 December 1947; bur St Catherine's Church, Alexandria

---

UMBERTO II   MAY–JUNE 1946

---

b Racconigi 15 September 1904, only son of King Victor Emmanuel III; Lieutenant-General of the Realm 5 June 1944; s his father on his

abdication 9 May 1946; left the country 13 June 1946; m Rome 8 January 1930 Marie José (b Ostende 4 August 1906), only dau of Albert I, King of the Belgians, and Elizabeth in Bavaria; 1 son, 3 daus; d Geneva 18 March 1983; bur Hautecombe

Victor Emmanuel II, 'il re galantuomo', the King of the risorgimento, was regarded as a hero by some and a monster by others. In temperament and tastes he could hardly have been less Italian, possessing no ear for music and being completely uninterested in art and literature. He was also completely lacking in warmth and exuberance and in this contrasted very unfavourably with his two arch-enemies, Pope Pius IX and King Ferdinand II of Naples, whose territories were conquered by Garibaldi in the war of Italian unification. Victor Emmanuel was content to remain behind the scenes while Garibaldi did the fighting and Count Cavour, an astute politician, conducted the government. As a result the King was able to proclaim himself King of Italy 'by the Grace of God and the will of the Nation' in 1861, although thanks to the heroic stand put up by the papal forces, aided by the French until their defeat in the Franco-Prussian War, he was unable to enter Rome until July 1871. The Pope became the 'Prisoner of the Vatican' and Victor Emmanuel took up residence in the Quirinal Palace.

His first wife, an Austrian Archduchess who was also his first cousin, had died in 1855, and in 1869 he married his mistress of long standing, who had already borne him a son and a daughter. She was Rosa Vercellana, the daughter of a drum-major and Victor Emmanuel gave her the romantic-sounding title of Countess di Mirafiori e Fontanafredda. In January 1878 the King fell ill with pneumonia and died at the Quirinal aged fifty-seven. The vast monument erected to his memory is one of the sights of Rome.

Umberto I, who succeeded his father, was completely dominated by his wife, Queen Margherita, a born Princess of Savoy and his first cousin. She was tall, beautiful and fair-haired with artistic, literary and musical tastes, but possessed a will of iron. The principal task which lay before the King and Queen was to consolidate the monarchy and place it on a firmer footing since it was still regarded as a revolutionary one in many quarters. A Triple Alliance with Germany and Austria was one way of doing this. The dream of colonial expansion, however, was shattered when the Italian army sent to conquer Ethiopia was completely destroyed at Adowa in 1896. Four years later in July 1900 King Umberto was shot and killed by an anarchist named Bresci while attending a sports meeting in the stadium at Monza. He was succeeded by his only child.

The diminutive King Victor Emmanuel III was thirty at his accession and had been married since 1896 to the statuesque Princess Elena of Montenegro, who towered above him. The disparity in height between the King and Queen made them the butt of many ill-natured jokes, but both were capable of great dignity. They were a devoted couple and led an extremely happy married life. The King had been well educated and was an avid numismatist, assembling an important collection of coins and medals. Italy joined the allies during the First World War and King Victor Emmanuel spent much time at the front, fearlessly visiting the trenches and encouraging his troops when under fire.

Umberto I, the second King of United Italy, who was assassinated by an anarchist at Monza in July 1900.

King Umberto never abdicated or renounced his rights. He had married Princess Marie José of Belgium in 1930 and they had a son and three daughters, but they had always been quite unsuited to each other temperamentally and after going into exile an amicable separation took place, the Queen going to live in Switzerland and the King going to Portugal. There, faithfully attended by the very aged Count Olivieri, who had entered the service of the House of Savoy as a page to Umberto's grandmother Queen Margherita many years before, he settled into the comfortable Villa Italia at the coastal resort of Cascais, north of Lisbon, and maintained a close interest in Italian affairs for the rest of his life. His day was mapped out to a strict timetable and part of it was allocated to giving audiences to his former subjects who would call to pay their respects. It became quite customary for young Italians on honeymoon to call upon the King to ask his blessing. King Umberto was very popular, too, with the younger members of Europe's royal families, to whom he was known as 'Uncle Beppo'. He became seriously ill with bone cancer in 1982 and after spending some time in the London Clinic was flown to Geneva to be as close as possible to his native land. Negotiations were opened to make it possible for him to return to Italy to die, but before they could be completed he breathed his last with the word 'Italia' on his lips.

The present head of the House of Savoy is King Umberto's only son, Victor Emmanuel, Prince of Naples, who was born in 1937. He is married and has one son.

The years between the wars saw the rise of Mussolini who became an all-powerful dictator reducing the King to a mere cipher. *Il Duce*, as Mussolini became known, conducted a series of campaigns to extend Italy's possessions. In 1935 Adowa was avenged by the conquest of Ethiopia and Victor Emmanuel was proclaimed Emperor, and in 1939 the little Balkan kingdom of Albania was invaded and annexed to the Italian crown.

Thanks to Mussolini, Italy became embroiled in the Second World War as an ally of Nazi Germany and it was not until 1943 that King Victor Emmanuel managed to engineer Mussolini's downfall and take steps to withdraw from a war which was proving disastrous to his country. Had he then also abdicated in favour of his only son Umberto the Italian monarchy might have been saved, but he left it far too late and did not do so until May 1946.

King Umberto II, a charming and cultured man, had always disliked Mussolini and been against Italy's participation in the war as an ally of Germany. He would have made a splendid King, but unfortunately never had the chance as a plebiscite held on 2 June 1946 resulted in 12,717,923 votes being cast in favour of a republic and 10,719,284 in favour of the continuation of the monarchy. Abiding by this decision, the King and royal family left the country on 13 June 1946, and a provisional government was elected on 28 June.

ETRURIA

LOUIS I	1801–1803

b Piacenza 5 July 1773, elder son of Ferdinand, Duke of Parma, and Maria Amelia of Austria; proclaimed King of Etruria 28 July 1801; entered Florence 10 August 1801; *m* Madrid 25 August 1795 his 1st cousin, Maria Louisa, Queen Regent of Etruria 27 May 1803 to 10 December 1807, Sovereign Duchess of Lucca 22 November 1817 to 13 March 1824 (*b* San Ildefonso 6 July 1782; *d* Rome 13 March 1824), 4th dau of Carlos IV, King of Spain, and Maria Louisa of Bourbon-Parma; 1 son, 1 dau; *d* Florence 27 May 1803; *bur* Church of San Lorenzo, Florence; transferred to El Escorial 1808

LOUIS II	1803–1807

b Madrid 22 December 1799, only son of King Louis I; *s* his father 27 May 1803 under his mother's regency; ceased to reign when Etruria was ceded to Emperor Napoleon I 10 December 1807; *s* his mother as (Charles Louis) Duke of Lucca 13 March 1824; abdicated 15 October 1847; *s* as (Charles II) Duke of Parma and Piacenza on the death of Archduchess Marie Louise 17 December 1847; abdicated 14 March 1849; *m* proxy Turin 15 August, in person Lucca 5 September 1820, Maria Theresa (*b* Rome 19 September 1803; *d* San Martino, nr Lucca, 16 July 1879), 5th dau of Victor Emmanuel I, King of Sardinia, and Maria Theresa of Austria-Este; 1 son, 1 dau; *d* Nice 16 April 1883

In 1796 the French Republican army under Bonaparte overran the Duchy of Parma and forced its ruler, Duke Ferdinand, to pay an indemnity of six million lire and deliver up some of his art treasures in exchange for being allowed to keep a life interest in the Duchy, which was annexed to the French Republic after his death on 9 October 1802. Meanwhile, Ferdinand's only surviving son and heir Louis had settled in Spain, where he married his cousin the Infanta Maria Louisa and had two children. In 1801 Bonaparte set up a puppet kingdom of Etruria, formed from the erstwhile Grand Duchy of Tuscany, and Louis was proclaimed its King on 28 July 1801, entering Florence, his capital, on 10 August 1801. He was a delicate young man and only survived his elevation by a little less than two years, dying on 27 May 1803, aged twenty-nine. His three-year-old son Charles Louis succeeded him as King Louis II with his mother Queen Maria Louisa as Regent. Almost all that remains to mark their reign of four and a half years is a very handsome coinage, some pieces displaying the busts of the King and his mother side by side, others showing them face to face.

In December 1807 the kingdom of Etruria was abolished by Napoleon and annexed to his kingdom of Italy. The young King and his mother went into exile. After the fall of Napoleon, Maria Louisa was compensated with the Duchy of Lucca in 1817. She ruled it until her death in 1824 when Charles Louis succeeded her until driven out by an insurrection on 15 September 1847, which forced him to abdicate and cede the Duchy to the Grand Duchy of Tuscany on 15 October. Two months later he succeeded Napoleon's widow Marie Louise in his ancestral heritage of Parma and Piacenza, but only enjoyed it for a matter of months before he was driven out on 19 April 1848. He retired to his estates in Saxony where he abdicated in favour of his only son Charles III on 14 March 1849.

Duke Charles II, three times a sovereign of three different realms, lived very happily in exile, wandering about Europe, eccentrically changing his religion to that of the state in which he happened to be residing, collecting antique watches, and conducting a number of love affairs with well-born persons of both sexes. He died at Nice in April 1885 in his eighty-fourth year. He had outlived his son and successor and seen his grandson Duke Robert I lose his throne when the Duchy of Parma was incorporated into the new kingdom of Italy.

NAPLES AND SICILY

The kingdom of Sicily was founded by the Norman House of Hauteville, closely allied to the Dukes of Normandy. In 1072 Roger of Hauteville captured Sicily from the Arabs and ruled it as Count until his death in 1101. He was succeeded by his son Simon, who reigned until 1105 and was succeeded by his brother Roger II, who took the title of King in 1130 and died in February 1154. Roger's son and grandson, both named William, reigned next and were followed by Tancred of Lecce, a natural son of Roger II's eldest son Roger, who had predeceased his father. Tancred died in 1194 and his son William III was murdered the same year, probably at the instigation of Emperor Henry VI, who had married Roger II's daughter Constance and claimed Sicily in her right. Constance did not become pregnant until she was forty and to allay rumours that her pregnancy was false gave birth to her child in a tent set up in the market place of Apulia. The boy thus born was to become the great Hohenstaufen Emperor Frederick II as well as King of Sicily. He died in 1250 and was followed by his son Conrad and grandson Conradin. The latter was deposed by his illegitimate uncle Manfred, who usurped the throne but was defeated and killed by Charles of Anjou, son of King Louis VIII of France, who was granted Naples and Sicily by the Pope, but lost Sicily after the famous 'Sicilian Vespers' in 1282. Manfred's son-in-law King Pedro III of Aragon then gained the throne and Sicily remained under Aragonese rule until 1516 when it passed to the Spanish Kings of the House of Habsburg. In 1713 it was given to Victor Amadeus II, Duke of Savoy by the treaty of Utrecht, but he was obliged to exchange it for Sardinia in 1718 and it eventually returned to Spanish rule in 1735.

Naples had no separate history from Sicily until 1282 when Charles of Anjou lost Sicily but retained Naples. His son Charles II and grandson Robert followed him in succession and when the latter died in 1343 he was succeeded by his seventeen-year-old granddaughter Joanna I. A controversial figure, Joanna married four times and may have murdered one of her husbands. She was deposed and murdered by suffocation in 1382 by her second cousin Charles III (who was also Charles I, King of Hungary). Charles III was followed in 1386 by his son Ladislas, who died childless in 1414 and was succeeded by his sister Joanna II, a woman of evil reputation, who also died childless in 1435. She willed the throne to René of Anjou, 'Le Bon Roi René', in whose name the government was carried on until 1442, when Alfonso I, King of Aragon, who had been nominated in an earlier will of Joanna II, seized power. The Aragonese reigned until 1516, from which date, save for a few brief periods, Naples remained united with Sicily.

The Kings of the Two Sicilies

FERDINAND I	1759–1825

b Naples 18 January 1751, 3rd son of Carlos III, King of Spain; *s* his father as King (Ferdinand IV and III) of Naples and Sicily under a Council of Regency 6 October 1759; declared of age 13 January 1767; expelled from Naples by the French 1798; returned 1800; again expelled and went to Sicily 1806; returned 1815; assumed the style of Ferdinand I, King of the kingdom of the Two Sicilies 9 June 1815; *m* (1) proxy Vienna 7 April, in person Caserta 12 May 1768, Maria Carolina (*b* Schönbrunn 13 August 1752; *d* Schloss Hetzendorf, nr Schönbrunn, 8 September 1814), 10th dau of Francis I, Holy Roman Emperor, and Maria Theresa, Queen of Hungary and Bohemia; 7 sons, 11 daus; *m* (2) (morganatically) Palermo 27 November 1814 Donna Lucia Migliaccio, Duchess di Floridia (*b* Syracuse 19 July 1770; *d* Naples 26 April 1826), widow of Don Benedetto Grifeo, 8th Prince di Partanna, and dau of Don Vincenzo Migliaccio, Duke de Floridia, and Donna Dorotea Borgia dei Marchesi del Casale; no issue; *d* Naples 4 January 1825

FRANCIS I   1825–1830

b Naples 19 August 1777, 2nd but eldest surviving son of King Ferdinand I; *s* his father 4 January 1825; *m* (1) proxy Vienna 19 September 1790, in person Foggia 25 June 1797, Maria Clementina (*b* Poggio Imperiale 24 April 1777; *d* Palermo 15 November 1801), 3rd dau of Leopold II, Holy Roman Emperor, and Maria Louisa of Spain; 1 son, 1 dau; *m* (2) proxy Barcelona 6 July, in person Naples 6 October 1802, Maria Isabella (*b* Madrid 6 July 1789; *m* (2) Naples 15 January 1839 Don Francesco, Conte del Balzo (*d* 15 April 1882); *d* Portici 13 September 1848), 5th dau of Carlos IV, King of Spain, and Maria Louisa of Bourbon-Parma; 6 sons, 6 daus; *d* Naples 8 November 1830

FERDINAND II   1830–1859

b Palermo 12 January 1810, 2nd but eldest surviving son of King Francis I; *s* his father 8 November 1830; *m* (1) Voltri 21 November 1832 Maria Christina (*b* Cagliari 14 November 1812; *d* Caserta 31 January 1836; declared Venerable), yst dau of Victor Emmanuel I, King of Sardinia, and Maria Theresa of Austria; 1 son; *m* (2) proxy Trieste 9 January, in person Naples 27 January 1837, Maria Theresa (*b* Vienna 31 July 1816; *d* Albano 8 August 1867), elder dau of Archduke Charles of Austria, Duke of Teschen, and Henrietta of Nassau-Weilburg; 8 sons, 4 daus; *d* Caserta 22 May 1859

FRANCIS II   1859–1860

b Caserta 16 January 1836, eldest son of King Ferdinand II; *s* his father 22 May 1859; lost his throne when the kingdom of the Two Sicilies was declared annexed to the kingdom of Italy 17 December 1860; *m* proxy Munich 18 January, in person Bari 3 February 1859, Maria Sophia (*b* Possenhofen 4 October 1841; *d* Munich 19 January 1925), 3rd dau of Maximilian, Duke in Bavaria, and Ludovika (Luise) of Bavaria; 1 dau; *d* Schloss Arco, Tyrol, 27 December 1894

The Napoleonic Kings of Naples

JOSEPH NAPOLEON   1806–1808

b (Joseph Bonaparte) Corte, Corsica, 7 January 1768, 2nd son of Charles Marie Bonaparte and Marie Laetitia Ramolino; French Prince and Imperial Highness on the establishment of the First Empire 18 May 1804; Lieutenant-General of the kingdom of Naples 21 February 1806; King of Naples 30 March 1806; resigned the crown to his brother Emperor Napoleon I 6 June 1808, when he became King of Spain (*see further under* Spain)

JOACHIM NAPOLEON   1808–1815

b (Joachim Murat) La Bastide-Fortunière 25 March 1767, 5th and yst son of Pierre Murat and Jeanne Loubières; Marshal of the French Empire 1804; French Prince and Imperial Highness 1805; Grand Duke of Berg

and Cleves 30 March 1806 to 1 August 1808; King of Naples 1 August 1808; deposed 19 May 1815; *m* Mortefontaine 20 January 1800 (civil) and rue de la Victoire, Paris, 4 January 1802 (religious) Caroline, French Princess and Imperial Highness from 18 May 1804 (*b* Ajaccio, Corsica, 25 March 1782; *d* Florence 18 May 1839), sister of Emperor Napoleon I and yst dau of Charles Marie Bonaparte and Marie Laetitia Ramolino; 2 sons, 2 daus; *d* (shot) Castello di Pizzo, Calabria, 13 October 1815

The treaty of Rastadt awarded the kingdom of Naples and Sicily to the Emperor Charles VI in 1714, but in 1734 Naples was conquered by the eighteen-year-old Infante Don Carlos, son of King Philip V of Spain and his ambitious second wife Elizabeth Farnese. Carlos was confirmed in his possession by the treaty of Vienna in 1735. We have already encountered Carlos as King of Spain. His enlightened rule and patronage of the arts transformed Naples into one of the finest and most cultivated capitals of Europe. In 1759 Carlos succeeded his half-brother Ferdinand VI on the Spanish throne and resigned that of Naples to his own third son Ferdinand, as his eldest son Philip was far too peculiar to rule and the second Carlos was designated to succeed him in Spain.

Ferdinand IV, as he was at first styled, was only eight years old and a Council of Regency ruled for him, headed by Bernardo Tanucci, who, in spite of being a former professor of the University of Pisa, shamefully neglected the young King's education. Ferdinand grew up a lout, semi-literate and the boon companion of palace servants, stable-boys and gamekeepers. He spoke the broad Neapolitan dialect and was only interested in shooting and fishing. When he had made a good catch he was in the habit of auctioning it off in the fish market and distributing the proceeds to the poor. Ferdinand was very ugly with an enormous nose (which occasioned his nickname of *Nasone*), but his good nature and general *bonhomie* made him immensely popular.

In 1768, a year after he came of age, Ferdinand married Archduchess Maria Carolina of Austria, a sister of Marie Antoinette. She suited him very well and went one better than her mother the Empress Maria Theresa by producing eighteen children. Ferdinand's satisfied comment on his bride was, 'she sweats like a pig'. He was always very coarse and unrefined in his habits, as was only to be expected from his upbringing, and shocked his prim brother-in-law the Emperor Joseph II by breaking wind noisily when standing at his side on the palace balcony and, on seeing the pained expression on the Emperor's face, excusing himself by saying that it was for the good of his health.

Queen Maria Carolina had received a careful education and was almost the complete opposite of her husband in interests and temperament, but in spite of this their domestic life was fairly happy for a long time and the Queen supplied the necessary culture in court life. She formed an attachment for the wife of Sir William Hamilton, the British envoy in Naples, who was later to become so famous as Nelson's Emma. When the French invasion of Italy came in 1798 it was Nelson who conveyed the royal family to safety in Sicily during the course of a terrible storm. Poor little Prince Alberto, the royal couple's six-year-old son, died of seasickness before reaching Palermo. The royal family was able to return to Naples in 1800, but was driven out again in 1806. In Sicily the King adopted the style of Ferdinand III and settled down to await the time when he should be restored to his mainland kingdom.

Napoleon set up his brother Joseph as King of Naples and in 1808 moved him to Spain and replaced him in Naples by his brother-in-law Joachim Murat. King Joachim, the son of an inn-keeper, was not content just to be a puppet. He was a distinguished soldier and on Napoleon's downfall attempted to retain Naples. When Napoleon escaped from Elba, however, Joachim rallied to his support again and after Waterloo lost both his throne and his life.

Ferdinand was restored to Naples and in accordance with the terms of the Congress of Vienna assumed the style of Ferdinand I, King of the kingdom of the Two Sicilies. The British envoy Lord William Bentinck persuaded him to grant a Constitution. Queen Maria Carolina had gone to Austria and died there in September 1814 and two months later Ferdinand married his long-time mistress, the Duchess di Floridia, in a morganatic marriage. He spent the remainder of his reign indulging in his favourite sport of shooting and died in January 1825.

Francis I, who succeeded his father at the age of forty-seven, had acted as Viceroy of Sicily since 1816. He only reigned five years and was succeeded in 1830 by his son Ferdinand II.

King Ferdinand II has gained an unenviable reputation as 'King Bomba' and through Gladstone's condemnation of him as the 'negation of God'. He was one of the earliest victims of a malevolent press campaign levelled against him by the liberals, but was in fact a conscientious and caring ruler, under whom Naples gained the first railway and the first electric telegraph in Italy. His appearance was against him as he was excessively stout, coarse-featured and, in later life, sported a bushy black beard. In short, he looked everybody's idea of a typical Italian brigand. His nickname of 'Bomba' was occasioned by his ordering the bombardment of Messina when an insurrection broke out in Sicily in 1848. The troubles of that year led the King to grant a new Constitution, but matters were only made worse and fighting broke out in Naples itself. Order was eventually restored and Ferdinand showed great clemency in dealing with the rebels, less than ten of them being executed after fair trials.

King Ferdinand was an exemplary husband, never straying elsewhere. His first wife, Maria Christina of Savoy, died in childbirth at the age of twenty-three and was so saintly that she was declared Venerable by the Pope and a case for her beatification was initiated. The King's second wife, Maria Theresa of Austria, gave him a large family. Ferdinand died after a long and painful illness in May 1859 and was succeeded by his eldest son Francis II.

The new King was of as pious a disposition as his late mother and was altogether a weak, dispirited young man, quite incapable of withstanding the forces which were about to overwhelm his kingdom. His greatest asset was his Queen, Maria Sophia, a sister of the Empress Elizabeth of Austria. When Garibaldi's 'Thousand' invaded Sicily, which they took with little resistance, and then crossed to the mainland, it was the Queen who inspired the loyal troops. The King and Queen and their band took refuge in the fortress of Gaeta and withstood three months' siege. The heroic Queen tended the sick and wounded and appeared on the battlements to encourage the men, braving the bullets and shells of the besiegers. The situation was hopeless, of course, and in February 1861 the garrison capitulated and the kingdom of the Two Sicilies had ceased to exist.

The King and Queen were allowed to make their way to Rome, still under papal rule, and take up residence in the Farnese Palace, which was their property. It was there that their only child Christina was born in December 1869, but sadly she only lived for three months. The Queen found life in Rome intolerable after this and the royal couple moved to Paris. King Francis died while staying in the Austrian Tyrol in 1894, but Queen Maria Sophia lived on in Paris until the outbreak of the First World War when she returned to her native Bavaria. She died at Munich in January 1925. In April 1984 the bodies of King Francis, Queen Maria Sophia and their baby daughter were transferred from Rome and reburied in the basilica of Santa Chiara at Naples.

Francis II was succeeded as head of the royal house by his brother Alfonso, Count of Caserta, who died in his ninety-third year in 1934. The death of his son Ferdinand in 1960 was followed by an unedifying dispute regarding the succession of the headship of the royal house – a question so academic that the whole matter has been rendered ridiculous.

CENTRAL AND EASTERN EUROPE

BOHEMIA

To most people mention of Bohemia conjures up a vision of 'Good King Wenceslas' and his page trudging through the snow to succour the poor fuel-gatherer. The original of the King of the Christmas carol was in fact only a Duke, who ruled over Bohemia from 921 until he was murdered by his brother Boleslav in 929 and later canonized. Boleslav's great-grandson Bretislav I united Moravia and Bohemia and was succeeded by his son Spitihnev II in 1055. Spitihnev's brother and successor Vratislav II received the title of King for life in 1085 as a personal mark of favour from the Emperor Henry IV. He died in 1092 and his son Vladislav I, Duke from 1109, was raised to the Electoral dignity in 1114. Elector Vladislav II received the personal title of King from Emperor Frederick Barbarossa in 1158 and died in 1173.

A period of anarchy followed until 1198 when Elector Premysl Ottakar I had the royal title made hereditary by Emperor Otto IV. He died on 15 December 1230 and was succeeded by his son Vaclav or Wenzel (or Wenceslas) I. He was followed in 1253 by his son Premysl Ottakar II, a great King who defeated King Bela IV of Hungary in 1260 and acquired Austria, Styria, Carinthia and Carniola. His extended realm was shortlived as he refused to do homage to Rudolf of Habsburg for his conquered lands and was killed in battle at Marchfeld on 26 August 1278. His only son Vaclav II also occupied the Polish throne from 1296 and was succeeded by his son Vaclav III in 1305. Vaclav reigned for one year only and was assassinated. He left no sons and the succession was disputed until 1310 when John of Luxembourg, Vaclav's son-in-law, was elected King by the Bohemian nobles. He is the famous Blind King John who fell fighting at the battle of Crécy on 26 August 1346. His emblem of three feathers and motto *Ich Dien* (I serve) were appropriated by his vanquisher, Edward, Prince of Wales (the 'Black Prince') and have been borne by every Prince of Wales since.

John's son Charles was elected Emperor Charles IV in 1347. He founded the University of Prague and built the great Hradschin Palace. One of his daughters, Anne, married King Richard II of England, the son of the 'Black Prince' who had slain her grandfather. Charles died on 29 November 1378 and was succeeded in turn by his sons Vaclav IV and Sigismund, the latter also being Emperor and King of Hungary. His successors were his son-in-law and grandson and in 1457 George Podiebrad, a Czech noble, was elected King. His adherence to the Hussite heresy made things difficult for him and eventually he was excommunicated by Pope Paul II and faced with a revolt by his mainly Catholic subjects.

George died in 1471 and Bohemia passed to the Polish Jagellons (*see below*) and eventually to the Habsburgs in 1526, remaining united to Austria until the fall of the Austro-Hungarian Empire in 1918, save for a brief episode in 1619 when the Calvinists gained the ascendancy and chose the Elector Palatine Frederick V to fill the throne. He is known as the 'Winter King' and was married to Elizabeth, the daughter of King James I of England, through whom the British royal family derives its claim to the (British) throne.

HUNGARY

The Magyars, a nomadic people some 100,000 strong, first appeared in the fertile area between the Danube and the Theiss under the leadership of their Duke Almos in about 895 and established themselves there after defeating King Svatopluk of Moravia. Almos was succeeded by his son Arpad, whose name became that of the dynasty they founded. Arpad's son Zoltan and grandson Taksony followed him in succession and the latter was succeeded in 972 by his son Geza, who was baptized at Constantinople and married first Sarolta, daughter of Duke Gyula of Transylvania, and secondly a sister of Mieszko, Prince of Poland. Geza's and Sarolta's son Stephen was baptized by St Adalbert, Bishop of Prague. He succeeded his father in 997 and completed his country's conversion to Christianity. As a reward he was sent a royal crown by Pope Sylvester II with the right for himself and his successors to bear the title of Apostolic King and was crowned as Hungary's first King in 1001. Stephen married Gisela, a sister of the Emperor Henry II, and carefully trained their only son Emeric (Imre) to succeed him. The young man was killed in a hunting accident in 1031 and Stephen's last years were embittered by his squabbling relations vying for the succession. He died at Buda on the anniversary of his coronation 15 August 1038 and he and Emeric are both venerated as Saints.

Stephen was succeeded by his sister's son Peter, whose father was Ottone Orseolo, Doge of Venice. As a foreigner he was unpopular and he was driven out and replaced in 1041 by Samuel Aba, the husband of another of Stephen's sisters. The deposed Peter secured the aid of Emperor Henry III and returned to defeat and kill Samuel Aba in 1044, regaining the throne. Two years later he was deposed and blinded in a popular uprising which brought about a brief resurgence of paganism, resolved when the crown was offered to Andrew I, a cousin of St Stephen. He reigned until 1061 and was succeeded by his brother Bela I. King Andrew II, who reigned from 1205 to 1235, signed the Golden Bull, Hungary's Magna Carta, in 1222 and it was to be renewed by all his successors. The male line of the House of Arpad became extinct on the death of King Andrew III in 1301. His death was followed by a succession war from which Charles Robert of Anjou, a great-grandson of King Stephen V, emerged as the successful candidate in 1309. He was succeeded by his son Louis I the Great, one of the most powerful Continental monarchs of his day, who also became King of Poland in 1370 and died on 11 September 1382. He only left daughters and was succeeded in Hungary by the elder, Maria, and in Poland by the younger, Jadwiga. Maria married the Emperor Sigismund (of the

House of Luxembourg), who was acknowledged as King in her right and crowned in March 1387. He reigned until his death in 1437. Maria had died childless in 1395 and Sigismund married as his second wife Barbara of Cilly and by her had a daughter Elizabeth, whose husband Albert of Austria succeeded him on the Hungarian throne. Albert died in 1439 leaving two daughters and a pregnant widow, who duly gave birth to a son, the third person to be born a King whom we have encountered in these pages. The little Ladislaus (Laszlo) was soon forced to retire into Austria with his mother and was replaced by the Polish King Wladyslaw, who was killed by the Turks at the battle of Varna in 1444. After a short interregnum, Ladislaus was restored and John Hunyady acted as Regent from 1446 to 1453. He became one of Hungary's great national heroes by successfully repelling the invading Turks.

Ladislaus died suddenly, probably poisoned, in 1457 in his Bohemian kingdom, and Matthias Corvinus, the son of Hunyady, was elected to succeed him in Hungary in 1458. He founded the University of Buda and, a warrior like his father, also battled successfully with the Turks. His death on 6 April 1490 was followed by a period of national decline. The nobles elected the son of King Casimir IV of Poland by Elizabeth, sister of King Ladislaus, and he reigned as Ladislaus II until his death in 1516. His only son and successor, King Louis II, fell bravely fighting the Turks at the battle of Mohacs on 19 August 1526 and Hungary passed to his sister Anna's husband Ferdinand of Austria (later Emperor Ferdinand I). It was to remain under Austrian rule until the break up of the Austro-Hungarian Empire at the end of the First World War in 1918. The last Emperor of Austria and Apostolic King of Hungary was the saintly Charles, whose widow Zita, the last crowned Apostolic Queen, is still alive in her nineties. Her eldest son Otto is the present heir to Austria and Hungary and as Dr Otto von Habsburg is a very active member of the European parliament.

POLAND

The first dynasty to reign in Poland, the House of Piast, took its name from a semi-legendary ancestor of that name, who was followed by his son Ziemowit, grandson Leszko, great-grandson Ziemomysl, and great-great-grandson Mieszko I, the first historical ruler whose reign is documented. He was reigning by 963 and in 965 married Dubravka, daughter of Duke Boleslav I of Bohemia. She was a Christian and the pagan Mieszko was baptized the year after his marriage. In politics Mieszko allied himself to the Holy Roman Emperor Otto III. His daughter Gunhild was married to King Sweyn Forkbeard of Denmark and became the mother of Canute the Great. When Mieszko died in 992 he was succeeded by his son Boleslaw I the Brave, who banished his half-brothers (the sons of Mieszko's second marriage to the German Oda) and thus kept the country united. Like his father, he was an ally of Emperor Otto III, whom he entertained

Stanislaw Augustus Poniatowski, the last elected King of Poland, owed his election to Empress Catherine the Great of Russia, whose lover he had once been. He lived to see his country partitioned between Austria, Prussia and Russia.

with great magnificence at Gniezno in 1000. He also indulged in some King-making among his Bohemian cousins.

The last Piast King, Casimir III the Great, died in 1370 and was succeeded by his sister's son Louis of Anjou, who was already King of Hungary. Louis's younger daughter Jadwiga conveyed Poland to her husband Wladyslaw Jagellon of Lithuania and the Jagellon dynasty ruled Poland until 1572, when the crown became elective. Many of Poland's elected Kings have already found some mention in these pages (*see* France, Sweden and Saxony). The great King John III Sobieski, who saved Europe from the Turkish menace in the last quarter of the seventeenth century, was elected in 1674 and reigned until his death in 1696. Among other things, he was the maternal great-grandfather of Bonnie Prince Charlie.

In the eighteenth century two successive Electors of Saxony reigned as Kings of Poland and the last King, elected in 1764 through the influence of Catherine the Great of Russia, whose lover he had been, was Stanislaw II Poniatowski. He lost the throne when his country was finally partitioned between Russia, Prussia and Austria in 1795. Poland was later annexed to Russia after the Napoleonic Wars and did not regain its independence until after the First World War when it became a Republic.

THE BALKANS

Boundaries of the Balkan States
after the Treaties of London
and Bucharest 1913

AUSTRIA – HUNGARY

MOLDAVIA

ROUMANIA

DALMATIA

HERZEGOVINA

BOSNIA

WALLACHIA

SERBIA

MONTE-
NEGRO

BULGARIA

EASTERN RUMELIA

ALBANIA

THRACE

MACEDONIA

SALONICA

LIVADIA

GREECE

MOREA

ALBANIA

ZOG I	1928–1939

b Burgajet, Mati, 8 October 1895, son of Xhemal Zogu Pasha, Hereditary Governor of Mati, and his 2nd wife Sadijé Toptani; Prime Minister of Albania 3 December 1922 to 10 June 1924 and 6–21 January 1925; President of Albania 21 January 1925 to 1 September 1928; proclaimed King of the Albanians by the Albanian National Assembly 1 September 1928; left the country following the Italian invasion 8 April 1939; *m* Tirana 27 April 1938 Geraldine (*b* Budapest 6 August 1915), elder dau of Count Gyula (Julius) Apponyi de Nagy-Appony, and Gladys Virginia Steuart; 1 son; *d* Paris 9 April 1961

King Zog of Albania.

The small country of Albania bordering the Adriatic coast of the Balkan peninsula has had a somewhat chequered history. After the break-up of the Roman Empire it fell to the Goths, later became part of the Depostate of Epirus under the Byzantine Empire, and after being ruled by Serbs, Normans from Sicily, and Serbs again, was overwhelmed by the Turkish expansion into Europe. The Muslim Turks were long resisted by the Christian native chieftains, the foremost of whom was George Castriota, Bey of Dibra, better known as Scanderbeg (a corruption of the Turkish Iskander Beg), who has become Albania's national hero. He wrested a measure of independence from the Turks in 1443 and ruled Albania until his death in 1467. His horned helmet was used as the heraldic crown of the Zogu family. Scanderbeg's son was unable to maintain his position for long and Albania reverted to Turkish rule for a period of four hundred and fifty years.

Albanian independence was officially declared by Ismail Qemali on 28 November 1912 and confirmed by the terms of the treaty of London in May 1913 at the end of the Balkan Wars. The Great Powers decided on a monarchical form of government for Albania on 21 December 1913 and, pending the election of a ruler, power was exercised by Essad Pasha. Roumania sponsored the candidature of Prince William of Wied (a small German principality), a nephew of the eccentric Queen Elisabeth of Roumania, and he accepted the throne on 6 February 1914. William assumed the title of *Mbret* (derived from the Latin *Imperator*), the only word in the Albanian language for a ruler. It was generally rendered as Prince in other languages, although William was occasionally referred to as King by the foreign press and was listed as a King in Ruvigny's *Titled Nobility of Europe*, published in 1914.

Prince William landed at Durazzo on 11 March, accompanied by his wife Princess Sophie and their two young children; but he found the country in such a state of anarchy and unrest that it was quite impossible for him to govern. The outbreak of the First World War in August 1914 made his position quite untenable and on 3 September the Prince and Princess left the country, although William retained full exercise of his power until 5 September and never renounced his rights. The regency was resumed by Essad Pasha, who remained in power until he was assassinated on 13 March 1920. A Council of Regency was

nominally in charge until 1925, during which period there was a power struggle between the young Ahmed Bey Zogu and Bishop Fan Noli. At length Zogu triumphed and on 21 January 1925 was proclaimed President of the Republic of Albania. He retained that title until 8 April 1928 when the National Assembly proclaimed him King and he took the style of Zog I, King of the Albanians. At the same time the title of Queen Mother was bestowed on Zog's mother Sadijé and his six sisters became Princesses, while his indolent but good-natured elder half-brother, who passed his time in marrying, divorcing and begetting children, became a Prince.

King Zog was a strong and efficient ruler and did much to modernize what had been a very backward country. His six sisters, referred to rather unkindly as 'the ugly Zoglets' by members of other European royal families who regarded their elevation with an amused tolerance, took to their new role like ducks to water. They modelled themselves on the Hollywood stars of the day, whose films they would watch for hours on end, and the three youngest Princesses delighted in parading about in white uniforms, looking like nothing so much as the chorus from a production of *The Desert Song*. An amusing story is told of the Princesses staying in the south of France and being politely saluted by a young man who entered their hotel lift. They ignored him entirely and were later asked by their equerry if they had not recognized the Archduke Otto of Austria. The Princesses shrugged their shoulders; '*il est tombé*', they commented. Their own fall was to come only too soon.

King Zog had been so busy running the country that he had had no time to marry and think about providing a direct heir to the throne. It was generally assumed that his heir was his nephew Tati Bey Kriziu, the promising young son of his second sister Princess Nafijé, whose husband, sometime Albania's Minister of Foreign Affairs, had been assassinated in Prague in 1927. In 1937 King Zog met and fell instantly in love with the half-American Hungarian Countess Geraldine Apponyi, a girl of great charm, poise and intelligence with a strength of character to match. She has admitted that for her, too, there was to be no other man once she had seen the dashing King, twenty years her senior, and the couple became engaged and were married at Tirana in April 1938. The ceremony had to be a civil one only as the King was a Muslim and his bride a Roman Catholic. A year later Queen Geraldine gave birth to a son and heir on 5 April 1939. The little Prince was only two days old when the Italians invaded Albania and the King, Queen, their infant son, and the Princesses (Queen Mother Sadijé had died in 1934) left the country. It was a nightmare journey for the Queen, who was suffering from puerperal fever, but safety in Greece was reached at last.

In Albania the Constituent Assembly proclaimed King Victor Emmanuel III of Italy King on 16 April 1939, a title which he was to renounce on 3 September 1943. By the end of the Second World War the Communist party had gained control in the country and a Socialist Republic was proclaimed on 11 January 1946 and has remained in power ever since, dashing all hopes King Zog had of returning to his throne.

King Zog was to spend the rest of his life in exile in Greece, England, Egypt, and finally France. He died at Paris on 9 April 1961 and his devoted and heroic wife Queen Geraldine sold her diamond engagement ring to pay for the building of his tomb in the Thiais Cemetery, Val-de-Marne.

On 15 May 1961 an Albanian National Assembly in exile, meeting in Paris, proclaimed Zog's son Leka King of the Albanians. The title is not quite as empty as it might seem as there are more Albanians living in exile all over the world than the actual population of Albania itself, and most of them regard Leka as their King. In 1975 he married an Australian lady, Susan Cullen-Ward, and they have a son, Leka Anwar Zog Reza Baudouin, who was born at Johannesburg, South Africa, on 26 March 1982 and is the future hope of Albanian monarchists.

BULGARIA

FERDINAND I · (1887) 1908–1918

b Vienna 26 February 1861, yst son of Prince Augustus of Saxe-Coburg and Gotha and Clementine of Bourbon-Orleans (dau of Louis Philippe I, King of the French); elected Prince of Bulgaria 7 July 1887; proclaimed himself King (Tsar) of the Bulgarians 5 October 1908;

abdicated in favour of his elder son 3 October 1918; *m* (1) Lucca 20 April 1893 Marie Louise (*b* Rome 17 January 1870; *d* Sofia 31 January 1899), eldest dau of Robert I, Duke of Parma, and his 1st wife Maria Pia of Bourbon-Two Sicilies; 2 sons, 2 daus; *m* (2) Coburg 28 February (Catholic) and Schloss Osterstein, Gera, 1 March (Protestant) 1908 Eleonore (*b* Trebschen, nr Züllichau 22 August 1860; *d* Euxinograd 12 September 1917), elder dau of Heinrich IV, Prince Reuss-Köstritz, and Louise of Saxe-Altenburg; no issue; *d* Coburg 10 September 1948

BORIS III · 1918–1943

b Sofia 30 January 1894, elder son of King Ferdinand I; *s* his father on his abdication 3 October 1918; *m* Assisi 25 October 1930 Giovanna (*b* Rome 13 November 1907), 3rd dau of Victor Emmanuel III, King of Italy, and Elena of Montenegro; 1 son, 1 dau; *d* Sofia 28 August 1943

SIMEON II · 1943–1946

b Sofia 16 June 1937, only son of King Boris III; *s* his father 28 August 1943; left the country following a Communist-rigged plebiscite 16 September 1946; *m* Lausanne 20 January (civil) and Vevey 21 January (religious) 1962 Margarita (*b* Madrid 6 January 1935), only dau of Don Manuel Gomez-Acebo y Modet and Doña Mercedes Cejuela y Fernandez; 4 sons, 1 dau

Bulgaria has a very ancient history. The Bulgars were a Hunnish tribe living in the Caucasus in an area on the Sea of Azov known as Old Great Bulgaria. They were ruled by Khans, of whom the first on record was Kubrat, or Kurt, reigning during the first half of the seventh century. His son, or more probably grandson, Asperuch, led his followers westwards, ending up in modern Bulgaria, where he established himself in about 680 after defeating a Byzantine Imperial army sent to check his advance. Several dynasties of pagan Khans or Kings ruled for the next two hundred years and in 865 Boris I was converted to Christianity. He died on 2 May 907 and his son Simeon I proclaimed himself Emperor of the Romans and the Bulgars in 925, obtaining papal recognition the following year. The state declined under his successors and by 1018 the Byzantine Emperor Basil II in a series of campaigns managed to incorporate Bulgaria into his Empire and earn himself the sobriquet of *Bulgaroktonos* (the Bulgar-slayer). Byzantine domination lasted until 1186 when the brothers Peter and Iovan Assen re-established Bulgarian independence. The dynasty they founded ruled as Tsars (derived from the Roman *Caesar*) for the next hundred years and was conquered by the Ottoman Turks in 1393.

Bulgaria did not regain any measure of independence until 13 July 1878, when it was constituted an autonomous principality under the suzerainty of Turkey by the terms of the treaty of Berlin following on the Russo-Turkish War. On 29 April 1879 Prince Alexander of Battenberg was elected Prince of Bulgaria by the unanimous vote of the National Assembly. His troubled reign ended when he was forced to abdicate on 3 September 1886 by a party of military insurgents incited by Russia. Prince Ferdinand of Saxe-Coburg and Gotha was elected Prince of

Bulgaria (with hereditary right) on 7 July 1887.

Ferdinand, who soon earned himself the nickname of 'Foxy Ferdinand', was an astute, wily individual with small eyes, an enormous nose and a pointed beard. Through his mother he was a grandson of Louis Philippe, King of the French, and he had inherited many of his traits. He was witty, amusing and loved splendour and beautiful jewels, which he would caress and fondle with his long fingers. He was, in short, a complete voluptuary. Although twice married, he did not care for women and was far happier when able to indulge in flirtatious badinage with a handsome young equerry, though how far he actually went in that direction can only be surmised.

Ferdinand was twenty-six when he became Prince of Bulgaria and for the first seven years of his reign was obliged to leave the government in the hands of Stambouloff, his rabidly anti-Russian Minister. Ferdinand's election had not been recognized

very backward country and his great schemes for aggrandizement led him to proclaim himself King (Tsar) of Bulgaria in October 1908, the title being recognized by the Great Powers in April 1909. His involvement in the Balkan Wars and his backing the wrong side in the First World War led to his abdication in favour of his son Boris on 3 October 1918. He lived on to see the end of the Bulgarian monarchy after the Second World War and died in Coburg, a lonely, forgotten figure in September 1948.

Ferdinand married Princess Marie Louise, the eldest daughter of Duke Robert I of Parma in 1893. She was far from good-looking with a long, melancholy face. Ferdinand and his wife were both Catholics and their first two children, both boys, were baptized in that faith, but Ferdinand realized the expediency of having them brought up in the Orthodox faith of Bulgaria and in February 1896, in spite of his wife's protestations, he had them taken to the Orthodox Cathedral in Sofia and re-baptized.

Ferdinand I, King of the Bulgarians.

Boris III, King of the Bulgarians.

by Russia or Turkey and he came to realize that he would have to get rid of Stambouloff in order to gain their recognition. Accordingly, he dismissed him in 1894 and in the following year Stambouloff was assassinated in the streets of Sofia. There was a strong suspicion that Ferdinand's government was implicated in the crime. In 1896 Ferdinand was finally recognized by the Powers and granted the qualification of Royal Highness by Turkey. In the course of his reign he did much to develop his

Princess Marie Louise, deeply religious like most of her family, never got over the blow and died the day after the birth of her younger daughter Nadejda in 1899. In 1908 Ferdinand decided that his four children needed a stepmother, his mother Princess Clementine, who had filled that function, having died in 1907. Being also on the verge of proclaiming himself King, he felt that Bulgaria needed a Queen, too. He chose Princess Eleonore Reuss-Köstritz, who was aged forty-seven and had a haughty pug-faced expression. In spite of her rather forbidding appearance, she made an excellent Queen and a kind stepmother and was sincerely regretted when she died in September 1917 after a long illness. Knowing what we do of Ferdinand's proclivities, it is practically certain that his second marriage was one in name only and was never consummated.

Ferdinand's elder son and successor took the style of Boris III, taking into account the two medieval Bulgarian Kings of that name. He was twenty-four years old at his accession and, although not very good-looking, had inherited much of his father's brilliance and none of his unpleasanter characteristics. He was an excellent linguist and his ruling passion was driving steam trains on the Bulgarian railway system. In 1930 he married the shyly attractive Princess Giovanna of Savoy, one of the daughters of King Victor Emmanuel III of Italy, and they had a son and a daughter. When the Second World War broke out

Simeon II, King of the Bulgarians.

King Boris hoped to remain neutral, but in 1941 he was compelled to join the Axis Powers. In August 1943 he was summoned to a meeting with Hitler, was taken ill during his flight home and died soon after landing. His death, which was officially attributed to heart failure, was regarded with great suspicion and there was a widespread belief that he had been poisoned on Hitler's orders for refusing to join in the war against Russia.

Boris's son, Simeon II, was only six when his father's death made him King, so a three-man Council of Regency was set up, headed by his uncle Prince Kyril. In February 1945 the Communists seized power and the Regents were murdered. The following year a rigged referendum resulted in the abolition of the monarchy and the proclamation of The People's Republic of Bulgaria on 16 September. King Simeon left the country with his mother and sister. He never abdicated or renounced his rights and today lives in Madrid with his Spanish wife Queen Margarita, whom he married in 1962. They have four sons and one daughter who all bear alliterative old Bulgarian names beginning with the letter K.

GREECE
The House of Wittelsbach

OTTO I	1832–1862

b Salzburg 1 June 1815, 2nd son of Ludwig I, King of Bavaria, and Therese of Saxe-Hildburghausen; elected King of Greece 7 May 1832; accepted the crown 5 October 1832; mounted the throne 6 February 1833; under regency until 1 June 1835; left the country 24 October 1862; *m* Oldenburg 22 November 1836 Amalia (*b* Oldenburg 21 December 1818; *d* Bamberg 20 May 1875; *bur* Theatinerkirche, Munich), eldest dau of August, Grand Duke of Oldenburg, and his 1st wife Adelheid of Anhalt-Bernburg-Schaumburg; no issue; *d* Bamberg 26 July 1867; *bur* Theatinerkirche, Munich

The House of Oldenburg

GEORGE I	1863–1913

b Copenhagen 24 December 1845, 2nd son of Christian IX, King of Denmark, and Louise of Hesse-Cassel; elected King of the Hellenes 6 June 1863; declared of age 27 June 1863; landed at Piraeus 30 October and began to reign 31 October 1863; *m* St Petersburg 27 October 1867, Olga, Queen Regent of Greece October to December 1920 (*b* Pavlovsk 3 September 1851; *d* Rome 18 June 1926; *bur* Tatoi), elder dau of Grand Duke Constantine Nikolaievitch of Russia and Alexandra of Saxe-Altenburg; 5 sons, 2 daus; *d* (assassinated) Salonika 18 March 1913; *bur* Tatoi

CONSTANTINE I	1913–1917 and 1920–1922

b Athens 2 August 1868, eldest son of King George I; *s* his father 18 March 1913; abdicated for himself and his eldest son June 1917; resumed the throne following a plebiscite 19 December 1920; again abdicated in favour of his eldest son 27 September 1922; *m* Athens 27 October 1889 Sophie (*b* Potsdam 14 June 1870; *d* Frankfurt am Main 13 January 1932; *bur* Tatoi), 3rd dau of Frederick III, German Emperor and King of Prussia, and Victoria of Great Britain; 3 sons, 3 daus; *d* Palermo 11 January 1923; *bur* Tatoi

ALEXANDER I	1917–1920

b Tatoi 1 August 1893, 2nd son of King Constantine I; *s* his father on his abdication June 1917; *m* Athens 4 November 1919 Aspasia (*b* Athens 4 September 1896; *d* Venice 7 August 1972), dau of Col Petros Manos and Maria Argyropoulos; 1 dau; *d* Athens 25 October 1920; *bur* Tatoi

GEORGE II	1922–1924 and 1935–1947

b Tatoi 19 July 1890, eldest son of King Constantine I; *s* his father on his second abdication 27 September 1922; left the country 25 March 1924; restored to the throne 3 November 1935; *m* Bucharest 27 February 1921 (*m* diss 1935) Elizabeth (*b* Pelesch 12 October 1894; *d* Cannes 14 November 1956), eldest dau of Ferdinand I, King of Roumania, and Marie of Great Britain; no issue; *d* Athens 1 April 1947; *bur* Tatoi

PAUL I	1947–1964

b Athens 14 December 1901, 3rd and yst son of King Constantine I; *s* his brother King George II 1 April 1947; *m* Athens 9 January 1938 Frederika (*b* Blankenburg, Harz, 18 April 1917; *d* Madrid 6 February 1981; *bur* Tatoi), only dau of Ernest Augustus, Duke of Brunswick, and Victoria Louise of Prussia; 1 son, 2 daus; *d* Tatoi 6 March 1964; *bur* Tatoi

CONSTANTINE II	1964–1974

b Psychiko 2 June 1940, only son of King Paul I; *s* his father 6 March 1964; left the country 13 December 1967; deposed 1 June 1973, but remained nominally King until a plebiscite decided against his return 8 December 1974; *m* Athens 18 September 1964 Anne-Marie (*b* Copenhagen 30 August 1946), 3rd and yst dau of Frederick IX, King of Denmark, and Ingrid of Sweden; 3 sons, 2 daus

The struggle for Greek independence from Turkey began in 1821 and a National Assembly convened at Astro in 1823 adopted a constitution. Fighting persisted for several years until the Turkish and Egyptian fleets were destroyed by the British, French and Russians at the battle of Navarino on 20 October 1827. The London Protocol of 1830 declared Greece to be an independent kingdom and, pending the election of a monarch, Count Joannis Capo d'Istria exercised power as President of the National Assembly; but his autocratic government led to his assassination in 1831. The crown was offered to Prince Leopold of Saxe-Coburg and Gotha (later first King of the Belgians), who declined, and then to Prince Otto of Bavaria, who accepted it on 5 October 1832 and landed at Nauplia on 6 February 1833. A Council of Regency held power until he had completed his twentieth year on 1 June 1835.

Otto was a very personable young man and at first his new subjects were delighted with him. Although he was full of good intentions, however, he was completely unable to understand the Greek temperament and never took the trouble to learn the language properly. He added to his growing unpopularity by maintaining a band of Bavarian troops and appointing Bavarian Ministers. In 1836 he married Amalia of Oldenburg, having transferred the seat of government from Nauplia to Athens the preceding year. A large palace was built in neo-classical style and the King and Queen took up their residence there and incurred further unpopularity by the grandeur of their court, which was regarded as an unnecessary extravagance for a poor and undeveloped country. Otto and Amalia did their best to win popularity by dressing as often as possible in the national costume, but it was of little avail and their childlessness also added to their troubles. After ten years a revolution forced the King to dismiss his Bavarian troops and grant a new constitution. His well-meaning attempts to add to Greek territory during the Crimean War were thwarted by the Great Powers and provoked another revolution in 1862, when he and the Queen were forced to leave the country in a British warship and return to Bavaria, where Otto died five years later.

The Greek throne was declared vacant and the Greek National Assembly set about electing a new King. Their first choice was Queen Victoria's second son Prince Alfred, but as Britain was one of the three Protecting Powers he was ruled out as ineligible. The Assembly's choice then fell on the seventeen-year-old Prince William of Denmark, second son of the heir to the Danish throne (soon to succeed as King Christian IX). Prince William is said to have learnt of his election by reading the newspaper wrapping the sardine sandwiches which he took to the Naval Academy for his lunch. He was filled with enthusiasm at the prospect and after overcoming his father's slight misgivings, the Greek throne was accepted on his behalf by King Frederick VII of Denmark on 6 June 1863. The National Assembly declared him of age and he landed at Piraeus on 30 October 1863, commencing his reign the next day. Prince William took the style of George I, King of the Hellenes, and at once set out to gain the affections of his subjects. He had a pleasant personality, was reasonably good-looking and took the pains to learn to speak Greek fluently. The only thing he did not do was convert to the Greek Orthodox faith; he remained a staunch Lutheran to the end of his life. King George spent the first four years of his reign travelling all over the country and never once leaving it, although he must often have been desperately lonely and homesick for Copenhagen. As a result he really gained a true understanding of the Greek people and their problems.

In 1867 King George married the sixteen-year-old Grand Duchess Olga of Russia. The Greeks took her to their hearts and she remained a truly loved Queen for the rest of her days. The marriage was a supremely happy one and was blessed with eight children born over a period of twenty years. The King and Queen led a simple family life, being happiest at Tatoi, a country estate which they bought in 1871. In the Athens Palace their growing family found the ballroom a suitable place for practising roller-skating and bicycling during the winter months.

King George reigned for fifty years and after the Balkan War of

King George I and Queen Olga of the Hellenes with six of their children. Back row, Prince Nicholas, Crown Prince Constantine and Prince George; in front, Princess Marie, Queen Olga, Prince Andrew, Princess Alexandra, King George.

1912 was visiting the newly liberated town of Salonika when he was shot by an assassin while walking through the streets of the town with a few companions.

George I was succeeded by his eldest son Constantine, a tall man of commanding appearance, who was married to Princess Sophie of Prussia, sister of the German Emperor William II and a granddaughter of Queen Victoria. The new King and Queen were popular and had everything to recommend them, but the King's equivocal attitude during the First World War provoked a rift between him and his Prime Minister, Eleutherios Venizelos, who wished Greece to enter the war on the side of the Allies, whereas the King wished to remain neutral. An extremely difficult political situation soon developed and in 1917 the King and the Crown Prince were forced to abdicate and renounce their rights in favour of Constantine's second son Alexander, who was left in Athens with only his grandmother Queen Olga, the rest of the royal family going into exile in Switzerland. The twenty-four-year-old King was merely a cipher, the real power being completely in the hands of Venizelos. In 1919 King Alexander fell in love with a young Greek lady of good family named Aspasia Manos. She reciprocated his feelings and they were married quietly on 4 November 1919. The marriage was

not made public and it was decided to defer the bride being acknowledged as Queen until more auspicious times. Ten months later King Alexander attempted to intervene when his dog was attacked by a pet monkey belonging to one of the gardeners at Tatoi. The monkey bit him, blood poisoning developed and he died in great agony on 25 October 1920. His widow was pregnant and gave birth the following March to a daughter (later Queen Alexandra of Yugoslavia).

On the King's death his grandmother Queen Olga was appointed Regent and Venizelos was obliged to hold an election in which his party was overwhelmingly defeated so that he was forced to resign and leave the country. A plebiscite held in December called for King Constantine's return and he and the rest of the royal family entered Athens to a tumultuous welcome. Things were still unsettled and far from easy; Venizelos was plotting and to avert a civil war King Constantine abdicated again on 27 September 1922. His marriage had long ago fallen apart and he retired to Sicily, where, exhausted and broken in spirit, he died in the arms of his mistress Paola Lottero, Countess von Ostheim, the ex-wife of Prince Hermann of Saxe-Weimar, on 11 January 1923.

Constantine's second abdication was in favour of his eldest son George, who had been forced to renounce his rights at the time of his father's first abdication. King George II reigned for eighteen months and was then compelled to abdicate in his turn in March 1924, when a republican government was proclaimed. The King settled in London, where he lived at Brown's Hotel. His childless marriage to Princess Elizabeth of Roumania broke up and he formed a sincere attachment for an English lady which was to endure and greatly sustain him for the rest of his life. The Greek republic was not a success and King George was recalled to the throne in November 1935 following yet another plebiscite.

The first year after the restoration saw a Communist bid for power which the Prime Minister General Metaxas effectively put down by asking the King to proclaim martial law. Five stable years followed until the German invasion forced the King to leave the country on 23 April 1941 after conducting a heroic but futile defence. At the end of the Second World War, King George's return was delayed by the tactics of his enemies and the anti-monarchists who were able to persuade the British government not to allow any of the royal family to return until the inevitable plebiscite had been held. The regency was exercised in the meantime by Archbishop Damaskinos, and when the plebiscite was held in September 1946, sixty-five per cent favoured the return of King George. His last reign was to be the shortest as he died very suddenly of a heart attack while taking an afternoon nap on 1 April 1947.

King George's successor was his brother Paul, who, with his wife Frederika of Hanover, had enjoyed great popularity as Crown Prince and Princess. They energetically carried on the war against the Communists and by 1949 the country had been cleared of all guerrilla forces. The King and Queen also did much to relieve the victims of a series of floods and earthquakes which afflicted parts of the country and gave their help and encouragement to repairing the ravages of war. Sadly, the Queen's popularity began steadily to decline and it was generally believed that she interfered too much in politics and was far too despotic by nature. King Paul fell ill with cancer and died after a long illness on 6 March 1964, when he was succeeded by his only son Constantine II.

The new King was an extremely attractive young man of twenty-four and his popularity was greatly enhanced when he married Princess Anne-Marie of Denmark, the youngest daughter of King Frederick IX, in the September following his accession. The wedding was the occasion of the last great royal gathering held in Athens. A little over three years later a group of army officers staged the 'Colonels' Coup' which sent the King and Queen into exile in Rome. King Constantine was deposed on 1 June 1973, but remained nominally in power until a plebiscite on the question of his return went against him on 8 December 1974 and Greece was once again proclaimed a republic.

Today King Constantine and Queen Anne-Marie live in London with their five children. The Greek monarchy has suffered more vicissitudes than any other in modern Europe and bearing in mind the unpredictably changing moods of the Greek people one can never preclude the possibility of another recall to the throne in the years to come.

MONTENEGRO

NICHOLAS I	(1860) 1910–1918 (1921)

b Njegoš 7 October 1841, only son of Mirko Petrović-Njegoš, Grand Voivode of Montenegro, and Stana Martinović; s his uncle Prince Danilo I as Prince of Montenegro 13 August 1860; assumed the qualification of Royal Highness 19 December 1900; proclaimed King of Montenegro 28 August 1910; refused to accept the annexation of Montenegro to the kingdom of the Serbs, Croats and Slovenes 13 November 1918 and maintained a government in exile until his death; m Cetinje 8 November 1860 Milena, Queen Regent of Montenegro (in exile) for her grandson King Michael 7 March 1921 to 13 July 1922 (b Cevo 4 May 1847; d Cap d'Antibes 16 March 1923), dau of Voivode and Senator Peter Vukotić and Elena Voivodić; 3 sons, 9 daus; d Cap d'Antibes 1 March 1921

[DANILO I	1–7 MARCH 1921]

b Cetinje 29 June 1871, eldest son of King Nicholas I; assumed the title of King on the death of his father 1 March 1921; abdicated in favour of his nephew Michael 7 March 1921; m Cetinje 27 July 1899 Jutta (Milica) (b Neustrelitz 24 January 1880; d Rome 17 February 1946), yr dau of Adolphus Frederick V, Grand Duke of Mecklenburg-Strelitz, and Elizabeth of Anhalt; no issue; d Vienna 24 September 1939

[MICHAEL I	1921–1922]

b Podgorica 14 September 1908, 3rd but eldest surviving son of Mirko, Grand Voivode of Grahovo and Zetà (2nd son of King Nicholas I), and Nathalie Constantinović; s as nominal King of Montenegro on the abdication of his uncle King Danilo I 7 March 1921; under the regency of his grandmother Queen Milena until 13 July 1922, when the Ambassadors' Conference in Paris recognized the annexation of Montenegro to the kingdom of the Serbs, Croats and Slovenes; m Paris 27 January 1941 (m diss 1949) Geneviève (b St Brieuc, Côtes-du-Nord, 4 December 1919), dau of François Marie Prigent and Blanche Bitte; 1 son; d Paris 24 March 1986

The tiny mountain kingdom of Montenegro on the Adriatic coast north of Albania was perhaps the most colourful of the Balkan states. Because of its inaccessibility it became a refuge for the Serbs who fled before the Turkish invaders after the battle of Kossovo in 1389. It was ruled by two native dynasties, the Balsa and the Crnojević, until 1516, when the Voivode George II retired to live in Venice and resigned the temporal power to Bishop Babylas. The Bishops (Vladikas) of Montenegro were elective until 1696, when Vladika Danilo I, of the Petrović-Njegoš family, was empowered to nominate his successor from his own family to ensure some continuity of government.

Vladika Peter I (1782–1830) obtained recognition of Montenegrin independence from Sultan Selim III in 1799 after winning a great victory over the Turks at Krusa in 1796 and taking the head of the Turkish commander to ornament his study. His nephew and successor Peter II was a great poet who wrote an historical verse drama relating the history of Vladika Danilo I and his struggle against the Turks. Peter II died on 31 October 1851 and was succeeded by his kinsman the twenty-five-year-old Danilo II. Danilo refused to be consecrated Bishop and assumed the title of Danilo I, Prince of Montenegro, on 8 January 1852. In 1855 he married Darinka Kvekić and on 13 August 1860 he was assassinated at Cattaro. He left an only daughter, Olga, so was succeeded by his nephew Nicholas.

Nicholas, a tall well-built man, was never seen except in the picturesque Montenegrin national costume, topped by the characteristic pillbox hat. He married the handsome, dark-haired and sloe-eyed Milena Vukotić, who also looked splendid in the national dress, and they had a large family of three sons and nine daughters. The daughters soon became known as their country's most valuable exports and their father shared with King Christian IX of Denmark the title of 'Father-in-law of Europe'. The eldest daughter married Prince Peter Karadjordjević, who after her death became King Peter I of Serbia; the second and third daughters married Russian Grand Dukes; the fourth daughter died young; the fifth daughter married King Victor Emmanuel III of Italy; the sixth daughter married Prince Francis Joseph of Battenberg; the seventh daughter died young; and the eighth and ninth daughters died unmarried.

Prince Nicholas was a keen exponent of paternalism and did much to advance his country's standard of literacy and improve communications by constructing roads and railways. When he went on a European tour he was a great success with his fellow monarchs and became a particular favourite with Queen Victoria, ever an admirer of a well-set-up man. In December 1900 Prince Nicholas began upgrading himself by assuming the qualification of Royal Highness, and ten years later he marked the fiftieth anniversary of his accession by taking the title of King. In the First World War King Nicholas joined forces with his son-in-law King Peter of Serbia, but in November 1918 his grandson Crown Prince Alexander of Serbia drove King Nicholas out of Montenegro and churlishly annexed it to the newly enlarged kingdom of the Serbs, Croats and Slovenes. The old King protested vehemently at his grandson's high-handed action and refused to recognize the annexation. He maintained a government in exile until his death at Cap d'Antibes in March 1921, when he was succeeded theoretically by his eldest son Crown Prince Danilo. Danilo, a curious man who played tennis with a loaded revolver thrust through his belt and enjoyed lying in his bath while his manservant cooked and served him spaghetti, had no wish to rule, even in exile, and abdicated one week later in favour of his nephew Michael, the son of his deceased brother Mirko. Queen Milena assumed the regency and it was only on 13 July 1922, when the Conference of Ambassadors at Paris recognized the union with Serbia, that the claims of the Petrović-Njegoš family were relinquished. King Michael lived quietly in Paris for the rest of his life, earning his living as a trade inspector. To his great credit he refused to return to Montenegro as a puppet ruler under German and Italian auspices in the Second World War. He died on 24 March 1986. His marriage to a Frenchwoman, Geneviève Prigent, had ended in divorce years before, but there was one son, Nicholas, the present head of the family, who is married and has a son and a daughter.

ROUMANIA

The House of Hohenzollern

CAROL I	(1866) 1881–1914

b Sigmaringen 20 April 1839, 2nd son of Charles Anthony, Prince of Hohenzollern-Sigmaringen, and Josephine of Baden; elected Prince of Roumania 20 April 1866 (recognized by the Powers 24 October 1866); assumed the qualification of Royal Highness 25 October 1878; proclaimed King of Roumania 26 March 1881; crowned Bucharest 22 May 1881; m Neuwied 15 November 1869 Elisabeth (b Neuwied 29 December 1843; d Curtea de Arges 3 March 1916), only dau of Hermann, 4th Prince of Wied, and Marie of Nassau; 1 dau; d Castle Pelesch, Sinaia 10 October 1914

FERDINAND I	1914–1927

b Sigmaringen 24 August 1865, 2nd son of Leopold, Prince of Hohenzollern, and Antonia of Portugal; Crown Prince of Roumania 18

March 1889; s his uncle King Carol I 10 October 1914; crowned Alba Julia 15 October 1922; m Sigmaringen 10 January 1893 Marie (b Eastwell Park, Kent, 29 October 1875; d Castle Pelesch, Sinaia, 10 July 1938), eldest dau of Alfred, Duke of Saxe-Coburg and Gotha, Prince of Great Britain and Ireland, Duke of Edinburgh, and Grand Duchess Marie Alexandrovna of Russia; 3 sons, 3 daus; d Sinaia 20 July 1927

MICHAEL I	(FIRST REIGN) 1927–1930
CAROL II	1930–1940

b Castle Pelesch, Sinaia, 15 October 1893, eldest son of King Ferdinand I; renounced his rights of succession to the throne 28 December 1925 (made law 4 January 1926); returned to Roumania and was reinstated in his rights 6 June 1930; proclaimed King 8 June 1930; abdicated in favour of his son Michael 6 September 1940; m (1) Odessa 31 August 1918 (m annulled 8 January 1919) Joana Maria Valentina (Zizi) (b Roman, Roumania, 3 October 1898; d Paris 11 March 1953), dau of Col Constantine Lambrino and Euphrosine Alcaz; 1 son; m (2) Athens 10 March 1921 (m diss 21 June 1928) Helen (b Athens 2 May 1896; d Lausanne, Switzerland, 28 November 1982), eldest dau of Constantine I, King of the Hellenes, and Sophie of Prussia; 1 son; m (3) Rio de Janeiro 3 June 1947 Elena (Magda) (b Jassy 15 September 1895; d Estoril, Portugal, 28 June 1977), formerly wife of Ion Tampeanu, and dau of Nicholas Wolf (Lupescu) and Elizabeth —; no issue; d Villa Mar y Sol, Estoril, Portugal, 4 April 1953

MICHAEL I	(SECOND REIGN) 1940–1947

b Pelesch 25 October 1921, son of King Carol II and his 2nd wife Helen of Greece and Denmark; s his grandfather King Ferdinand I under a regency 20 July 1927; replaced by his father 8 June 1930; again s on his father's abdication 6 September 1940; forced to abdicate and leave the country 30 December 1947; m Athens 10 June 1948 Anne (b Paris 18 September 1923), only dau of Prince René of Bourbon-Parma and Margrethe of Denmark; 5 daus

The principality of Roumania came into being on 5 November 1859 when the Danubian principalities of Moldavia and Wallachia, which had for centuries been ruled by elected Princes as Turkish tributaries, were united under one ruler, Alexander John Cuza. The union was recognized by Turkey in December 1861, but in February 1866 the Prince was forced to abdicate, his autocracy and dissolute private life having made him no longer acceptable. He is said to have signed his abdication using the bare back of his mistress as a writing table.

The Roumanian parliament, led by the powerful Minister Ion Bratianu, determined to elect a foreign Prince as the next ruler. Their first choice was Philip, Count of Flanders, the younger brother of King Leopold II of the Belgians, but he declined to accept, and the next choice was Prince Charles of Hohenzollern-Sigmaringen, an officer in the Prussian army, who accepted with Bismarck's backing. The election took place on 20 April 1866 and was recognized by the Powers on 24 October. Prince Charles adopted the Roumanian form of his name, Carol, and settled down to rule his principality. He was an unspectacular but capable man and had to keep a careful balance in his relations with his neighbours, Austria, Russia and Turkey. The Russo-Turkish War gave Roumania complete independence from Turkey and on 25 October 1878 Prince Carol assumed the qualification of Royal Highness. On 26 March 1881 he was proclaimed King following a unanimous decision of the Chamber of Deputies and on 22 May he crowned himself at Bucharest with an iron crown fashioned from Turkish cannon captured at the siege of Plevna, where Carol had commanded his troops in person.

Roumania is a rich, fertile country, producing corn, iron, coal and oil, and soon became the most prosperous Balkan state under King Carol's development of its natural resources.

As a personality, King Carol was completely overshadowed by his wife, the romantic Queen Elisabeth. A tall, stately lady with prematurely white hair, she dressed in flowing white draperies, which she had adopted as mourning after the loss of her only child, Princess Marie, who died of scarlet fever and diphtheria at the age of four. The Queen was an intellectual and wrote poetry and fairy stories using the pen-name of Carmen Sylva. She was completely tone-deaf, but would give her patronage to every hack musician or vocalist who applied to her, listening enraptured to their often tuneless cacophony. She took her position as Queen very seriously and would stand on the terrace of her seaside palace calling out blessings through a megaphone to the passing ships. Her world was a fantasy one and her husband and the other members of the royal family regarded her actions with an amused and admiring tolerance.

As King Carol had no son he adopted his nephew Ferdinand as his heir in 1889. Ferdinand married the beautiful Princess Marie of Edinburgh in 1893 and they had six children. Marie was quite as romantic as Queen Elisabeth and also a writer, but had a far more practical side to her and was able to organize cholera camps and field hospitals during the Balkan and First World Wars. King Carol I died in October 1914 and was succeeded by Ferdinand, who was completely dominated by Queen Marie. Roumania fought with the Allies in the First World War and at its end it was Queen Marie who attended the peace conference in Paris, using her beauty and personality to gain Roumania's ends, although her frivolity was to shock the primly austere President Wilson. In October 1922 the deferred coronation of the King and Queen took place at Alba Julia in Transylvania and Marie devised a highly theatrical costume and crown for herself, based on those of the old Byzantine Empire.

The heir to the throne was the royal couple's eldest son, Prince Carol, and he began to give them a lot of anxiety and trouble before he even grew out of his teens. His mother's cousin King George V of Great Britain would have described him as a cad and he would have been quite right. Carol was a womanizer and so weak willed that almost any woman could influence him. He became infatuated with a Roumanian girl of good family, 'Zizi' Lambrino, and eloped with her to Odessa, where he persuaded the Orthodox clergy to marry them in the Cathedral in August 1918. When the news reached Bucharest the King and Queen were furious with their son and demanded the immediate annulment of the marriage, which was effected in January 1919. Carol continued to live with 'Zizi' and in January 1920 she gave birth to a son in Bucharest. The child was not

King Carol II of Roumania, a photograph taken in 1924 when he was Crown Prince.

acknowledged by the King and Queen and they arranged for Carol to marry Princess Helen of Greece. The marriage took place at Athens in March 1921, but although the Princess was beautiful and accomplished Carol never loved her and soon left her after she had given birth prematurely to a son. His taste ran to more brassy and obvious women and in 1925 he caused another scandal by eloping with the red-haired, half-Jewish divorcée Elena (known as Magda) Lupescu, who some allege was an illegitimate daughter of King Carol I. Carol renounced his rights to the throne and the King and Queen accepted his renunciation with a sense of relief. King Ferdinand died two years later in July 1927 and was succeeded by his six-year-old grandson Michael, the son of Carol and Princess Helen, whose marriage was dissolved the following year. Michael reigned under a three-man Council of Regency headed by his uncle Prince Nicholas until June 1930, when his father returned to Roumania at the invitation of the Prime Minister and was proclaimed King Carol II. Michael was demoted from King to Crown Prince.

King Carol was still completely under the influence of Magda

Lupescu and behaved in very cavalier fashion towards his mother and other members of the royal family. However, he did restore the country to prosperity and proved himself a patron of the arts, rebuilding the royal palace in a somewhat flamboyant style in which he showed himself a true son of his mother. By 1940 he had become an absolute monarch and on 6 September that year he was forced to abdicate at Hitler's instigation in favour of his son Michael. Carol became a royal wanderer, always accompanied by the Lupescu. In June 1947 they were in Rio de Janeiro when Magda fell ill, allegedly with pernicious anaemia, and was reported to be on her deathbed. A tearful Carol married her in a moving bedside ceremony. The next day she began miraculously to mend and soon made a full recovery. Carol decided that she should take the title of Princess of Hohenzollern with the qualification of Royal Highness and got his kinsman the Prince of Hohenzollern to agree to this. The couple eventually settled in the Portuguese resort of Estoril, a favourite haven for royal exiles, and Carol died at their villa there in April 1953. Magda lived on until June 1977. Her coffin lies beside Carol's in the burial chapel of his Bragança ancestors, awaiting the day when they can be returned to Roumania.

King Michael's second reign lasted seven years, but he really never had a chance. After the Second World War the Communists gained control in Roumania and he was at last forced to abdicate and leave the country on 30 December 1947. When attending the wedding of Princess Elizabeth (now HM Queen Elizabeth II) in London in November 1947, Michael met and fell in love with Princess Anne of Bourbon-Parma and they married in Athens in June 1948. They made their home in Lausanne, Switzerland, where King Michael earns his living as an executive with a brokerage firm. The royal couple have five daughters.

SERBIA AND YUGOSLAVIA

The House of Obrenović

MILAN I (1868) 1882–1889

b Marasesci, Roumania, 22 August 1854, only son of Milosh Obrenović and Elena Maria Catargi; s his first cousin once removed Prince Michael Obrenović III as Milan Obrenović IV, Prince of Serbia, and was proclaimed 2 July 1868; under regency until 22 August 1872; proclaimed Serbia independent of Turkey 22 August 1878; proclaimed King of Serbia 6 March 1882; abdicated in favour of his only surviving son 6 March 1889; m Belgrade 17 October 1875 (m diss 1888; reconciled 1893) Nathalie (b Florence 14 May 1859; d Paris 8 May 1941), dau of Col Peter Ivanovitch Kechko and Princess Pulcheria Sturdza; 2 sons; d Vienna 11 February 1901

ALEXANDER I 1889–1903

b Belgrade 15 August 1876, elder and only surviving son of King Milan I; s his father on his abdication 6 March 1889; under regency until he proclaimed himself of age 13 April 1893; m Belgrade 5 August 1900 Draga (b Jornji Milanovac 23 September 1867; d (assassinated) Belgrade 10 June 1903), widow of Col Svetozar Mashin and dau of Andrej Lunyevica and Anja Kiljenić; no issue; d (assassinated) Belgrade 10 June 1903

The House of Karadjordjević

PETER I 1903–1921

b Belgrade 11 July 1844, 3rd but eldest surviving son of Alexander Karadjordjević, Prince of Serbia, and Persida Nenadović; elected King of Serbia by the Skupština 15 June 1903; crowned Belgrade 21 September 1904; proclaimed King of the Serbs, Croats and Slovenes at Zagreb 24 November 1918; m Cetinje 1 August 1883 Zorka (b Cetinje 23 December 1864; d Cetinje 28 March 1890), eldest dau of Nicholas I, Prince (later King) of Montenegro, and Milena Vukotić; 3 sons, 2 daus; d Belgrade 16 August 1921; bur Oplenac

ALEXANDER I 1921–1934

b Cetinje 16 December 1888, 2nd son of King Peter I; Crown Prince of Serbia on his elder brother's renunciation 28 March 1909; Regent and Commander-in-Chief 24 June 1914; s his father 16 August 1921; assumed the title of King of Yugoslavia 3 October 1929; m Belgrade 8 June 1922 Marie (b Gotha 8 January 1900; d London 22 June 1961; bur Frogmore, nr Windsor), 2nd dau of Ferdinand I, King of Roumania, and Marie of Edinburgh; 3 sons; d (assassinated) Marseilles 9 October 1934

PETER II 1934–1945

b Belgrade 6 September 1923, eldest son of King Alexander I; s his father 9 October 1934; under the regency of his father's cousin Prince Paul until 27 March 1941, when he assumed power; left the country following the German invasion June 1941; lost his throne when the Constituent Assembly abolished the monarchy 29 November 1945; m London 20 March 1944 Alexandra (b Athens 25 March 1921), only dau of Alexander I, King of the Hellenes, and Aspasia Manos; 1 son; d Denver, Colorado, USA, 3 November 1970; bur Libertyville

Serbia enjoyed two hundred years as the dominant power in the Balkans under the Nemanyid dynasty before falling to the Turks at the battle of Kossovo on 15 June 1389. It then remained under Turkish domination until January 1804 when a movement for independence was begun under the leadership of George Petrović, better known as Karadjordje (Black George), a former pig dealer. The Serb National Assembly chose him as Supreme Leader on 5 February 1804 and he led them so successfully that

King Milan of Serbia, the first King of modern Serbia, proclaimed in 1882.

ruled until Milan came of age at eighteen in 1872 and, following the Russo-Turkish War, Serbia obtained complete independence in 1878. On 6 March 1882 the Prince was proclaimed King Milan I.

He was a typical Balkan, a giant of a man with a loud voice and a penchant for political intrigue, intent on bringing the whole of the Balkans under his rule. In 1875 he married his second cousin Nathalie Kechko, the daughter of a Russian army officer. She was slight, dark-haired and sloe-eyed and possessed a smouldering temper which was exacerbated by King Milan's roving eye. The marriage was doomed to failure from the start and the King and Queen were not above conducting their marital rows in public. On one occasion Milan slapped Nathalie's face while they were attending a service in Belgrade Cathedral and she stormed out to the embarrassment of the assembled courtiers. Two sons were born in the early years of the marriage, but only the elder Alexander survived. By 1888 matters between the King and Queen reached a head and there was a divorce which created a great scandal throughout Europe and gave Russia the looked-for excuse to force Milan's abdication in March 1889.

The new King, Alexander I, was only twelve so a Council of Regency had to be appointed once again. Alexander was completely unlike his father, a physical weakling with bad eyesight, but he was not unintelligent. As he grew up he came to resent the regency and on 13 April 1893 he staged a coup and proclaimed himself of age, although still under seventeen. He invited his father to return and there was a nominal reconciliation between his parents. The former King became Commander-in-Chief of the Serbian army in 1898 and served his son with great loyalty and devotion, making no attempt to recover the throne for himself.

Milan was anxious for Alexander to marry and beget an heir and began looking round for a suitable German Princess; but Alexander had other ideas. When visiting his mother at her villa in Biarritz he had met and fallen in love with one of her ladies-in-waiting, a plump widow of mature years and a somewhat dubious reputation. He brought her back to Belgrade with him and determined on marrying her in spite of parental opposition. The wedding took place in August 1900 and Milan showed his disapproval by at once resigning as Commander-in-Chief and going to Vienna, where he died the following February. The King's marriage made him extremely unpopular with all his subjects, especially when it became apparent that Queen Draga was unable to bear children and Alexander was rumoured to be contemplating the appointment of one of her brothers as heir-presumptive. A conspiracy of army officers (the brother of Draga's first husband among them) pledged themselves to overthrow the King and replace him with Peter Karadjordjević of the rival dynasty. On the night of 10/11 June 1903 the conspirators struck. The Palace was surrounded while the King and Queen slept and an entry was forced. Alexander and Draga were aroused by the clamour and vainly endeavoured to take refuge in a secret compartment behind a cupboard in their bedroom, where they were found, dragged forth and butchered by the swords of the conspirators, their bodies thrown out of the window to the lawn below. They lay exposed on the grass while

most of Serbia had been liberated by 1811, when George was confirmed as leader with the right of succession vested in his family. In 1813, however, he was abandoned by his Russian allies and the Turks were able to drive him out of the country. In 1815 a new liberation movement was headed by Milosh Obrenović, who had been one of Black George's lieutenants. In 1817 George returned to Serbia and was murdered by the Mayor of Vouitza, possibly with Milosh's connivance. From that date onwards the Karadjordjevićs and the Obrenovićs were deadly rivals.

Milosh was elected Prince of Serbia in November 1817 and abdicated in 1839, being succeeded in turn by his sons Milan and Michael. In 1842 Michael was forced to leave the country when there was a rising in favour of Black George's son Alexander, who reigned until 1858, when he was driven out and old Milosh was restored and recognized as Prince by Turkey. He reigned until his death in 1860 when his son Michael re-ascended the throne. Michael was assassinated near Belgrade in June 1868 and was succeeded by his fourteen-year-old kinsman Milan, a grandson of Milosh's brother Yephrem. A Council of Regency the soldiers caroused around them, and were finally taken back into the Palace at the instance of the Russian Minister.

Queen Nathalie lived on for many years after the death of her son. There was a false report of her death in 1934, but she actually died in German-occupied Paris in May 1941, a sad, forgotten figure.

Peter Karadjordjević was acclaimed as King and his succession was confirmed by the Skupstina on 15 June 1903. Having waded to the throne through the blood of his predecessor (although not involved himself in any way in the assassination), Peter was regarded with a certain disdain by his fellow sovereigns, who had been shocked by the brutality of the crime. The year following his accession it was decided to consolidate his dynastic rights by holding a coronation ceremony, the first to take place in Serbia since the middle ages. On 21 September 1904 the crowned and robed King rode on horseback through the streets of Belgrade. With his fierce bushy white moustache and straight back he made a most imposing figure (as can be seen from photographs of the event).

King Peter's wife Zorka, the eldest daughter of Prince (later King) Nicholas of Montenegro, had died many years before he became King, three weeks after the birth of their youngest child. Crown Prince George, their eldest son, was a violent-tempered man of eccentric disposition and in March 1909 was persuaded to renounce his rights in favour of his more stable brother Alexander. In June 1914 Alexander was appointed Regent because of King Peter's failing health. During the First World War he distinguished himself as Commander-in-Chief of the Serbian army, fighting in the trenches beside his men. At the end of the war King Peter was proclaimed King of the Serbs, Croats and Slovenes and was reigning over a greatly enlarged kingdom which had also taken over Montenegro from his father-in-law King Nicholas. Peter I died in August 1921 and was succeeded by Alexander who changed the name of the kingdom to Yugoslavia on 3 October 1929. Unfortunately, the country now lacked national unity as the Croats and Slovenes did not

agree with the Serbs. In 1928 the King suspended the Constitution and made an attempt to solve matters by absolute rule, but things became no easier. In October 1934 he went on a state visit to France and soon after landing at Marseilles was shot and killed by a hired assassin in the pay of a Croatian terrorist organization.

King Alexander had married the plump, stolid Princess Marie of Roumania, a daughter of King Ferdinand and Queen Marie, and they had three sons. The eldest, who now became King Peter II, was only eleven and the regency was headed by King Alexander's cousin Prince Paul, a handsome man of cultured tastes, who was married to the beautiful Princess Olga of Greece. When the Second World War reached the Balkans, the Regent, although pro-British, signed a pact with Germany and Italy in March 1941, fearing domination by Soviet Russia. His act provoked a military revolt which overthrew the government and declared King Peter of age although still six months short of his eighteenth birthday. Hitler at once ordered the invasion of Yugoslavia and after a fortnight of intensive bombing King Peter surrendered and went into exile, heading a free Yugoslav government in London. While there he fell in love with a fellow exile, Princess Alexandra of Greece, and they were married in 1944. After the war Tito's partisans seized power in Yugoslavia and King Peter's return was prevented by the Communist takeover. The rest of his life in exile was a sad one. He and Queen Alexandra separated and he went to live in America, where his health slowly deteriorated through his attempts to drown his sorrows with strong drink. He died alone at Denver, Colorado, in November 1970.

The present head of the Royal House of Yugoslavia is King Peter's only child, Crown Prince Alexander, who was born in London on 17 July 1945. Now a highly successful business man in London, he wisely pursues no active claim to his ancestral heritage. He has been married twice and has three sons by his first marriage.

APPENDIX

GENEALOGICAL TABLES

KEY TO ABBREVIATIONS

b	born	granddau(s)	granddaughter(s)
bur	buried	jure (uxoris)	by right (of the wife)
cr	created	k	killed
d	died	m	married/marriage
dau(s)	daughter(s)	s	succeeded
diss	dissolved	surv	surviving, survived
div	divorced	unm	unmarried
dsp	died without issue	yr	younger
dvp	died in the lifetime of the father	yst	youngest

1 PORTUGAL: THE HOUSE OF BURGUNDY

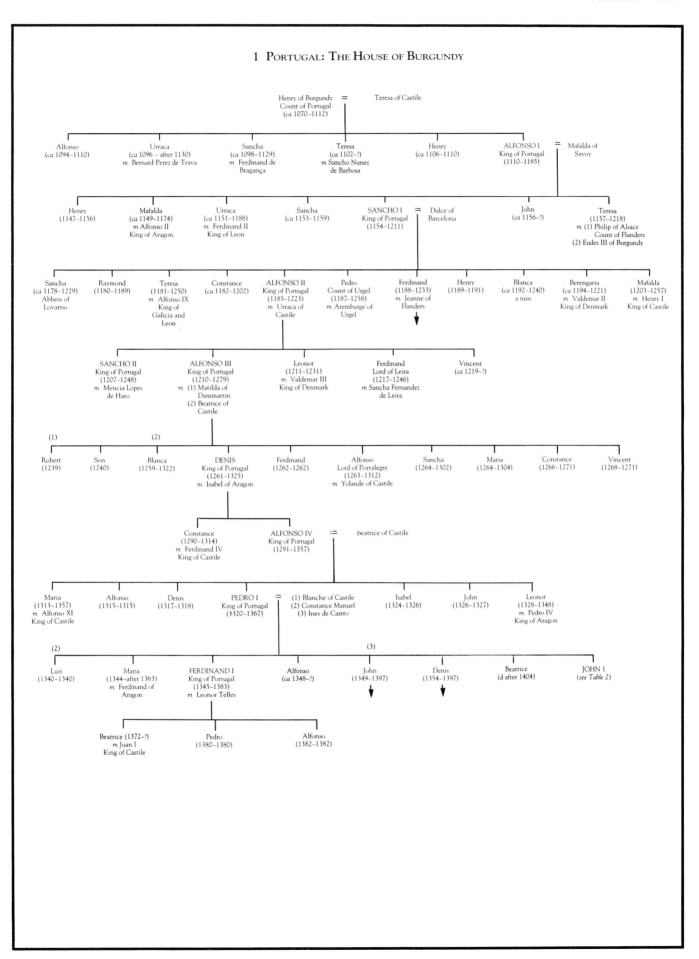

2 PORTUGAL: THE HOUSE OF AVIS

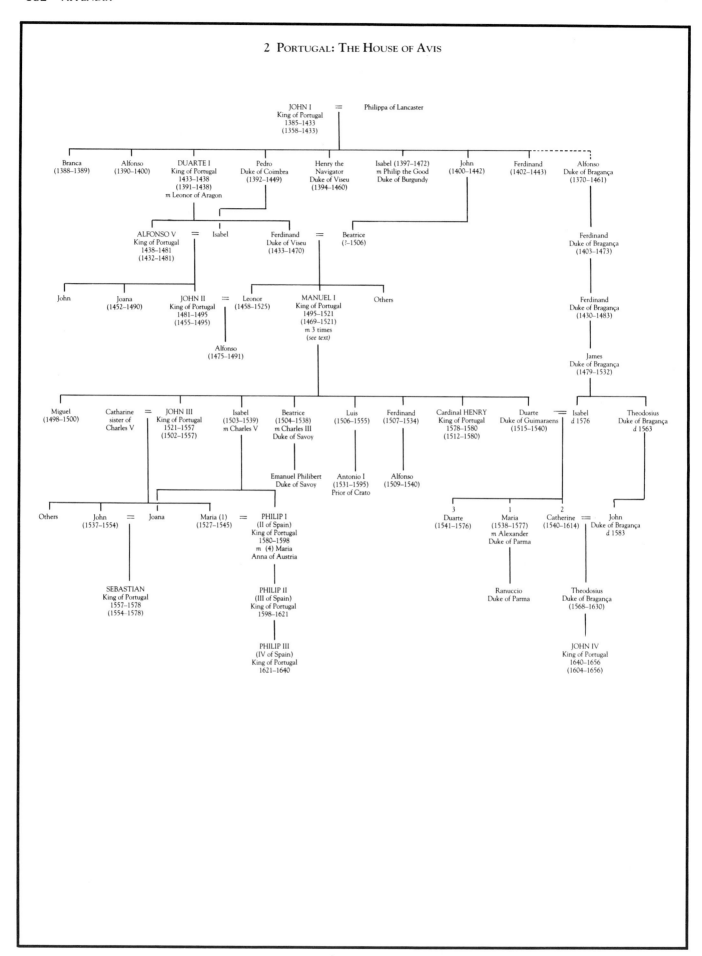

3 PORTUGAL: THE HOUSE OF BRAGANÇA

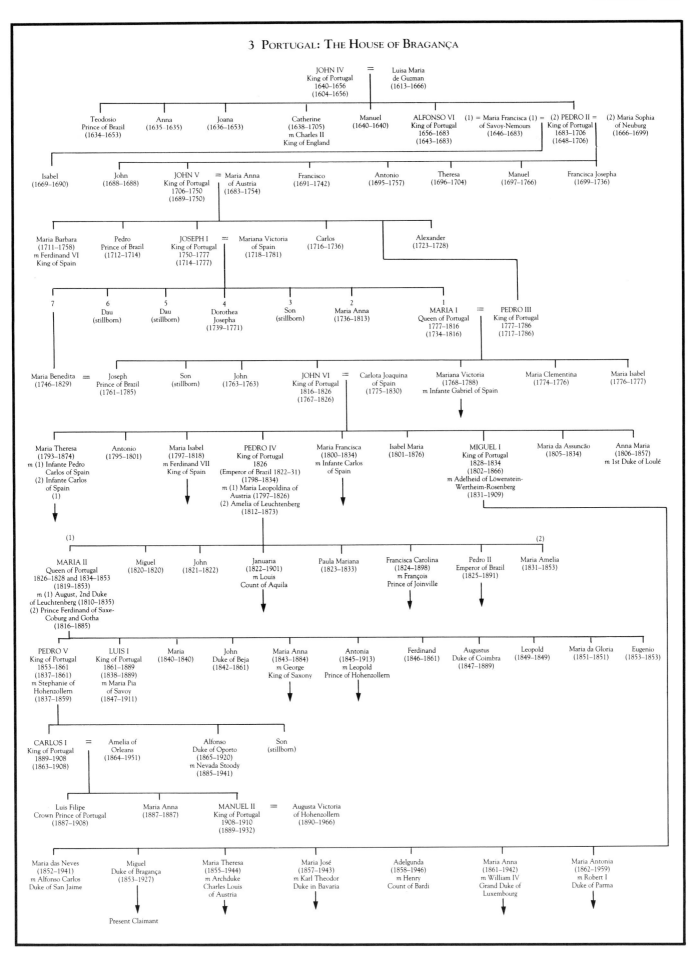

4 SPAIN: THE KINGS AND QUEENS OF CASTILE AND LEON

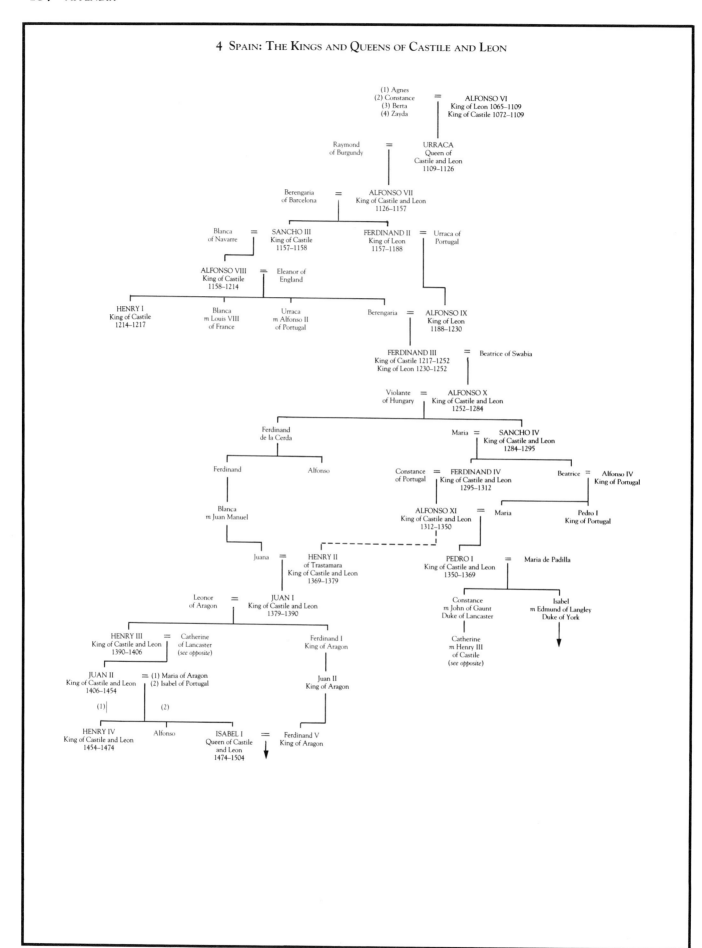

5 SPAIN: THE KINGS AND QUEENS OF NAVARRE

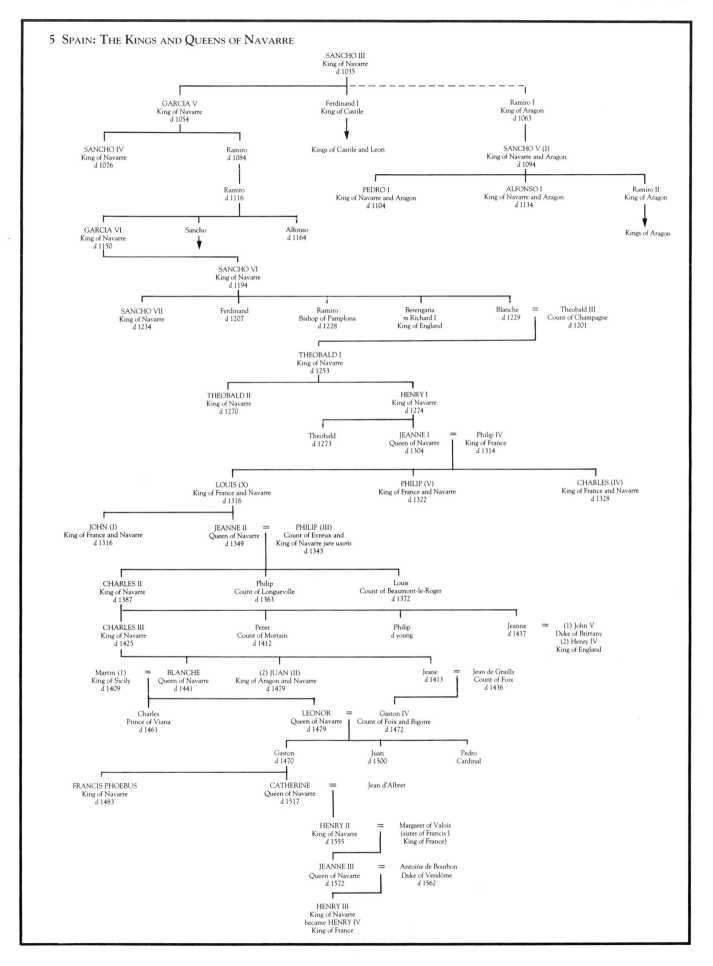

6 THE BOURBON KINGS OF SPAIN (1)

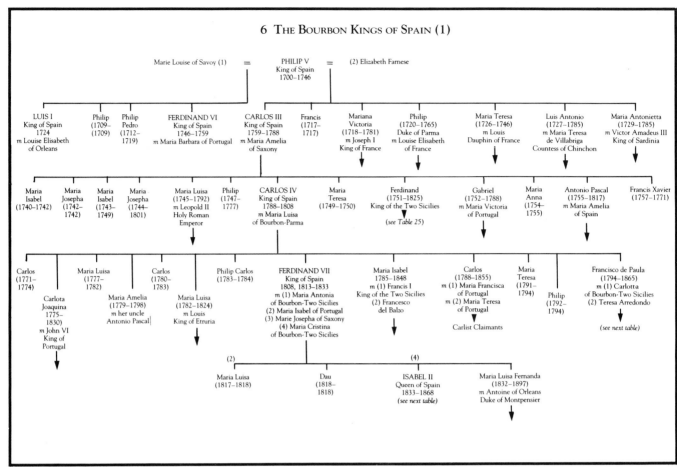

7 THE BOURBON KINGS OF SPAIN (2)

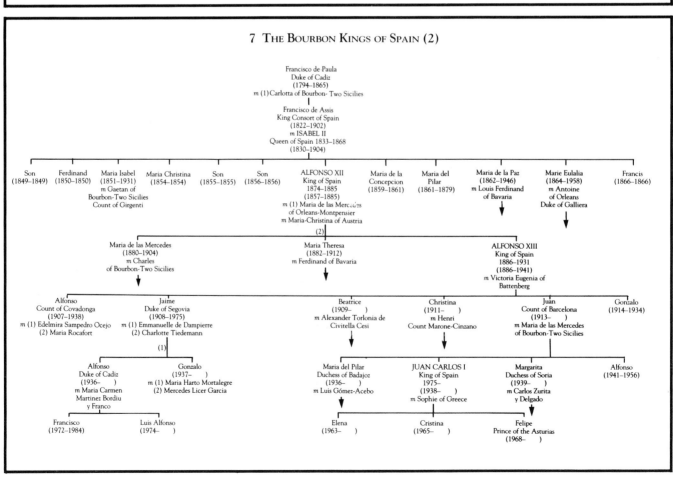

8 FRANCE: THE MEROVINGIAN KINGS

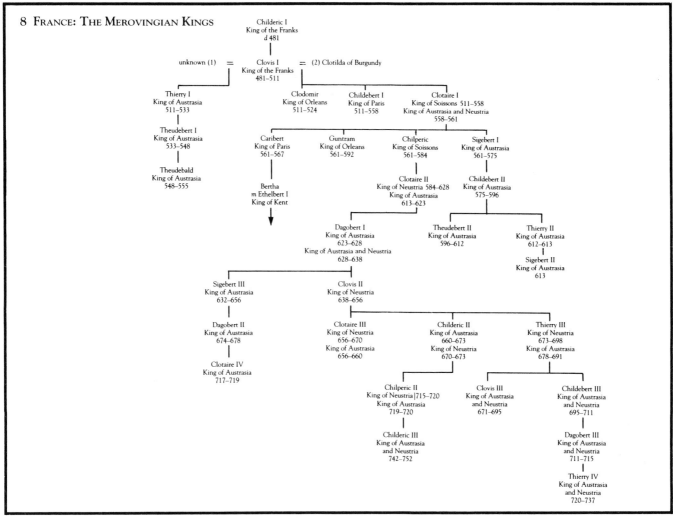

9 FRANCE: THE CAROLINGIAN KINGS

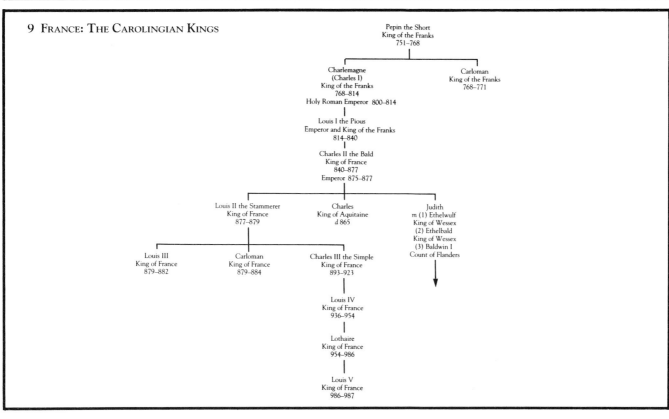

10 FRANCE: THE CAPETIAN KINGS

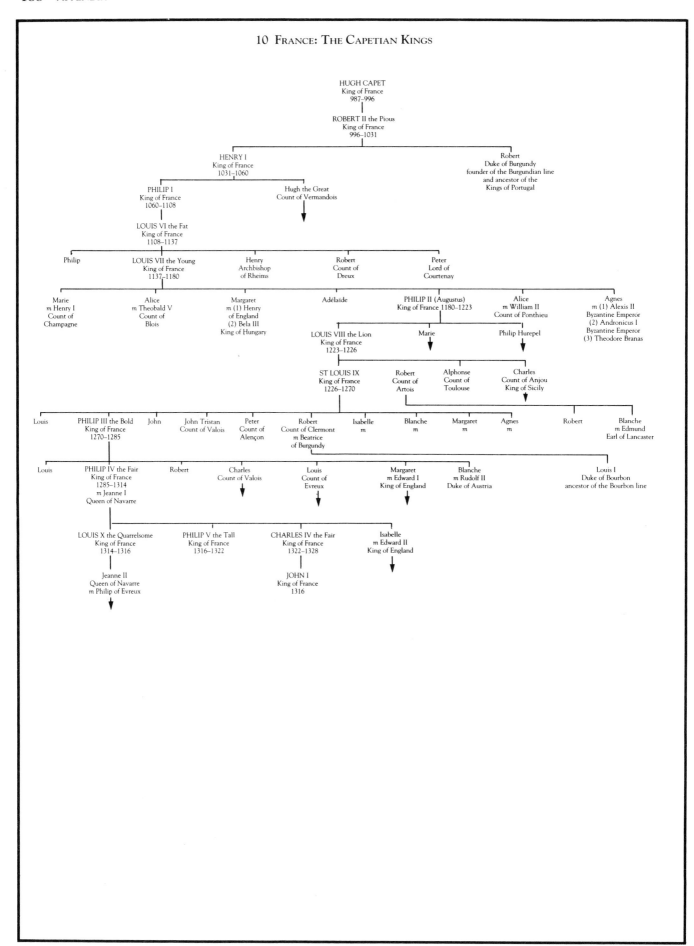

11 FRANCE: THE HOUSE OF VALOIS

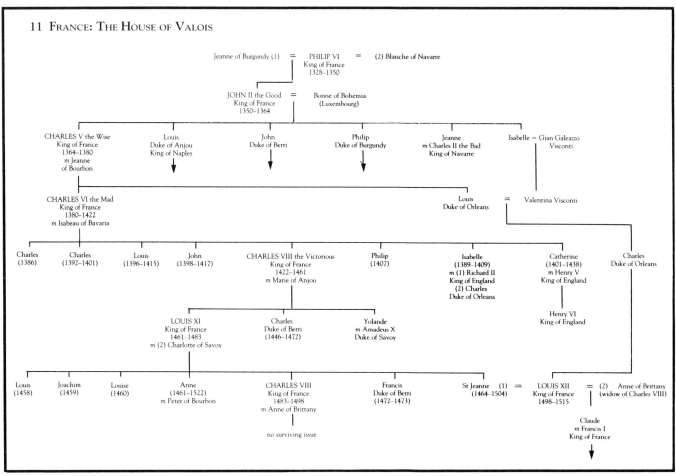

12 FRANCE: THE HOUSE OF VALOIS-ORLEANS

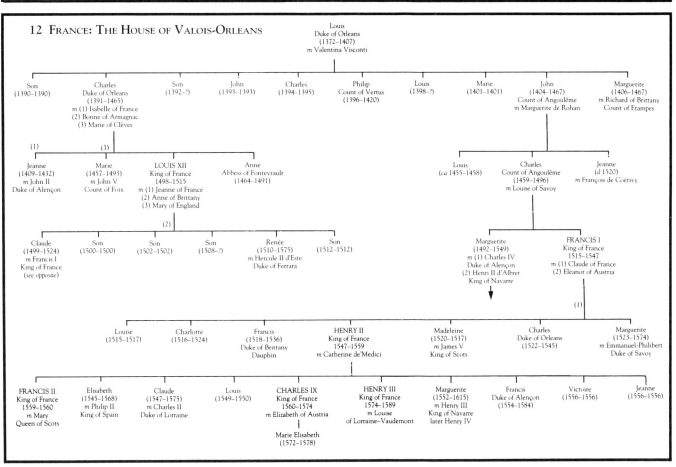

13 FRANCE: THE HOUSE OF BOURBON

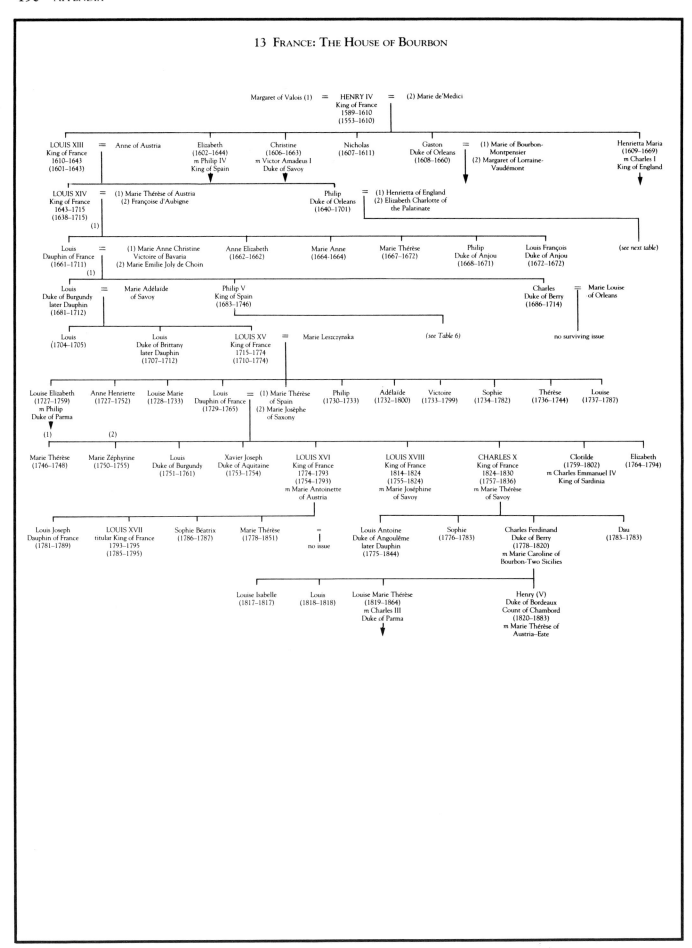

14 FRANCE: THE HOUSE OF BOURBON-ORLEANS

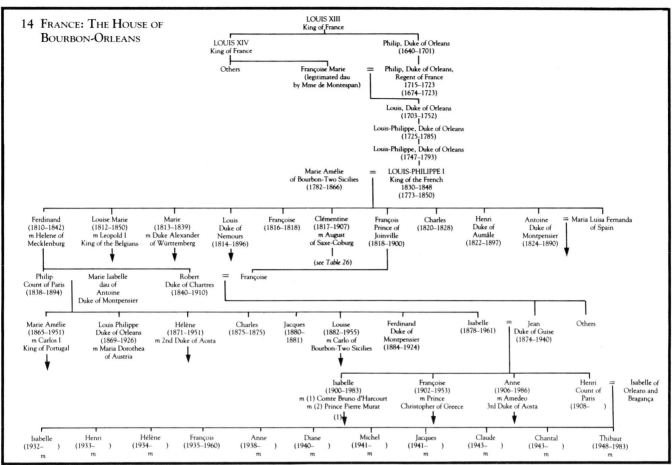

15 THE KINGS OF THE BELGIANS

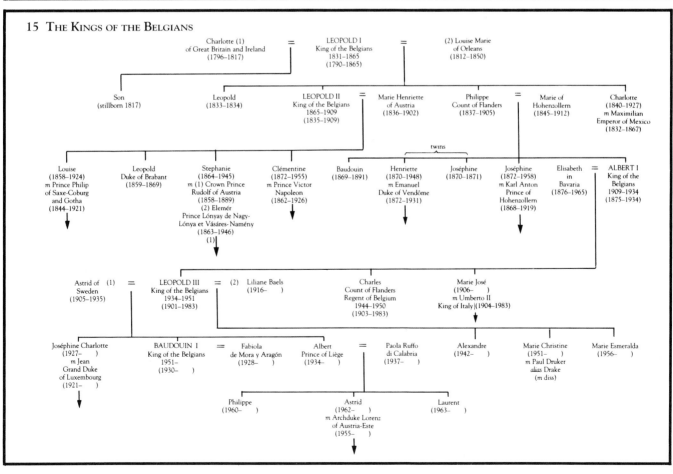

16 THE KINGS AND QUEENS OF THE NETHERLANDS

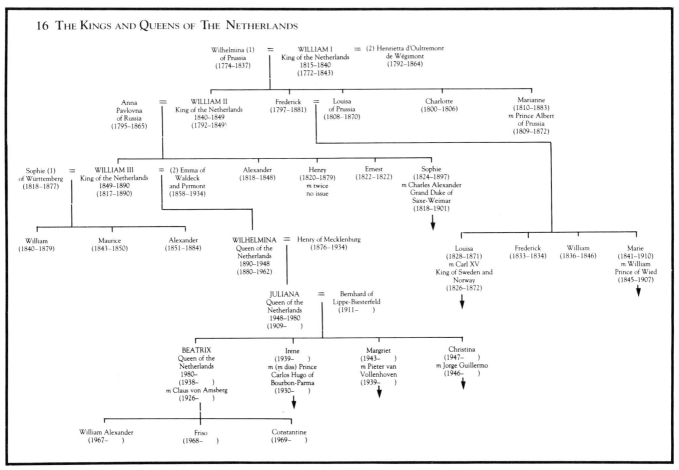

17 THE KINGS AND QUEENS OF DENMARK

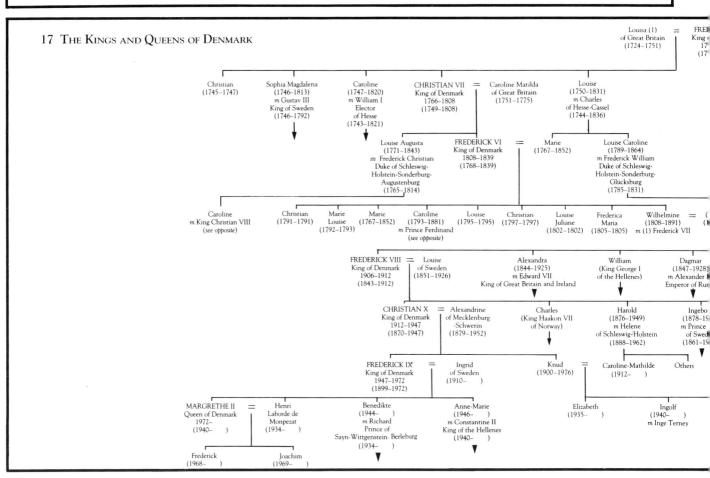

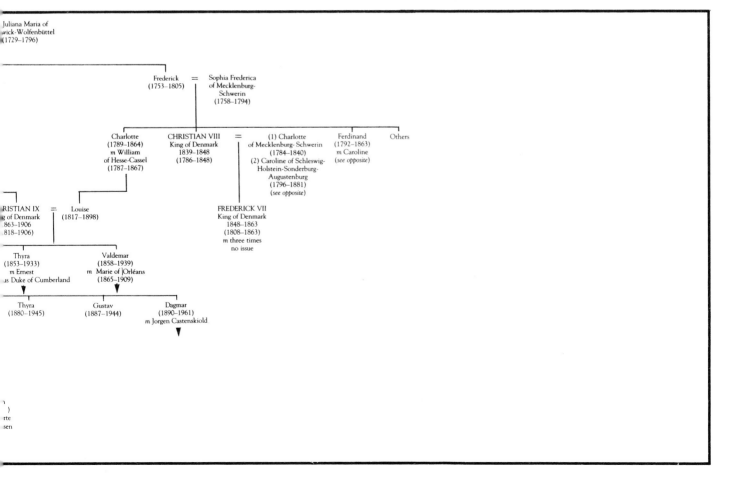

Juliana Maria of
...wick-Wolfenbüttel
(1729–1796)

Frederick
(1753–1805) = Sophia Frederica
of Mecklenburg-
Schwerin
(1758–1794)

Charlotte
(1789–1864)
m William
of Hesse-Cassel
(1787–1867)

CHRISTIAN VIII
King of Denmark
1839–1848
(1786–1848) = (1) Charlotte
of Mecklenburg-Schwerin
(1784–1840)
(2) Caroline of Schleswig-
Holstein-Sonderburg-
Augustenburg
(1796–1881)
(see opposite)

Ferdinand
(1792–1863)
m Caroline
(see opposite)

Others

...RISTIAN IX
...g of Denmark
...863–1906
...818–1906) = Louise
(1817–1898)

FREDERICK VII
King of Denmark
1848–1863
(1808–1863)
m three times
no issue

Thyra
(1853–1933)
m Ernest
...us Duke of Cumberland

Valdemar
(1858–1939)
m Marie of Orléans
(1865–1909)

Thyra
(1880–1945)

Gustav
(1887–1944)

Dagmar
(1890–1961)
m Jorgen Castenskiold

...)
...rte
...sen

18 THE KINGS
AND QUEENS
OF SWEDEN

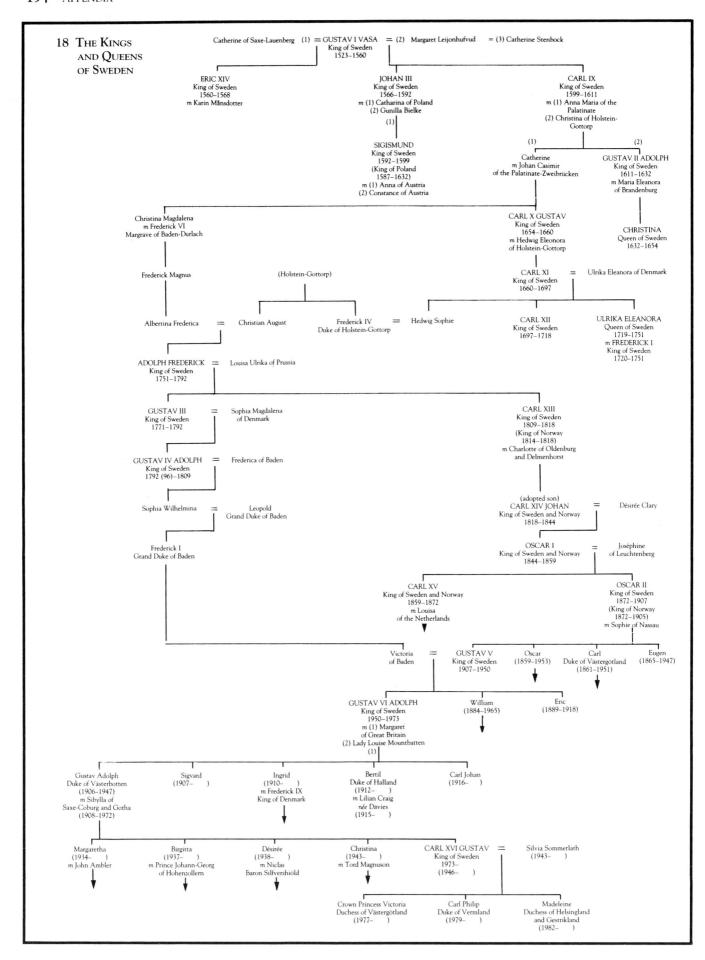

19 GERMANY: THE KINGS OF PRUSSIA

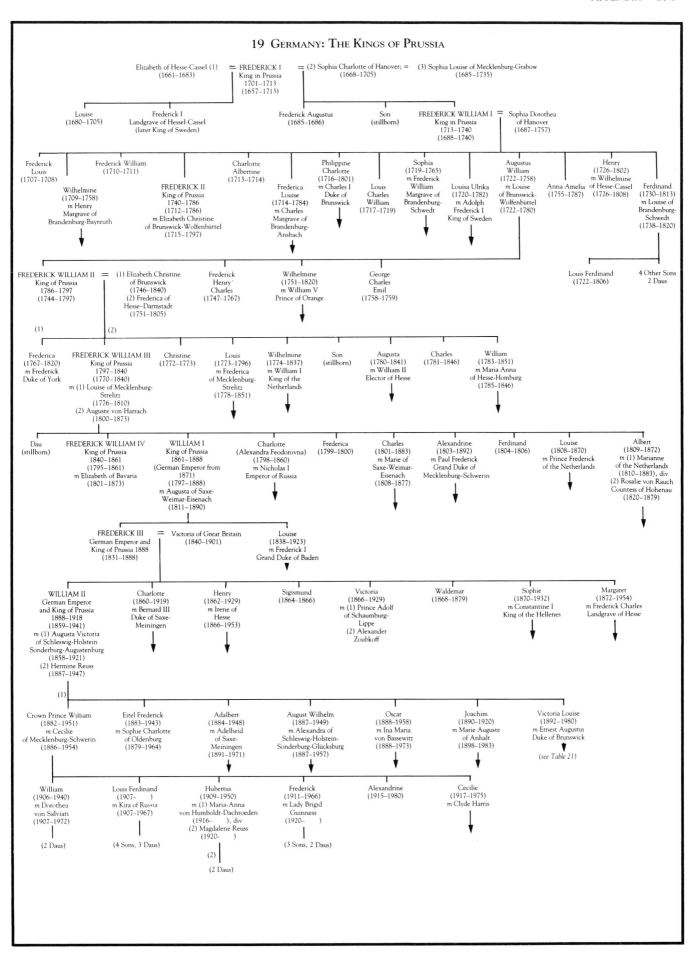

20 GERMANY: THE KINGS OF BAVARIA

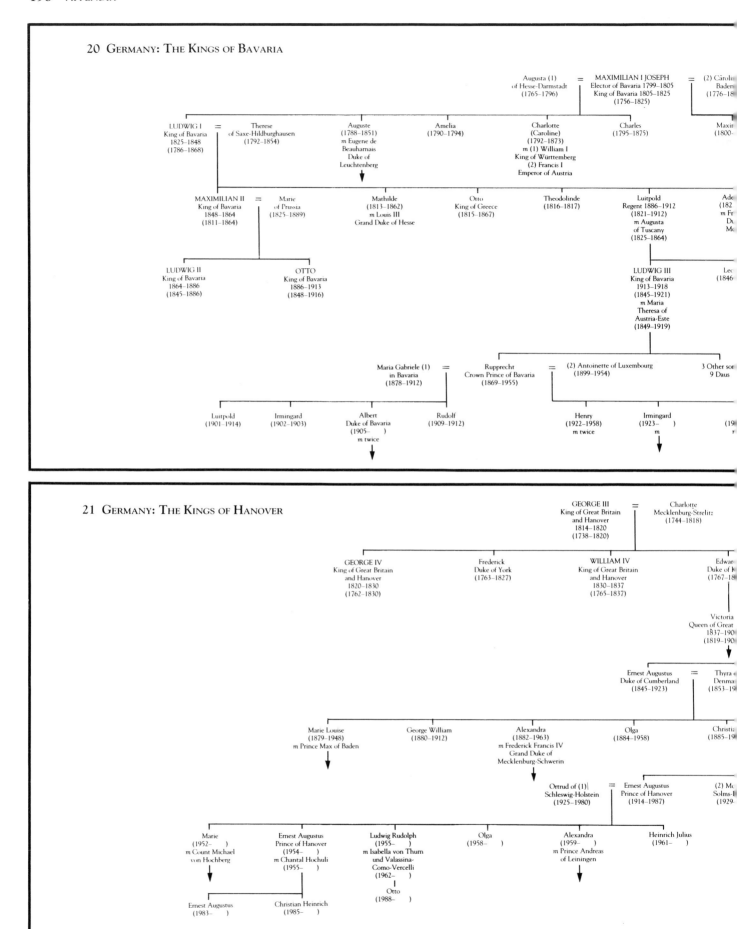

Augusta (1)
of Hesse-Darmstadt
(1765–1796)
=
MAXIMILIAN I JOSEPH
Elector of Bavaria 1799–1805
King of Bavaria 1805–1825
(1756–1825)
=
(2) Caroli
Bade
(1776–18

LUDWIG I
King of Bavaria
1825–1848
(1786–1868)
=
Therese
of Saxe-Hildburghausen
(1792–1854)

Auguste
(1788–1851)
m Eugene de
Beauharnais
Duke of
Leuchtenberg

Amelia
(1790–1794)

Charlotte
(Caroline)
(1792–1873)
m (1) William I
King of Württemberg
(2) Francis I
Emperor of Austria

Charles
(1795–1875)

Maxir
(1800–

MAXIMILIAN II
King of Bavaria
1848–1864
(1811–1864)
=
Marie
of Prussia
(1825–1889)

Mathilde
(1813–1862)
m Louis III
Grand Duke of Hesse

Otto
King of Greece
(1815–1867)

Theodolinde
(1816–1817)

Luitpold
Regent 1886–1912
(1821–1912)
m Augusta
of Tuscany
(1825–1864)

Ade
(182
m Fr
Du
Me

LUDWIG II
King of Bavaria
1864–1886
(1845–1886)

OTTO
King of Bavaria
1886–1913
(1848–1916)

LUDWIG III
King of Bavaria
1913–1918
(1845–1921)
m Maria
Theresa of
Austria-Este
(1849–1919)

Leo
(1846

Maria Gabriele (1)
in Bavaria
(1878–1912)
=
Rupprecht
Crown Prince of Bavaria
(1869–1955)
=
(2) Antoinette of Luxembourg
(1899–1954)

3 Other son
9 Daus

Luitpold
(1901–1914)

Irmingard
(1902–1903)

Albert
Duke of Bavaria
(1905–   )
m twice

Rudolf
(1909–1912)

Henry
(1922–1958)
m twice

Irmingard
(1923–   )
m

(19

21 GERMANY: THE KINGS OF HANOVER

GEORGE III
King of Great Britain
and Hanover
1814–1820
(1738–1820)
=
Charlotte
Mecklenburg-Strelitz
(1744–1818)

GEORGE IV
King of Great Britain
and Hanover
1820–1830
(1762–1830)

Frederick
Duke of York
(1763–1827)

WILLIAM IV
King of Great Britain
and Hanover
1830–1837
(1765–1837)

Edwar
Duke of K
(1767–18

Victoria
Queen of Great
1837–190
(1819–190

Ernest Augustus
Duke of Cumberland
(1845–1923)
=
Thyra
Denma
(1853–19

Marie Louise
(1879–1948)
m Prince Max of Baden

George William
(1880–1912)

Alexandra
(1882–1963)
m Frederick Francis IV
Grand Duke of
Mecklenburg-Schwerin

Olga
(1884–1958)

Christi
(1885–19

Ortrud of (1)
Schleswig-Holstein
(1925–1980)
=
Ernest Augustus
Prince of Hanover
(1914–1987)
(2) Mo
Solms-
(1929–

Marie
(1952–   )
m Count Michael
von Hochberg

Ernest Augustus
Prince of Hanover
(1954–   )
m Chantal Hochuli
(1955–   )

Ludwig Rudolph
(1955–   )
m Isabella von Thurn
und Valassina-
Como-Vercelli
(1962–   )

Olga
(1958–   )

Alexandra
(1959–   )
m Prince Andreas
of Leiningen

Heinrich Julius
(1961–   )

Ernest Augustus
(1983–   )

Christian Heinrich
(1985–   )

Otto
(1988–   )

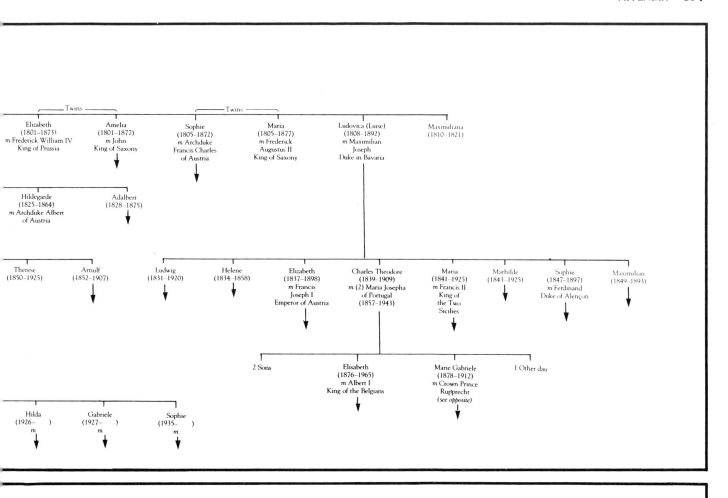

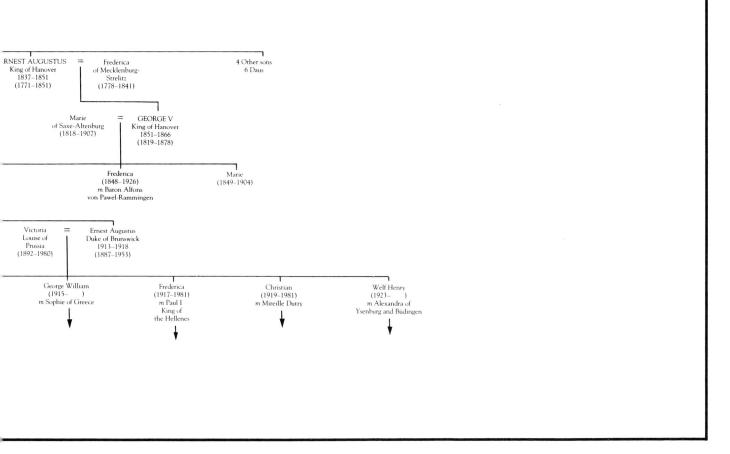

22 GERMANY: THE KINGS OF SAXONY

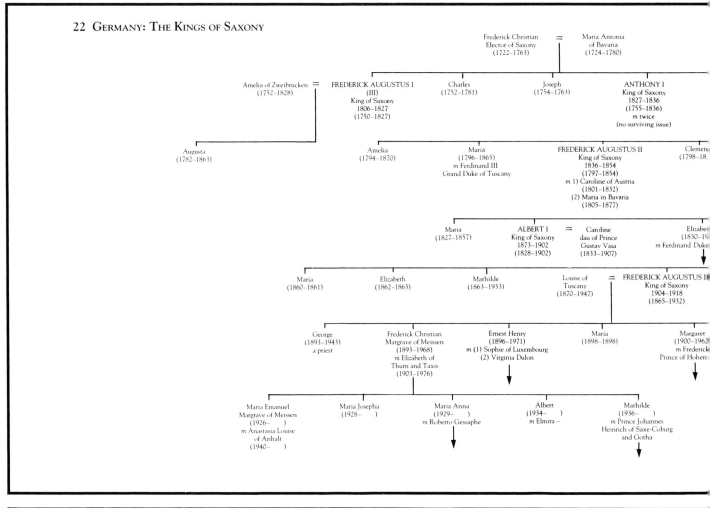

23 GERMANY: THE KINGS OF WÜRTTEMBERG

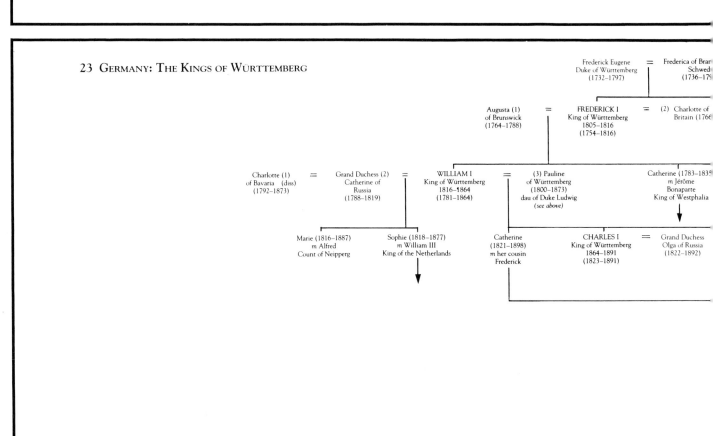

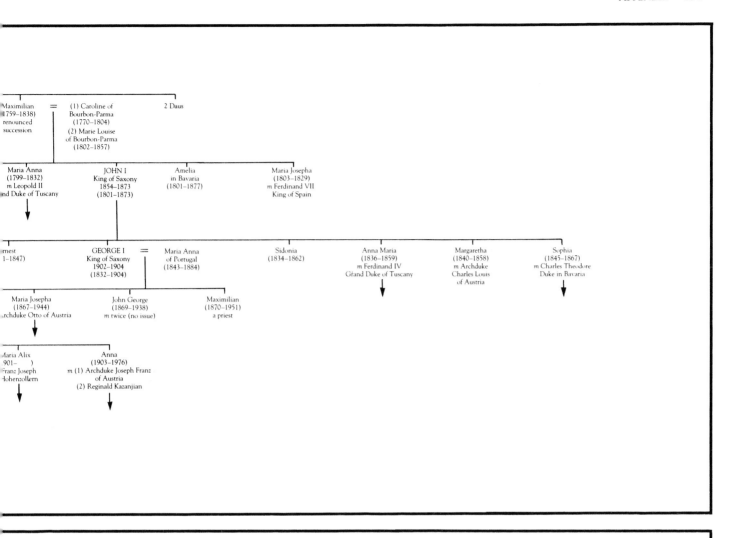

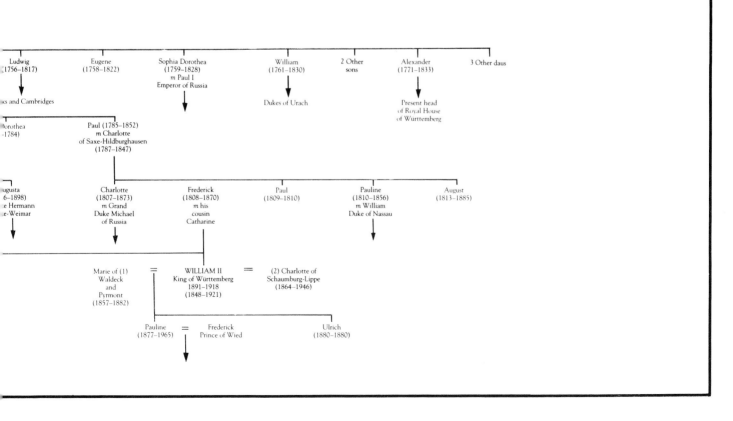

24 ITALY: THE HOUSE OF SAVOY

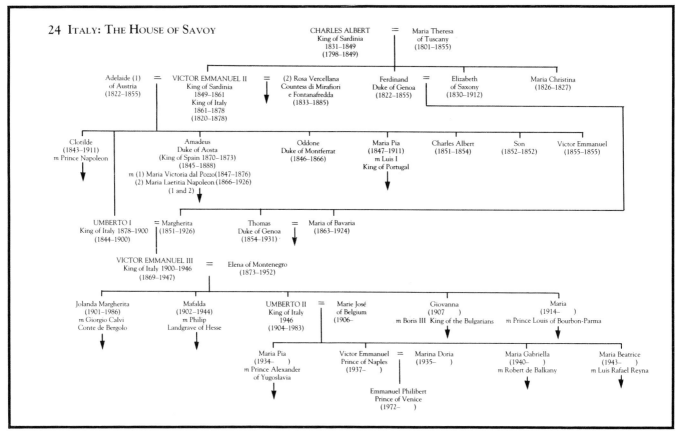

25 ITALY: THE KINGS OF THE TWO SICILIES

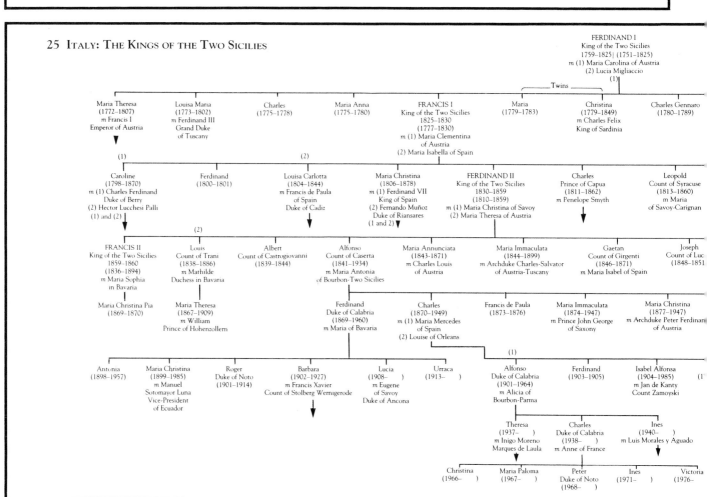

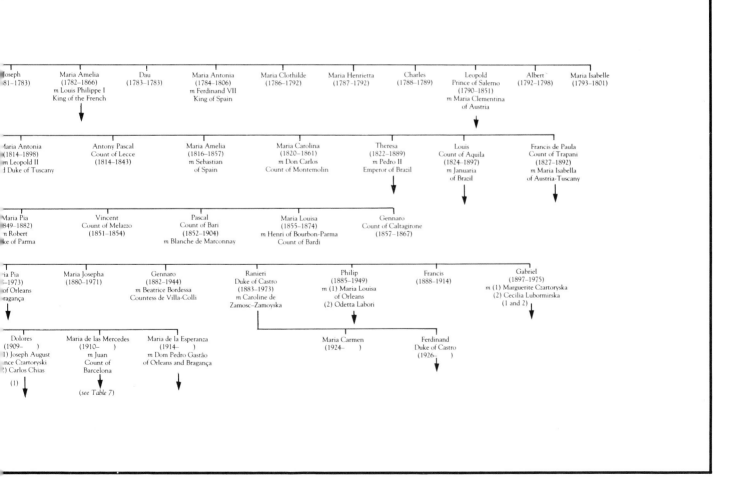

Joseph
(1781–1783)

Maria Amelia
(1782–1866)
m Louis Philippe I
King of the French

Dau
(1783–1783)

Maria Antonia
(1784–1806)
m Ferdinand VII
King of Spain

Maria Clothilde
(1786–1792)

Maria Henrietta
(1787–1792)

Charles
(1788–1789)

Leopold
Prince of Salerno
(1790–1851)
m Maria Clementina
of Austria

Albert
(1792–1798)

Maria Isabelle
(1793–1801)

Maria Antonia
(1814–1898)
m Leopold II
Duke of Tuscany

Antony Pascal
Count of Lecce
(1814–1843)

Maria Amelia
(1816–1857)
m Sebastian
of Spain

Maria Carolina
(1820–1861)
m Don Carlos
Count of Montemolin

Theresa
(1822–1889)
m Pedro II
Emperor of Brazil

Louis
Count of Aquila
(1824–1897)
m Januaria
of Brazil

Francis de Paula
Count of Trapani
(1827–1892)
m Maria Isabella
of Austria-Tuscany

Maria Pia
(1849–1882)
m Robert
Duke of Parma

Vincent
Count of Melazzo
(1851–1854)

Pascal
Count of Bari
(1852–1904)
m Blanche de Marconnay

Maria Louisa
(1855–1874)
m Henri of Bourbon-Parma
Count of Bardi

Gennaro
Count of Caltagirone
(1857–1867)

Maria Pia
(1878–1973)
m of Orleans
Bragança

Maria Josepha
(1880–1971)

Gennaro
(1882–1944)
m Beatrice Bordessa
Countess de Villa-Colli

Ranieri
Duke of Castro
(1883–1973)
m Caroline de
Zamosc–Zamoyska

Philip
(1885–1949)
m (1) Maria Louisa
of Orleans
(2) Odetta Labori

Francis
(1888–1914)

Gabriel
(1897–1975)
m (1) Marguerite Czartoryska
(2) Cecilia Lubormirska
(1 and 2)

Dolores
(1909–   )
1) Joseph August
nce Czartoryski
2) Carlos Chias

(1)

Maria de las Mercedes
(1910–   )
m Juan
Count of
Barcelona

(see Table 7)

Maria de la Esperanza
(1914–   )
m Dom Pedro Gastâo
of Orleans and Bragança

Maria Carmen
(1924–   )

Ferdinand
Duke of Castro
(1926–   )

26 THE KINGS OF THE BULGARIANS

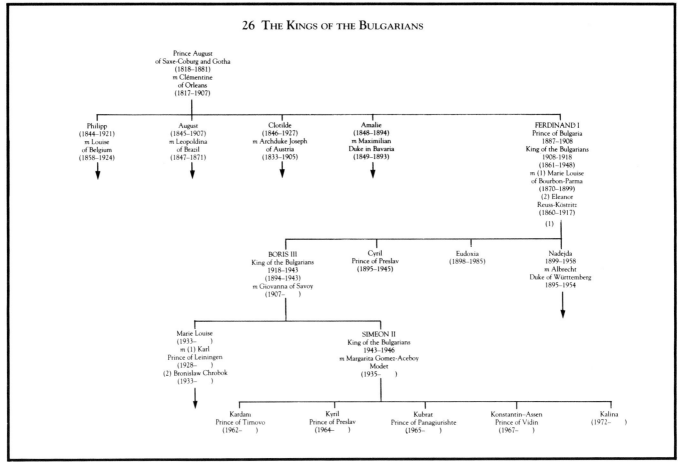

27 THE KINGS OF THE HELLENES

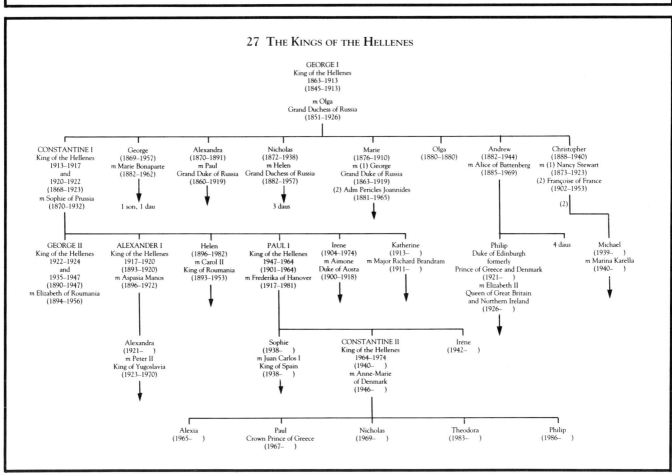

28 The Kings of Roumania

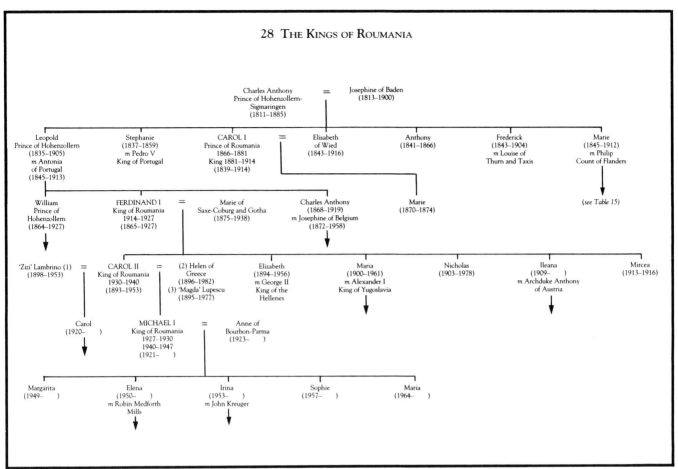

29 The Kings of Yugoslavia

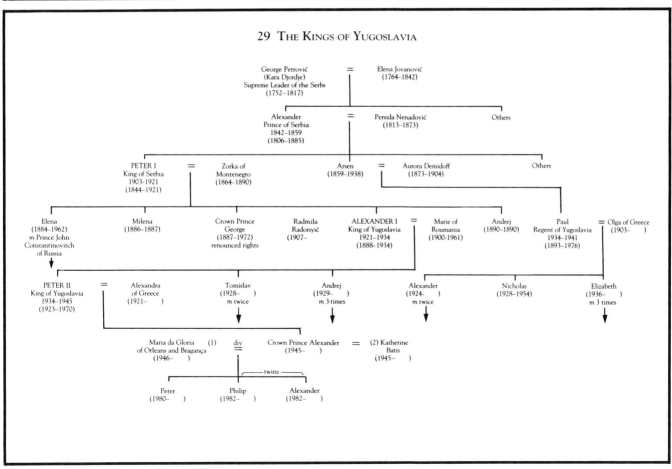

BIBLIOGRAPHY

ACTON, HAROLD *The Bourbons of Naples* (1956)
The Last Bourbons of Naples (1961)
ADDINGTON, A C *The Royal House of Stuart*, 3 vols (1969–76)
ANDERSSON, INGVOR *History of Sweden* (1956)
ATKINSON, EMMA WILLSHER *Memoirs of the Queens of Prussia* (1858)
BADDELEY, ST CLAIR *Queen Joanna I of Naples, Sicily, and Jerusalem, Countess of Provence, Forcalquier and Piedmont – An Essay on Her Times* (1893)
BARING-GOULD, S *Germany* (1893)
BERTAUT, JULES *Le Roi Jérôme* (1954)
BIRCH, J H S *Denmark in History* (1938)
BLUNT, WILFRID *The Dream King – Ludwig II of Bavaria* (1970)
BOYESEN, HJALMAR H *A History of Norway from the earliest times* (1900)
Burke's Guide to the Royal Family (1973)
Burke's Royal Families of the World, Volume I Europe and Latin America (1977)
CARPENTER, CLIVE *The Guinness Book of Kings, Rulers & Statesmen* (1978)
CARTWRIGHT, JULIA *Christina of Denmark, Duchess of Milan and Lorraine 1522–1590* (1913)
CASTRIES, DUC DE *The Lives of the Kings & Queens of France* (translated by Anne Dobell) (1979)
CHANNON, HENRY *The Ludwigs of Bavaria* (1933)
CHEKE, MARCUS *Carlota Joaquina, Queen of Portugal* (1947)
CORTI, EGON CAESAR, COUNT *Leopold I of Belgium* (1923)
CORYN, M *House of Orleans* (1936)
CURLEY, WALTER J P *Monarchs in Waiting* (1975)
DAVID-DARNAC, MAURICE *The True Story of the Maid of Orleans* (1969)
DURUY, VICTOR *A Short History of France*, 2 vols (1917)
ELSBERRY, TERENCE *Marie of Roumania* (1973)
Encyclopaedia Britannica, 13th edition (1926)
EULENBERG, HERBERT *The Hohenzollerns* (1928)
FENYVESI, CHARLES *Splendour in Exile – The Ex-Majesties of Europe* (1979)
FINESTONE, JEFFREY *The Last Courts of Europe* (1981)
FRYXELL, ANDERS *The History of Sweden* (ed Mary Howitt) (1844)
Führer Durch di Fürstengrüfte Münchens (1958)
FUNCK-BRENTANO, FR *The Earliest Times* (The National History of France, Vol I) (1927)
GEORGE, ANITA *Memoirs of the Queens of Spain*, 2 vols (1850)
GIBSON, PETER *The Concise Guide to Kings and Queens – A Thousand Years of European Monarchy* (1985)
GRAHAM, STEPHEN *Alexander of Jugoslavia, Strong Man of the Balkans* (1938)
GREECE, HRH PRINCE CHRISTOPHER OF *Memoirs* (1938)

GREGORY OF TOURS *The History of the Franks* (translated with intro by Lewis Thorpe) (1974)
HACKETT, FRANCIS *Francis the First* (1934)
HAMEL, FRANK *The Dauphines of France* (1909)
HARDING, BERTITA *Amazon Throne – The Story of the Braganzas in Brazil* (1942)
HÊTE, THIERRY LE *Les Capétiens – Le livre de millénaire* (1987)
HUBERTY, M, GIRAUD, A, and MAGDELAINE, F and B *L'Allemagne Dynastique, Tomes I–IV* (1976)
HUME, MARTIN *Modern Spain* (1906)
ISENBURG, PRINCE WILHELM KARL VON *Stammtafeln zur Geschichte der Europäischen Staaten*, 2 vols (1937)
KATZ, ROBERT *The Fall of the House of Savoy* (1972)
LANE, H M *The Royal Daughters of England*, 2 vols (1910)
LANGER, WILLIAM L (ed) *An Encyclopaedia of World History* (1940)
LAW, JOY *Fleur de Lys – The Kings and Queens of France* (1976)
LEE, ARTHUR S GOULD *The Royal House of Greece* (1948)
LIVERMORE, H V *A History of Portugal* (1947)
LORING, ULICK, and PAGE, JAMES *Yugoslavia's Royal Dynasty* (1976)
LOUDA, JIŘÍ, and MACLAGAN, MICHAEL *Lines of Succession – Heraldry of the Royal Families of Europe* (1981)
LUCAS, NETLEY EVELYN (EVELYN GRAHAM) *Albert the Brave, King of the Belgians* (1934)
LUISA OF TUSCANY (EX-CROWN PRINCESS OF SAXONY) *My Own Story* (1911)
MADOL, HANS ROGER *Christian the Ninth* (1939)
MANSEL, PHILIP *Louis XVIII* (1981)
MAYR-OFEN, FERDINAND *Ludwig II of Bavaria – The Tragedy of an Idealist* (translated by Ella Goodman and Paul Sudley) (1937)
MIJATOVICH, CHEDOMILLE *A Royal Tragedy – The Assassination of King Alexander and Queen Draga of Servia* (1906)
MILLER, TOWNSEND *Henry IV of Castile 1425–1474* (1972)
MITFORD, NANCY *The Sun King* (1966)
Frederick the Great (1970)
PETRIE, SIR CHARLES *The Spanish Royal House* (1958)
King Alfonso XIII (1963)
POLNAY, PETER DE *A Queen of Spain – Isabel II* (1962)
POPE-HENNESSY, JAMES *Queen Mary* (1959)
PRUSSIA HRH PRINCESS FRIEDRICH LEOPOLD OF *Behind the Scenes at the Prussian Court* (1939)
RALL, HANS and MARGA *Die Wittelsbacher in Lebensbildern* (1986)
REDDAWAY, W F, PENSON, J H, HALECKI, O, and DYBOSKI, R (eds) *The Cambridge History of Poland to 1696* (1950)
REIFENSCHEID, RICHARD *Die Habsburger in Lebensbildern – Von Rudolf I. bis Karl I.* (1984)
ROBYNS, GWEN *Geraldine of the Albanians – The Authorised Biography* (1987)

ROMANOFF, PRINCE DIMITRI *The Orders, Medals and History of Montenegro* (1980)

The Orders, Medals and History of the Kingdom of Bulgaria (1982)

The Orders, Medals and History of Greece (1987)

ROUMANIA, QUEEN MARIE OF *The Story of My Life* (1934–35)

RUNCIMAN, STEVEN *A History of the First Bulgarian Empire* (1930)

RUVIGNY, MARQUIS OF *The Titled Nobility of Europe* (1914)

SEWARD, DESMOND *The Bourbon Kings of France* (1976)

SOISSONS, COUNT DE *The Seven Richest Heiresses of France* (1911)

Six Great Princesses (ND)

STEPHENS, H MORSE *Portugal* (1891)

STOKVIS, A M *Manuel d'Histoire, de Généalogie et de Chronologie*, 3 vols (1888–91)

SVANSTRÖM, R, and PALMSTIERNA, C F *A Short History of Sweden* (1934)

TAPSELL, R F (compiler) *Monarchs, Rulers, Dynasties and Kingdoms of the World* (1983)

VALYNSEELE, JOSEPH *Les Enfants Naturels de Louis XV* (1953)

Les Laborde de Monpezat et leurs Alliances (1975)

VAMBÉRY, ARMINIUS *Hungary in Ancient, Mediaeval, and Modern Times* (1889)

VAN KERREBROUCK, PATRICK *La Maison de Bourbon 1256–1987* (1987)

VITELLESCHI, THE MARCHESA *The Romance of Savoy*, 2 vols (1905)

WARREN, RAOUL DE *Énigmes et Controverses Historiques: Les Prétendants au Trone de France* (1947)

WATTS, HENRY EDWARD *Spain: Being a Summary of Spanish History from the Moorish Conquest to the Fall of Granada (711–1492 A.D.)* (1894)

WIEL, ALETHEA *The Romance of the House of Savoy*, 2 vols (1898)

WILKINS, W H A *Queen of Tears: Caroline Matilda, Queen of Denmark and Norway and Princess of Great Britain and Ireland*, 2 vols (1904)

WILLIAM II, EX-EMPEROR OF GERMANY (sic) *My Early Life* (1926)

WILLIAMS, H NOEL *Last Loves of Henri of Navarre* (ND)

A Rose of Savoy – Marie Adélaïde of Savoy, Duchesse de Bourgogne, Mother of Louis XV (1909)

WILLIAMSON, DAVID *Debrett's Kings and Queens of Britain* (1986)

WILLIS, G M *Ernest Augustus, Duke of Cumberland and King of Hanover* (1954)

WILSON, MRS NORTHESK *Belgrade, the White City of Death – The History of King Alexander and Queen Draga* (1903)

WINDSOR, HRH THE DUKE OF *A King's Story* (1951)

YOUNG, GEORGE *Portugal Old and Young – An Historical Study* (1917)

YUGOSLAVIA, QUEEN ALEXANDRA OF *For a King's Love* (1956)

ZORRILLA, FRANCISCO JAVIER *Genealogía de la Casa de Borbón de España* (1971)

PICTURE CREDITS

INDEX

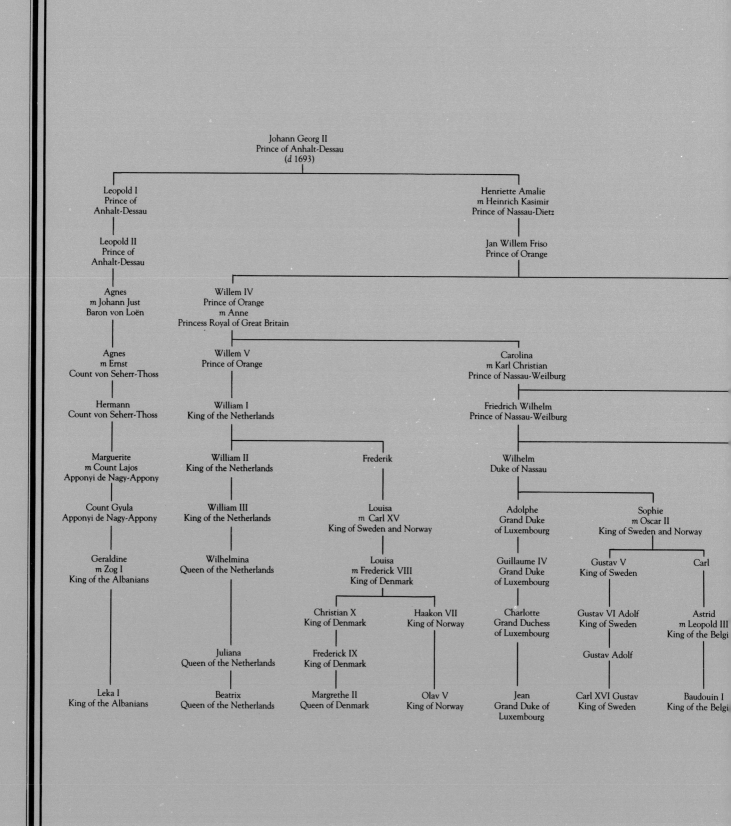

Johann Georg II
Prince of Anhalt-Dessau
(d 1693)

Leopold I
Prince of
Anhalt-Dessau

Henriette Amalie
m Heinrich Kasimir
Prince of Nassau-Dietz

Leopold II
Prince of
Anhalt-Dessau

Jan Willem Friso
Prince of Orange

Agnes
m Johann Just
Baron von Loën

Willem IV
Prince of Orange
m Anne
Princess Royal of Great Britain

Agnes
m Ernst
Count von Seherr-Thoss

Willem V
Prince of Orange

Carolina
m Karl Christian
Prince of Nassau-Weilburg

Hermann
Count von Seherr-Thoss

William I
King of the Netherlands

Friedrich Wilhelm
Prince of Nassau-Weilburg

Marguerite
m Count Lajos
Apponyi de Nagy-Appony

William II
King of the Netherlands

Frederik

Wilhelm
Duke of Nassau

Count Gyula
Apponyi de Nagy-Appony

William III
King of the Netherlands

Louisa
m Carl XV
King of Sweden and Norway

Adolphe
Grand Duke
of Luxembourg

Sophie
m Oscar II
King of Sweden and Norway

Geraldine
m Zog I
King of the Albanians

Wilhelmina
Queen of the Netherlands

Louisa
m Frederick VIII
King of Denmark

Guillaume IV
Grand Duke
of Luxembourg

Gustav V
King of Sweden

Carl

Christian X
King of Denmark

Haakon VII
King of Norway

Charlotte
Grand Duchess
of Luxembourg

Gustav VI Adolf
King of Sweden

Astrid
m Leopold III
King of the Belgi

Gustav Adolf

Juliana
Queen of the Netherlands

Frederick IX
King of Denmark

Leka I
King of the Albanians

Beatrix
Queen of the Netherlands

Margrethe II
Queen of Denmark

Olav V
King of Norway

Jean
Grand Duke of
Luxembourg

Carl XVI Gustav
King of Sweden

Baudouin I
King of the Belgi